D1072133

Discovering American Folklife

Studies in Ethnic, Religious, and Regional Culture

American Material Culture and Folklife

Simon J. Bronner, Series Editor

Professor of Folklore and American Studies
The Pennsylvania State University at Harrisburg

Other Titles in This Series

"We Gather Together": Food and Festival in American Life	Theodore C. Humphrey and Lin T. Humphrey, eds.
Exploring Western Americana	Austin E. Fife
Cultural History and Material Culture: Everyday Life, Landscapes, Museums	Thomas J. Schlereth
Cemeteries and Gravemarkers: Voices of American Culture	Richard E. Meyer, ed.
Appalachian Images in Folk and Popular Culture	W. K. McNeil, ed.
Reading the Visible Past: Social Function in the Arts	Alan Gowans
By the Work of Their Hands: Studies in Afro-American Folklife	John Michael Vlach

Discovering American Folklife

Studies in Ethnic, Religious, and Regional Culture

by
Don Yoder

With a Foreword by
Henry Glassie

Ann Arbor / London

Unless otherwise credited, historical photography by Theodore Brinton Hetzel.

Produced and distributed by
UMI Research Press
an imprint of
University Microfilms Inc.
Ann Arbor, Michigan 48106

Library of Congress Cataloging in Publication Data

Yoder, Don.
Discovering American folklife : studies in ethnic, religious, and regional culture / by Don Yoder.
p. cm.—(American material culture and folklife. Masters of material culture)
Includes bibliographical references.
ISBN 0-8357-1973-1 (alk. paper)
1. United States—Social life and customs. 2. Material culture—United States. 3. Folklore—United States. 4. Pennsylvania Dutch—Social life and customs. 5. Pennsylvania—Social life and customs.
I. Title. II. Series.
E161.Y63 1989
306.4'0973—dc20 89-20236
CIP

British Library CIP data is available.

To all my students,
and especially to my doctoral children,
1946–1990

Contents

Foreword

Integrity is the virtue of folklife. While the people of the conventional historical record are swept up in storms of event and driven from fashion to fashion, each more trivial than the last, the people at the center of folklife studies maintain their integrity and draw our admiration by holding to traditions that enable them simultaneously to express themselves and to meet their social responsibilities.

The people we get to know as part of our study should inspire our own work, as the career of Don Yoder proves, for his has been a scholarly life of the highest integrity. While scholars around him have veered from theory to theory, from topic to topic like the shades of hypocrisy out of a Dantean nightmare, Don Yoder has preserved over time an approach, a vision of scholarly procedure, that is sensible, solid, and constantly fresh.

Don Yoder's program is founded on a concept free of generic bias. Literary scholars seeking to apply their skills in new spheres are drawn naturally to certain formulations. Folk expressions that parallel great literature have entrapped their attention and retarded the growth of the folklorist's discipline. But inspired by European models of scholarship and owing no prior allegiance to literature, Don Yoder was able to pioneer in articulating the idea of folklife, of the study of folk culture however expressed—in work as well as play, in craft as well as speech, in belief as well as proverb. His paper, "The Folklife Studies Movement," now more than a quarter of a century old, remains the single best statement of the idea, and its influence has been great. Through his work and the work of his students and colleagues (Warren Roberts, Louis Jones, and Austin Fife were also there at the beginning), folklife has become an integral and major part of modern folklore scholarship. The word itself—*folklife*—has become a common part of our language, and scholars today comfortably study, as Don Yoder always has, folk culture however it appears in the world, as song or story, as house or garden or religious observance.

Time is the second feature of his program. While anthropologically oriented scholars imported the idea of the synchronic into folklore research and then struggled to relocate culture's manifest diachronic dimensions, Don Yoder has always attended at once to culture's contemporary unfolding and to its historical realities. His studies of a wide range of cultural facts, with his explorations of foodways providing an excellent series of examples, have always admirably integrated the ethnographic with the historical in a way wholly congruent with contemporary philosophy.

Now add a spatial dimension. Excessive concentration on abstract method in folkloristic education has led young scholars into the assumption that, having mastered method, all they have to do is apply it in some place among some people and success will be theirs. But successful application requires a committed saturation in a place's history and geography, a people's literature and language. A native of Pennsylvania, the American state with the greatest cultural diversity, Don Yoder has spent a lifetime building an inward understanding of the state's people, their history, their religions, and languages. In full possession of the big picture, he has been able to frame his own small pictures with richness and accuracy. Owing to his knowledge, his studies, and to the years he gave to editing *Pennsylvania Folklife,* Pennsylvania, despite its complexity, is the state best understood by modern American folklorists.

Committed to the study of folk culture in all of its manifestations, to history as well as ethnography, to the study of one large and remarkable place, Don Yoder's program has preserved its integrity and inspired us all. But one other aspect of his commitment has served to fuse his work into coherence. Religion is the deep force of what we call tradition. Faith is the foundation of folk culture; an idea of the sacred powers folk action. Don Yoder's training in religious thought and his constant attention to religion have enabled him to press past surfaces into the depths of cause, notably in his studies of costume and folk art.

Put all these concerns together and you have the reason why *Pennsylvania Spirituals* is a wholly satisfying work, one of a tiny number of nearly perfect studies that the discipline of folklore has produced. It treats song as a cultural expression, it approaches song both ethnographically and historically, it grounds expression in place and in faith.

Just as culture and personality do not separate in folk practice, so, too, is a scholarly program a part of the scholar's own being. Integrity is the great virtue of Don Yoder's scholarship and it is also a feature of his personality. Having known him for decades, I know that to be true, and I would sketch out of my experience other parts of the man. That he possesses a nimble, inquisitive mind his works clearly demonstrate. Once we went off for a taste of fieldwork together in his home region and it was a pure pleasure to feel that mind taking in facts and bringing them into significant order. It might not be as obvious from his writings that he has a sweet, puckish sense of humor. I appreciated that when I was his student (it inspired cartoons among my class notes), and when I was his chairman, charged with organizing an annual introductory set of lectures for graduate students, I always looked forward to his slide talks on the Quakers or the Pennsylvania Dutch, not only because they were constantly enlightening, but as well because I could count on delightful flickers of humor that would rise in an impish smile before they flashed happily through the dark room.

Generosity, too, is a part of him. When as a graduate student I was writing *Pattern in the Material Folk Culture of the Eastern United States,* he warmly opened his vast private library to me. There is probably something in the fact that so many of us who are the students of oral literature are mad collectors of books. There is certainly something for us to learn from the way Don Yoder brought his marvelous library into class in bits and pieces and made it available to his multitude of students. It was a way for him to exemplify the virtue of generosity in an academic setting, just as his works, his gifts to us, exemplify through scholarship the personal virtue of integrity.

Henry Glassie

Introduction

I have often wondered what path my career would have taken had I been born outside Pennsylvania. With the exception of my graduate school years at the University of Chicago and my first teaching job at Union Theological Seminary in New York City, and frequent visits to Europe, my life has been spent thus far entirely in Pennsylvania. Roots are decisive, and my cultural and family roots trail back through Central Pennsylvania, where I was born, to Southeastern Pennsylvania, where all of my immigrant ancestors—except for the Hudson Valley DeLongs and the Delaware Garretsons, both Holland Dutch—had settled from William Penn's time until the 1790s.

All of my historical and ethnographic research has grown out of my fascination with Pennsylvania and its rich composite ethnic and regional cultures. My research has, of course, not been limited to Pennsylvania subjects, for I have studied and taught graduate courses dealing with the wider American cultural scene in religious history, particularly sectarian and cultic movements; in folk-religious phenomena, including religious folk art and folk music; in regional and ethnic cultures; and in the history of folklife studies.

Since 1950 I have made almost annual research visits to Western Europe, where I have familiarized myself with European backgrounds of American culture and with the archival and folk-cultural research institutions in Germany, Switzerland, Austria, France, Holland, Belgium, Spain and Portugal, Italy, Scandinavia, and the British Isles. My acquaintance with Eastern Europe includes research visits to Poland, Czechoslovakia, Romania, and East Germany. And a memorable sabbatical in the spring semester of 1969 took me for several months to the major cities of Latin America, to visit the anthropological museums and acquaint myself with university colleagues there who are engaged in studying their own cultures. An ethnographic journal I kept during that memorable sabbatical, detailing my explorations in the German-speaking settlements of Brazil's southernmost province, Rio Grande do Sul, is, alas, too lengthy for inclusion in this volume, but I trust it will see publication elsewhere.

But in my work I have used the bountiful historical and folk-cultural resources of Pennsylvania, its ethnic groups and regional cultures and its complex religious patterns, as the major source of examples for my teaching and writing. As my students and colleagues know, my two major research areas are the Pennsylvania German (Pennsylvania Dutch) culture of Southeastern, Central, and Western Pennsylvania—where it originally covered an area the size of Switzerland; and the Quaker sectarian culture of the Delaware Valley, covering a three-state area centering around the city of Philadelphia.

In an autobiographical essay the late West German statesman Theodor Heuss states that he became conscious of his place in culture from the difference in outlook between his Swabian father and his Rhineland mother. My own cultural consciousness is based on a similar dichotomy. The fact that I was born not in the heart of the Pennsylvania Dutch culture area of Southeastern Pennsylvania, but in the extension of it in the Allegheny Mountains of Central Pennsylvania, made me aware in growing up that the two strands in my family were very different culturally. What made me aware of the difference were those many childhood summers when I visited my grandmother's farm—later owned by my father—in Eastern Pennsylvania. As a city boy, this experience on a legitimate farm, with its fields and orchards and gardens, its creek and woods and sawmill that my father and his brothers delighted in, made me aware of the basic rural patterns of life that, until the twentieth century, most Americans have known personally and shared. The seasonal round of work—the spring and fall plowing, the midsummer harvests, the great day when the threshing machine separated the summer's wheat from the chaff and piled the straw stacks high in the barnyard—this view of the yearly round of work on the farm, the feel of the seasons, became an indispensable ingredient in my life and an irreplaceable part of my memory.

I thought of all this during a long summer day in 1959 that I spent talking with Richard Weiss of the University of Zurich, at his home at Küssnacht on the Lake of Zurich. As we talked of traditional culture and the problems of researching it in Switzerland and Pennsylvania, he told me that his boyhood experiences on his grandfather's alpine farm in Graubünden helped to guide him into his folk-cultural research career. His book on the complex folk-cultural patterns of Switzerland, *Volkskunde der Schweiz* (1946), has had a major influence on my own career, and one I am happy to acknowledge.

Naturally, I could have absorbed formative influences on farms in Ohio, Indiana, or Iowa, where distant cousins lived. But what made my boyhood visits to grandmother's farm decisive for me was the fact that my father's family was Pennsylvania Dutch or Pennsylvania German (the terms are interchangeable) and all of their everyday culture was a living complex of ideas, framed in the Pennsylvania Dutch dialect but completely American in its ramifications. To this day I can call up a Dutch expression or proverb from the rich store imparted to me while growing up by my father and his brothers and sisters, who spoke Pennsylvania Dutch all their lives and whose memories were stocked with all the traditional lore of special days in the calendar, proverbial sayings and bywords, folk tales and legends, and above all, songs.

The best example of my growing awareness of the difference in Pennsylvania's cultural regions and how this shaped my own research career is my work in the Pennsylvania Dutch folksong field. I soon discovered that my father and his brothers and sisters, particularly my Dutch aunts who had stayed on the farm, knew what I, as a budding "folklorist," was learning to call folksongs. My mother and her generation on her side of the family had none of this. In the area of Central Pennsylvania where my mother had grown up, the dialect had died out, and the Dutch culture had mingled with Scotch-Irish and Quaker elements. The only songs that she and her generation of schoolmates seemed to know were the rural church's hymns and gospel songs, and the popular culture songs of the First World War era, including the one about the "long, long trail a-winding," and the song requesting "a Lucifer to light my fag"—which always seemed to me incongruous in a Protestant rural culture that disapproved of cigarette smoking. It was plain that the culture of my mother's family was mostly Anglo-American, although distinctive Pennsylvania Dutch culture elements lingered on, especially in the traditional foods that were served at our table.

Of all the American regional and ethnic cultures, then, the Pennsylvania Dutch world with its living, vibrant culture came to be my principal research focus. In collecting folksongs and folktales in those early years, I first became fascinated with the linguistic element of my own culture. The Pennsylvania Dutch dialect—*Deitsch,* as it was called—was there to learn, and I learned to use it, along with standard German, as a research tool, although I must admit my spoken "Deutsch" is often flavored with telltale elements of "Deitsch."

Fifty years ago, when I was beginning my study of things Pennsylvania Dutch, I made a point of seeking out, meeting, and talking with the living scholars who had contributed vital treatments of the culture. In 1937 I joined the newly founded Pennsylvania German Folklore Society. I still have my first membership card, signed by the treasurer, the irascible Edwin M. Fogel of the University of Pennsylvania, whom I came to know at the time. I sought out Preston A. Barba of Muhlenberg College, in whose weekly columns in the Allentown *Morning Call, 'S Pennsylfawnisch Deitsch Eck,* in 1946 and 1947, there appeared several of the very first of my ethnographic writings. Also, at Muhlenberg College, where I taught briefly in the 1940s, there was the delightful Harry Reichard, one of the leaders of the current dialect revival, who was not above performing weekly in a dialect comedy show over the radio that was faithfully listened to by my father every Sunday after church, and by myself whenever I was home. With my cousin Albert F. Buffington of Penn State and Walter Boyer, then a country preacher in the Mahantongo Valley, later also a professor at Penn State, I joined forces to produce the first complete folksong book dealing with the Pennsylvania Germans, *Songs along the Mahantongo* (1951; second edition, 1964). This was based on joint fieldwork with folksingers from our own home area, the Mahantongo culture region of Schuylkill, Northumberland, and Dauphin Counties in the central Susquehanna Valley north of Harrisburg—an area celebrated for its decorated furniture and other distinctive Pennsylvania Dutch traits.

Two younger scholars, Alfred L. Shoemaker and J. William Frey, became close associates when I joined them in 1949 in founding what we chose at the time to call the Pennsylvania Dutch Folklore Center at Franklin and Marshall College, and in the publication of a tabloid-format periodical with the very ethnic title of *The Pennsylvania Dutchman.* The Center was modeled on the folklore/folklife institutes of the European universities. The periodical was unique in America, for its purpose was to publish materials on one ethnic/regional culture and stimulate research from its readers. We developed questionnaires and encouraged and engaged in field work. We also abstracted and indexed published materials and fed the results into a massive card file, much like those of the European institutes in the precomputer age.

The term "folklife" appeared only sporadically among American folklorists at that time. The term was used only minimally, for example, at the Indiana University folklore conference of 1946, in a paper by Sven Liljeblad on Swedish research. But certainly Louis Jones, Austin Fife, Warren Roberts, and other scholars who were concerned not only with folklore in its narrow definition but with material culture, were aware of it. The term "folklife" had even made a single, indeed a unique appearance, in the nineteenth century, in the title of an article on German peasant life, published in an American magazine in 1873. This single use, which was obviously a translation of the German *Volksleben,* had no influence on the research world. There were also, as Simon Bronner has pointed out in articles and books, folklife scholars in Victorian America long before there was a concerted folklife studies movement in the twentieth century. Their work is on record, but alas, their efforts seem to have had little or no effect in broadening the research program of the infant science of American folklore to include more of what we today call American folklife.

Research techniques have long roots. In those exciting days of the 1940s and 1950s the term and concept of "folklife" began to take its place alongside "folklore" in the United States. In looking back over the past four decades, it would seem that much of the present wide usage of the term is the direct result of its pioneer official use in Pennsylvania. At that time the term "folklife" in its Swedish form *folkliv* (obviously a Swedish adaptation of the earlier German term *Volksleben*) was crossing the waters to the British Isles where it came into use in Ireland, England, and other areas. The principal link between this European usage and America was my long-time associate Alfred L. Shoemaker, who in the late 1940s, after the close of the war, investigated the folk-cultural research institutes in Sweden and in Ireland, and brought the refined folklife research techniques developed there to Pennsylvania. But for some time after that the term "folklife" maintained a low profile and we were still "folklorists."

After 1950, when I made the first of my annual research visits to Europe and got my own firsthand impressions of folklife research and its possibilities for application here, we became increasingly dissatisfied with the term "folklore" for the broader, culture-oriented research we were conducting. The break came in 1958, when we incorporated the center, changing its name to the Pennsylvania Folklife Society, and the title of our periodical to *Pennsylvania Folklife,* inclusive of all the cultures that made up Pennsylvania.

It is important to underscore the fact that these changes followed or paralleled similar changes in the British Isles, with the founding in 1961 of the Society for Folk Life Studies by members of the Folklore Society, to do justice, as the founders intended, to aspects of British Isles traditional culture that had been neglected through the years by the parent society and its periodical. A bit earlier, and providing a model for our name change, the journal called *Ulster Folklife* was founded in 1955, representing the same scholarly direction for another culture of extreme importance for establishing backgrounds for Pennsylvania's Scotch-Irish settlement areas. Also, in 1955 the Arnhem Conference on Folk Culture came out with the statement that, in its opinion, the term and concept of "folklore" should be subsumed under the obviously broader term and concept "folklife."

What is important about the folklife studies movement, as I saw it in 1963 and still see it, is that it was and is intended to teach American students to look at their own culture, as European folk-cultural scholars had been doing for decades. This is somewhat different from the anthropological, Margaret Mead approach of living one's way into an understanding of an alien culture. Growing up in a culture and then applying objective research techniques to it gives one, in a sense, a double vision which involves multi-layered understanding of the culture's meaning, the way it is conveyed by its society, the way it works in everyday life, and the way the individual expresses it in his own identity.

In limiting the geographical focus of our research to Pennsylvania, we were in no way limiting our research horizons, since these involved the place of the Pennsylvania culture in the overarching American culture (Henry Glassie's Southeastern Pennsylvania "culture hearth" idea), as well as the spread of Pennsylvanian cultural phenomena to other parts of the United States and Canada through migration. Also involved here was the acculturation of European, Indian, Black and general American phenomena on the cultural soil of Pennsylvania. In a very real sense Pennsylvania's cultural pluralism, brought about by William Penn's invitation to English and Welsh Quakers, Scotch-Irishmen, Rhinelanders, Swiss, and anyone else who wanted to come, made Penn's Woods the basic prototype, the colonial model, for the pluralistic America that we have today.

As I view my own work—and this volume represents only a small part of my total production—it has grown organically out of my own background as a Pennsylvanian, and my delight, since high-school days and my first driver's license, in roving these Pennsylvania valleys, visiting cousins in a dozen counties in Eastern and Central Pennsylvania, photographing and recording aspects of farming and small-town life in the area, interviewing in their country kitchens informants who soon became friends, and writing about it all.

The second formative influence on my career has been my annual research visits to Europe, where I made it a point to make contact with the major folk-cultural research institutions and colleagues there, to acquaint myself with their own and their students' research specialties and techniques.

Among the European scholars whose work has helped mine are Martha Bringemeier, Günter Wiegelmann, and Hans Teuteberg of the University of Münster; Lutz Röhrich of Freiburg; Hermann Wellenreuther and Rolf-Wilhelm Brednich of Göttingen; Hermann Bausinger of Tübingen; Martin Scharfe, Peter Assion, and Ingeborg Weber-Kellermann of Marburg; Klaus Beitl of Vienna; Edith Hörandner and Elfriede Grabner of Graz; Roger Pinon of Liege and P. J. Meertens of Amsterdam; Arnold Niederer and Paul Hugger of Zurich; Hans Trümpy and, above all, the late Robert Wildhaber of Basel. There are others that I could mention, as for example Phebe Fjellström of Uppsala; Carl-Herman Tillhagen of Stockholm; Olav Bø of Oslo; Gustav Henningsen of Copenhagen; and Nils-Arvid Bringéus of Lund, who invited me to participate in the First International Symposium on Ethnological Food

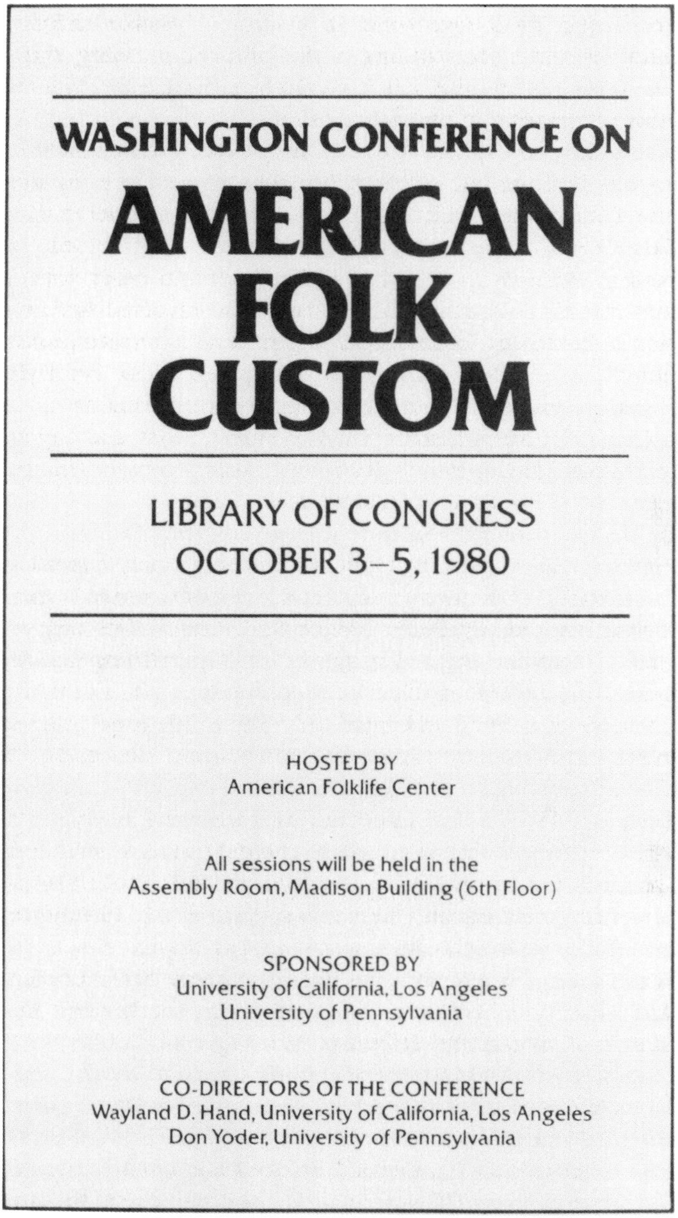

WASHINGTON CONFERENCE ON

AMERICAN FOLK CUSTOM

LIBRARY OF CONGRESS
OCTOBER 3–5, 1980

HOSTED BY
American Folklife Center

All sessions will be held in the
Assembly Room, Madison Building (6th Floor)

SPONSORED BY
University of California, Los Angeles
University of Pennsylvania

CO-DIRECTORS OF THE CONFERENCE
Wayland D. Hand, University of California, Los Angeles
Don Yoder, University of Pennsylvania

Figure I.1. The Washington Conference on American Folk Custom (1980) was co-directed by Wayland D. Hand and Don Yoder and sponsored jointly by UCLA and the University of Pennsylvania.

Research, at Lund, in 1970. In the British Isles I must mention Iorwerth Peate and Geraint Jenkins of the Welsh Folk Museum; Alexander Fenton of the National Museum of Scottish Antiquities; and Estyn Evans of Queens University, Belfast, with whom I have had many pleasant contacts in Northern Ireland and Pennsylvania, and whose work has influenced both Henry Glassie's and my own.

Some of these scholars have been my academic guests at the University of Pennsylvania, and I have had the pleasure of driving many of them up into the Dutch Country to show them something of my own research area. I have also sent students to some of them, to study or to consult on projects, and some of them have sent students my way as well. This has been and continues to be an exciting international exchange which has enriched my life and, through my teaching, that of my students.

What have I learned through these European contacts and interconnections? First of all, I sensed that Europeans were generations ahead of Americans in recording the details of their own cultures, and archiving the results. Secondly, there were obvious specialities in European folklife studies that had scarcely begun to register in American scholarship. Several of these, the study of folk religion, folk medicine, folk cookery and foodways, and folk costume, fitted in with my own interests and I was able to write what were at the time considered "definitive" introductions to these areas, tracing their research history both in Europe and the United States, outlining fields into subfields, and calling for concerted investigation into these topics in all the American cultural subregions. In folk medicine and folk custom I joined hands with the American pioneer in these areas, Wayland D. Hand, and enjoyed participating in his U.C.L.A. Conference on American Folk Medicine, December 13–15, 1973, the first such conference where folklorists and medical historians discussed together areas of their common interest. And then it was a pleasure to join Wayland as co-director of the Washington Conference on American Folk Custom, held at the Library of Congress, October 3–5, 1980.

A third emphasis that I share with my European folklife colleagues is my strong interest in the historical background of the present culture. While my work has involved much fieldwork or current ethnography, it has also made use of the method of historical ethnography, analyzing historical documentation to reconstruct past levels of the culture on which one is focusing. One of my models here is Karl-Sigismund Kramer of the University of Kiel, whose historical ethnographies of Franconia in West Germany from 1500 to 1800 are exemplary. Various American social histories and Annalist productions of the Braudel school in France can also be cited as models.

In the United States my historical interests have brought me into close relationships with our American Civilization Department at the University

QUAKER
CULTURE
IN THE
DELAWARE
VALLEY

Figure I.2. The Winterthur Conference on Quaker Culture in the Delaware Valley (1979) grew out of Don Yoder's Winterthur Fellowship.

QUAKER CULTURE IN THE DELAWARE VALLEY

DECEMBER 1, 1979

COPELAND LECTURE HALL

9:30 A.M.	Introduction –*Scott T. Swank*, Winterthur Museum
9:45	"Quaker Culture in the Delaware Valley" –*Don Yoder*, University of Pennsylvania
10:45	Break
11:00	"The Quaker Aesthetic" –*Raymond V. Shepherd*, Cliveden
11:30	"Quaker Printing and Bookbinding" –*Willman Spawn*, American Philosophical Society
12:00 NOON	Lunch
1:00 P.M.	"Quaker Meetinghouse Architecture" –*Francis J. Puig*, Ph.D. Candidate, Yale University
1:30	"Quaker Domestic Architecture" –*Bernard L. Herman*, University of Delaware
2:00	"Quaker Gardens and Botany" –*Julia F. Davis*
2:30	Break
2:45	"Quaker Needlework" –*Margaret Schiffer*
3:15	"Quaker Culture in the Midwest" –*Willard B. Moore*, Minnesota Historical Society
3:45	Panel and Discussion

Figure I.3. Eight papers illustrated the expression in culture of Quaker religious ideals, "plain" aesthetic, and concern for nature and the environment.

of Pennsylvania, for whom I have taught for over a decade graduate courses on the history and ethnography of the Pennsylvania Germans, and, every other year, a matching course in Delaware Valley Quaker culture. My long-time mentor and friend in that department, Anthony N. B. Garvan, helped to make the university's American Civilization program the broadest in the country by adding the dimension of material culture to the discipline's original limited lens of American literature. He also pioneered in the area of museum studies and historic preservation, in which some of my own students, Jay Anderson for example, have been involved in both teaching and practice.

My own training in American history and the history of religion in America has been immensely useful in one of my major specialties—the study of American folk religion. While some old-line folklorists have attempted to treat "superstition" as a folklore "genre" and continue to use that (in my opinion) outmoded and questionable term, my work centers on the relations of traditional culture, with its strong components of folk belief, to organized religion, and the tensions between them. My conception of folk religion is derived principally from two prior research areas, the European field called variously "religiöse Volkskunde" and "religion populaire," and Redfield's discovery of "folk Catholicism" in Yucatan and elsewhere. My teaching in this field began in 1957, when I offered a pioneer course in folk religion at the University of Pennsylvania. I have taught this course frequently since, alternating it every other year with another favorite course of mine, American Sectarian and Cultic Movements. This involves fieldwork in local religious group cultures and in fact focuses on the concept of sectarian culture, which I treat as a subfield in folklife studies. After three decades of researching and teaching in the field of American folk religion I have been pleased to see several of my doctoral children—Gerald Pocius and Leonard Primiano for two examples out of many—teaching courses in the subject.

Because of the importance of this area for folklorists and folklife research I have included in this volume my essay "Toward a Definition of Folk Religion," which was given as a paper at the meeting of the American Folklore Society in Washington, D.C., in 1971, and published in 1974 in my Symposium on Folk Religion in *Western Folklore.* My own work in this research area continues, especially in the area of religious folk art. A major paper, "Religion and Folk Art: Trends in and Directions for Research," which was presented as the keynote address at the conference, Reflections of Faith: Religious Folk Art in America, sponsored by the Museum of American Folk Art in 1985, is to appear later this year in the volume of conference papers to be published by the Popular Press for the Museum of American Folk Art.

Also scheduled for publication in 1989 is the folk art book, *Lamp of My Heart: The Picture-Bible of Ludwig Denig,* under the imprint of the Hudson Hills Press, New York, in association with the Museum of American Folk Art and the Pennsylvania German Society. Ludwig Denig (1755–1830), a native Pennsylvania Dutchman who served in the Revolution, put together in 1784 a two-hundred-page manuscript book, in German, of lay sermons on the Passion of Christ, and meditations on symbolic drawings in the style of the seventeenth-century emblem books. His work contains sixty full-page watercolor drawings of emblems and Bible scenes. These show delightful touches of contemporaneity such as portraying the Wise and Foolish Virgins appareled in long dresses, capes and little white caps just like the Lancaster ladies of the 1780s, and King Herod and his courtiers at his birthday party, seated in Windsor chairs.

Denig's texts reveal a thoroughly Pietist approach to church affairs, with numerous asides critical of current ministers whom he does not consider "Sons of Thunder" in the New Testament sense. These texts are unusual in that they are the products of a layman's experience—he was a shoemaker in Lancaster—rather than the product of a clergyman's mind. The work is to appear in two volumes, elegantly boxed, the first volume a color facsimile of the original manuscript, the second my analysis of the artist and his world and the book and its pictorial and textual sources, plus my translation of the sermons and meditations. This manuscript emblem book by a layman is unique both in the world of eighteenth-century America and in the world of Pennsylvania German art, and will add a major figure to our growing galaxy of early American folk artists.

It has been interesting to watch the increased use of the term folklife and the concept of folklife studies in the United States, in the public sector as well as the academic world, following its pioneer official usage by the Pennsylvania Folklife Society and its periodical *Pennsylvania Folklife* in the 1950s. Some of these uses were natural developments in American scholarship with only an indirect connection with the Pennsylvania folklife movement, but others appear to be direct influences.

First of all, the term was adopted in Washington and used in the title of the Smithsonian Institution's Folklife Festival on the Mall, beginning in 1967. For over two decades now the annual programs of the festival have provided scholarly analyses of the nation's state and regional cultures, ethnic and occupational groups. The festival is now operated jointly by the National Park Service and the Smithsonian Institution. The Smithsonian agency that supervises the event and sponsors other folklife projects is the Office of Folklife Programs, founded in 1977.

It was also in 1967 that a folklife conference was held at the Library

Figure I.4. The Pennsylvania Dutch Folk Festival at Kutztown was founded in 1950 by Alfred L. Shoemaker, J. William Frey, and Don Yoder, who had initiated the Pennsylvania Dutch Folklore Center in 1949. The festival was unique among American festivals in that it pioneered the public display and discussion of a single ethnic/regional culture.

of Congress, where American scholars were joined by Europeans like Robert Wildhaber to discuss the possibilities of folklife research in the United States. Beginning in 1969, plans were laid for a national folklife research institute, under United States government sponsorship, to investigate folklife patterns in various states and cities. Plans at first were aimed at establishing this center under the aegis of the Smithsonian Institution, as part of its research empire. But as it worked out, the American Folklife Center, as it came to be called, was adopted by the Library of Congress in the bicentennial year 1976. The first board of trustees, chosen in 1976, included Wayland D. Hand and myself.

Secondly, a number of states have established government-funded folklife research centers. Examples are the Bureau of Florida Folklife; the Vermont Folklife Center; the Western Folklife Center in Utah; the Washington State Folklife Commission; the Southwestern Folklife Center in Arizona; and Pennsylvania's State Office of Folklife Programs, directed by Amy Skillman, under the Governor's Heritage Commission headed by Shalom Staub. There are other such programs involved in folklife research, although not all of them use the term in their titles. Examples include the Missouri Cultural Heritage Center, Chicago's Urban Traditions Program, and the Baltimore Traditions Program. Two most noteworthy institutions are found in Texas: the influential Institute of Texan Cultures at San Antonio, now part of the University of Texas; and the new Program for Regional Studies at Baylor University. Two additional institutions that can serve as models for the regional research centers needed in other sections of the country are the Center for New England Folklife in New Hampshire, and the Center for the Study of Southern Culture at the University of Mississippi, which is headed, I am proud to say, by one of my former students, William Ferris. There is also the Middle Atlantic Folklife Association, which has stimulated research in the Middle States area through its annual meetings. And finally, some of the state arts councils, as well as the National Endowment for the Arts, have sponsored folklife projects through their folk arts divisions.

Thirdly, the term "folklife" has registered in the academic world since 1966, when at the University of Pennsylvania the recently established (1964) Department of Folklore was expanded into a Department of Folklore and Folklife, and I was named chairman by Graduate Dean Roy F. Nichols. Graduates from this program are now teaching courses dealing with aspects of American folklife such as material culture, vernacular architecture, folk medicine, folk religion, and folk art, in various universities in the United States and Canada.

It is also a pleasure to note the upswing in research into American material culture. Whether done by folklore/folklife students, cultural anthropologists, historical archeologists, American civilization graduates, under whatever aegis it has been conducted and published, material culture research forms a welcome adjunct to folklife studies in the United States. I particularly applaud, among many younger scholars whom I could mention in detail, the work of Thomas Schlereth of Notre Dame and Simon Bronner of the Pennsylvania State University. Dr. Schlereth's books—*Artifacts and the American Past* (1980), *Material Culture Studies in America* (1982), and *Material Culture: A Research Guide* (1985)—are indispensable for students in the field. The same is true of Professor Bronner's volumes, *American Material Culture and Folklife: A Prologue and Dialogue* (1985) and *Folklife Studies from the Gilded Age: Object, Rite, and Custom in Victorian America* (1987). In addition, it is a pleasure to salute my colleagues at various other institutions whose work in material culture and folklife has already produced volumes in this series—Warren Roberts, Austin Fife, and Michael Owen Jones.

At the same time that American research was broadening to take in more folklife-oriented projects, under a variety of names and flags, new developments in the field have come in Europe. European scholars are as active as ever in researching their own cultures, but on the continent the folk-oriented terms are being questioned. This questioning springs not only from the misapplication of the folk concept in the Third Reich (several conferences have been held recently in West Germany to analyze this usage, with its complex motivation), but also from its cheapening and tarnishing through use in connection with tourism, festivals, folk revivals, and what Europeans call "applied" folklore, a different usage than our "public sector" folklore. This current flurry of new opinion reflects not only the constant need for redefinition in any discipline, but also the hope to stabilize the terminology by setting it more firmly in the established academic area of ethnology. Hence the increased use of the terms "European ethnology" or "regional ethnology" for the academic field, as evidenced in titles of many academic departments at European universities, and in the periodicals *Ethnologia Europea*, *Ethnologia Scandinavica*, *Ethnologia Slavica*, and *Ethnologie Française*.

In a very real sense, a teacher exists for his students. From my childhood days I always wanted to become a teacher, and I certainly became the first professor, but not the first teacher or even the first Ph.D., in my immediate families. All of my Pennsylvania forebears down to my father and mother were farmers, surveying the world from their own fields and woods and streams, and taking their part in rural communities. But beginning in the early nineteenth century many of my farmer forefathers became country

Figure I.5. Student field trip to the Fallsington and Bucks County Quaker settlements of the seventeenth and eighteenth centuries (1985).
(Photo: Theodore B. Hetzel)

Figure I.6. Student field trip to Lancaster County. Don Yoder analyzes baroque tombstone design at the Bergstrasse Church near Ephrata (1982).
(Photo: Theodore B. Hetzel)

Figure I.7. University field trip (1986) to the William Brinton House (1704).
(Photo: Helen W. Congdon)

Figure I.8. Students examine the architecture of the William Brinton House (1704), south of West Chester, near Dilworthtown in the heart of the Chester-Delaware County Quaker settlement (1986). This room is the basement kitchen, complete with built-in bakeoven at the left of the huge fireplace.
(Photo: Theodore B. Hetzel)

schoolmasters, teaching in the winters, farming in the summers. Both my father and mother taught country school—all eight grades in one room—before going on to higher education, careers, and marriage.

The students who have worked with me at the University of Pennsylvania since 1956 have been varied in talents and interests. From all of them I have learned much along the way, and friendships continue long after degrees are achieved. My doctoral children now number over forty (fifty, counting those who are still laboring at dissertations), and it has been a distinct pleasure to work with all of them through the years. The dissertations I have directed fall into four disciplines: Folklore and Folklife, American History, American Civilization, and Religious Studies. Most of my doctoral progeny are—like their mentor—teaching, as for example Gerald Pocius at Memorial University in Newfoundland and Bernard Herman at the University of Delaware; Kathryn Morgan at Swarthmore and John Burrison at Georgia State; Bonita Freeman-Witthoft at West Chester and Angus Gillespie at Rutgers; Richard Candee at Boston University and Carter Craigie at Cabrini College. Some have gone into museum careers, like the inimitable Yvonne Lange of the Museum of International Folk Art at Santa Fe, Scott T. Swank of the Henry Francis duPont Winterthur Museum, and Jay A. Anderson, who has directed the Colonial Pennsylvania Plantation as well as historical farm museums for both Iowa State University and Utah State University. Others have found influential posts in the public sector as directors of state folklife programs, like Charles Camp, or state and national arts councils, like Robert Teske. And finally there is David Hufford, who of all my students is doing most to advance the field of folk medicine. His position at the Hershey Medical Center of Pennsylvania State University involves teaching future physicians the importance of knowing alternative medical systems with a folk or ethnic or religious base. Dealing with such problems, and pressing on with research in one of my own specialties, religious healing, David Hufford is the first folklore/folklife specialist to teach in a medical school in the United States.

Finally, it is a pleasure to record the fact that my interest in pointing students toward the study of their own cultures—the cultural landscapes around them—has resulted in dissertations on various phases of Pennsylvanian (and American) traditional culture. Heavy hints dropped in class as to open research areas have occasionally led to doctoral dissertations. In her dissertation Barbara Reimensnyder admitted that, although she comes from a Pennsylvania Dutch family and grew up in a Pennsylvania Dutch county, she had never really heard about "powwowing" (Pennsylvania Dutch folk medicine) until she heard the term in one of my classes. Returning home, she asked her mother about it, and yes, Union County, Pennsylvania turned out to be an area where powwowing was widely known, hence Barbara decided to do her dissertation on the subject.

Likewise Thomas E. Graves, a New York Yankee who has lived in the Dutch Country for at least a decade, decided to do his dissertation on "The Pennsylvania German Hex Sign: A Study in Folk Process" (1984). We collaborated on a traveling exhibit on hex signs for the Museum of American Folk Art in New York and on the book *Hex Signs: Pennsylvania Dutch Barn Symbols and Their Meaning,* published in 1989 by E. P. Dutton in collaboration with the Museum of American Folk Art. In fact, we both had the pleasure recently of opening the exhibit at the Reading Museum, accompanied by two hex sign painters of the present, Johnny Claypoole and Ivan Hoyt, both featured in our book.

Two of my current crop of *Doktoranden,* as my German colleagues would call them, deserve special mention. First there is Mario Montaño, whose dissertation deals with a food-related event, the Barbacoa de Cabeza, in his own Mexican-American culture of South Texas. Lastly, Susan Isaacs, through extensive fieldwork over the past several years, has analyzed the production and marketing of the work of the four leading potters in the current Pennsylvania German pottery revival. As my teaching assistant, her help was invaluable in arranging, for those of my students who requested it, classes in the Pennsylvania Dutch dialect. And finally, Susan Isaacs has taken her turn in editing the new periodical, *New Jersey Folklife.*

I could go on reminiscing about my doctoral children, whose friendship along the academic path and interchange of ideas has been an important aspect of a professor's career. I have listed all of my doctoral students and their dissertation titles at the end of the book. I dedicate the book to these, and beyond them, to all my students who have participated in my classes since I first began formal teaching in 1946.

It would not be proper to close these academic reminiscences without a word of thanks to my student, former colleague, and one-time department head, Henry Glassie, who graciously consented to write the foreword to this collection of essays. Henry was a member, along with Jay Anderson and Archie Green, of my very first class in Folklife Studies at the University of Pennsylvania in 1966—a stellar group indeed. I do not know what Henry could possibly have added to his knowledge of American folklife from my classes, since he had come to us, in a sense like Athena from Zeus, thoroughly trained from the Cooperstown Program under Louis E. Jones, Bruce Buckley, and other mentors. He had also met along the way the cultural geographer Fred Kniffen, and already had surveyed the folk cultures of the eastern United States. This survey developed into his book, *Pattern in the Material Folk Culture of the Eastern United States,* which was published by the University of Pennsylvania Press in 1968. In fact, we accepted this book in printed form as his Ph.D. dissertation, an unusual but perfectly legal procedure.

Through the years Henry Glassie has been an inspiration to my own work and thinking about traditional cultures in the American landscape. One of our collaborations needs to be mentioned here. In 1966 I took him with me to the Bald Eagle Valley in Centre County, Pennsylvania, to record two hundred years of rural culture that was shortly to be wiped from the map by a new dam construction. The new "recreational" lake now covers ten miles of a valley settled in the 1790s. In it we found and photographed numerous log houses and barns—even double-crib (southern!) barns—from the pioneer period of the valley's history, and nineteenth-century farmhouses and outbuildings worthy of the National Register. A selected number of these structures Henry measured in his painstaking way. We also came unexpectedly on a rattlesnake den, but that is another story.

Alas, the task of publishing the results of this fieldwork was put on the back burner by both of us. Henry has since gone on many research tracks, most notably to that winsome, unexcelled book, *Passing the Time in Ballymenone,* and has also adopted Turkish culture as one of his comparative specialties. But the Bald Eagle project would still make a good monograph, as a model of how to record a vanishing or threatened American cultural landscape.

In conclusion, let me say how exciting it has been to participate in the shaping and redefinition of an important academic area in the United States. It has been rewarding also to work with all of my students over the past four decades, and to all of them I wish developing careers and exciting research projects. Students exist to go beyond their teachers, so go, students, go! To my colleagues, it has been and continues to be a pleasure to work with all of you—Roger Abrahams, Kenneth Goldstein, Dan Ben-Amos, Margaret Mills, John Roberts, Brian Sutton-Smith, Robert St. George, and David Hufford. I wish you all continued progress in your own valuable and exemplary work. For myself, I hope to press onward in the various research areas on which I have put my mark, and to expand the bibliography with which this volume of mine closes.

Foundations of Folklife Studies

Foundations of Folklife Studies

The two articles with which the book opens speak for themselves. What Henry Glassie has called my "folklife manifesto" of 1963, "The Folklife Studies Movement," called for at the time and still calls for concerted American research on the full range of folk-cultural data in all of America's ethnic, regional, and sectarian cultures. The article traces the history and transit of the terms and concepts of folklife and folklife studies from European scholarship to the British Isles and across the Atlantic to the United States. The article appeared in *Pennsylvania Folklife* and is published here in full except for the omission of the detailed materials on the Pennsylvania Folklife Society and its regionally limited program.

The article "Folklife Studies in American Scholarship" was the introduction to my bicentennial offering to my colleagues and students in 1976, the volume entitled *American Folklife.* It carries my argument further, and broadens my definition of American folklife to include all the ethnic groups who contributed to its makeup. It is offered here with the hope that it will continue to be of use as a guide and stimulus to American research in the future.

It is obvious that my principal concern in these early writings on folklife studies was to provide American students with research tools, methods, and models, and to challenge them to undertake a systematic study of their own traditional cultures and their roots here and abroad. It should be equally obvious that these methods are by no means limited to Europe and America, but can indeed be applied all over the world, to study traditional and regional elements in complex societies.

1

The Folklife Studies Movement

The folklife studies movement is a twentieth-century addition to scholarship. The term "folklife," an English adaptation of the Swedish term *folkliv,* is building about itself a new and exciting discipline, which has already influenced research in the British Isles, from whence it has begun to make itself felt in the United States.

"Folklife Studies" or "Folklife Research"—Swedish *folklivsforskning,* German *Volkslebenforschung* or *Volkskunde*—is a total scholarly concentration on the folk levels of a national or regional culture. In brief, folklife studies involves the analysis of a folk culture in its entirety.

By folk culture is meant in this case the lower (traditional or "folk" levels) of a literate Western (European or American) society. Folk culture is traditional culture, bound by tradition and transmitted by tradition, and is basically (although not exclusively) rural and preindustrial. Obviously it is the opposite of the mass-produced, mechanized, popular culture of the twentieth century.

"Folklife" is a term of Swedish origin, from *folkliv,* coined by scholars in the nineteenth century, following the already established German term *Volksleben.* The term "folklife research" *(folklivsforskning)* was coined in 1909 at the University of Lund when Sven Lampa began lectures in *Svensk Folklivsforskning* (Swedish Folklife Research). The term *Folkslivsforskning* is an exact equivalent of the German term *Volkskunde* and probably was coined with that intention.[1]

To those who are beginning to use it in Britain and the United States, the term "folklife" is intended to include the total range of the folk culture, material as well as oral or spiritual. It is consciously intended to be a term of broader range than the English word *folklore*, which, as is commonly known, was coined in England in 1846 by W. J. Thoms, to express in "basic Anglo-Saxon" what the English at the time meant by "popular antiquities."

This article originally appeared in *Pennsylvania Folklife* 13 (3) (July 1963): 43–56.

Thoms' definition of his new word was "the study of traditions, customs and superstitions current among common people in civilised countries." Following the definition favored by the English Folklore Society, folklore has been, with a few exceptions which we will discuss later, limited in range to the *literary* aspects of folk culture—the folktale, the folksong, the proverb and other oral literature—in other words, the "lore" in folklore.

In a sense "folklore" and the folklore movement represent a nineteenth-century discovery, in the English-speaking lands, of isolated bits of folk-cultural memoranda—in other words, a partially conceived folk culture, basically oral tradition. In working on his specialties, whether they were folksongs, folktales, or "superstitions," the folklorist did discover the folk level of his culture, but in limiting himself to oral aspects of culture he very frequently missed the setting of the songs or tales themselves in the total culture of his area. He performed the valuable function of preserving the songs, or tales, of a culture, but was rarely concerned to relate them functionally, sociologically, and psychologically to the culture that produced them.

The folklife studies movement is the twentieth-century rediscovery of the total range of the folk culture (folklife). Folklore is not so much its parent as is anthropology, especially what Americans call cultural anthropology and Europeans ethnology or ethnography. The cultural anthropologist studies *all* aspects of a culture—farming, cooking, dress, ornament, houses, settlements, handicrafts, trade, transportation, amusements, art, marriage, family, religion—to list a few of the subjects included as chapter headings in any basic recent text.

The twentieth-century rediscovery of folklife and the consequent emergence of the academic discipline of Folklife Studies would seem to be a converging of several older academic disciplines. Basically, as we have said, it represents the application of the techniques of cultural anthropology—used so successfully with primitive cultures—to the folk levels of the literate cultures of Northern Europe, the British Isles, and now the United States. In addition to anthropology, geography, linguistics, religion, psychology, parapsychology, and sociology have all contributed to the creation of the new discipline of folklife studies. Scholars from all of these fields are involved. Before looking at the emergence and progress of the folklife studies movement, let us take a more detailed look at the vocabulary of the movement.

"Folklore" and "Folklife"

There are three terms that we must look at as background for the folklife studies movement. These are "folklore," "folklife," and the German term *Volkskunde,* which antedates both. The term "folklore" seems to have been coined independently of the already existing German word *Volkskunde* which had made its appearance in 1806.[2] In England the term "folklore"—originally hyphenated as "folk-lore"—was given widespread attention through the foundation of the Folk-Lore Society in London in 1877, and in America through the foundation of the American Folklore Society in 1888.

The creator of the term "folk-lore," W. J. Thoms, in 1846 described it as "that department of the study of antiquities and archaeology which embraces everything relating to ancient observances and customs, to the notions, beliefs, traditions, superstitions and prejudices of the common people."[3] The definition adopted by the Folk-Lore Society of Britain is "the oral culture and traditions of the folk, that is folk-beliefs, customs, institutions, pastimes, sayings, songs, stories, and arts and crafts, both as regards their origin and their present social functions."[4] The second of these definitions is broader than the first. It attempts to broaden "folklore" to include not only custom and oral tradition, but also something of material culture (arts and crafts).

There are of course as many definitions of "folklore" as there are scholars working in the field.[5] But basically there are two main trends in definitions of the term. One trend attempts to limit folklore to the spiritual folk culture, the other attempts to stretch folklore to include both spiritual and material folk culture. An example of the first is the Arnhem Congress definition (1955) of folklore as "the *spiritual* tradition of the folk, particularly oral tradition, as well as the science which studies this tradition."[6] An example of the second or stretched definition of folklore is Stith Thompson's, who would have folklore involve "the dances, songs, tales, legends, and traditions, the beliefs and superstitions, and the proverbial sayings of peoples everywhere," as well as customs, practices, buildings, utensils, etc., if these latter belong to the materials of culture in a literate society.[7]

The stretching of the term folklore to include the totality of folk culture would seem to be a recent trend, a belated admission of the insufficiency of the term, as usually defined in the English-speaking countries, to deal with folk culture as a whole. For instance, Lord Raglan, in his presidential address before the British Folklore Society in 1946, suggested that it was high time that the society live up to its broadened definition of folklore.[8] While "arts and crafts" were included in the society's definition of folklore they had at that time yet to make their appearance in the society's journal, "the contributions to which are almost entirely confined to superstition and what is known as oral literature." He goes on to suggest the need for study of the material culture—cart types and rural architecture, for two examples. "It should, in my opinion, be the task of this Society to collect, and publish in convenient form, information on all aspects of folk life, using that term in its widest sense, in the hope of enabling us to find out how and why changes in custom and fashion come about, and therefore developing a real science of folklore."

The American Folklore Society, like its British parent, has also wrestled with the definition of folklore and has tried to broaden its sights. The results have been disappointing. In a 1957 symposium, "A Theory for American Folklore," there is not a single reference to the "folklife" approach and its possible relation to the "folklore" approach. The key article by Richard Dorson pays lip-service to "folk culture" and the contributions anthropologists can make to folklore studies, but the image of "folklore" that one retains after reading his suggestions is still limited to oral literature plus custom plus folk art (he does mention "Pennsylvania Dutch *fraktur*").[9]

In his "prepared comments" on Dorson's address, Melville J. Herskovits praises Dorson's "consideration of the relevance of cultural anthropology for the study of American folklore" and then goes on to make two very interesting criticisms. The first one is this: "I have a friend who has a great interest in the barns found in different parts of the United States, particularly the migration to the Middle West of the type of barn where the upper level is reached by a built-up ramp that represents a survival of the New England structure which makes use of the hillside against which the barn is built for this purpose. In his studies of barns, is my friend doing folklore?" Obviously most literary or humanistic folklorists, as Dorson calls them, would say "no," and most anthropological folklorists or folk anthropologists would say "yes." Seriously, Herskovits comments that "what is sometimes alluded to as 'folk custom' does enter into Dorson's paper, but it is given distinctly minor emphasis. If the amount of space devoted to this aspect of the subject is compared with the discussion of narrative and song and proverb and tall tale and legend, its relevance strikes me as no more than tangential."[10]

In more recent years, the symposium "Folklore Research around the World," which fills the entire October-December issue of the *Journal of American Folklore* for 1961, shows almost total unawareness of folklife research. The one article that does mention several Scandinavian folklife research institutions makes no attempt to differentiate them in method and range from the earlier folklore institutions.[11]

May it be that, despite the American and British attempt—halfhearted at that—to stretch the term folklore to include material culture, scholarship in the English-speaking countries has been seriously hindered, is hindered, and will continue to be hindered by the psychological limitations of the word "folklore" itself, whereas European scholars schooled in the *Volkskunde* and *folkliv* concepts, have without embarrassment accepted material culture as well as oral culture as their natural field of study?

The German term *Volkskunde* is related to both "folklore" and "folklife." It is the oldest of the three. In fact "folklore" is an attempt—not a successful one, as time seems to be proving—to find an equivalent in English. "Folklife" (Swedish *folkliv*) is a successful rendering which preserves the total range of interest expressed in the highly developed science of *Volkskunde.*

Perhaps the late Richard Weiss, the outstanding Swiss folklife scholar and one of the shapers of the contemporary folklife movement, can help to clarify American as well as British thought on the subject of the relation of folklore and folklife. According to Richard Weiss, "*Volkskunde* (which I would translate 'Folklife Studies') is the science of folklife. Folklife consists of the mutual relations operative between folk and folk culture, so far as they are determined by community and tradition."[12]

Sigurd Erixon, a founder of "folklife research" as an academic discipline, defines it as "the science of man as a cultural being.... Folklife research is essentially to be regarded as a branch of general anthropology or ethnology and may therefore be called ethnology.... The subject of the folklife research we are concerned with is, in my opinion, a comparative culture research on a regional basis, with a sociological and historical orientation and with certain psychological aspects."[13] The regional delimitation has led Erixon and others to suggest the alternate name "Regional Ethnology" or "European Ethnology."

In the recent ethnological dictionary issued by UNESCO, Prof. Hultkrantz of the University of Stockholm comments on Erixon's definition as follows. Folklife research focuses upon the whole range of culture—material, social, and spiritual. Hence it is not an equivalent to "folklore." It is best to say that folklife research *includes* folklore. In comparing it, however, with general ethnology, folklife research has a regional basis—its aim is to study folk culture in civilized countries. Hultkrantz suggests modestly that for the United States it may prove a better term than "folklore"—"it could (better than the vague or more limited term folklore) serve as a name for that discipline which studies the indigenous culture of the white settlers in its totality."[14]

The term "European Ethnology" has been proposed, and used by some scholars, for the discipline of folklife studies.[15] The advantage of the terminology is that it does set the discipline against its background in anthropology. A disadvantage is that while the term is useful in Europe, to "translate" it into "American Ethnology" brings confusion since ethnology in America has normally been associated with the study of the native Indian cultures of North America, as for instance in the publications of the Bureau of American Ethnology, founded in 1879 specifically to study the American Indian and his culture.

Folklife Studies in Europe

Among the institutions for research in folklife which have arisen in Europe are (1) the International Association for European Ethnology and Folklore, (2) regional folklife societies such as the Ulster Folklife Society (1960) and the Society for Folk Life Studies (1961), (3) the folklife institute and archive, usually in connection with a university, and (4) the open-air museum. Let us look at each of these phases.

Out of the working together of Scandinavian, Continental, and British Isles scholars has come the International Ethnological (*Volkskunde* or *Folklivsforskning*) Association for Central, Northern, and Western Europe—usually referred to as "The International Association for European Ethnology and Folklore"—which resulted from a conference at Lund in November, 1935. Its purpose is "to facilitate researches in cultural and folkloristic subjects over an extensive field, ultimately projected to embrace all Europe, by the exchange of information among constituent countries and by the co-ordination of research methods and results wherever possible."[16]

At the Association's first international congress, at Edinburgh in 1937, Prof. H. Geijer of Uppsala, in the presidential address, suggested that the work with which the congress scholars were occupied "is devoted to sciences that are still young. These sciences are not yet in a satisfactory and definite state, in relation to the older sciences. Our studies are concentrated round human nature and the development of mankind, but from other points of view than those with which the older sciences mostly deal. The most usual and accessible men—that is, the men of our own countries—are the latest to be made objects of scientific interest and research. The exotic and the prehistoric races have occupied the minds of the scientists more than those nearer home." Not only must science turn to the human cultures closer to home, i.e., the folklife approach—but the materials of folklore and folklife must be studied in relation to the culture as a whole. The Association adopted as its official organ the periodical *Folkliv.*[17]

Regional folklife societies have arisen in Britain in particular as a conscious effort to interest scholars as well as lay collectors in the concept of folklife. In 1960 the Ulster Folklife Society was organized, whose aim is "to encourage the study of local history and the collecting and recording of material relating to the folklife and traditions of Northern Ireland." It grew out of the Committee on Ulster Folklife and Traditions which had been organized in 1952. The Society has taken over the publication of the Committee's annual volume, *Ulster Folklife,* founded 1955 and now in its ninth year. The first annual meeting of the Ulster Folklife Society was held in the spring of 1961.

In the fall of 1961 the first meeting of the (British) Society for Folk Life Studies was held at University College, London, with the second meeting at the University of Reading in September, 1962. Its purpose is "to further the study of traditional ways of life in Great Britain and Ireland and to provide a common meeting point for the many people and institutions engaged with the varied aspects of the subject."[18] The first number of the annual journal of the society, *Folk Life,* appeared in the summer of 1963.

The basic unit in European folklife research, however, is not the international association or the national folklife society, but the folklife institute and archive. These are national or regional institutions. There are many names for this type of institution: for examples, there are the *Folklivsarkivet* (Lund), *Institutet for Folkelivsgransking* (Oslo), *Volkskundliche Kommission* (Münster/Westfalen), *Institut voor Volkskunde* (Amsterdam), and the *Schweizerisches Institut für Volkskunde* (Basel). Some of these "institutes" and "archives" are connected with universities, others with national societies or academies of science, some are state supported and others are privately supported. But basically all these institutions have a common approach and a common set of research techniques. They house, first of all, research libraries which, with few exceptions, put American university folklore collections quite in the shade. Furthermore, sizable permanent staffs are engaged in collecting materials in the field and archiving these materials in the central archive. Most of these institutes are also involved in museum work, especially open-air museum work.

The common approach of these institutions is the folklife approach—whether it is called folklife, *Volkskunde,* or Regional Ethnology. The common techniques are the questionnaire, the local collector and informant, the *Kartei* indexing of the materials brought in from the field, and the cartographical method (Folk Atlas) with its distribution maps of terms, customs, and types of material objects (house-types, barn-types, cart-types, etc.).[19]

The exciting thing about these institutions, apart from their revolutionary concept of the holistic approach to regional folk culture, is that they are oriented in two directions. A great many of them are connected with universities—the *Folklivsarkivet* at Lund and the *Volkskundliche Kommission* at Münster for two examples. The staffs are on the university staff and supervise research in this growing field.[20] In 1961–62, for instance, five doctoral dissertations in folklife studies resulted from the work of the *Volkskundliche Kommission* in Münster. The second orientation of these institutions is that they are rooted in the population through the local informants who either contribute oral recorded or written answers to the printed questionnaires which are sent out on every possible subject in folk-cultural studies. Holland's *Institut voor Volkskunde* has, under the direction of Dr. P. J. Meertens, over 2000 local collaborators—school teachers and others—in every area of Holland, who are constantly sending in materials that they have collected in their home areas.[21] In some cases also the institutes are related to the public schools. For example, the Irish Folklore Commission has used reports on folktales written down on their request by school children in the Gaeltacht.

While the original folklife institutions are Scandinavian and Continental, the movement and its methods spread to the British Isles beginning with the creation of the Irish Folklore Commission in 1935 by Prof. James H. Delargy. Admittedly influenced by and based on Scandinavian, particularly Swedish, techniques for folklife study, the Commission has in turn influenced research in "these islands"—as the Scots and Irish are now somewhat over-tactfully calling what used to be known as the "British Isles." There are also the School of Scottish Studies at the University of Edinburgh, the Welsh Folk Museum at St. Fagan's, Cardiff, and the Ulster Folklife Society and Ulster Folk Museum, connected through its leadership with Queen's University, Belfast, and now the latest offspring of the Swedish-Irish-Scottish chain of influence—the Folk Life Survey at the University of Leeds in Yorkshire, initiated in 1960 and headed by Professor Stewart F. Sanderson, who was trained in the School of Scottish Studies.[22]

And so the influence continues. The research impulse and techniques generated in the *Volkskunde* movement in Germany and the *Folklivsforskning* movement in Sweden are applied to the British Isles and eventually to the United States.

The Open-Air Museum

So far we have spoken only of research institutions of the library-archive-institute type. Many of these, however, have an adjunct institution, an annex called the "folk museum" or "open-air museum."[23] To illustrate the material aspects of the folk culture, a new type of museum was developed in Scandinavia beginning in the 1890's—the "open-air museum" or sometimes, simply, "folk museum."

American tourists are familiar with the oldest of these institutions, the Skansen Open-Air Museum located magnificently on a hilltop on one of Stockholm's wooded islands. Here, beginning in 1891 under the inspiration of the founder, Dr. Artur Hazelius, were rebuilt typical farmhouses, manor-houses, barns and other outbuildings, and a magnificent folk church, brought from all parts of Sweden and representative of regional variant types. Hazelius had earlier founded the Nordic Museum *(Nordisk Museet)* to study Swedish peasant culture, of which Skansen is a public annex whose purpose is to display to the public, in their natural settings, rural and town buildings from all parts of Sweden.[24]

With Skansen as the model, the open-air museum has spread throughout Sweden and the rest of Scandinavia. In Sweden over 400 communities maintain open-air museums or smaller folk museums to display aspects of the regional culture. For instance, at Harnösand, an eighty-building open-air museum deals with the Lapp culture. The Culture-Historical Museum *(Kulturhistoriska Museet)* at Lund is a town museum, with town houses and conventional museum buildings of exhibits.[25] Some small towns have parish museums, some estate owners have private open-air museums. And then there are the craft museums, as that for the glass-making craft at Växjö. This frenzy of museum activity—much, though not all of it, directed toward the study and display of the folk level of culture—has led in Sweden to mass collecting of objects of the material culture and to the creation of an able corps of officially commissioned and university-trained museum men.

From Sweden the open-air museum has spread to Denmark, Norway, Finland, and the Continent, where it combines with the German museum movement in which *Volkskunde* scholars have long since united with regional historians in the highly developed German study of *Heimatkunde*.[26] Many small German, Swiss, and Austrian communities have a *Heimatmuseum* which displays materials from the folk or peasant level of the regional culture along with emphasis on regional history, architecture, arts, and costume. Most of these, however, are not open-air museums but folk museums of the more usual museum-building sort. The largest and best open-air museum on the continent of Europe south of Scandinavia is the 220-acre *Nederlands Openlucht Museum* (Dutch Open-Air Museum) at Arnhem in Gelderland, Netherlands, founded in 1912 and formally opened in 1918.[27]

In the British Isles the first folk museum of the open-air variety was the museum of Highland culture begun by Isabel F. Grant on Iona in 1936—since 1944 "Am Fasgadh" (The Shelter) at Kingussie, Invernessshire, Scotland.[28] In 1955 the management was taken over by the four universities of Scotland, in collaboration with the Royal Scottish Museum. Other folk museums in the British Isles are the Welsh Folk Museum at St. Fagan's Castle, Cardiff, opened 1946; Blaise Castle House, Bristol, opened 1949; the Museum of English Rural Life at the University of Reading, opened 1950; the Manx Museum at Cregneash on the Isle of Man; the West Yorkshire Folk Museum at Halifax, opened 1953; and the Ulster Folk Museum near Belfast in Northern Ireland, opened 1955.

In the United States the trend has been toward the "pioneer village" or "restoration village" type of open-air museum. The pioneer here was that for Norwegian-American life at Decorah, Iowa, founded in 1925—an example of Scandinavian influence. The most spectacular of the restoration projects is Colonial Williamsburg, begun in 1926. The Farmer's Museum operated by the New York State Historical Association at Cooperstown, New York, deals with a wide range of folk-cultural subjects in its displays and annual seminars for research students. Old Sturbridge Village in Massachusetts and the Shelburne Museum in Vermont are open-air museums dealing with New England culture. The Greenfield Village at Dearborn, Michigan, is an open-air museum but on the historical-museum plan, with "association items" moved to the site.

Regional Folk Cultures in America

In suggesting the possibilities for folklife studies in the United States, we must first point out that folklife studies is a very young discipline, and, like all new systems of scholarship, it has to make its way amid the earlier and already established approaches to the study of American life. These already existing approaches study American life on the national, regional, and local levels, and include (1) the old-line historical approach with historical societies and historical journals interested in basically military and political history, with some emphasis upon "social history" which begins to approach folklife studies. There is (2) the sociological approach which studies American civilization as a whole. There is (3) the folklore approach which has been crystallized into several academic schools and departments of folklore—those at the Universities of California, Indiana, and Pennsylvania being the principal examples. There is (4) the young and growing discipline of American Civilization, which has however basically concentrated on urban rather than on rural America, and on creative rather than folk culture, leaving the rural field of traditional regional culture free for the development of folklife studies.[29]

Folklife Studies is a new approach. We in America who are concerned with the new discipline feel very much as Dr. Iorwerth Peate did when he stated, in 1958, in an address before the British Association for the Advancement of Science, that "the study of folk life is a new discipline and one so far unrecognized by all universities in Britain."[30] So far this is true also in America. There are plenty of scholars working in the field, who look for inspiration to the organized movements in Scandinavia and the British Isles, but thus far there are no departments or schools of folklife studies connected with any American university. However, since Dr. Peate made his statement, a chair of Folk Life Studies has been founded at the University of Leeds in 1960. Possibly during the 1960s progress can be made also in the United States in the recognition of folklife studies as an academic discipline.

One of the difficulties is that one *can* study *"American* folklore"—basically folksongs sung or folktales told in America—but to study *"American* folklife" one has to divide the folk level of American culture into its regional components. There just is no "American folk culture" as a whole, in the same sense that one can speak of a Swedish folk culture, or a Welsh folk culture, or a Highlands folk culture.

New England with its Puritan-Yankee culture—its native types of farmhouses, barns, and meetinghouses, its baked beans and boiled dinners, its accent and folkspeech—is one of these. This regional culture has influenced Long Island, Central and Western New York, Northern Pennsylvania, and the Midwest, as well as the Maritimes in Canada. The area of Holland Dutch settlement (New York, New Jersey, Pennsylvania, and Delaware) can offer certain visible signs of a Netherlands-American folk culture—the hay barrack being the best specific example.[31] The Upland South and the Deep South had and have differing folk cultures.[32] The study of these American regions, and the others, can be aided greatly by concentration on folk-cultural concepts.

The Pennsylvania folk culture is important to the nation for two basic reasons. Here the American process of acculturation—the trading and adjusting of emigrant cultural gifts—was vastly more important than in New England or the South, with their more homogeneous populations. For instance, the Swiss and German settlers built two-story barns (Swiss, bank, or Pennsylvania barns) which were copied as early as the eighteenth century by the Quakers, who called them "cellar barns." House patterns went in the other direction—from the British Isles settlers to the settlers of Continental origin, so that by 1800 the Pennsylvania Dutch groups were building English-style Georgian houses. The influence of food specialties is an example of the same transfer. The Quakers, even in Philadelphia, made crocks of "pickled cabbage" and came to call it "sourcrout" like their Dutch neighbors; they made "scrapple" at butchering time and came to call it, some of them, "ponhors" or "ponhaws" like the upcountry Dutch. Pennsylvania is important folk-culturally because of this early acculturation process which can be so thoroughly documented in the eighteenth- and nineteenth-century sources.

Pennsylvania is important folk-culturally to the nation for a second reason. Pennsylvania was the source of a great migration in the eighteenth and nineteenth centuries. The main thrusts of this migration went (1) southward as far as the Carolinas beginning in the 1740s and 1750s; (2) northward through the Genesee Country, the Niagara Peninsula and Central Ontario after the Revolution; and (3) westward through Ohio as far as Iowa and Kansas, from the Revolution to the Civil War. This Pennsylvania migration has influenced all of these areas folk-culturally—Dutch dialect and

Dutch-English expressions, barn, farmhouse, and springhouse patterns, cookery habits (sauerkraut, smearcase, scrapple, etc.), all made their way south, north, and west with the migrating Pennsylvanians., With the exception of Pennsylvania's three basic contributions to the American frontier—log architecture, the Conestoga wagon, and the Kentucky rifle—these folk-cultural influences of Pennsylvania upon the nation have never been fully studied.

The Application of the Folklife Concept

The application of the folklife concept in the United States could, first of all, provide the necessary corrective to the undisciplined or commercially slanted "collecting" of "folk art" and "antiques." In Pennsylvania and elsewhere the "collector" has set his sights on commercially valuable pieces—i.e., items that could be displayed decoratively in the urban home—and left the remaining aspects of the folk culture behind to disintegrate. The "antique" collectors of the nineteenth and twentieth centuries ripped individual pieces out of their settings, the "folk art" collectors did the same. The collecting was valuable, as far as it went, and many collections are now in public institutions where, at last, proper attention can be given to their functional relation to the entire culture.

The folklife studies movement can also eventually correct the definitely pseudo use of regional "folk" themes in connection with America's rapidly growing tourist industry.[33] Pennsylvania provides several instructive examples here. The tourist identification of "Amish" with "Pennsylvania Dutch," the perpetuation of false fictional Dutch-English expressions on menus as typical of Dutchdom, the too-facile popularization of regional cookery—all these need correction. Actually, as we have pointed out, the real work on folk cookery, historically based, still remains to be done. We need cookery atlases as well as linguistic atlases of the eastern seaboard, and unfortunately the work on these has only now begun.

Thirdly, folklife research can eventually enrich the teaching of state and regional history, and early American history, in the public schools. American history as taught in the public schools has too often been linear—1775 to 1861 to 1941—with heavy emphasis on military and political phases. History, like our study of literature, has concentrated on the "great men" approach to the past. It has concentrated on the few creative individuals—the Lincolns in history and the Emersons in literature. Their lives have of course influenced others, and have symbolic value as representatives of past ages and areas. But the horizontal or cultural approach to history, to the history of the folk culture, has only in part, through the twentieth-century emphasis on "social history," been seen as worthy of attention. We have studied Greek temples and Gothic cathedrals in Europe and for the most part neglected to look at our farmhouses, barns, and meetinghouses—which European travelers of the nineteenth century noted with amazement as distinctive of our regional culture.

Fourthly, folklife research, if introduced into the university level of study, could tie together here, as it has done in Europe, the related work of folklorists and cultural anthropologists, of regional historians and human geographers.

Fifthly, the application of the folklife concept, the folk-cultural approach to history, could revitalize, even revolutionize, our local historical societies and local museums. Our county historical societies contain a corps of the most likely persons to be interested in folk culture, but until very recently, most individual interests were motivated by genealogical, straight-historical concerns, or for the rest, membership in the county historical society is simply one of several "status symbols" in our county towns. Possibly a basic reason why urban historical society members have not been attracted to the folklife approach is that they prefer to forget the earlier rural roots of their families. Also, the D.A.R. emphasis, which views the past genealogically, concentrates on the Revolutionary era; it presents a filtered view of American history which overemphasizes 1775–1783 and deemphasizes the long building of American life with the plow and the flail, the husking peg and the hominy block, the schoolhouse and the meetinghouse.[34]

The county historical societies have done a good job of connecting local history with the general framework of American history—the county's participation in the Revolution, the county's response to the Civil War—all this in the wake of the nationalist historiography that followed the Centennial of 1876. In the Central Pennsylvania societies, transportation history and the iron industry are well covered—the history of agriculture and rural life almost completely neglected.

In museum work also the folklife approach could revolutionize the local historical societies. Some of the rooms now lined with Civil War swords might well be used to illustrate the settlement history of the county, accenting its rural culture from pioneer days through the nineteenth century. A beginning has been made in such excellent research institutions as the historical societies of Bucks County, with the Mercer Museum in Doylestown with its magnificent displays of material culture;[35] the Chester County society, with its splendid museum of period rooms, its seasonal displays of Christmas, Easter, and Valentine materials, and its restoration of a typical West Chester town house, the Townsend House, and the oldest rural house in Chester County—the Brinton House of 1704; the Berks County society with its excellent museum facilities; and the York County society, with its recent new museum building with period rooms, shops, and exhibits on settlement history.

Sixthly, concern with folklife—with the folk levels of American culture—could teach us to look with new eyes at what we still have with us of the folk-cultural past. The stump fences and log barns of the Allegheny Mountain counties of Central Pennsylvania, the snake fences, the remaining bake-ovens, springhouses, the barn patterns, log and stone and brick farmhouses, the cookery, the folkspeech—all the things, in fact, that *Pennsylvania Folklife* has been interested in—deserve full study as phases of American folk culture.

Lastly, the chief value of folklife studies is that its data show us the range of human thought, more basically perhaps than history, literature, and other already accepted studies. In showing us what life was like before urbanization and industrialization, we are shown the long roots of the life that we share. E. Estyn Evans, folklife scholar at Queen's University in Belfast, has made the statement: "Nothing less than the whole of the past is needed to explain the present."[36] And Ruth Benedict, speaking of folk belief and folk custom, makes clear the value of our investigation of it in these words: "More than any other body of material it makes vivid the recency and the precariousness of those rationalistic attitudes of the modern urban educated groups which are often identified with human nature."[37]

Perhaps a flail can teach us more about man than a Civil War sword.

Notes

1. Information from the Folklivsarkivet, University of Lund, Sweden, letter from Dr. Brita Egardt, 26 March 1963, which suggests that the earliest documented use of "folkliv" in Sweden came with Lovén's book, *Folklivet i Skytts härad* (The Folklife of the Jurisdictional District of Skytt), published 1847. In 1878 it was used in the title of a new periodical, *Svenska Landsmål och Svenskt Folkliv* (Swedish Dialects and Swedish Folklife), which is still in publication. Of "folklife research" *(folklivsforskning),* Åke Hultkrantz's new dictionary, *General Ethnological Concepts* (Copenhagen, 1960), vol. 1 of the "International Dictionary of Regional European Ethnology and Folklore," says only that it was "coined in Sweden in 1909."

2. For the history of the word *Volkskunde,* see Oswald A. Erich and Richard Beitl, *Wörterbuch der deutschen Volkskunde,* 2d ed. by Richard Beitl (Stuttgart, 1955), 799–809; Grimm, *Deutsches Wörterbuch,* R. Meiszner, ed., Bd. 12, 2. Abt., 4.Lieferung (Leipzig, 1932), "Volkskunde," columns 486–87; Will-Erich Peuckert and Otto Lauffer, *Volkskunde: Quellen und Forschungen seit 1930* (Bern, 1951); Friedrich Kluge, *Etymologisches Wörterbuch der Deutschen Sprache,* 18th ed. by Walther Mitzka (Berlin, 1960), "Volkskunde"; Karl Meisen, "Europäische Volkskunde als Forschungsaufgabe," *Rheinisches Jahrbuch für Volkskunde* 3 (1952): 7–40; and Wolfgang Steinitz, "Volkskunde und Völkerkunde," *Deutsches Jahrbuch für Volkskunde* 1 (1955): 269–75.

3. For the term "Folk-Lore," which first appeared in the *Athenaeum* for 22 August 1846, in a letter by "Ambrose Merton" (W. J. Thoms), see the *Oxford English Dictionary,* vol. 4:

390. For Thoms and his defense of the originality of his coinage against charges that it was borrowed from the German, see Duncan Emrich, "'Folk-Lore': William John Thoms," *California Folklore Quarterly* 5 (1946): 355–74.

4. Lord Raglan, "The Scope of Folk-Lore," Presidential Address delivered before the Folk-Lore Society, 20 March 1946, in *Folk-Lore* 57 (1946): 98.

5. Compare the twenty or more definitions listed in Maria Leach, ed., *Funk & Wagnalls Standard Dictionary of Folklore, Mythology and Legend* (New York, 1949), vol. 1; also Hultkrantz, *Ethnological Concepts,* 135–41.

6. The Arnhem Congress, which met at the Dutch Open-Air Museum at Arnhem in Gelderland, 20–24 September 1955, was called by Director Winfred Roukens of the Open-Air Museum for the specific purpose of determining upon international terminology for the folklore-folklife field of research. Roukens proposed the problem in his article, "Folklore. Ein Name und eine Gefahr?" *Bijdragen en Mededelingen* 20 (1955): 2–9. At the congress, certain delegates favored "Ethnology" or "European Ethnology" for the international name of the science they were creating. However, the West German, Austrian, and Swiss representatives, who came from the highly scientific development of *Volkskunde,* opposed the merging of the term *Volkskunde* into ethnology, which would have meant a serious loss of prestige for the *Volkskunde* movement. The congress emphasized the pressing need for an international term corresponding to the Scandinavian *Folklivsforskning.* For the Arnhem Congress, see the *Deutsches Jahrbuch für Volkskunde* 2 (1956): 264; also *Volkskunde* 56 (1955): 139–43.

7. Hultkrantz, *Ethnological Concepts,* 136. See also Stith Thompson, ed., *Four Symposia on Folklore* (Bloomington, Indiana, 1953), for debates on the scope of folklore at the Midcentury International Folklore Conference, held at Indiana University in the summer of 1950. This was perhaps the first national forum at which the term "folklife" was given attention in the United States, principally through the participation of Sigurd Erixon. However, as late as 1953 Stith Thompson complained that "both folklorists and ethnologists in America have failed to make adequate systematic studies of the material culture and customs of the dominant white groups, mostly of European origin. Folk-life in the sense in which the Europeans use it has seldom seemed to be the business of either, but it must be hoped that some of the problems now so well worked on by Swedes, Finns, Irish, French, and others who will be assembling in the Ethnological Congress in Vienna this summer may appeal to our own investigators. It matters little whether they call themselves folklorists or ethnologists or anthropologists" (Stith Thompson, "Advances in Folklore Studies," in A. L. Kroeber, ed., *Anthropology Today: An Encyclopedic Inventory* (Chicago, 1953), 592–93.

8. Lord Raglan, "Scope of Folk-Lore," 98, 105. See also his "The Origin of Folk-Culture," *Folk-Lore* 58 (1947): 250–60, which regrets that the study of folklore has failed to attract the attention of leading British medievalists and social historians.

9. Richard M. Dorson, "A Theory for American Folklore," *Journal of American Folklore* 72 (1959): 197–215. Dorson's valuable suggestions as to the use of folk materials in immigration, frontier, and regional history have been further elaborated in his now standard American volume on the folklore approach, *American Folklore* (Chicago, 1959).

10. Melville J. Herskovits, "Prepared Comments," *Journal of American Folklore* 72 (1959): 216–20. Herskovits was more specific in an earlier article, "Folklore after a Hundred Years: A Problem in Redefinition," *Journal of American Folklore* 59 (1946): 89–100,

which does contain a brief mention of the "folk-life" or "Nordic Ethnology" approach in Scandinavia, and points out the fact that from the very beginning *Volkskunde* has had a far wider scope than folklore. See also William R. Bascom, "Folklore and Anthropology," *Journal of American Folklore* 66 (1953): 283–90: "Folklore, to the anthropologist, is a part of culture but not the whole of culture. It includes myths, legends, tales, proverbs, riddles, the texts of ballads and other songs, and other forms of less importance, but not folk art, folk dance, folk music, folk costume, folk medicine, folk custom, or folk belief" (285).

11. "Folklore Research around the World: A North American Point of View," Richard M. Dorson, ed., *Journal of American Folklore* 74 (1961): 287–460. The one article that makes specific reference to folklife research is Warren E. Roberts, "Folklore in Norway: Addendum," 321–24.

12. Richard Weiss, *Volkskunde der Schweiz* (Zurich, 1946). *"Volkskunde ist die Wissenschaft vom Volksleben. Das Volksleben besteht aus den zwischen Volk und Volkskultur wirkenden Wechselbeziehungen soweit sie durch Gemeinschaft und Tradition bestimmt sind."* Richard Weiss (1907–1962) has had deep influence upon folklife *(Volkskunde)* scholarship in the German-speaking lands, through his writings on *Volkskunde*-theory, principally the work cited, and his teaching at the University of Zurich. His untimely death in 1962 has deprived the folklife studies movement of one of its principal leaders. For a summary of his importance in the movement, see *Schweizerisches Archiv für Volkskunde* 58 (4) (1962): 185–99.

13. Hultkrantz, *Ethnological Concepts,* 133.

14. Ibid., 133–34.

15. On the varying uses of "ethnology" and "ethnography" see T. K. Penniman, *A Hundred Years of Anthropology* (New York, 1936).

16. *The Proceedings of the Scottish Anthropological and Folklore Society* 2 (3) (October, 1937): 1. This society and its proceedings, vols. 1–4 (1935–1956), were until 1956 one of the most active evidences in Britain of the folklife movement. Since 1956, however, the Society has been replaced by the School of Scottish Studies at the University of Edinburgh and the proceedings are succeeded by *Scottish Studies.*

17. Jan de Vries, in his Introduction to *Folk-Liv* 1 (1938): 8–9, speaks of the amalgamation in the new journal of "the two sides of our activity, ethnology and folklore proper, together covering the whole domain of the material, social and mental life," so that both are "assured of a platform." Other European folklife journals are *Laos* (Stockholm, 1951 ff.), *Folk* (Copenhagen, 1959 ff.), *Folkkultur* (Lund, 1941–1946), and *Folklivsstudier* (Helsinki, 1945 ff.). Unfortunately the holdings of these important journals in American libraries are extremely scanty.

18. At the organization meeting in 1961, Dr. Iorwerth C. Peate, Curator of the Welsh Folk Museum, and J. Geraint Jenkins of the same institution were elected President and Honorary Secretary. The papers read were all on the theme "Folk Life and Its Related Disciplines." The papers were entitled: "The Study of Folk Life," by Prof. Sigurd Erixon of Stockholm; "Language and Folk Life," by David Murison, Editor, Scottish National Dictionary; "Archaeology and Folk Life," by Basil R. S. Megaw, Director, School of Scottish Studies, University of Edinburgh; "Architecture and Folk Life," by Dr. R. B. Wood-Jones, University of Manchester; and "Geography and Folk Life," by Dr. R. H. Buchanan, Queen's University, Belfast.

19. For the questionnaire, developed in the nineteenth century by Mannhardt, and the *Volkskundeatlas,* see Beitl, *Wörterbuch,* 804, 34–38; for the atlas method, see Walther Mitzka, "Die Methodik des Deutschen Sprachatlas und des Deutschen Volkskundeatlas," *Hessische Blätter für Volkskunde* 41 (1950): 134–49. The linguistic atlas technique has been applied to America by Hans Kurath, although so far the *Volkskundeatlas,* while it has spread to Switzerland, Holland, and Scandinavia, has no progeny in the United States.

20. Brita Egardt, *Folklivsarkivet i Lund: Historik och Vägledning* (Lund, 1957), 16 pp., gives the history of the archive, accenting von Sydow's work as head of the archive and Professor of Scandinavian and Comparative Folklife Research at the University. At his death in 1946 he was succeeded by Professor Sigfrid Svensson.

21. The institute is a division of the Royal Dutch Academy of Sciences and was initiated in 1934 by Prof. Dr. Joseph Schrijnen and other scholars. For the work of the institute, see P. J. Meertens, "De Nederlandsche Volkskunde-Commissie," *Volkskunde,* n.s. 1 (1940): 60–63; also K. C. Peeters, "De Nederlandse Volkskunde-Atlas," *Volkskunde,* n.s. 19 (1960): 108–18.

22. For the program of the Folk Life Survey, see Stewart F. Sanderson, "Yorkshire in a New Folk-Life Survey," *Transactions of the Yorkshire Dialect Society,* Part 60, vol. 10 (1960): 21–34.

23. On the history and spread of the open-air museum, see Sigurd Erixon, "Nordic Open-Air Museums and Skansen," The Im Thurm Memorial Lecture (1937), *The Proceedings of the Scottish Anthropological and Folklore Society* 2 (3) (October, 1937): 31–45. See also Douglas A. Allen, "Folk Museums at Home and Abroad," ibid., 5 (3) (1956): 91–120, plus plates. For "Regional and Local Museums" in Europe, see *Museum* 10 (3) (1957); for "Regional Museums in the United States of America," *Museum* 11 (1958): 147–63.

24. For the Swedish museum movement, see *Museum* 2 (1) (1949), entire issue.

25. *Den Gamle By* (The Old Town) at Aarhus in Jutland, begun in 1909, is also an open-air museum of the town variety, balancing the rural folk museum at Lingby near Copenhagen, the *Dansk Frilandsmuseet.*

26. For *Heimatkunde* and *Heimatmuseum* concepts, see Beitl, *Wörterbuch,* 314–17; also Wilhelm Pessler, "Heimatmuseen of Germany," *Museum* 4 (1951): 95–103.

27. Belgium has recently opened its first open-air museum, at Bokrijk in Limburg. See Josef Weyns, "Bokrijk: The First Open-Air Museum in Belgium," *Museum* 12 (1959): 18–22.

28. See I. F. Grant, *Highland Folk Ways* (London, 1961).

29. There is a fifth approach, regional rather than national and often amateur rather than academic—the filiopietistic ethnic-genealogical approach represented by the ethnic societies—which have stressed "Scotch-Irishness," "Huguenotness," or "Pennsylvania Germanness" rather than folk culture as such. This approach is related to the D.A.R. approach to American history, which is highly selective in what it considers of value in the American heritage. The Pennsylvania Folklife Society is concerned not with genealogical heritage but with culture, principally folk culture. For some of the problems raised by the ethnic approach to history, see John J. Appel, "Immigrant Historical Societies in the United States, 1880–1950," unpublished Ph.D. dissertation in American Civilization, University of Pennsylvania, 1960. For the D.A.R. approach, see Wallace E. Davies, *Patriotism on Parade: The Story of Veterans' and Hereditary Organizations in America, 1783–1900* (Cambridge, Massachusetts, 1955), chap. 3, "Blue Blood Turns Red, White, and Blue."

30. Iorwerth C. Peate, "The Study of Folk Life: and Its Part in the Defense of Civilization," *The Advancement of Science* 15 (58) (September, 1958): 86–94, quotation from page 87.

31. Cf. Alfred L. Shoemaker, "Barracks," *Pennsylvania Folklife* 9 (2) (Spring, 1958): 2–11. This was the first article in the United States on this important regional hay-barn type.

32. The best introduction to the cultural diversity of the Colonial South is Thomas Jefferson Wertenbaker's *The Old South: The Founding of American Civilization* (New York, 1942).

33. The use of the term "folklore" in European tourism also gives it a slightly tarnished name everywhere. And the present "folksinging" revival—presenting a mischmasch of international songs as "American folklore"—is under serious question, academically speaking.

34. This is perhaps the same reason why such groups as the Presbyterians and the Quakers have little interest in their own folk-cultural background—although their Scotch-Irish and Quaker forebears created two of the most important sub-cultures in early America—with influences upon American architecture, folkspeech, cookery—the whole range of folk-cultural influence. What happened in the case of Quakerism is that the Philadelphia variety has been accepted as standard, and the related but different pattern of life created by rural Quakers goes completely unrecognized.

35. See Gary S. Dunbar, "Henry Chapman Mercer, Pennsylvania Folklife Pioneer," *Pennsylvania Folklife* 12 (2) (Summer, 1961): 48–52.

36. E. Estyn Evans, *Irish Folk Ways* (London, 1957), xiv.

37. Ruth Benedict, "Folklore," *Encyclopedia of the Social Sciences* 6:288.

2

Folklife Studies in American Scholarship

Folklife studies (regional ethnology) is a subject of recent development in the United States. Essentially it is the application to the American scene of the European discipline called *folklivsforskning*, or regional ethnology, in the Scandinavian lands (particularly in Sweden where the term *folkliv* was coined) and *Volkskunde* in the German-speaking areas of Europe. Folklife studies, or folklife research, has penetrated American academia both directly from the Scandinavian sources and indirectly from the British Isles, where the term *folklife* is used for scholarly journals, societies, and university programs.[1]

The concept of folklife studies was developed in Europe to study the native European cultures, focusing on the traditional aspects of these cultures. As an academic migrant it has come to the American scene at an unusually favorable moment in the development of American scholarship. With the present concern of Americans, particularly American youth, to determine their identity as it relates to ethnic, national, and world loyalties, we are witnessing at our universities a growth of ethnic studies programs which focus on the experience and acculturation of the diverse groups that make up the American people. Ethnic consciousness is certainly one of the motivating forces in the search for their meaning in the larger picture so evident in the lives of students today. While black consciousness is the most conspicuous of these movements toward self-understanding on the American human landscape, the focus on civil rights and the rights to ethnic heritage and language have aroused many of our ethnic enclaves, from the Mexican Americans of the southwest to the French Canadians of the northeast. What we are witnessing is a re-ethnicizing of America, a final ground

---

This article originally appeared in *American Folklife*, Don Yoder, ed. (Austin: University of Texas Press, 1976), 3–18.

swell of denial of the old "melting pot" concept of American history, and in its stead a vigorous vote of confidence for the concept of cultural pluralism.[2]

America will soon be celebrating the two-hundredth anniversary of her political birth. The cultural conception of America is of a much earlier date and involves the acculturation of three elements without which America cannot be explained—the native American Indian cultures, the European cultures of the immigrants (Oscar Handlin's "uprooted"), and the African cultures of the blacks. These are the peoples, along with the more recent arrivals from the Orient, that have made the American people, and as such they are, in Ward Goodenough's phrase, the proper focus of American folklife research.

By "American" folklife we mean essentially the regional cultures of North America with principal focus upon the United States, but with attention also to our neighbors in the North American experience of organizing New World cultures out of native American, European, African, and Asian components. These are, in particular, Canada, Mexico, and the Caribbean island nations. Canadian culture is an especially valuable check on American studies, since some of the same ethnic ingredients produced different cultural results there than in the States. Mexico, indeed all Latin America, is of increasing cultural importance to the United States for the understanding of our entire southwestern Spanish culture from Texas to California. The Caribbean, closer to us psychologically in the days of the clipper ships and the triangular trade, which left a deposit of Caribbean street names in our seaport towns and Caribbean foods on our urban tables, has become important once again, among other reasons, for providing additional keys to black acculturation in the United States.

At the present moment, it is difficult to define the terms "folklife" and "folklife studies" to the satisfaction of all elements interested in the subject matter.[3] There are those who, starting with "folklore" in its usual Anglo-American sense, define "folklife" by default, as material culture only. This is not the boundary set for it by its European creators. To Sigurd Erixon, folklife research was "the science of [European] man as a cultural being."[4] As such Erixon saw it as a regional branch of general anthropology, and in fact he often preferred to call it regional ethnology or, in its wider reaches, European ethnology. Its subject matter involves material, social, and spiritual culture, thus including what in the Anglo-American world has usually been called "folklore." In its methodology "historical, descriptive, and reconstructive studies alternate with functional studies of culture, society, and the individual." The most useful British manual of folklife research defines it broadly as the study of the interaction of man (in this case British man) with his environment, hence, "British ethnography."[5] And Richard Weiss of the University of Zurich in 1946 defined *Volkskunde,* the continental European parent of American folklife studies, as "the study of the interrelationships between the folk and folk culture, in so far as they are determined by community and tradition."[6] Weiss differentiates folk culture from mass culture, but locates "the folk-cultural," that is, traditionally mediated attitudes and beliefs, within the mind of the individual, where it coexists alongside other elements from different cultural levels. Thus Weiss prefers to speak not of "folk" levels of society or "folk" classes as wholes, but essentially of the folk-cultural element in the individual. It all goes back, of course, to that thorny word *folk* and the difficulty one faces in attempting to define it. The important point to note in all these definitions is that, in distinction to Anglo-American folklore studies, which have been until recently genre-oriented, folklife research is oriented toward holistic studies of culture regionally delimited and toward "life," the life of the society under study and of the individual within that society.

If definitions of the subject matter of folklife studies were difficult in the opening stages of its development as a university discipline, it was equally difficult—as is the case with every developing discipline—to relate the new study to already existing sciences. Richard Weiss, whom we have already cited, was one of the shapers of folklife studies in Europe. In his model ethnography of Switzerland, *Volkskunde der Schweiz,* he wrestled with the interdisciplinary character of his subject. He marveled at the great range of subject matter involved in folklife monographs and asked whether there is a common bond that unites all these different approaches. "Is there such a spiritual bond, which makes a unified science of folklife studies? Or is folklife studies a product of addition, made up of research on settlement patterns, house types, costumes, customs, folksongs, tales, legends, legal aspects, and folk piety? Are these disciplines simply fringe fields in other sciences—geography, cultural history, and the sciences of literature, law, and religion? Or can folklife studies bring them all into fruitful and necessary cooperation?"[7]

Obviously, the focus on the regional and national cultures of Switzerland combined the tributary disciplines into a unified scientific study. With their more fully developed sense of homeland and heritage—national, regional, even local—and their recognition of national character, the European nations began early in the nineteenth century to develop archives, academic programs, and, finally, museums to record and study the traditional aspects of regional European existence. In a distinguished series of research institutions from north to south, from Nordiska Museet in Stockholm to the Museo Nationale dell' Arte e Tradizione Popolari in Rome, and in a chain of ethnographic museums from Moscow and Bucharest on the east to Dublin and Lisbon on the west, European folklife scholarship has analyzed the traditional genius of Europe. But what began as a by-product of the Romantic Movement, with its focus on cultural nationalism, developed gradually into the cooperative science of European folk-cultural studies. National boundaries were early seen as nondeterminative in folk-cultural phenomena, as the European atlases of folk culture make clear. Folklife studies, under whatever name it is known, has developed within its European parameters into a university discipline in almost every European nation, and in the understanding of European life it is a potent ally of the historical, sociological, and anthropological sciences.[8]

In general, folklife studies stands particularly close to cultural and social anthropology, and, as we have suggested, in many European countries it is referred to as European ethnology. The major difference between the disciplines is that folklife studies insists on historical as well as ethnographic methodology. In the American academic world, folklife studies shares subject matter not only with cultural anthropology but also with the two historical disciplines, the older American history and the newer American civilization or, as it is frequently called, American studies. In the academic locales where it is taught in the United States, folklife studies is most closely associated with folklore and folkloristics, a division reminiscent of the Scandinavian distinction between *folkliv* and *folkminne* and in the distinction between *folklore* and (regional) *ethnology* in the Europeanist organization Société Internationale d'Ethnologie et de Folklore (SIEF). In the Anglo-American world a minority of folklorists prefer to stretch the word *folklore* to include *folklife*. I prefer to follow Åke Hultkrantz[9] and the Arnhem Congress[10] of 1955 in subsuming *folklore* (defining it after William Bascom[11] as the verbal arts of a society) under *folklife*, as only one aspect of folk culture.

Among the other disciplines that are related to folklife studies in sharing subject matter and that, in analyzing American culture, are potential allies of folklife studies in the academic world are agricultural history, rural sociology, human relations, ethnohistory, oral history, ethnomusicology, social psychology and parapsychology, medical history, art history, architectural history, history of diet and nutrition, cultural geography, medieval studies, historical archaeology, industrial archaeology, history of technology, and dialectology and linguistic geography.

In focusing upon traditional forms of life, folklife studies thus far in its development in Europe and the United States has offered three essentially different approaches: (1) the study of the historical past, (2) the study of the past as surviving in and influencing the present, and (3) the study of the ethnographic present. Let us look at these approaches one after the other.

Historical Folklife Studies

A great many researchers in traditional culture, particularly those in Europe, prefer to approach their subject matter completely oriented to past levels of the culture, reconstructing them through the use of the tried-and-true, if conservative, methods of analyzing historical texts and material artifacts. Europeans, more so than Americans, have turned to their abundant historical source materials to reconstruct the past levels of their own cultures. State and local archives are developed to a higher degree, and in most cultures the scholar has available every possible historical source from medieval charters to the present-day newspaper. What the Germans call *rechtliche Volkskunde* (legal ethnology) is a good example of this approach. The laws and edicts, the sumptuary legislation, the criminal and civil codes comprise one fruitful source of dated material on folklife from the early Middle Ages to the present that Europeans have thoroughly studied.[12] Church records, almost entirely neglected here as a source even for social history, have been abstracted and used not only for local history and genealogy, as here, but also for the highest level of social and regional history.[13]

What is called for in this country is a democratizing of historiography. The strongest rationale for such a democratizing of American history has come from Theodore Blegen, whose work, based at the University of Minnesota, on ethnic studies (concentration on Norwegian Americana) and regional history (with focus on Upper Mississippi Valley cultures) has put him in the forefront of American historians in our field. "The pivot of history is not the uncommon," writes Blegen, "but the usual, and the makers of history are 'the people, yes.' ... This is the essence of grass roots history. It grapples, as history should grapple, with the need of understanding the small, everyday elements, the basic elements, in large movements. It recognizes, as maturely conceived history should recognize, the importance of the simple, however complex and subtle the problem of understanding the simple may be."[14] This broadening of historiography to include the life of all classes has still not been completely achieved even in social history. Lynn White, Jr., writing of medieval history, makes the point that, "from its beginnings until very recently, written history has been a history of the upper classes by the upper classes and for the upper classes." Our culture is not completely democratic, because of our long-inherited tradition of aristocratic scholarship. We need, he insists, "the history of all mankind including the hitherto silent majority, and not merely that of the tiny vocal fraction which dominated the rest." In his own field of medieval studies, this means new concentration upon peasant life, using every source available from medieval literature to agrarian archaeology.[15]

Historical folklife studies has great potential for our discipline because, when our historical source materials are abstracted and archived, we will at last have on hand some basic diachronic documentation for our ethnographic studies. This "accumulation of micro-regional-ethnological studies," as Alexander Fenton puts it, will in time allow a comparative view of the development of the country under study, as well as providing material of international comparative value.[16] Every area of folklife research and many of the related disciplines will profit from such documentation. To give one example, the historical dictionaries of American English were constructed on the policy of using only printed citations in tracing the history of American words.[17] In the case of many Americanisms, earlier datings than those in Mathews turn up constantly in manuscript source materials. The wills and inventories, one widespread manuscript source, that exist by the hundreds of thousands in the courthouses of the older settled parts of the country, need to be abstracted systematically for early American culture and its vocabulary. Wills and inventories, which are dated and official yet intensely personal documents, shed light on every aspect of regional folk culture in the United States.[18] The full range of historical source material—travel accounts, newspapers, diaries, autobiographies, collections of letters, local histories—will eventually have to be plowed through and abstracted if we are to understand the full development of our regional cultures.

Of the regional file systems set up thus far to archive historical materials, three deserve special mention: (a) the Index of American Cultures, dealing with colonial urban America (Boston, 1675–1725, and Philadelphia, 1725–1775), directed by Dr. Anthony N. B. Garvan at the University of Pennsylvania in connection with the Human Relations Area Files;[19] (b) the Index of American Folk Belief (including folk medicine), initiated by Dr. Wayland D. Hand at the University of California at Los Angeles; and (c) the Pennsylvania Folk-Cultural Index of the Pennsylvania Folklife Society, now on deposit at the Myrin Library, Ursinus College, Collegeville, Pennsylvania. The first represents an urban area study, the second a topical research area within folklife studies, and the third a regional cultural approach.

Folklife Studies and Survivals

For those who define folk culture as the culture of preindustrial, pre-urban groups in Western civilization, the approach has been to look at the present but to focus upon existing remnants of the "true" folk cultures of the past.[20] *Survival* is a suspect word these days due to its earlier overuse, but one literal survival from all our regional pasts is our older architecture—man's most visible alteration of his environment. Unfortunately, this is now rapidly disappearing from sight and memory, giving way to the bulldozer, the superhighway, and the suburban developer (as well as less permanently to the Permastone salesman). The necessity of preserving at least some of America's earlier architectural forms is recognized by scholarly groups the nation over, from the Society for the Preservation of New England Antiquities to the National Trust. Much education is still needed in the local field to encourage appreciation of local and regional examples of architecture. Preservation efforts should involve not only the George-Washington-slept-here types of houses, important because of their historical associations, but also the best surviving examples of regional types—not only homes, but also civil, ecclesiastical, and farmstead architecture. Such examples serve literally as "landmarks" in our culture, as way-stations to the present and to our own understanding of ourselves.

In the long run the historical environment may be as important to us psychologically as is the natural environment. Regional architecture has teaching value in orienting us to the meaning of our own situation in the cultural-historical spectrum. European cultures have seen this value most intelligently, both in preservation programs and in teaching institutions, such as the open-air museums that developed out of folklife studies. Unfortunately, the American ethos has a built-in derogation of the past, from the Pilgrims' rejection of Europe to Henry Ford's classic evaluation, "History is bunk." Unfortunately, too, the American business motto that "progress is our most important product," as well as our "conspicuous consumption" and "planned obsolescence" syndromes, have long been blinding forces in preventing preservation. A kind of passive barbarism, as Iorwerth Peate puts it, has developed in the West, just as destructive of heritage as what he calls the active barbarism of the East.[21]

The past is important, and our historic man-made environment of urban, rural, and village architecture, of farmstead and town layouts, of settlement patterns in general is important for Americans to recognize as part of their heritage, as keys to self-understanding.

Folklife Studies and the Ethnographic Present

The third approach to folklife scholarship is the ethnographic, focusing on the present and scientifically describing the contemporary forms of American traditional culture. Field work is the method of this approach, and field work in fact is the primary need in American folklife scholarship today.

When American folk-cultural scholarship is compared with its European model, one of the gravest complaints is that we are half a century behind Europe in gathering the raw materials for understanding our own traditional cultures. In only a few areas of traditional culture, for example folksong and folktale, do we have even a relatively complete national selection. It is true that the European university and museum worlds have been recording their own cultures since the beginning of the nineteenth century. My favorite example of the many European folk-cultural research institutions is Nordiska Museet in Stockholm, founded in 1871 to record Scandinavian and, in particular, Swedish culture. One single research department of the museum, the Archive of Swedish Folk Belief, directed by Dr. Carl-Herman Tillhagen since 1945, today has a staff of over two dozen persons and several million references in its catalogue, derived from field work and informant questionnaires from every area of Sweden.[22] Sweden is an especially good example of the academic cooperation that has developed in Europe to study traditional cultures of a national area. Supplementing the Folklore Archive of Nordiska Museet are the equally impressive Folklife Archive at the University of Lund and the Dialect Archive at the University of Uppsala.

The common quest for social relevance in scholarship has in the last decades brought new emphases to folklife studies. The new, or "contemporary folklife," approach arose largely in Germany since World War II, in part through the necessity of coming to grips with the acculturation problems of resettled German-speaking groups from Eastern Europe. The lore and customs of these displaced persons were immediately forced into acculturation with the customs and lore of the new settlements. The important focus of research was recognized as not the Germanic "survivals" but the contemporary patterns of human life in an industrialized and urbanized world. Not peasant cultures as such, but the impact of the industrial revolution as social process, in which both traditional culture and individual are caught up inexorably, was seen as the proper focus for folklife scholarship.[23] The modern locus of both folklore and folklife was seen as the city, and the concepts of "urban folklife" and "industrial folklife" have already taken their place beside the concepts of peasant, regional, and ethnic cultures. In Germany the work of Hermann Bausinger at Tübingen,[24] of Walter Hävernick and Herbert Freudenthal at Hamburg,[25] and of Gerhard Heilfurth and his associates at Marburg[26] point folk-cultural scholarship in this direction.

An example of this updating of European folklife research methodology is the recent criticism of the folk-cultural questionnaire technique. According to Rudolf Schenda of Tübingen, questionnaires have made no substantial progress since the nineteenth century, when they were based on the ideas of "primitive uniformity" of the groups studied, the concept of "cultural relics," and the principle of "continuity" from past to present.[27] Questions and answers were directed not at the reality of today, the social facts as they exist, but at an ideal picture, a projection of the vanished past. Finally, the folk-cultural questionnaires have been material oriented rather than problem oriented. In general they need to be geared into the research methods of the social sciences. Instead of focusing on the remnants of primitive culture "still alive today," we need to focus on the individual in the midst of social conflict, the present, and the future.

This would seem to be a widespread new orientation in European folklife research. In his inaugural lecture at the University of Lund in 1967, Professor Nils-Arvid Bringéus called for what amounts to a complete updating of folk-cultural research method. Following Erixon's lead, he emphasized the necessity of observing the present. "Our only opportunity of obtaining an all-round study of folklife is still and always will be the present way of life itself." And again:

> In the future we must not simply be content with reminiscences instead of testimonies, we must also study what is alive. We must learn to find easier ways of getting into homes, not just old people's homes, to densely populated areas instead of to the sparsely populated ones. The ethnologist is looking for the normal situation.
>
> Superficially this may mean that ethnology becomes less historical. But its objectives in the study of society must still be to demonstrate the part played by tradition as the mortar in our culture. Consequently, a historical perspective is needed in an analysis of the present and in planning the future.[28]

In many areas of everyday life, what is now increasingly called "popular culture" turns out to be an extension of or development from the older traditional forms of culture.[29] This is brought graphically to focus in the folklife films in the series Deutsche Volkskunde, edited by Dr. Ingeborg Weber-Kellermann of the University of Marburg. One of the films deals with the concept of *Volkslesestoff,* or everyday reading matter. In the eighteenth century the average German read chapbook lives of saints and legends of popular heroes. In the nineteenth century they read the "trivial romance," in installments in the newspapers and the family periodicals.[30] In the twentieth century their descendants read comic books and look at TV westerns. The forms and manners of distribution have changed—from market stalls, peddlers, *Bänkelsänger,* and colporteurs—but the function in the group involved and in the individual life remains the same.

It seems clear that we continue to need both the historically oriented reconstructions of earlier stages of our present culture and sociologically and anthropologically oriented analysis of present-day forms of culture, urban or rural, that are equivalent or analogous to the earlier folk forms. Which emphasis will take priority in North American scholarship remains to be seen.

In conclusion, let us take a brief overview of the ways in which folklife scholarship is represented in the American academic world today. Courses in American folk culture, its regional versions and branches, are offered at the State University of New York at Oneonta-Cooperstown, Indiana University, University of California at Los Angeles, University of Pennsylvania, University of Texas at Austin, University of North Carolina, Vanderbilt University, Pennsylvania State University, Utah State University, Western Kentucky University, and others. Several of the institutions mentioned offer folklife programs as such, while others offer folklife courses under the aegis of folklore, anthropology, American studies, cultural geography, and other departments. In some cases, branches of folklife studies or specialties within folklife are featured. For example, courses in folk art are offered at the University of California at Los Angeles, folk architecture and architectural preservation at Columbia, and cookery and foodways at the Capitol Campus of Pennsylvania State University. Area studies in European and American ethnography, regional culture courses, and work in ethnic and immigration history are given at an increasing number of American universities and colleges.[31]

The research programs and folk-cultural archives of many of these institutions accent, as is the case in Europe, the local regional cultural materials as well as comparative materials from other cultures both here and abroad. For example, the University of Maryland has an archive that deals with Maryland materials, the University of Maine has one that deals heavily though not exclusively in materials from Maine, Western Kentucky University channels Appalachian materials into its archive, and UCLA features California and western materials. In addition, the larger university programs sponsor research in particular phases of folklife studies. The Institute of Urban Ethnography at the University of Pennsylvania has sponsored research in the cultures of many American ethnic enclaves. The Center for Comparative Folklore and Mythology at UCLA has sponsored the *American Dictionary of Superstitions and Popular Beliefs,* edited by Wayland D. Hand on the model of the *Handwörterbuch des Deutschen Aberglaubens,* and is the principal research institution in the United States at the present time for folk medicine.

In addition to these academic institutions, museums conduct much folklife research, particularly the open-air museums that have been founded in the United States and Canada on the Scandinavian model.[32] The principal examples here are Colonial Williamsburg in Virginia, Old Sturbridge Village and Plimoth Plantation in Massachusetts, the Farmers Museum at Cooperstown, N.Y., the Pennsylvania Farm Museum at Landis Valley in Pennsylvania, Mystic Seaport in Connecticut, and the Black Creek Village and Upper Canada Village in Ontario. Old Sturbridge Village, for one example, has a staff of some thirty full-time researchers working on various phases of New England life in the period of the museum, 1790–1840, on every subject from religion to agriculture, from cookery to rural dress. In addition, specialized museums, such as the Henry Francis du Pont Winterthur Museum, cultivate specialties that are useful to folklife studies, such as Winterthur's emphasis on early American decorative arts. Its sister institution, the Hagley Museum, also founded by the du Ponts, specializes in early American crafts and technology. The American folk arts are represented in major collections in many of the fine arts museums of the country, as, for example, the Karolik Collection at the Boston Museum of Fine Arts and the Garbisch Collection in the National Gallery in Washington, while American and other folk arts are featured in the Museum of American Folk Art in New York and the Museum of International Folk Art at Santa Fe.

Of the national museums of Canada and the United States, the National Museum of Man in Ottawa and the Smithsonian Institution both express increasing interest in folklife materials. The Canadian Centre for Folk Culture Studies at the National Museum of Man is essentially a collecting institute for ethnographic data, artifacts, and audiovisual materials from all of Canada's current ethnic populations.[33] The Smithsonian Institution has several divisions that are working in folklife materials—the Center for the Study of Man, the Division of Preindustrial Cultural History, the Division of Agricultural History, the Division of Ethnic and Western Cultural History, and the Division of Performing Arts. Out of the latter's interest in American crafts has come the Festival of American Folklife,[34] now in its eighth year, which is reflected on the state level by such newer festivals as the Texas Folklife Festival founded in 1972 by the Institute of Texan Cultures at San Antonio. While festivals are attempts at displaying folk culture to the public in a different way than is possible in the older museum format, what is most exciting is the solid research preparation that goes into them. For example, in connection with the Smithsonian festival entire states have each year been surveyed to determine the current status of folk craftsmanship. Particularly healthy also in this newer movement is the Smithsonian festival's emphasis not only upon rural crafts, but also upon the contemporary urban labor union craftsman as the modern equivalent of the older village artisan.[35]

In the new world of ethnic studies in the United States and Canada, contributions are being made to folklife scholarship by the various ethnic institutes and historical societies, some of them connected with academic institutions, others independent.[36] Four examples out of many that could be cited are the American Swedish Historical Foundation in Philadelphia, as well as its homeland counterpart, the Emigrant Institute at Växjö in Sweden; the Norwegian-American Historical Society in Minneapolis, which, under the leadership of Theodore Blegen, revived ethnic history of the best sort in the twentieth century and provided a model for all ethnic historiography; the work of the various Pennsylvania German organizations headed by the Pennsylvania German Society, founded in 1891; and the Yivo Institute in New York for the study of Jewish immigrant culture and, principally, the Yiddish language culture of the Eastern European Jews in America.

On the national level, two general institutions now exist in the United States with the broad purpose of surveying all ethnic groups. These are the Center for Migration Studies located on Staten Island, which has begun a distinguished series of ethnic bibliographies, and the Balch Institute in Philadelphia, which is becoming the depository for records of historical societies of many ethnic groups. Equally promising for their breadth of purpose are two statewide organizations, the Institute of Texan Cultures at San Antonio, organized under the University of Texas, and the Ethnic Culture Survey of Pennsylvania at Harrisburg, organized under the Pennsylvania Historical and Museum Commission.

In the American academic field there are also many journals, mostly quarterlies, that publish, at least occasionally, articles of folk-cultural interest. These range from folklore (for example, the *Journal of American Folklore* and the various state and regional folklore journals) through anthropology, ethnology, ethnohistory, sociology, agricultural history, the history of technology, to geography. Museum publications, such as the *Winterthur Portfolio,* carry folklife articles along with others. Many state and county historical society publications show increasing interest in folk-cultural data, everyday life—in other words, the historical ethnographic approach.

From this point on, statewide programs and national coordination of folklife research will be increasingly necessary. National vision demands national programs, here as in Europe. Plans for an American Folklife Foundation reached the stage of hearings before the Ninety-first Congress (1971), and, as the American Folklife Center to be established under the aegis of the Library of Congress, the project is marshaling support in the Ninety-second Congress (1973).[37] Plans for an atlas of American folk culture have also been broached.[38]

Folklife studies, in conclusion, is a newer holistic approach that analyzes traditional cultural elements in a complex society—whether these elements are defined as folk, ethnic, regional, rural, urban, or sectarian—viewing them in the context of that larger unifying society and culture of which all subgroups and traditions are functioning parts. It can focus upon the individual, the group, single cultural traits or complexes, or the culture as a whole. As the regional ethnology of North America—American ethnology in the widest sense of that term—it takes its place beside European ethnology in researching the continuing role of tradition in Western civilization.

Notes

1. For the history of folklife research, see Sigurd Erixon, "European Ethnology in Our Time," *Ethnologia Europaea* 1 (1) (1967): 3–11; Ronald H. Buchanan, "A Decade of Folklife Study," *Ulster Folklife* 10 (1965): 63–75; Ingeborg Weber-Kellermann, *Deutsche Volkskunde zwischen Germanistik und Sozialwissenschaften;* and Don Yoder, "The Folklife Studies Movement," *Pennsylvania Folklife* 13 (3) (July 1963): 43–56. The best manual on the subject thus far, although unfortunately not available in English, is Sigfrid Svensson, *Introduktion till Folklivsforskningen.* For the history of the terms *folkliv* and *folklivsforskning,* see Sigurd Erixon, "Benämningen på Sven Lampas docentur och den svenska folklivsforskning," in *Kulturspeglingar,* Ernst-Folke Lindberg, ed., 67–74.
2. For recent summaries of the "melting pot" and "cultural pluralist" theories, see Milton M. Gordon, *Assimilation in American Life.*
3. The best collection of definitions thus far is included in Åke Hultkrantz, ed., *General Ethnological Concepts,* 126–44.
4. Erixon, cited in ibid., 133–34. See also Åke Hultkrantz, "The Conception of 'Folk' in Sigurd Erixon's Ethnological Theory," *Ethnologia Europaea* 2–3 (1968–1969): 18–20.
5. J. W. Y. Higgs, *Folk Life Collection and Classification,* 4–7.
6. Richard Weiss, *Volkskunde der Schweiz,* 11.
7. Ibid., 45–49: "Die Volkskunde und ihre Nachbarwissenschaften."
8. The most recent report on the academic organization of folklife studies in Europe is "The Academic Position of European Ethnology," *Ethnologia Europaea* 1 (4) (1967): [243]–323.
9. Hultkrantz, *General Ethnological Concepts,* 133–34.
10. *Actes du Congrès International d'Ethnologie Régionale.*
11. William R. Bascom, "Folklore and Anthropology," *Journal of American Folklore* 66 (1953): 283–90; also, "Verbal Art," *Journal of American Folklore* 68 (1955): 245–52.
12. For a brief summary in English, with German references, see Hermann Baltl, "Folklore Research and Legal History in the German Language Area," *Journal of the Folklore Institute* 5 (2–3) (1968): 142–51.
13. Historical ethnography is highly developed in Europe. One model example that can be cited out of many is the work of Karl-Sigismund Kramer, *Volksleben im Fürstentum Ansbach und seinen Nachbargebieten (1500–1800),* which draws upon every available type of historical source. My two favorite examples of historical ethnography on a regional basis from the United States are Guion Griffis Johnson, *Ante-Bellum North Carolina,* and Solon J. and Elizabeth Buck, *The Planting of Civilization in Western Pennsylvania.*
14. Theodore C. Blegen, *Grass Roots History,* vii.
15. Lynn White, Jr., "The Life of the Silent Majority," in *Life and Thought in the Early Middle Ages,* Robert S. Hoyt, ed., 85–100.
16. Alexander Fenton, "Historical Ethnology in Scotland," *Ethnologia Europaea* 1 (2) (1967): 125–29.

17. Mitford M. Mathews, ed., *A Dictionary of Americanisms on Historical Principles.*

18. Unfortunately, the abstracts of wills in our historical societies were done mostly by and for genealogists, and they lack the materials needed by the folklife scholar. The best published collection of American inventories thus far is Abbott Lowell Cummings, *Rural Household Inventories Establishing the Names, Uses and Furnishings in the Colonial New England Home, 1675–1775.*

19. For the Human Relations Area Files, see George P. Murdock et al., *Outline of Cultural Materials.* For the Index of American Cultures, see Anthony N. B. Garvan, "Historical Depth in Comparative Culture Study," *American Quarterly* 14 (2), part 2 (Summer 1962 Supplement): 260–74.

20. For a series of models illustrating the relation of historical reconstruction of past levels of a culture and ethnographic research into its present level, see Nils-Arvid Bringéus, "Probleme und Methoden ethnologischer Nahrungsforschung im Lichte jüngster schwedischer Untersuchungen," *Ethnologia Scandinavica* 1 (1971): 20–23.

21. Iorwerth C. Peate, "The Study of Folk Life and Its Part in the Defence of Civilization," *Advancement of Science* 15 (58) (September 1958): 86–94.

22. Carl-Herman Tillhagen, "Folklore Archives in Sweden," *Journal of the Folklore Institute* 1 (1–2) (1964): 20–36. For the program of Nordiska Museet in general, see Mats Rehnberg, *The Nordiska Museet and Skansen.*

23. The volume by Rudolf Braun, *Industrialisierung und Volkskultur,* dealing with the impact of the Industrial Revolution on the Zürcher Oberland, is a model of research using precisely this concept. For more general perspectives on this whole problem, see Hermann Bausinger, *Volkskultur in der technischen Welt.*

24. Hermann Bausinger, "Folklore Research at the University of Tübingen: On the Activities of the Ludwig-Uhland-Institut," *Journal of the Folklore Institute* 5 (2–3) (1968): 124–33.

25. Walter Hävernick, "The Hamburg School of Folklore Research," *Journal of the Folklore Institute* 5 (2–3) (1968): 113–23.

26. Gerhard Heilfurth, "The Institut für mitteleuropäische Volksforschung at the University of Marburg," *Journal of the Folklore Institute* 5 (2–3) (1968): 134–41.

27. Rudolf Schenda, "Einheitlich–Urtümlich–Noch Heute: Probleme der volkskundlichen Befragung," in *Abschied vom Volksleben,* Klaus Geiger, Utz Jeggle, and Gottfried Korff, eds., 124–54.

28. Nils-Arvid Bringéus, "Det etnologiska perspectivet. Installations-föreläsning vid Lunds universitet den 9 mars 1968," *Rig,* 1968.

29. In the field of American popular culture, the works of Carl Bode and Russell B. Nye have pioneered. The *American Quarterly* has published articles on this subject, and more recently Ray B. Browne has established the useful *Journal of Popular Culture.* For boundaries and relations between "folk" and "popular" cultures, see Henry Glassie, *Pattern in the Material Folk Culture of the Eastern United States.*

30. On these genres of popular culture, see Dorothee Bayer, *Der triviale Familien- und Liebesroman im 20. Jahrhundert;* and Hermann Fischer, *Volkslied–Schlager–Evergreen.*

31. A selective listing of institutions, personnel, and specialties taught is given in Paul Leser, "The Academic Position of European Ethnology in North America," *Ethnologia Europaea* 1 (4) (1967): 320–22.

32. *The Official Museum Directory: United States-Canada, 1971* lists open-air museums under history, agriculture, and other categories. For agricultural museums, see Darwin P. Kelsey, "Outdoor Museums and Historical Agriculture," in *Farming in the New Nation*, Darwin P. Kelsey, ed., pp. 105–27. For the new concept of the "living historical farm," see the article by John T. Schlebecker, "Curatorial Agriculture," in ibid., 95–103.

33. For the centre's program, see Carmen Roy, *Canadian Centre for Folk Culture Studies: Annual Review 1972.*

34. The seven printed programs of the Festival of American Folklife provide an excellent record of the geographical areas, craft specialties, and ethnic groups featured in the seven years since the festival's foundation in 1967. For the philosophy of the festival as a "living museum," see the foreword by S. Dillon Ripley in the *1973 Festival of American Folklife*, 4. Starting in 1973 the festival has been jointly sponsored by the Smithsonian Institution and the National Park Service, which has in its many historic-sites museums over the country featured for decades the concept of "living history."

35. See the section "Working Americans" in the *1973 Festival of American Folklife*, 38–43. The emphasis on industrial folklore and folklife was pioneered in this country by such scholars as George Korson and Archie Green, whose volumes on miners' songs and their context are models of their kind.

36. For ethnic historiography in the United States and the various movements that have shaped it, see John J. Appel, "Immigrant Historical Societies in the United States, 1880–1950," Ph.D. dissertation.

37. *American Folklife Foundation Act. Hearing before the Subcommittee on Education of the Committee on Labor and Public Welfare, United States Senate, Ninety-First Congress, Second Session, on S. 1591: To Establish an American Folklife Foundation, and for Other Purposes. May 18, 1970.* For the current bills (S. 1844, H.R. 8770, H.R. 8781) to provide for the establishment of an American Folklife Center in the Library of Congress, see the *Congressional Record*, May 17, 1973, and June 18, 1973.

38. William F. H. Nicolaisen, formerly of the School of Scottish Studies, Edinburgh, now at the State University of New York, Binghamton, addressed the November 1970 meeting of the American Folklore Society on the possibilities of an American folklore atlas, and at the 1971 and 1972 sessions he conducted panel discussions of the atlas plans. He is at present organizing a national committee to consider the steps necessary to establish such an atlas research program. Unfortunately, there are no prior regional atlases here as in Europe, except for the linguistic atlases, of which the most useful is Hans Kurath's *Linguistic Atlas of New England.*

Bibliography

"Academic Position of European Ethnology," *Ethnologia Europaea* 1 (4) (1967): [243]-323.

Actes du Congrès International d'Ethnologie Régionale, Arnhem, 1955. Arnhem: Rijksmuseum voor Volkskunde, 1956.

American Folklife Foundation Act. Hearing before the Subcommittee on Education of the Committee on Labor and Public Welfare, United States Senate, Ninety-First Congress, Second Session, on S. 1591: To Establish an American Folklife Foundation, and for Other Purposes. May 18, 1970. Washington, D.C.: U.S. Government Printing Office, 1970.

Appel, John J. "Immigrant Historical Societies in the United States, 1880–1950." Ph.D. Diss., University of Pennsylvania, 1960.

Bach, Adolf. *Deutsche Volkskunde.* 3d ed. Heidelberg: Quelle & Meyer, 1960.

Baltl, Hermann. "Folklore Research and Legal History in the German Language Area." *Journal of the Folklore Institute* 5 (2–3) (1968): 142–51.

Bascom, William R. "Folklore and Anthropology." *Journal of American Folklore* 66 (1953): 283–90.

———. "Verbal Art." *Journal of American Folklore* 68 (1955): 245–52.

Bausinger, Hermann. "Folklore Research at the University of Tübingen: On the Activities of the Ludwig-Uhland-Institut." *Journal of the Folklore Institute* 5 (2–3) (1968): 124–33.

———. *Volkskultur in der technischen Welt.* Stuttgart: W. Kohlhammer, 1961.

———. *Volkskunde: Von der Altertumsforschung zur Kulturanalyse.* Das Wissen der Gegenwart: Geisteswissenschaften. Berlin-Darmstadt: Carl Habel Verlagsbuchhandlung, 1970.

———, ed. *Populus Revisus: Beiträge zur Erforschung der Gegenwart.* Volksleben 14. Tübingen: Tübinger Vereinigung für Volkskunde, 1966.

Bayer, Dorothee. *Der triviale Familien- und Liebesroman im 20. Jahrhundert.* Volksleben 1. Tübingen: Tübinger Vereinigung für Volkskunde, 1963.

Blegen, Theodore C. *Grass Roots History.* Minneapolis: University of Minnesota Press, 1947.

Braun, Rudolf. *Industrialisierung und Volkskultur: Sozialer und Kultureller Wandel in einem ländlichen Industriegebiet.* Erlenbach-Zurich: Eugen Rentsch Verlag, 1960.

Bringéus, Nils-Arvid. "Det etnologiska perspectivet: Installations-föreläsning vid Lunds universitet den 9 mars 1968." *Rig,* 1968. Reprinted in *Artikelsamling i folklivsforskning,* 33–41. Lund: Studentliteratur, 1970.

———. "Probleme und Methoden ethnologischer Nahrungsforschung im Lichte jüngster schwedischer Untersuchungen." *Ethnologia Scandinavica* 1 (1971): 19–36.

Brunvand, Jan H. *The Study of American Folklore: An Introduction.* New York: W. W. Norton & Co., 1968.

Buchanan, Ronald H. "A Decade of Folklife Study." *Ulster Folklife* 10 (1965): 63–75.

———. "Geography and Folk Life." *Folk Life: Journal of the Society for Folk Life Studies* 1 (1963): 5–15.

———. "The Study of Folklore." *Ulster Folklife* 1 (1955): 8–12.

Buck, Solon J., and Elizabeth H. Buck. *The Planting of Civilization in Western Pennsylvania.* Pittsburgh: University of Pittsburgh Press, 1939.

Carvalho-Neto, Paulo de. *The Concept of Folklore.* Jacques M. P. Wilson, trans. Coral Gables: University of Miami Press, 1971.

Cocchiara, Giuseppe. *Storia del Folklore in Europa.* Turin: Einaudi, 1952.

Cummings, Abbott Lowell. *Rural Household Inventories Establishing the Names, Uses and Furnishings in the Colonial New England Home, 1675–1775.* Boston: Society for the Preservation of New England Antiquities, 1964.

Dalton, George. "Peasantries in Anthropology and History." *Current Anthropology* 13 (1972): 385–415.

Dégh, Linda. "Folklore and Related Disciplines in Eastern Europe." *Journal of the Folklore Institute* 2 (1965): 103–19.

———. "Survival and Revival of European Folk Cultures in America." *Ethnologia Europaea* 2–3 (1968–1969): 97–107.

Dorson, Richard M., ed. *Folklore and Folklife: An Introduction.* Chicago: University of Chicago Press, 1972.

———, ed. *Folklore Research around the World: A North American Point of View.* Port Washington, N.Y.: Kennikat Press, 1973.

Erich, Oswald A., and Richard Beitl, eds. *Wörterbuch der deutschen Volkskunde.* 2d ed., rev. by Richard Beitl. Stuttgart: Alfred Kröner Verlag, 1955.

Erixon, Sigurd. "Benämningen på Sven Lampas docentur och den svenska folklivsforskning."

In *Kulturspeglingar: Studier tillägnade Sam Owen Jansson 19 mars 1966,* Ernst-Folke Lindberg, ed., 67–74. Stockholm: Nordiska Museet, 1966.

———. "European Ethnology in Our Time." *Ethnologia Europaea* 1 (1) (1967): 3–11.

———. "Folklife Research in Our Time: From a Swedish Point of View." *Gwerin* 3 (1962): 275–91.

———. "An Introduction to Folk Life Research or Nordic Ethnology." *Folkliv* 14–15 (1950–1951): 5–15.

"Erixoniana: Contributions to the Study of European Ethnology in Memory of Sigurd Erixon." *Ethnologia Europaea* 2–3 (1968–1969); 4 (1970).

Fél, Edit, and Tamás Hofer. *Proper Peasants.* Viking Fund Publications in Anthropology 46. Chicago: Aldine Press, 1969.

Fenton, Alexander. "Historical Ethnology in Scotland." *Ethnologia Europaea* 1 (2) (1967): 125–29.

———. "Material Culture as an Aid to Local History Studies in Scotland." *Journal of the Folklore Institute* 2 (1965): 326–39.

Fenton, William H., L. H. Butterfield, and Wilcomb E. Washburn. *American Indian and White Relations to 1830: Needs and Opportunities for Study.* Chapel Hill: University of North Carolina Press, 1957.

Fife, Austin, Alta Fife, and Henry H. Glassie, eds. *Forms upon the Frontier: Folklife and Folk Arts in the United States.* Monograph Series 16 (2). Logan: Utah State University Press, 1969.

Fischer, Hermann. *Volkslied—Schlager—Evergreen: Studien über das lebendige Singen aufgrund von Untersuchungen im Kreis Reutlingen.* Volksleben 7. Tübingen: Tübinger Vereinigung für Volkskunde, 1965.

Garvan, Anthony N. B. "Historical Depth in Comparative Culture Study." *American Quarterly* 14 (2), part 2 (Summer 1962 Supplement): 260–74.

Glassie, Henry. *Pattern in the Material Folk Culture of the Eastern United States.* University of Pennsylvania Monographs in Folklore and Folklife 1. Philadelphia: University of Pennsylvania Press, 1968.

———. "The Types of the Southern Mountain Cabin." Appendix to *The Study of American Folklore: An Introduction,* by Jan H. Brunvand. New York: W. W. Norton & Co., 1968, 338–70.

Gordon, Milton M. *Assimilation in American Life: The Role of Race, Religion, and National Origins.* New York: Oxford University Press, 1964.

Haug, Jörg. *Heimatkunde und Volkskunde.* Volksleben 22. Tübingen: Tübinger Vereinigung für Volkskunde, 1970.

Hävernick, Walter. "The Hamburg School of Folklore Research." *Journal of the Folklore Institute* 5 (2–3) (1968): 113–23.

Heilfurth, Gerhard. "The Institut für mitteleuropäische Volksforschung at the University of Marburg." *Journal of the Folklore Institute* 5 (2–3) (1968): 134–41.

Higgs, J. W. Y. *Folk Life Collection and Classification.* London: Museums Association, 1963.

Hultkrantz, Åke. "The Conception of 'Folk' in Sigurd Erixon's Ethnological Theory." *Ethnologia Europaea* 2–3 (1968–1969): 18–20.

———. "Historical Approaches in American Ethnology: A Research Survey." *Ethnologia Europaea* 1 (2) (1967): 96–116.

———, ed. *General Ethnological Concepts.* International Dictionary of Regional European Ethnology and Folklore 1. Copenhagen: Rosenkilde and Bagger, 1960.

Jenkins, Geraint, ed. *Studies in Folk Life: Essays in Honour of Iorwerth C. Peate.* New York: Barnes and Noble, 1969.

Jenson, Merrill, ed. *Regionalism in America.* Madison: University of Wisconsin Press, 1965.

Jocher, Katharine, ed. *Folk, Region, and Society: Selected Papers of Howard Washington Odum.* Chapel Hill: University of North Carolina Press, 1964.

Johnson, Guion Griffis. *Ante-Bellum North Carolina.* Chapel Hill: University of North Carolina Press, 1937.

Kelsey, Darwin P. "Outdoor Museums and Historical Agriculture." In *Farming in the New Nation: Interpreting American Agriculture, 1790–1840,* Darwin P. Kelsey, ed., 105–27. Washington, D.C.: Agricultural History Association, 1972.

———, ed. *Farming in the New Nation: Interpreting American Agriculture, 1790–1840.* Washington, D.C.: Agricultural History Association, 1972.

Kramer, Karl-Sigismund. "Volkskunde jenseits der Philologie." *Zeitschrift für Volkskunde* 64 (1968): 1–29.

———. *Volksleben im Fürstentum Ansbach und seinen Nachbargebieten (1500–1800): Eine Volkskunde auf Grund archivalischer Quellen.* Würzburg: Kommissionsverlag Ferdinand Schöningh, 1961.

Kurath, Hans, ed. *Linguistic Atlas of New England.* 3 vols. Providence, R.I.: Brown University Press, 1939–1943.

———. *A Word Geography of the Eastern United States.* Studies in American English 1. Ann Arbor: University of Michigan Press, 1949.

Leser, Paul. "The Academic Position of European Ethnology in North America." *Ethnologia Europaea* 1 (4) (1967): 320–22.

Lindberg, Ernst-Folke, ed. *Kulturspeglingar: Studier tillägnade Sam Owen Jansson 19 mars 1966.* Stockholm: Nordiska Museet, 1966.

Lutz, Gerhard. "Volkskunde, 'Lehre vom Volke' und Ethnologie: Zur Geschichte einer Fachbezeichnung." *Hessische Blätter für Volkskunde* 62–63 (1971–1972): 11–29.

Maget, Marcel. "Problèmes d'Ethnographie Européenne." In *Ethnologie Générale,* Jean Poirier, ed., 1247–1338. Encyclopédie de la Pléiade 24. Paris: Éditions Gallimard, 1968.

Marden, Charles F., and Gladys Meyer, eds. *Minorities in American Society.* 3d ed. New York: American Book Company, 1968.

Mathews, Mitford M., ed. *A Dictionary of Americanisms on Historical Principles.* Chicago: University of Chicago Press, 1951.

Murdock, George P., et al. *Outline of Cultural Materials.* 4th rev. ed. New Haven, Conn.: Human Relations Area Files, 1961.

Murphey, Murray G. "An Approach to the Historical Study of National Character." In *Context and Meaning in Cultural Anthropology,* Melford E. Spiro, ed., in honor of A. Irving Hallowell. New York: Free Press, 1965.

Niederer, Arnold. "Zur gesellschaftlichen Verantwortung der gegenwärtigen Volkskunde." In *Kontakte und Grenzen: Probleme der Volks-, Kultur- und Sozialforschung. Festschrift für Gerhard Heilfurth zum 60. Geburtstag,* Hans Friedrich Foltin, Ina-Maria Greverus, and Joachim Schwebe, eds., 1–10. Göttingen: Verlag Otto Schwartz, 1969.

Odum, Howard W., and Harry E. Moore. *American Regionalism: A Cultural-Historical Approach.* New York: Henry Holt and Co., 1938.

The Official Museum Directory: United States-Canada, 1971. New York: American Association of Museums and Crowell-Collier Educational Corp., 1970.

Peate, Iorwerth C. "The Study of Folk Life and Its Part in the Defence of Civilization." *Advancement of Science* 15 (58) (September 1958): 86–94; reprinted in *Gwerin* 2 (1959): 97–109.

———. *Tradition & Folk Life: A Welsh View.* London: Faber and Faber, 1972.

Poirier, Jean, ed. *Ethnologie générale.* Encyclopédie de la Pléiade 24. Paris: Éditions Gallimard, 1968.

Rasmussen, Holger. "Classification Systems of European Ethnological Material." *Ethnologia Europaea* 4 (1970): 73–97.

Redfield, Robert. *Peasant Society and Culture: An Anthropological Approach to Civilization.* Chicago: University of Chicago Press, 1956.

Rehnberg, Mats. *The Nordiska Museet and Skansen: An Introduction to the History and Activities of a Famous Swedish Museum.* Stockholm: Nordiska Museet, 1957.

Riedl, Norbert F. "Folklore and the Study of Material Aspects of Folk Culture." *Journal of American Folklore* 79 (1966): 557–63.

Roy, Carmen. *Canadian Centre for Folk Culture Studies: Annual Review 1972.* Mercury Series, Canadian Centre for Folk Culture Studies 6. Ottawa: National Museum of Man, National Museums of Canada, 1973.

Saintyves, P. *Manuel de Folklore.* Paris: Librairie Émile Nourry, 1936.

Sanderson, Stewart F. "The Work of the School of Scottish Studies." *Scottish Studies* 1 (1957): 3–13.

Schenda, Rudolf. "Einheitlich—Urtümlich—Noch Heute: Probleme der volkskundlichen Befragung." In *Abschied vom Volksleben,* Klaus Geiger, Utz Jeggle, and Gottfried Korff, eds., 124–54. Volksleben 27. Tübingen: Tübinger Vereinigung für Volkskunde, 1970.

Schlebecker, John T. "Curatorial Agriculture." In *Farming in the New Nation: Interpreting American Agriculture, 1790–1840,* Darwin P. Kelsey, ed., 95–103. Washington, D.C.: Agricultural History Association, 1972.

Smithsonian Institution, Division of Performing Arts. *Festival of American Folklife.* Annual Programs. Washington, D.C.: Smithsonian Institution, 1967–1973.

Svensson, Sigfrid. *Introduktion till Folklivsforskningen.* Stockholm: Natur och Kultur, 1969.

Thomas, Charles. "Archaeology and Folk-Life Studies." *Gwerin* 3 (1960): 7–17.

Tillhagen, Carl-Herman. "Folklore Archives in Sweden." *Journal of the Folklore Institute* 1 (1–2) (1964): 20–36.

Trindell, Roger T. "American Folklore Studies and Geography." *Southern Folklore Quarterly* 34 (1) (March 1970): 1–11.

Utley, Francis Lee. "A Role for Folk Life Study in the United States." *Ethnologia Europaea* 4 (1970): 150–54.

Varagnac, André. *Civilisation traditionnelle et genres de vie.* Sciences d'aujourd'hui. Paris: A Michel, 1948.

Wagner, Philip L., and Marvin W. Mikesell, eds. *Readings in Cultural Geography.* Chicago: University of Chicago Press, 1962.

Weber-Kellermann, Ingeborg. *Deutsche Volkskunde zwischen Germanistik und Sozialwissenschaften.* Stuttgart: J. B. Metzlersche Verlagsbuchhandlung, 1969.

Weiss, Richard. *Volkskunde der Schweiz: Grundriss.* Erlenbach-Zurich: Eugen Rentsch Verlag, 1946.

White, Lynn, Jr. "The Life of the Silent Majority." In *Life and Thought in the Early Middle Ages,* Robert S. Hoyt, ed., 85–100. Minneapolis: University of Minnesota Press, 1967.

Whitten, Norman E., Jr., and John F. Szwed, eds. *Afro-American Anthropology: Contemporary Perspectives.* New York: Free Press, 1970.

Wiegelmann, Günter. "Möglichkeiten ethnohistorischer Nahrungsforschung." *Ethnologia Europaea* 1 (3) (1967): 185–94.

Yoder, Don. "The Folklife Studies Movement." *Pennsylvania Folklife* 13 (3) (July 1963): 43–56.

———. "Historical Sources for American Foodways Research and Plans for an American Foodways Archive." *Ethnologia Scandinavica* 1 (1971): 41–55.

———. "Pennsylvania German Folklore Research: A Historical Analysis." In *The German Language in America,* Glenn G. Gilbert, ed., 70–105, 148–63. Austin: University of Texas Press, 1971.

———, ed. "Symposium on Folk Religion." *Western Folklore* 33 (1) (January 1974): 1–87.

Genres of Folklife

Genres of Folklife

If folklorists have divided their field of interest into what they call "genres," folklife scholars have followed suit with some of their specialties. My own work in American folklife has branched into several special subfields in folklife studies, principally folk religion, folk cookery/foodways, and folk costume. My students assure me that my work in these three areas has pioneered and helped to generate research interest in America. In two additional fields, folk medicine and religious folk music or folk hymnody, my own research was influenced by prior work by such scholars as Wayland D. Hand in folk medicine and George Pullen Jackson in folk hymnody, but my fieldwork in both these areas has filled in significant gaps in the national research picture.

This section begins appropriately with my paper, "Toward a Definition of Folk Religion," which introduced my symposium on folk religion at the sessions of the American Folklore Society at Washington, D.C., November 14, 1971. It appeared with the other symposium papers, mostly by students of mine, in *Western Folklore.* I have, however, omitted the "Introductory Bibliography on Folk Religion" which accompanied it, including 268 items in English, German, French, Italian, Spanish, Portuguese, Dutch, and Swedish. It is basic in the field and I plan to expand it and publish it elsewhere with annotations.

The article on "Folk Medicine" was one of three that I contributed to Richard M. Dorson's *Folklore and Folklife: An Introduction.* The other contributions were my general introductions to "Folk Costume" and "Folk Cookery."

"Historical Sources for American Traditional Cookery" was read as a paper at the First International Symposium on Ethnological Food Research, at the University of Lund, Sweden, August 20–26, 1970. A shortened version, entitled "Historical Sources for American Traditional Cookery and Plans for an American Foodways Archive" appeared in *Ethnologia Scandinavica.* This version, copiously illustrated, appeared in *Pennsylvania*

Folklife. In my opinion it is one of my most important articles making use of the method of historical ethnography and, in fact, while using Pennsylvania German examples, forms an introduction to the types of documentation available in American culture for such research.

The essay on "Sectarian Costume Research in the United States" likewise grew out of my participation in a conference, the first Fife Conference on Folklife and Folk Arts, held at Utah State University, Logan, Utah, July 26–27, 1968. It appeared, with a different set of illustrations, in *Forms upon the Frontier: Folklife and Folk Arts in the United States,* edited by Austin and Alta Fife and Henry H. Glassie. Its importance is, in my opinion, that it provides a comparative study of the motivation of religious costume in three contexts, Roman Catholic, Jewish, and Protestant, and offers several theories on the origins of "plain" costume in the world of Protestant sectarianism. This is obviously not my final word on the subject, since I have been working for some years on a volume that I have named *Plain Pennsylvanians.* This will analyze the Puritan-Quaker-Anabaptist concept of "plainness" and trace its striking influence in the colorful world of Pennsylvania's Protestant sectarians in the past as well as the present.

The final article in this section, "Another Look at George Pullen Jackson," appeared as the Foreword to the new edition of Dr. Jackson's last volume, *Another Sheaf of White Spirituals* (1952), reprinted in 1981 by the Folklorica Press of New York and Philadelphia. In addition to reviewing the volume, the article analyzes the continuing and expanding research in the field of American religious folk music. For my more complete biographical review of Dr. Jackson, whose work influenced mine and who kindly transcribed some of the tunes for my volume *Pennsylvania Spirituals* (1961), see "George Pullen Jackson (1874–1953)," the Foreword to the reprint edition of *White Spirituals in the Southern Uplands: The Story of the Fasola Folk, Their Songs, Singings, and "Buckwheat Notes"* (Hatboro, Pennsylvania: Folklore Associates, 1964), pp. i-xv.

3

Toward a Definition of Folk Religion

The concept of folk religion in the academic world has at least two major roots. The first is the study of what German scholarship has named *religiöse Volkskunde*, for which I have two translations: the religious dimension of folk-culture, or the folk-cultural dimension of religion. The second root is the anthropological study of syncretisms between two forms of religion on different levels of civilization, as for example the melange of African beliefs and Roman Catholicism that is called "voodoo" in Haiti, or the syncretism of Catholicism and native Indian religious beliefs and practices in Central and South America.

The format of this paper will involve a threefold division: (1) a brief review of the development of the concept of folk religion from these two roots; (2) a look at selected problems in defining folk religion; and (3) an attempt to define folk religion.

According to German scholarship the term *religiöse Volkskunde* was coined in 1901 by a Lutheran minister named Paul Drews.[1] In that year he published an article entitled "Religiöse Volkskunde, eine Aufgabe der praktischen Theologie." His concern was to investigate, as he put it, "religious folklife" in its totality, its psychological and sociological dimensions and its many-sided expressions. The reason for his concern: so that young ministers fresh from seminary education could better deal with the people in their rural congregations, whose conception of the Christian religion was often radically different from the official doctrinal versions represented by the clergy. The term thus came out of an attempt, within organized religion, to narrow the understanding gap between pulpit and pew, but has moved out of religion proper into the general academic world, where it has

This article originally appeared in *Western Folklore* 33 (1) (January 1974): 1–15.

created a strong subcategory in the European discipline of folk-cultural studies.

While the term was coined in 1901, the discovery of folk religion in Europe had come at the time of the eighteenth-century Enlightenment, when rationalist clergy attacked folk "superstitions" in sermons and ministerial periodicals.[2] In the nineteenth century the German founder of scientific *Volkskunde,* Wilhelm Heinrich Riehl, looked sympathetically at folk-religious elements in culture, and German folk-cultural scholarship came to include folk religion as a concept in the overarching discipline of Volkskunde. By the 1930s there were good theoretical studies of *religiöse Volkskunde,* among them the volumes by Josef Weigert (1924), Werner Boette (1925), and Max Rumpf (1932). All of these focused on peasant culture, and the German shaper of folk community studies and the functionalistic approach to folk culture, Julius Schwietering, saw in religion a creative force in the community culture of the German villages.

Scholars interested in the religious aspects of folk culture in Europe created a massive literature in the twentieth century. Roman Catholic scholars focused upon the pilgrimage system and the practices and folk arts associated with the shrines (the *ex voto* and the *geistliches Lied,* for example), upon hagiography (the study of the saints), and heortology (the study of the church year), including its peasant-level manifestations. Among the scholars in Germany who led the field of Catholic folk religion research were Georg Schreiber[3] of Münster, who founded an Institut für religiöse Volkskunde; Heinrich Schauerte[4] of Paderborn, who has taught many generations of students as docent and professor in this area of study both at Paderborn and Münster; and Rudolf Kriss,[5] the leading German scholar of *Wallfahrtsvolkskunde* or the ethnography of the pilgrimage, the shrine, and related subjects. Principal among the theorists in defining the differences between Catholic and Protestant folk cultures was the Swiss scholar Richard Weiss.[6]

The most thorough regional activity in recording folk religion in a Protestant culture has come in Sweden. At the University of Lund, an Institute for Church History with an Archive for Swedish Church History *(Kyrkohistoriska Arkivet)*, was founded, headed by Hilding Pleijel, which has over the years gathered both historical and ethnographical documentation on Swedish folk-religious beliefs and practices.[7] Pleijel's chapter, "Der Religions- und Kirchengeschichtliche Hintergrund der schwedischen Volkskultur," pp. 64–86 in the symposium edited by Gösta Berg et al., *Schwedische Volkskunde* (Stockholm, 1961), gives a basic overview and a thorough bibliography. See also his *Das Luthertum in schwedischen Volksleben: Einige Entwicklungslinien* (Lund, 1958), and his monograph, *The Devotional Literature of the Swedish People in Earlier Times* (Lund,

1955), which deals with the place the Bible, catechism, hymnbook, and other devotional works had among the Swedish peasantry.

The other tributary strand in folk religion studies is the work of cultural anthropologists, most of them American, in studying the syncretistic cultures of the Caribbean and Central and South America. Here Redfield was the pioneer, with his *Tepoztlán: A Mexican Village* (1930). His fruitful analyses of peasant culture and his distinctions between little and great traditions, folk and urban societies, produced terms and concepts that are still being debated and reshaped in American scholarship. The concept of "folk religion" in tension with "official religion" grew out of the concern of anthropologists to show the interrelatedness of types of culture in a complex society, the relationships between the larger society with its official and sophisticated culture and the little societies that existed in partial isolation, in partial relationship, to the larger societies. Obviously religion as a system was involved in both levels of the culture hierarchy, the "official" and the "folk."

While it is impossible at this time to state definitively where and when the term "folk religion" was first used in English, I suspect that it may have been modeled on the German term *Volksreligion.* Certainly the concept appears in the anthropological literature, as for example Redfield's distinction between "formal Catholicism" and "folk Catholicism."[8]

One of the earliest "official" uses of the term "folk religion" appears to have been by Joshua Trachtenberg, who used it in the title of his early work on *Jewish Magic and Superstition: A Study in Folk Religion* (1939). It has become a fairly widespread term in comparative religion as well, for example, the volume by Ichiro Hori, *Folk Religion in Japan: Continuity and Change* (1968). Martin Nilsson's small paperback on *Greek Folk Religion* and Charles Leslie's reader entitled *Anthropology of Folk Religion* have likewise registered the increased academic acceptance of the term. And in the academic world courses in folk religion have been taught in various universities; John Messenger's at Indiana University and my own (since 1957) at the University of Pennsylvania furnishing two examples.

Two recent volumes, dealing with non-American contexts, have used the term "folk religion" in their titles and both provide some insight into the problems of defining the term. Hori's book sees Japanese folk religion existing in special relationships with the high-cultural forms of Japanese religion:

> Japanese folk religion, unlike Buddhism or Confucianism, is extremely diverse in character and difficult to define precisely. It is made up of vague magico-religious beliefs, many of which are survivals or successors of archaic and primitive elements; these beliefs or primitive elements themselves remain unsystematized theoretically and ecclesiastically

> but in many ways have penetrated and become interrelated with institutionalized religions.[9]

And again Hori provides us with this insight: "I believe that the essence of Japanese folk religion lies in the interaction of two belief systems: a little tradition, which is based on blood or close community ties; and a great tradition, introduced from without, which is adopted by individual or group choice. The belief patterns found everywhere in Japanese rural society are complex, multilayered, and syncretistic."[10]

Leslie's *Anthropology of Folk Religion* (1960) helps us particularly in its chapters on India and Yucatan. In the sections dealing with India (by McKim Marriott) we have folk religion as the interpretation by the little community of the religion of the great tradition (what Toynbee refers to as the process of "parochialization" rather than "universalization").[11] In the chapters of Yucatan (from Redfield) we have folk religion as the syncretization of the religions of two civilizations.[12]

The problems in defining folk religion are first of all conditioned by the preconceptions held by various disciplines in relation to nonstandard religious phenomena in culture. Two disciplines in the United States whose subject matter shades over into the area of folk religion—folklore and religious studies—have shown comparatively less interest in the area than have their European counterparts, the folk-cultural and history of religion fields.

In the field of religious studies in the United States the interest in folk-religious phenomena has been minimal. The teaching of religious studies in the United States has concentrated largely on the theological and institutional level, which either neglects folk practices and folk interpretations of religion as unimportant or because the discipline has too rigid a framework to include such phenomena. In the standard church history journal for the United States, *Church History,* in contrast to the European church historiographical journals, there has never been the slightest interest in practices or beliefs which depart from the theological and liturgical norm. This was graphically displayed in the sobersides program of the American Society of Church History which met several years ago in Nashville, the center of country and gospel music, with its hand on the pulse of the basic religious character of Mid-America. The papers of the session indicated no concern whatsoever with any aspects of either folk or popular religion. In contrast, European journals of ecclesiastical history include all levels and types of religious expression.[13]

The tensions between "high" or official religion and folk religion are of course discoverable in any complex society. E. R. Leach, in his recent volume, *Dialectic in Practical Religion* (1968), distinguishes between

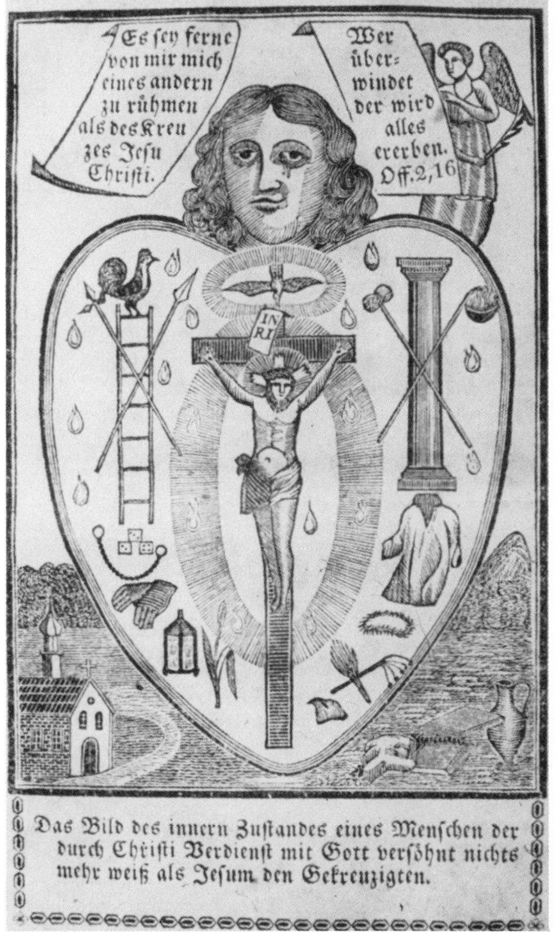

Figure 3.1. The "Heart Book" was a Pennsylvania German imprint of the early nineteenth century based on European models. It portrayed the human heart on the way from sin to salvation. Its woodcut illustrations are an American example of religious folk art. *(Courtesy Roughwood Collection)*

"philosophical" and "practical" religion.[14] The first is the religion of the intellectual elite, by which the religion is usually judged by scholarship, the latter is the "religious principles which guide the behavior of an ordinary churchgoer." In the field of comparative religion the common failure to distinguish between philosophical religion and practical religion has often led to serious misunderstanding. The Western interpretation of Buddhism, for example, was almost entirely derived from the Pali texts, with little attention paid to the ordinary everyday practice of Buddhism. This is also true of Hinduism. Does one, for example, judge Hinduism as a religious complex by the Upanishads or by what anthropology calls "village Hinduism"?

I mentioned Joshua Trachtenberg's excellent study of Jewish magic. In his foreword he states the problem of formal versus folk religion:

> But alongside this formal development [legalism] there was a constant elaboration of what we may call "folk religion"—ideas and practices that never met with the whole-hearted approval of the religious leaders, but which enjoyed such wide popularity that they could not be altogether excluded from the field of religion. Of this sort were the beliefs in demons and angels, and the many superstitious usages based on these beliefs, which by more or less devious routes actually became a part of Judaism, and on the periphery of the religious life, the practices of magic, which never broke completely with the tenets of the faith, yet stretched them almost to the breaking-point. If we call these "folk religion" it is because they expressed the common attitude of the people, as against the official attitude of the Synagogue, to the universe.[15]

The rabbis, representatives of official religion, attempted either (1) to eradicate some of these practices, or (2) to transmute their "offensive features."

Trachtenberg admits the neglect of the folk level of belief in the study of Judaism in these words:

> Everywhere the common folk has existed on an intellectual and spiritual plane all its own, and it is only in the most recent centuries that true science and religion have made inroads into folk conceptions of the universe and brought them closer—if only a little—to what we call our modern, rationalist viewpoint. In Jewish scholarship this phase of folk religion and folk science has been sorely neglected. The tendency has been to impute to the Jewish people as a whole the ideas of a few advanced thinkers, to investigate philosophy and mysticism and law, the cultural and religious creations of the intellectual elite—valuable studies which, however, provide no insight into the inner life of the people themselves.[16]

If religious scholarship has neglected the study of what Trachtenberg calls "the inner life of the people themselves," so, unfortunately, has much of our folklore scholarship in this country. The chief reason for the slow

DECEMBER 12th Month.

Weeks and Days.	Remarkable Days.	H. w. h	Moon R. & S. h m	Moons Place.	Moon south.	Miscellaneous Particulars.	SUN fast. m	SUN rises. h m	SUN sets. h m	O. style
Tuesday	1 Longinus	9	morn.	11	6 41	☿ rises 6 29 ☊	11	7 19	4 41	19
Wednesd	2 Candidus	9	12 26	23	7 25	☿ gr. dist. west	10	7 19	4 41	20
Thursday	3 Fr. Xavier	10	1 39	5	8 6	☌☽♂ ♂ rises 1 40	10	7 20	4 40	21
Friday	4 Barbara	11	2 48	17	8 49	☽ in apo. ☌☽♃	10	7 20	4 40	22
Saturday	5 Abigail	12	3 59	0	9 31	☍ ♄ sets 9 12	9	7 21	4 39	23
49]	2d *Sunday in Advent.*		Luke. 22.			Days' length 9 hours 18 min.				
Sunday	6 *St. Nicholas*	12	5 10	12	10 20	♃ rises 2 26	9	7 21	4 39	24
Monday	7 Agathon	1	6 19	25	11 5	☌☽☿ Reg. ri. 10 21	8	7 22	4 38	25
Tuesday	8 *Conc. V. M.*	2	sets.	8	11 50	8. ♀ in ☊ ☌☽♀	8	7 22	4 38	26
Wednesd	9 Joachim	3	5 26	21	12 42	☌♀☉ inferior	7	7 23	4 37	27
Thursday	10 Judith	3	6 36	5	1 22	Sirius ris. 8 28 ☋	7	7 23	4 37	28
Friday	11 Barsabas	4	7 46	19	2 2	Orion rises 6 11	6	7 23	4 37	29
Saturday	12 Ottilia	5	8 41	5	2 41	☌☽♄ ♄ sets 8 51	6	7 24	4 36	30
50]	3d *Sunday in Advent.*		Matth. 11.			*Days' length* 9 *hours* 12 *min.*				
Sunday	13 Lucian	6	9 43	19	3 40	♂ rises 1 23	5	7 24	4 36	D
Monday	14 Nicasius	7	10 44	3	4 38	Aldeb. so. 11 12	5	7 25	4 36	2
Tuesday	15 Ignatius	8	11 46	16	5 34	☌♃ ♃ ri. 1 50	5	7 25	4 35	3
Wednesd	16 *Emberday*	9	morn.	0	6 31	16. Ri.s. 11 33	4	7 25	4 35	4
Thursday	17 Lazarus	10	12 56	14	7 32	Regulus ris. 9 32	4	7 25	4 35	5
Friday	18 Arnold	11	2 16	28	8 31	☌☿♀ Sir. ris. 7 51	3	7 25	4 35	6
Saturday	19 Abraham	12	3 34	12	9 32	☊ ♄ sets 8 26	3	7 25	4 35	7
51]	4*th Sunday in Advent.*		*John* 1.			*Days' length* 9 *hours* 10 *min.*				
Sunday	20 Ammon	1	4 46	26	10 31	☽ per. ♃ ris. 1 25	2	7 25	4 35	8
Monday	21 *St. Thomas*	1	5 59	9	11 30	☉ enters ♑ *Sh.d.*	2	7 26	4 34	9
Tuesday	22 Beata	1	rises.	21	morn.	22. *Wint. co.*	1	7 25	4 35	10
Wednesd	23 Dagobert	2	5 22	5	12 26	♂ ris. 1 4 ☊	1	7 25	4 35	11
Thursday	24 Adam, Eve	3	6 23	18	1 10	Altair sets 8 0	slower.	7 25	4 35	12
Friday	25 *Christmas*	4	7 20	1	1 52	♄ sets 8 4		7 25	4 35	13
Saturday	26 Stephen	5	8 10	14	2 32	♀ ri. 5 44 morn. st.		7 25	4 35	14
52]	*Sunday after Christmas.*		*Luke* 2.			*Days' length* 9 *hours* 10 *min.*				
Sunday	27 *John, Evan.*	5	8 55	26	3 20	Arietis so. 7 36	1	7 25	4 35	15
Monday	28 H. Innocents	6	9 46	7	4 4	♀ stationary	2	7 25	4 35	16
Tuesday	29 Noah	7	10 48	19	4 56	♃ rises 12 45	2	7 24	4 36	17
Wednesd	30 David	8	11 49	1	5 50	30. ♂ ri. 12 56	3	7 24	4 36	18
Thursday	31 Sylvester	9	morn.	13	6 49	☽ in perigee	3	7 24	4 36	19

VENUS is on the 9th inferior with the Sun, and passes from Evening to Morning Star.
THE TRANSIT OF VENUS occurs on the 8th of December 11 o'clock 14 min. in the evening; invisible in the United States.

Figure 3.2. The *Farmer's Almanac* was a folk-cultural document of the first importance. It included the calendar for the year, listing saints' days and holidays, phases of the moon, signs of the zodiac, and other material connected with folk religion. Note journal notations at bottom of page. *(Courtesy Roughwood Collection)*

development of the study of folk religion in this country by folklorists has been, as I see it, the thorny question of definition of the field of folklore. Most American definitions of folklore provide no categories in which to include religious phenomena, unless it includes them under that impossible survival from the Enlightenment, the word *superstition,* which blocks any sympathetic understanding of the belief elements in folk religion. "Religion" is obviously not a "genre," and cannot therefore be included in the old-fashioned genre-oriented definitions. With the newer culture-oriented definitions obviously religion can be included as it has been in Europe.

The term "superstition," as we all know, has its defenders. It was even used in its German form, *Aberglaube,* in the title of the best work on folk beliefs produced in Europe, the *Handwörterbuch des deutschen Aberglaubens,* all ten volumes, although it was minimally used in the text itself. European scholars who oppose *Aberglaube* as a value judgment, understandable solely in relation to a system of hard orthodoxy which sees truth only in its own terms, have of course proposed the neutral substitute term *Volksglaube,* which is now also widely current in its English form "folk belief."[17]

The second difficulty in the term "folk religion" is that to some minds the term "religion" suggests what we normally mean by organized religion, or the official religious institutions of a culture. Durkheim appears to be the father of this viewpoint. In differentiating magic from religion, he suggests that religion always forms what is sociologically known as a "church," an association of believers; magic forms no "church" in this sense. Those who limit the term "religion" to organized forms prefer the term "folk belief" to designate the body of phenomena that we are attempting to define. Olof Pettersson provides strength for this argument in a recent essay. In analyzing an early attempt at "constructing" a "folk religion" (Albrecht Dieterich, *Mutter Erde: Ein Versuch über Volksreligion* [1905]), Pettersson comes to the conclusion that it is more advisable to speak of "folk-cultural elements of a religion" than of a delimited, settled entity called "folk religion."[18]

A final difficulty in defining "folk religion" is posed by the sociological use of the term as the opposite of "universal religion," as documented, for example, by the sociologists Schneider and Mensching.[19] "A folk religion, as the name suggests," writes Louis Schneider, "is bound to a particular people, folk or tribe, just as the particular people, folk or tribe is bound to the particular religion." Universal religions, on the other hand, are "detached from a folk base. They address themselves to individual men anywhere and everywhere."

> In the emergence of universal religion a process of structural differentiation is clearly at work. Religion in the folk case has as it were one house, one dwelling, one box from

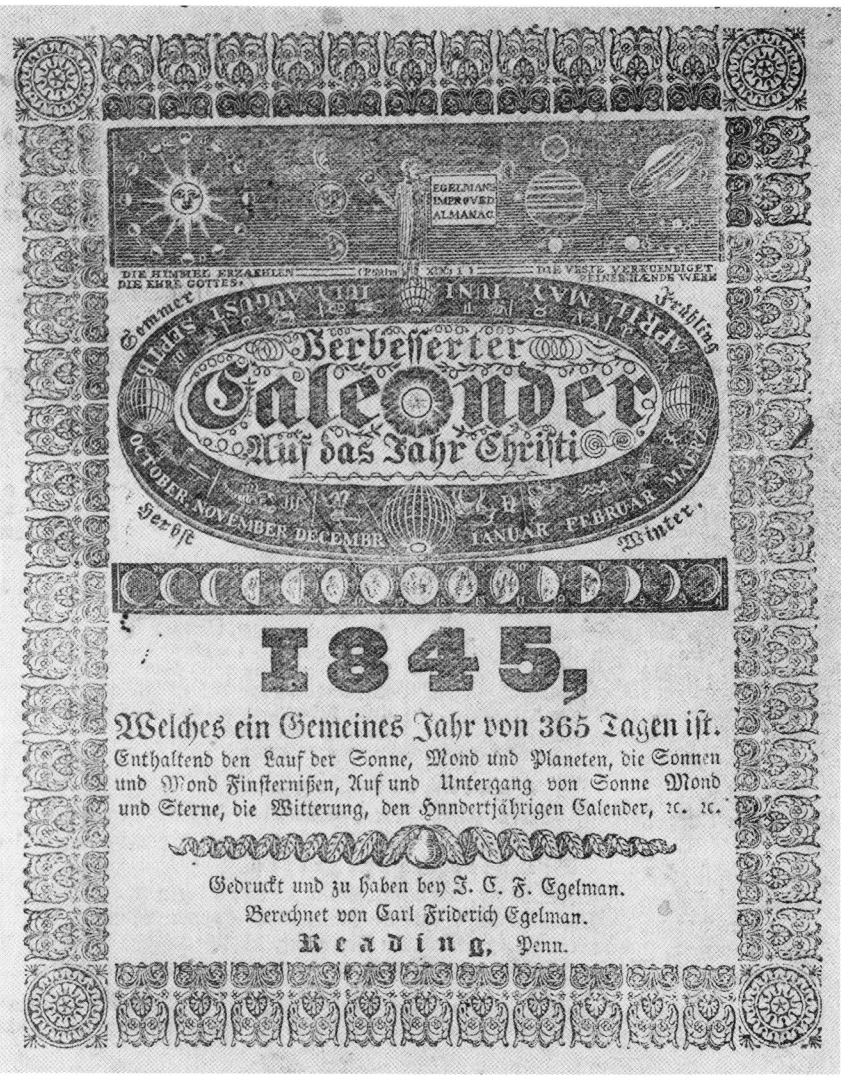

EGELMAN'S IMPROVED ALMANAC

DIE HIMMEL ERZAEHLEN DIE EHRE GOTTES. (Psalm XIX, 1.) DIE VESTE VERKUENDIGET SEINER HÆNDE WERK

Verbesserter Calender Auf das Jahr Christi

1845,

Welches ein Gemeines Jahr von 365 Tagen ist.

Enthaltend den Lauf der Sonne, Mond und Planeten, die Sonnen und Mond Finsternißen, Auf und Untergang von Sonne Mond und Sterne, die Witterung, den Hundertjährigen Calender, ꝛc. ꝛc.

Gedruckt und zu haben bey J. C. F. Egelman.
Berechnet von Carl Friderich Egelman.
Reading, Penn.

Figure 3.3. Almanac for 1845 from Reading, Pennsylvania. Note engravings of heavenly bodies, signs of the zodiac, and phases of the moon, all the work of the Pennsylvania German engraver and almanac editor Carl Friderich Egelman.
(Courtesy Roughwood Collection)

> which it is inseparable. In the universal case, it comes out of the folk matrix and may theoretically "strike" anywhere—in any folk, or tribal or national locus. It may then be said to have a house of its own—a distinctively religious house.[20]

In general I prefer the use of the terms "tribal" or "national" religion to "folk religion" for this particular concept. These terms will serve for living religions; for the now-defunct religions which influenced earlier stages of European civilization (Greco-Roman, Celtic, Germanic, and Slavic religions) perhaps the term "archaic" is adequate. The confusion involved in the sociological use of the term as outlined above is found in other institutions as well, stemming from the secondary (primary?) usage in some European cultures of the term "folk" for "national," as in the Scandinavian term "folk school." The German term *Volksreligion* has been used in both ways: (1) as the opposite of "universal religion" in the sense of national religion of an entire people, and (2) as the folk-level opposite of sophisticated, official, institutionalized levels of religion *(Hochreligion)* in a complex society.[21] It is of course this second sense of the word that we are concerned with.

In my own conceptualization of folk religion I differentiate it from organized religion, primitive religion, popular-level religion, and sectarian religion. Folk religion exists in a complex society in relation to and in tension with the organized religion(s) of that society. Its relatively unorganized character differentiates it from organized religion. Its part-cultural setting differentiates it from primitive religion which, as the religion of a people, is in a sense official religion. Neither is folk religion "popular religion" of the Norman Vincent Peale level, although there have been unsuccessful attempts in American religion to label such phenomena as Pealeism as "folk religion," obviously a misnomer in the academic world.[22] Finally folk religion can be differentiated from sectarian religion. The sects and cults represent organized and therefore official religion with churches and congregations. Hence I feel it improper to refer to the religion of any organized sect as a "folk religion." We have to speak instead of folk-religious aspects of sectarian religion. Obviously sects as small groups and still more as counter-cultures achieve and defend a culture of their own, and some of the component elements in sectarian culture may be folk elements.

Finally, how can we define "folk religion"? Can we construct a usable definition that will fit the American situation? As I see it, there are five possibilities.

1. Is folk religion, in the European context, as Charles G. Leland once defined it in the last century, "the old religion" *(la vecchia religione),*[23] that is, survivals in the present of pre-Christian forms of religion? This is the

evolutionist, survivalist, *gesunkenes Kulturgut* approach. According to this definition folk religion in Catholicism would be the acculturated elements from the pre-Christian religions, while in Protestantism folk religion would consist of survivals carried over by the people from medieval Catholicism (including the healing cults, witchcraft, saints' days, and calendric customs, as well as common peasant attitudes such as the *do ut des* contractual relationship with God). If, according to Santayana, Catholicism was paganism spiritualized,[24] official Protestantism is a truncated form of medieval Catholicism. The austerity and intellectuality of much of official Protestantism forced the people to develop in some contexts a folk Protestantism of their own, and even official Protestantism was forced to develop Protestant substitutes for Catholic values exscinded at the time of the Protestant Reformation. An example of the former is the survival in Protestant contexts of the medieval practice of magico-religious healing, an example of the latter is the development of the personal diary and religious autobiography as substitute for, among other values, the Catholic element of confession.[25] To construct a definition from this approach, folk religion is essentially the survival, in an official religious context, of beliefs and behavior inherited from earlier stages of the culture's development.

2. Is folk religion, secondly, in the Caribbean or Latin American context, as defined by Métraux, the mixture *(mélange)* of an official "high" religion (Catholicism) with "native" or "primitive" religion (in this case either African belief systems or indigenous Indian religion)?[26] This is the syncretist approach, growing out of acculturation theory. Obviously this is similar to the first definition, although as usually applied, the survivalist definition involves a kind of static view of "survivals" as identifiable, researchable things, whereas this acculturationist view or syncretist definition is dynamic, suggesting the process whereby the present forms of the religion came about. To construct, then, a definition: folk religion is essentially a syncretistic system built up through the interpenetration of two or more forms of religion in a complex society.

3. Is folk religion, thirdly, as folklorists have largely described it, certain fringe phenomena in religion, the unpermitted, the unsanctioned, that is, superstitions? This is an attempt to create a genre out of the folk elements in religion, but unfortunately it cannot do justice to thé full range of folk-religious phenomena and attitudes. There has been some attempt to justify this definition on a psychological basis, by suggesting that the individual's attitude to "superstition" is different from his attitude to "religion," but this does not get us very far from the old debate about "magic" and "religion." In general, as suggested above, I prefer to scrap the word "superstition" and substitute "folk belief." Certainly in a functioning culture the common people's attitudes to a supposed division of labor between "magic" and

A LETTER

— WRITTEN BY —

GOD HIMSELF, AND LEFT DOWN AT MAGDEBURG

It was written in golden letters, and sent by God through an Angel; to him, who will copy it, it shall be given; who despiseth it, from him will part THE LORD.

Whoever works on Sunday, is cursed. Therefore, I command you that you do not work on Sunday, but devotedly go to church; but do not adorn your face; you shall not wear strange hair, and not carry on arrogance; you shall give to the poor of your riches, give plenty and believe, that this letter is written by my own hand and sent out by Christ himself, and that you will not act like the dumb beast; you have six days in the week, during which you shall carry on your labors; but the seventh day (namely, Sunday,) you shall keep holy; if you do not do that, I will send war, famine, pest and death among you, and punish you with many troubles. Also, I command you, every one, whoever he may be, young or old, small and great, that you do not work late on Saturday, but you shall regret your sins, that they may be forgiven you. Do not desire silver and gold; do not carry on sensualities and desires; do think that I have made you and can destroy you.

Do not rejoice when your neighbor is poor, feel moreover sorry with him, then you will fare well.

You children, honor father and mother, then you will fare well on earth. Who that doth not believe these and holds it, shall be damned and lost. I Jesus, have written this myself with my own hand; he that opposes it and scandalizes, that man shall have to expect no help from me; whoever hath the letter and does not make it known, he is cursed by the christian church, and if your sins are as large as they may be, they shall, if you have heartily regretted and repented of them, be forgiven you.

Who does not believe this, he shall die and be punished in hell, and I myself will on the last day inquire after your sins, when you will have to answer me.

And that man who carries this letter with him, and keeps it in his house, no thunder will do him any harm, and he will be safe from fire and water; and he that publishes it to mankind, will receive his reward and a joyful departure from this world.

Do keep my command which I have sent through my Angel. I, the true God from the heavenly throne, the Son of God and Mary. Amen.

This has occured at Magdeburg, in the Year 1783.

Figure 3.4. The *Himmelsbrief*, or Letter from Heaven, was a widespread phenomenon among the Pennsylvania Germans, although examples turn up in other ethnic cultures as well. It was a paper amulet that was believed to protect the bearer, or any building in which it was placed. Part of its appeal to the believer was that it represented the concept of post-biblical revelation. *(Courtesy Roughwood Collection)*

THE TWO MASTERS.

Jesus
The Believer's Master,
IS
ALMIGHTY,
GOOD,
KIND,
TRUTHFUL,
A SAVIOUR.

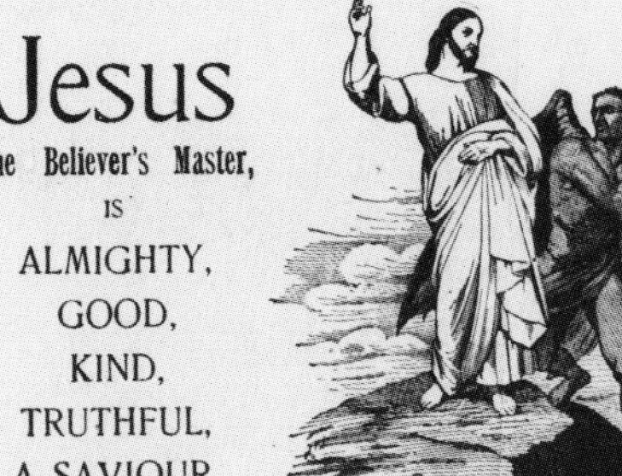

Satan
The Sinner's Master,
IS
MIGHTY,
WICKED,
CRUEL,
A DECEIVER,
A DESTROYER.

His Servants are | The Angels, The Saved, The Holy.

They | Love Him, Serve Him, Will Reign with Him forever.

HIS FREE GIFT:

Eternal Life!

But now
Being made free from sin,
and
Become servants to God,
ye have
Your fruit unto holiness,
and the end
EVERLASTING LIFE. Rom. 6:22.

His Servants are | Devils, The Unsaved, The Unholy.

They | Are deceived by him, Serve him, Will suffer with him forever.

His Awful Wages:

Eternal Death!

Know ye not that
To whom ye yield yourselves servants to obey, his servants ye are to whom ye obey,
whether of
Sin unto death,
or of
Obedience unto Righteousness? Rom. 6:16.

The flight of time, the nearness of Death, the certainty of the Judgment, the duration of Eternity, the woes of Hell, the wealth of Heaven, the sinfulness of Sin, the joys of Salvation, and the love of God all combine to make it of vital importance that every moment of our lives be spent in the service of Christ. Choose ye this day whom ye will serve. Decide for Jesus NOW!

You are Invited to the Revival Meetings!

Figure 3.5. Broadside invitation to revival meetings, contrasting in a highly dualistic manner the powers of Christ and the powers of Satan. This dualism was reflected in Protestant folk religion in America as well as (this example) in organized Protestantism of the evangelical variety. *(Courtesy Roughwood Collection)*

"religion" are very difficult to pry apart even for scientific analysis. All of man's self-initiated approaches to the supernatural (prayer, blessing, conjuration, and curse) as well as those phenomena believed to be "invasions" of the supernatural into the natural (revelation, vision, dream, prophecy, miracle, charisma, etc.), obviously operate in a unified organic system of belief. One of the best recent treatments of some of these problems is Irmgard Hampp's *Beschwörung Segen Gebet* (1961). And Caro Baroja's diagrams in *The World of the Witches* (1964) graphically display the overlapping of the common man's attitudes to magic and religion, priest and shaman. Perhaps we can construct a definition here by seeing folk religion as the interaction of belief, ritual, custom, and mythology in traditional societies.

4. Is folk religion, fourthly, the "folk interpretation and expression of religion"? This is a definition that involves religion among the expressive elements of a culture, and its application is particularly plain in the area of the folk arts, religious folk music, festivals, calendar customs, and other similar creations. In each of these areas the little community puts in its ingredient of self-expression, adds its own local coloration, to universally accepted official-religious forms. This definition is particularly apt for the area of folk religion for which the Germans have coined the term ***kirchliche Volkskunde,*** that is, those folk-cultural phenomena which are associated with or grow out of ecclesiastical phenomena.[27] The recent work by Latin American scholars on the *fiesta* as a total community event involving every aspect of culture from costume to foodways is an example of what can be done to study this positive or "creative" side of folk religion.[28] But can this definition include also the passive survivalist elements of folk belief, the witchcraft complex for example? Perhaps one way of reconciling this dichotomy is to invoke the term "folk religiosity."[29] This would result in the following definition: Folk religion is the deposit in culture of folk religiosity, the full range of folk attitudes to religion.

5. Perhaps in the last analysis we must construct a practical working definition to include all these component elements. My original translations of *religiöse Volkskunde* can serve here. Folk religion is "the folk-cultural dimension of religion," or "the religious dimension of folk-culture." This can include active/creative as well as passive/survivalist elements, it also certainly can suggest the element of tension existing between folk and official levels of religion in the complex society. Therefore we can phrase this practical definition in another way: Folk religion is the totality of all those views and practices of religion that exist among the people apart from and alongside the strictly theological and liturgical forms of the official religion.[30]

We have had scholarly precedent for all five of these views. Some,

Figure 3.6. Catholic devotional art focusing on the Wounds of Christ and the Sacred Hearts of Jesus and Mary (Vienna, late nineteenth century). These are officially sanctioned devotional cults in Roman Catholicism, but they shade over into folk-religious spirituality and devotional art. *(Courtesy Roughwood Collection)*

however, are narrower and some are broader. The broadest of all would appear to be no. 5. Under it could be included the passive phenomena of folk religion (witchcraft and magic, for example) as well as the active or creative phenomena (religious folk music, folk costume, folk art, even folk theology), the reinterpretations or expressions of the official religion on the folk level. This definition includes therefore both the ecclesiastical as well as the para-ecclesiastical phenomena, the elements related to official ecclesiastical forms on the one hand, and on the other, those which have a partially independent existence outside the boundary of orthodoxy. Finally, this definition can be applied, as Richard Weiss and others have done with folk culture in general, to the components of the individual mind, where rationalistic attitudes, orthodox religious opinions, and folk-religious reactions can coexist in the same person.[31]

Notes

1. For the history of the term and the scientific study of "religiöse Volkskunde," see particularly Albrecht Jobst, *Evangelische Kirche und Volkstum: Ein Beitrag zur Geschichte der Volkskunde* (Stuttgart, 1938), 203–32; and Heinrich Schauerte, "Entwicklung und gegenwärtiger Stand der religiösen Volkskundeforschung," *Historisches Jahrbuch* 72 (1953): 516–34. The only summary in English thus far is Wolfgang Brückner, "Popular Piety in Central Europe," *Journal of the Folklore Institute* 5 (1968): 158–74.

2. For general perspectives on the Enlightenment and folk religion, see Hermann Bausinger, *Volkskunde: Von der Altertumsforschung zur Kulturanalyse* (Berlin-Darmstadt, [1970]), 17–30; Leopold Schmidt, "Volkskunde, Gegenreformation, Aufklärung," *Deutsche Vierteljahrsschrift für Literaturwissenschaft und Geistesgeschichte* 16 (1938): 75–94; and Josef Dünninger, "Volkstum und Aufklärung in Franken: Beiträge zur fränkischen Volkskunde im ausgehenden 18. Jahrhundert," *Bayerisches Jahrbuch für Volkskunde 1957,* 29–42.

3. Georg Schreiber made massive contributions to the study of folk religion. His institute at Münster was followed by a similar institution at Salzburg founded by Hanns Koren. Schreiber created the term "kirchliche Volkskunde," edited *Volk und Volkstum: Jahrbuch für Volkskunde* and the *Forschungen zur Volkskunde,* and aided the study of Auslandsdeutschtum with his series, *Deutschtum und Ausland,* 65 numbers. For his books and contributions in general, see the estimate by Heinrich Schauerte, "Georg Schreiber und die Volkskunde," *Rheinisch-Westfälische Zeitschrift für Volkskunde* 9 (1962): 132–39.

4. For Schauerte's contributions, see Georg Wagner, "Heinrich Schauerte und sein volkskundliches Schaffen," *Rheinisch-Westfälische Zeitschrift für Volkskunde* 9 (1962): 278–80.

5. Kriss assembled the Sammlung Kriss, one of the largest collections of folk-religious art and material culture in Europe, now housed in the Bayerisches Nationalmuseum, Munich. For his publications, see Leopold Schmidt, comp., "Rudolf Kriss 70 Jahre: Eine Bibliographie seiner Veröffentlichungen von 1926 bis 1972," *Österreichische Zeitschrift für Volkskunde,* n.s. 27 (1973): 1–8; for a brief biography, see Leopold Schmidt, "Rudolf Kriss," ibid., 243–45.

6. Richard Weiss's indispensable *Volkskunde der Schweiz* (Erlenbach-Zürich, 1946) contains basic theory on folk religion and folk religiosity, and analyzes the differences between Catholic and Protestant folk cultures, a subject that Swiss folk-cultural scholars had to wrestle with. For the latter, see his essay "Zur Problematik einer protestantischen Volkskultur," *Beiträge zur Volkstumsforschung* 14 (1964): 27–46.

7. For the history of the institute and its work, see the series *Meddelanden från Kyrkohistoriska Arkivet i Lund*, Hilding Pleijel, ed. No. 1 is entitled *Kyrklig folklivsforskning* and includes the basic questionnaire on Swedish folk religion.

8. Cf. *The Folk Culture of Yucatan* (Chicago, 1941), 261, 267. Since there appears to be no summary of the development of the term "folk religion" in anthropological and sociological scholarship, I would appreciate citations from readers on earlier uses than Redfield's and Trachtenberg's.

9. Ichiro Hori, *Folk Religion in Japan: Continuity and Change* (Chicago, 1968), 1.

10. Ibid., 49.

11. Charles Leslie, *Anthropology of Folk Religion* (New York, 1960), chap. 4: "Little Communities in an Indigenous Civilization," by McKim Marriott.

12. Leslie, ch. 8: "Spanish and Indian: The Two Heritages," from Redfield, *Folk Culture of Yucatan*.

13. Cf. the *Blätter für Pfälzische Kirchengeschichte und religiöse Volkskunde*.

14. E. R. Leach, ed., *Dialectic in Practical Religion* (Cambridge, 1968), 1.

15. Joshua Trachtenberg, *Jewish Magic and Superstition: A Study in Folk Religion* (New York, 1939), vii-viii.

16. Ibid., viii. A similar note is struck by the French sociologist le Bras: "The folklife of Catholicism has been just as little observed by the historians of the Middle Ages and of the Ancien Régime as by our contemporaries. We have thousands of studies on doctrines, on monuments, on illustrious men . . . but how many monographs are there on the religious history of the French people, on the Christian life or lack of it of our forefathers, which merits perhaps just as much attention as a syllogism or a prehistoric flintstone and which can explain so many apparent mysteries?" (Gabriel le Bras, "De l'État présent de la pratique religieuse en France," *Revue de folklore français* 4 [1933]: 195.)

17. One of the most recent attempts to define the term scientifically, Karl E. Scheibe and Theodore R. Sarbin, "Towards a Theoretical Conceptualisation of Superstition," *British Journal for the Philosophy of Science* 16 (1965): 143–58, ends on the curious note: "A final point should be made that may seem surprising, in view of the title of this paper. Instead of using the term superstition more frequently, as would be necessary if we were to apply the term at all consistently, it should be used less frequently, and perhaps not at all. According to the major points outlined earlier regarding the psychological nature of superstitions as a category of belief, it should be apparent that they are ubiquitous; that even scientists have them though here they are often clothed in the dignified fabric of irreproachable mathematical or verbal symbolism. Moreover, superstitions, i.e., beliefs that are not inductively derived and not empirically checked, are psychologically necessary for existence. Thus, even though the category of beliefs called superstitions is a distinct and meaningful category, it turns out to be too inclusive a class of beliefs to bear the socially reprehensible label of Superstition. For the sake of equity and fairness, the term should be used not more, but less."

18. Olof Pettersson, "Der Begriff 'Volksreligion': ein religionsgeschichtliches Problem," *Ethnologia Europaea* 4 (1970): 62–66.

19. Gustav Mensching, *Soziologie der Religion* (Bonn, 1947), particularly 25–85.

20. Louis Schneider, *Sociological Approach to Religion* (New York, 1970), 73–74.

21. Alfred Bertholet, *Wörterbuch der Religionen* (Stuttgart, 1952), 508–9; Kurt Goldammer, *Die Formenwelt des Religiösen: Grundriss der systematischen Religionswissenschaft* (Stuttgart, 1960), 14.

22. A. Roy Eckhart, *The Surge of Piety in America: An Appraisal* (New York, 1958), deals with the "revival" of religion in the 1950s. Chapter 2 is entitled "Folk Religion: Its Ways and Works." He "suggests" the term "folk religion" for this phenomenon because the "return to religion" was "very much a popular movement." He seems to know nothing of the term's prior use in religious and folk-cultural scholarship.

23. Charles Godfrey Leland, *Etruscan Roman Remains in Popular Tradition* (London and New York, 1892), 2.

24. George Santayana, *My Host the World* (New York, 1953), 84.

25. Don Yoder, "The Saint's Legend in the Pennsylvania German Folk-Culture," in Wayland D. Hand, ed., *American Folk Legend: A Symposium* (Berkeley and Los Angeles, 1971), 157–83.

26. Alfred Métraux, *Voodoo in Haiti* (New York, 1959), or Leslie, chap. 9.

27. For this area of folk religion, see George Schreiber, "Kirchliche Volkskunde," *Deutsche Forschung: Aus der Arbeit der Notgemeinschaft der Deutschen Wissenschaft* 6 (1928): 65–73; Will-Erich Peuckert, "Kirchliche Volkskunde," *Zeitschrift für Kirchengeschichte* 58 (1939): 521–73; also Will-Erich Peuckert and Otto Lauffer, eds., *Volkskunde: Quellen und Forschungen seit 1930* (Bern, 1951), 47–50.

28. Latin American folklorists and ethnographers have written widely on the fiesta as a total community event. American scholars like Ralph Boggs, Américo Paredes, Paulo Carvalho-Neto, and Robert J. Smith have mediated this vast body of scholarship to the United States. See also Henry F. Dobyns, "The Religious Festival" (Ph.D. diss., Cornell University, 1960). For the larger aspects of the festival spirit within Christianity, see the recent work by Harvey Cox, *The Feast of Fools: A Theological Essay on Festivity and Fantasy* (Cambridge, Mass., 1970).

29. Again there appears to be German precedent in the terms *Volksreligiösität* and *Volksfrömmigkeit.*

30. This is modeled on the broad-gauge definition of folk medicine developed by Hanns O. Münsterer in his article, "Grundlagen, Gültigkeit und Grenzen der volksmedizinischen Heilverfahren," *Bayerisches Jahrbuch für Volkskunde 1950,* 9–20.

31. Weiss, *Volkskunde der Schweiz,* 6–9.

4

Folk Medicine

Folk Medicine and Modern Medicine

Folk medicine is related to three other levels or types of medicine practiced in the world. At the other end of the medical spectrum stands scientific, academic, or "modern" medicine, with which it has coexisted in increasingly uneasy tension since the eighteenth century. Folk medicine is related derivatively to the academic medicine of earlier generations. Certain ideas that were once circulating in academic medical circles and are now discarded have become part and parcel of the folk-medical viewpoint. Examples are the doctrine of "signatures," the seventeenth-century idea of "sympathy," and from earlier cultural strata, astrology and the doctrine of the four humors. It is true that these have long ago been scrapped by science, but they provide us with instructive examples that folk medicine, like certain other aspects of folk culture, has many *gesunkenes Kulturgut* items in its repertory. At the same time, there is much evidence that some medical practice went in the other direction, making modern medicine in part a derivative of primitive and folk medicine.

The other levels of medicine to which folk medicine has a relation are primitive medicine, with which it shares common elements of materia medica, techniques, and worldview, and popular medicine. While folk medicine and primitive medicine share worldview and magical techniques, they differ in social context: the classical primitive medicine (difficult to locate in the twentieth century) being the only type of medicine found natively in the culture, while folk medicine (representing the "little culture") shares the ground with and exists in tension with the higher forms of medicine (representing the "large culture"). Popular medicine is in a sense folk medicine gone commercial, the patent medicines and techniques of which it consists being frequently derived from the folk-medical repertory.

This article originally appeared in *Folklore and Folklife: An Introduction,* Richard M. Dorson, ed. (Chicago: University of Chicago Press, 1972), 191–215.

Of folk medicine there are essentially two varieties, or branches: (1) natural folk medicine, and (2) magico-religious folk medicine. The first of these represents one of man's earliest reactions to his natural environment, and involves the seeking of cures for his ills in the herbs, plants, minerals, and animal substances of nature. Natural medicine, which is sometimes called "rational" folk medicine, and sometimes "herbal" folk medicine because of the predominance of herbs in its materia medica, is shared with primitive cultures, and in some cases some of its many effective cures have made their way into scientific medicine. The second branch of folk medicine is the magico-religious variety, sometimes called "occult" folk medicine, which attempts to use charms, holy words, and holy actions to cure disease. This type commonly involves a complicated, prescientific worldview that we will describe in detail later.

Folk medicine, like folklore, has outgrown its strict identification with peasant cultures. Its clientele is drawn from a wide variety of groups and individuals. In the 1930s, writing of Franconia in central Germany, the medical historian Büttner described the clientele of the folk-medical practitioners as generally the older generation of the peasantry, plus the working classes and petty bourgeois of the cities. Folk-medical ideas of the older traditional sort were to be met most frequently in the mountainous areas that had little communication with the outside world, more in Catholic than in Protestant circles, and more among women than among men. The middle classes and working classes of the cities had turned away from folk medicine to the empirical and rational viewpoints, and now normally went first to the physician and only secondarily to the practical healers, the naturopaths, the quacks, and the magicians. Even among the classes with more formal education, the women especially patronized occult medicine, astrology, pseudo-radiology, and other modern cultic forms of popular medicine. In other words, a great many representatives of different classes and educational strata patronize nonscientific medicine.[1]

Writing of the situation in the United States in the mid-twentieth century, Wayland Hand points out that "superstition is not the preserve of the unlettered only, but is a state or a way of looking at things that may befall even the most sophisticated members of society. Professional people of all kinds, no less than tradesmen, are prone to many of the same popular conceits and mental errors to which, for want of formal education, members of the humbler classes have fallen heir."[2] He cites Eugen Mogk's formula that every *Kulturmensch* has within him the rudiments of a *Naturmensch.*[3] And Richard Weiss, who wrestled with this basic question of definition, finally defined "folk" not in terms of class or cultural level in society but as a way of thinking within the individual, always combined today with other levels and types of thinking.[4]

Perhaps this gives us insight into a simpler, more workable definition of folk medicine for the present time. Hanns Otto Münsterer's useful admonition points in this direction: "We must therefore resolve to describe folk medicine from the widest possible standpoint, as whatever ideas of combating and preventing disease exist among the people apart from the formal system of scientific medicine."[5] The editors of the recent *Wörterbuch der deutschen Volkskunde* come to the same conclusion, urging scholars to underplay the linear historical viewpoint of *gesunkenes Kulturgut* and stress the place of folk medicine in the folk-cultural milieu.

> The first question should not be, What did the people receive from above in the course of history, but rather: What viewpoints about sickness and health do the people possess on the ground of their own thinking? The answer to this question shows us that folk medicine has grown organically out of the whole of folk belief and custom, thought, life and speech. Medicine is older than doctors. Hence the definition: folk medicine is the substance of all the traditional viewpoints on sickness and the healing methods applied against disease which exist among the people.[6]

Folk-Medical Research in Europe and the United States

The history of the study of folk medicine has followed the same general pattern as other aspects of folk culture: first the literary or philological approach, followed by the sociological and functional approach. Pioneer European folklorists, fascinated with the philological aspects of folklore, collected charms in the nineteenth century, stressing their antiquity and their value for linguistic research. Ancient practices were discovered—in Germany the Merseburg formulas, in England the Anglo-Saxon leechdoms—and the horizon of folk medicine was pushed back to the early Middle Ages. At the same time the classical scholar became interested in the medical systems of classical antiquity, and the comparative religionist in the medical materials in the Vedas, which provided parallels from across the roof of the world to ancient European tribal forms of medicine.

The charm-collectors not only scoured medieval literature but also began to collect and analyze the manuscript charm-books that exist all over Europe, the *Zauberbücher,* or *Svartböcker,* which provided them with overall glimpses of the practice of the folk-healer, the conditions he attempted to cure, and the immediate documentary background of the living charms of the current practitioners who were found to exist in every area of Europe in the nineteenth century. Among the great European collections are Dr. A. Christian Bang's *Norske Hexeformularer og Magiske Opskrifter* (Kristiania, 1901–12); and F. Ohrt's collection of Danish formulae, *Danmarks Trylleformler* (Copenhagen and Christiania, 1917). The largest collection of Germanic charms was the Adolf Spamer Collection, now housed in the Institut für deutsche Volkskunde, Deutsche Akademie der Wissenschaften, at the Humboldt University in Berlin. This collection, now containing over 25,000 separate items, was built up largely by Spamer himself in forty years of collecting in every area of Germany.[7] Spamer's analysis of the major motifs in this unique corpus of material was edited by Dr. Johanna Jaenecke-Nickel, Spamer's successor at the institute, in the volume, *Romanusbüchlein: Historisch-philologischer Kommentar zu einem deutschen Zauberbuch* (Berlin, 1958).

The publication of national charm collections is still continuing, the most recent example from western Europe being Dr. Jozef van Haver's *Nederlandse Incantatieliteratuur: Een Gecommentarieerd Compendium van Nederlandse Bezwerings-formules* (Gent, 1964).

In addition to the national collections, there were, again, following a major trend in folklore in the nineteenth and early twentieth century, comparative studies of folk medicine. The largest of these, still of basic use, is the two-volume work by the Viennese physicians Oskar von Hovorka and Adolf Kronfeld, *Vergleichende Volksmedizin: Eine Darstellung volksmedizinischer Sitten und Gebräuche, Anschauungen und Heilfaktoren, des Aberglaubens und der Zaubermedizin* (Stuttgart, 1908). Vol. 1 is essentially a dictionary, from *Aal* to *Zwiebel;* vol. 2 is an analysis of all the branches of medicine from obstetrics to dermatology, with discussion of the folk cures and treatments comparatively from around the world and historically from antiquity to the present. Its Pan-European viewpoint is especially valuable, with useful comparative materials from the Germanic, Slavic, and Mediterranean culture areas.

But the great comparative product of European scholarship is the ten-volume *Handwörterbuch des deutschen Aberglaubens* (Berlin, 1927–42), edited by the Swiss scholars Hanns Bächtold-Stäubli and Eduard Hoffmann-Krayer with the assistance of the widest possible network of academic collaborators.

European studies of magic, from Frazer to Malinowski, have also widened our understanding of folk medicine in many directions. Particularly useful has been the definition of types of magic—imitative, contagious, homeopathic, sympathetic—and the analysis of the theory of magic in primitive and folk culture. A volume by Irmgard Hampp, *Beschwörung, Segen, Gebet: Untersuchungen zum Zauberspruch aus dem Bereich der Volksheilkunde* (Stuttgart, 1961) analyzes the close relation between conjuration, blessing, and prayer, which exist together in most folk-religious milieux. And the magnificent volume on amulets by Liselotte Hansmann and Lenz Kriss-Rettenbeck, *Amulett und Talisman: Erscheinungsform und Geschichte* (Munich, 1966), widely illustrated from every cultural level and geographical area, speaks authoritatively on fetish magic and its usage.

Recently there has been a stepping up of scholarly interest in folk medicine in Europe. Of the more recent studies to come out of this European academic activity, the two most valuable volumes are the symposium on folk medicine edited by Carl-Herman Tillhagen, ***Papers on Folk-Medicine Given at an Inter-Nordic Symposium at Nordiska Museet, Stockholm 8–10 May 1961*** (Stockholm, [1963]); and the extremely useful reader on folk-medical research edited by Elfriede Grabner, ***Volksmedizin: Probleme und Forschungsgeschichte*** (Darmstadt, 1967), in the series *Wege der Forschung*, vol. 63. As an English-language introduction to the problems involved in the study of folk medicine, the symposium is my choice for student use and should help to stimulate similar research in the United States.

The Scandinavian symposium grew out of the work of Carl-Herman Tillhagen, director of the Section on Folk Belief at Nordiska Museet, who earlier had produced what undoubtedly is the best single regional treatment of European folk medicine since World War II, ***Folklig Läkekonst*** (Stockholm, 1958). The symposium centered on the relationship between scientific and folk-medical traditions. A distinguished panel of twenty scholars from Sweden, Norway, Denmark, and Finland represented the disciplines of medicine, history of medicine, veterinary science, cultural anthropology, history of religions, and ethnography. The papers include analyses of the humoral-pathological system in folk medicine, medical magic in Linnaeus's dietetics, the personality and work of the "wise woman" as healer, the question of the effectiveness of folk medicine, rational folk medicine, Lapp medicine, and other topics. We will discuss several of these contributions during the course of this chapter.

Elfriede Grabner, specialist in folk-medical research at the Steirisches Volkskundemuseum in Graz and the author of several dozens of basic articles on problems of folk medicine, has reprinted twenty-two selections from 1913 to 1964, including the major essays on basic folk-medical theory and practice, including those by Jungbauer, Marzell, Diepgen, Münsterer, and others. Specialized treatments deal with folk-medical dentistry, ethnobotany in the light of modern antibiotic research, astrology and medicine, healing gestures in folk medicine, humoral-pathological theory in folk medicine, and other subjects. Three of the selections deal with Slovene and Serbo-Croatian folk-medical practices. Two essays (Weiser-Aall and Honko) are reprinted from Tillhagen. On the development of scholarly theories about the nature of folk medicine and its relation to academic medicine, this book is the indispensable introduction.

In the United States the gathering of folk-medical materials has been more sporadic. There was a flurry of interest around the turn of the century, when the *Journal of American Folklore* published many articles of folk-medical collectanea. A few statewide collections have been made, the best

THE

LONG LOST FRIEND.

A COLLECTION

OF

MYSTERIOUS & INVALUABLE

ARTS & REMEDIES,

FOR

MAN AS WELL AS ANIMALS.

WITH MANY PROOFS

Of their virtue and efficacy in healing diseases, &c., the greater part of which was never published until they appeared in print for the first time in the U. S. in the year 1820.

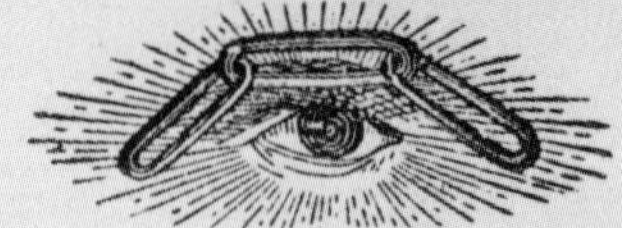

BY JOHN GEORGE HOHMAN.

HARRISBURG, PA.—1856.

T. F. Scheffer, Printer.

Figure 4.1. *The Long Lost Friend* by John George Hohman (Homan) is America's most widespread folk-medical manual. Its charms are those of Pennsylvania German powwowing or magical medicine. The first edition of the book was published in German in Reading, Pennsylvania, in 1819/1820. This edition appeared in Harrisburg in 1856. *(Courtesy Roughwood Collection)*

of which is the two-volume work by Wayland D. Hand in *The Frank C. Brown Collection of North Carolina Folklore,* vols. 6–7, *Popular Beliefs and Superstitions from North Carolina* (Durham, North Carolina: Duke University Press, 1961–64). Hand has collated each item with all the major printed studies from the United States, providing American scholars with the best comparative materials yet available on folk medicine and the related areas of witchcraft and weather lore. His introduction to volume 6 offers a valuable survey of American research in these areas and points out the basic reason for the differential in European and American research:

> Whereas European workers have been able to consider superstitions and folk beliefs as part of broad ethnological studies by country, region, or special occupational or ethnic groups, American folklorists have not been in any such enviable position. In default of full ethnological data, and in fear of losing what previous relics of folk life still remain, they have concentrated on the breadth of their collecting, not on its depth, nor on the meaning and connections of the material collected.[8]

Various ethnic and regional treatments have appeared in article or monograph form. Two of the most extensive studies deal with the Pennsylvania Germans: David E. Lick and Thomas R. Brendle's *Plant Names and Plant Lore among the Pennsylvania Germans,* Proceedings of the Pennsylvania German Society, vol. 33 (1923), and Thomas R. Brendle and Claude W. Unger's *Folk Medicine of the Pennsylvania Germans: The Non-Occult Cures,* Proceedings of the Pennsylvania German Society, vol. 45 (1935). For the southwest Spanish cultural area there have been many useful treatments, including Wilson M. Hudson, ed., *The Healer of Los Olmos and Other Mexican Lore* (Austin, Texas, 1951). For Negro healing practices, "conjuring" and "hoodoo," there is the pioneer work by Newell Niles Puckett, *Folk Beliefs of the Southern Negro* (Durham, North Carolina, 1926). Puckett's work stressed the acculturated character of Negro folk belief, with some Africanisms persisting, although his estimate was that four or five beliefs recorded among American Negroes were actually European in origin.

The most extensive research project in American folk-medical research is the "Dictionary of American Popular Beliefs and Superstitions," edited by Wayland D. Hand at the University of California, Los Angeles, on the plan and scale of the European *Handwörterbuch des deutschen Aberglaubens.* State research committees have been set up to gather regional materials for the work, so that it has become a national project.

The Two Varieties of Folk Medicine

Let us look first at natural, rational, or herbal healing, and secondly, at magico-religious healing.

Natural Folk Medicine

Natural or herbal folk medicine is undoubtedly as ancient as occult folk medicine and has been as widely practiced in the United States as in Europe. This type of healing in its commonest form is old-fashioned, domestic, household medicine, the kind our mothers and grandmothers normally practiced on the farms and in the villages of America, and in some cases in the cities. "Home remedies" were passed down from generation to generation. Herbs that were thought to have special curative ability were gathered in woodland and field, in the fall or on certain days of the church year, and the women planted herb gardens that were used for medical much more than for culinary purposes.

A large part of this branch of folk medicine was herbal, its materia medica drawn from the plants of woodland and field. "God Almighty never put us here without a remedy for every ailment," exclaimed one of Vance Randolph's informants in the Ozarks. "Out in the woods there's plants that will cure all kinds of sickness, and all we got to do is hunt for 'em."[9] In one of the best introductions to natural folk medicine in the United States, Randolph describes the use in Missouri and Arkansas of such herbs as mullein, horehound, horsemint, slippery-elm bark, spice-bush, dogbane, and sassafras. Almost every wild plant and many domestic plants had their curative uses. Most widespread were the decoctions or "teas" made from the various mints and wild plants and barks. Even tobacco had its medicinal value:

> Tobacco is used in other ways by the yarb doctors and granny-women. I have seen severe abdominal pain, later diagnosed as appendicitis and cured by surgery, apparently relieved at once with a poultice of tobacco leaves soaked in hot water. The tobacco poultice is very generally used for cuts, stings, bites, bruises, and even bullet wounds. A poultice of tobacco leaves is often applied to "draw the pizen" out of a boil or a risin'.[10]

In addition to the women of the average American household who gathered and cultivated herbs, there were sometimes herbal specialists in the community, usually men, the "yarb doctors" of the Ozarks, who gathered herbs widely—professionally, one may say. Sometimes, too, special occupational classes, like shepherds, had herbal as well as magical cures for their animals and their colleagues.

Herbs were not the only source of the materia medica of the natural healer. Minerals and animal substances were widely used, including such things as clay, mud, animal organs, and even human urine and excrement. There was even a time when the latter departments of natural medicine were dignified by being raised into a sort of scientific medical fad—in the late seventeenth century when the German doctor Paullini issued his now amusing *Dreckapotheke* or "Pharmacy of Filth."[11]

In many cases herbs and other rational cures were overlaid with magical ritual either in the preparation or in the healing technique. In most cases, as Hultkrantz points out in his recent study of healing methods among the Lapps, healers and clientele made no definite distinction between rational medicine and the irrational type.[12] Rational medicine may be "strengthened" by a magic spell and thus be drawn into the irrational zone. Examples of this process are found on a worldwide basis. Sympathetic prescriptions are followed in gathering herbs, bark, and roots. Leaves plucked upward from a plant have efficacy as an emetic; downward, as an enema. Randolph has described this belief in the Ozark regional setting:

> In scraping bark from a tree or shrub, the direction in which it is cut may make a vast difference as medicine. Peach-tree bark, for example, if the tree is shaved upward, is supposed to prevent vomiting, or to stop a diarrhea. But if the bark is scraped downward, the tea made from it is regarded as a violent purgative. In general, the old-timers say that if the pain is in the lower part of the body, it is best to scrape the bark downward, to drive the disease into the legs and out at the toes. If the bark in such a case were stripped upward, it might force the pizen up into the patient's heart, lungs, or head, and kill him instantly.[13]

The time of year in which the herb is picked and dried also was prescribed by folk-medical tradition. In some cases the plants had to be chosen in connection with some religious holiday in the church year, or again, in connection with the zodiacal positions or the phases of the moon. Not all of these prescriptions were nonsense from the scientific standpoint. As an example borne out by modern medicine, recent botanical studies have shown that the time when plants are picked does in some cases affect their medicinal efficacy.

Despite the derogatory terms for this type of medicine—"old wives' medicine" and *"Dreckapotheke"* being two favorite ascriptions—did any of the old traditional remedies have an efficacy? On just this point Lauri Honko warns us that we cannot understand folk or primitive medicine solely from the viewpoint of modern medicine, but must

> look upon this art from the point of view of its cultural background and its function in an authentic milieu. Problems then arising thus acquire medicinal interest, not only folkloristic. One can ask in all seriousness: Was the primitive art of medicine really

> effective in its own environment? Were the primitive healers able to treat successfully the same diseases as modern man suffers from and as are now treated by entirely different methods? Are there any special diseases or groups of diseases for which the popular methods were particularly suitable?[14]

The first factor in the success of folk medicine, as Honko sees it, was the use of "objectively effective medicines"—estimated at a possible twenty-five percent of the entire primitive pharmacopoeia. Examples: salicyl, aspirin, cocillana, cocaine, quinine, ephedrine, cascara. Second, effective folk techniques included compresses, scarification, hot baths and the sauna, primitive surgery, and even vaccination. On the other hand, these "natural" cures were rarely used without magical spells or rites to accompany them, and in the resultant "cures" there was no attempt made to differentiate the material and spiritual effects. Also, the primitive pharmacopoeia was in some cases harmful to the patient.

The great "herbals" of Elizabethan England and Renaissance Europe in a sense standardized the herb lore of the Middle Ages. In addition, other printed sources, like the colonial almanacs, made much of herbal remedies. Pastor Stoy's cure for rabies, a famous colonial remedy from the Pennsylvania German country, involves the use of pimpernel (*Anagallis arvensis* L.) and was widely reprinted in broadside form and presumably used.[15]

In a study of "Rational Folk-Medicine" in the Scandinavian countries, Olav Bø points out the neglect that this type of medicine has suffered from researchers, most of whom have concentrated on the more spectacular magical variety. Bø points to a wide variety of healers who used rational techniques, from *bonde-dokter* (peasant doctors) to *medisinkoner* (medicine women), the latter presumably so named because "they always provided their patients with medicine, herb concoctions they had prepared themselves." Bø's study is important for giving us historical guidelines on the types of medicine operative in peasant Norway in the nineteenth century. The years around 1850, he points out, formed a dividing line between scientific medicine and folk medicine.

> Not until that time was there any real progress in learned medicine and only then did the first trained doctors go out into the country districts to act as district physicians. But their practices were few and far between on account of the great distances in sparsely populated Norway, so a long time passed before any real order with regard to health matters was established. Apart from this the doctors demanded cash payment, too much in the people's opinion, and they turned therefore to those whom they knew both could and would help without demanding payment. It was typical of many of the good local doctors that they regarded their work as a Samaritan occupation and were not in it for profit. If they were paid, it was usually in kind, but this only applied to doctors who were themselves so poor that they had to be paid.

These lay practitioners were normally called "doctors." It was not until later that the Enlightenment word "quacks" *(Kvaksalvar)* was introduced, along with education, legislation, and medical usage. This was the derogatory expression of modern medicine for the popular forms, whether magic or rational.[16]

Magico-Religious Folk Medicine

An historical perspective on magico-religious healing in Western civilization can be provided by the following analysis. The principles of religious healing, rooted in antiquity, were channeled into Christianity, where healings in the name of the deity were permitted, and with the growth of the cult of the saints, a special category of saint arose, the healing saint. The powers of the healing saints could be tapped through prayer or even through contact with their material relics, tombs, holy places, chapels, and shrines. Miraculous intervention in healing was an important belief in the Middle Ages. In both Eastern Christendom and Roman Catholicism healing shrines and healing saints were recognized, and in most cases the people's drive toward connecting faith and healing was diverted into ecclesiastical, church-sanctioned channels.[17] Through its systems of blessings, benedictions, and its wide use of sacramentals (essentially expressing the belief in the holiness of material objects), the medieval church ministered to and encouraged the principles that we consider basic to folk medicine of the magico-religious sort: the ideas of the availability of supernatural powers for healing, and the mediation of that power through material objects as well as human healers.[18]

A radical change was initiated at the time of the Reformation. Saints in the Catholic sense, healing and non-healing, were exscinded from the Protestant worldview. In the process folk healing as such was driven underground, falling completely into the hands of lay practitioners, and within the purview of the church only formal churchly prayers for the sick were permitted. Hence all over Protestant Europe folk healing was driven underground, while it continued to be permitted, even blessed, in Catholic cultures. In the four hundred years since the Reformation, there has been a gradual restoration, so to speak, of magic healing apart from the churches, in such forms as conjuration, *Belezen, Brauchen,* powwowing—there are words for this phenomenon in all European cultures. Since belief in the possibility of healing through faith and prayer is a widespread human hope, this idea has occasionally emerged above ground and crept back into official Protestantism, first among the sects and cults, and now in the twentieth century among the churches. Two examples of faith healing becoming official in organized Protestantism are (1) the Pentecostal sects, which practice healing officially, gearing it into the worship services of the group; and (2) Christian Science, which teaches faith healing on a sophisticated, philosophical level.

It is unofficial religious healing, the type not connected with the churches, that we wish to analyze. In the United States the commonest word for this type of folk healing is "powwowing," which, according to the historical dictionaries of the English language, passed over into English usage from the Algonquin languages of New England in the first half of the seventeenth century. Other English words for "powwow" are to "charm," to "conjure" (Southern and Negro usage), to "try for" (Central Pennsylvania and Western Maryland), and to "use" (a direct translation of the German dialect word ***brauche*** reported from the Carolinas). The term "power doctor," used in the Ozarks and elsewhere,[19] appears to be a variant of the older term "powwow doctor," a change undoubtedly involving folk-etymology.

Powwowing is magico-religious healing, on the folk-cultural or traditional level, using words, charms, amulets, and physical manipulations in the attempt to heal the ills of man and beast.[20] It is based on the primitive worldview of the unity of all things, heaven, earth, man, animal, and nature. Within this unity there is a dualism between evil powers, concentrated in the Devil and his voluntary servitors the witches, and good powers, concentrated in God, the Trinity, the saints, and the powwower who is the channel for healing power from source to patient. Disease is believed to be demonic, "sent" by evil forces into the person or animal, hence it has to be removed by a "counterspell," which can be provided by ritual, written charms involving holy words, or prepared amulets. In most cases the powwower attempts to heal by ritual and spoken word; in cases of severe demonic action, he relies on paper amulets with elaborate occult texts or simple occult formulas such as the SATOR-formula, which he gives, usually for a fee that is understood rather than demanded, to his patient. The matter of fees is a touchy one, since set fees can bring arrests on the charge of practicing medicine without a license. Several of the powwowers from whom I have recorded in Pennsylvania never actually took money from the patient's hand, but suggested that they put it on the table, thus avoiding actual transfer of currency.

American folk-medical techniques of a magical character are discussed in a series of recent articles by Wayland D. Hand. In primitive as well as folk medicine, one of the commonest methods of ridding a person of disease is through transference of the disease, either by direct transfer or by way of an intermediary person or thing, into another person, an animal, a plant, or an object. The transference can be accomplished through contact or it can take place symbolically, as for example, "selling" a wart. One of the commonest examples of the "direct" method is the transfer of disease to trees or shrubs by means of plugging, wedging, or nailing. The practice and the idea behind it are connected with the transference of evil in general, to which so much attention has been paid, from biblical scapegoats to contemporary psychiatric transference.[21]

Folk diagnosis is kept to a minimum. While there are many folk names for diseases or conditions, generally it is conditions rather than precisely defined ailments that are recognized and "treated." In speaking of folk dermatology, Büttner makes the comment, "The folk do not differentiate these sicknesses. They name them according to the symptoms and rarely according to the etiology, which they do not know."[22] As we have pointed out, folk etiology ascribes sickness to supernatural or irrational causation. The ascriptions range from witchcraft to the predestinarian idea that "God causes sickness." Puckett's study of Negro medicine makes the statement that the first thing the conjure-doctor has to do "is to diagnose the case, tell the person whether he is conjured or not, or in Negro parlance, to find out who 'layed de trick.'" The "trick" (charm) has to be found and destroyed and the patient cured. If the patient wishes, the trick must also be turned back upon the one who set it.[23]

Of course folk medicine includes veterinary practice. This was, in fact, one of the larger branches of the art. More difficult than treating human beings, since the patient was incapable of self-diagnosis, it was of utmost importance on the rural scene. According to a German folk-medical historian, the livestock were the living capital of the peasants, who sometimes, it was rumored, paid more attention to the health of their stock than to that of their families. They also believed that animals, being without a soul, were more vulnerable to influence from witchcraft than persons, and misfortune in the stables was usually attributed to witchwork *(Unglück im Stall ist Hexenwerk).*[24] Elaborate rituals involving stall and stable as well as farmhouse and farmyard protected the animals on the farm. Special church-sponsored blessings were carried through under the aegis of the ancient medieval protector-saints, Saint Leonard for horses, Saint Patrick for cattle. Protection was furnished the cattle of the alpine pastures by the chanting of the *Alpsegen,* unforgettable to those who have heard it.[25] As these examples show, folk medicine and folk religion often overlap.

The Folk-Medical Practitioner and the Patient

In general, the research that has been done on the sociological background of the practitioner of magico-religious healing shows us that, like the primitive "shaman," the powwower and the conjurer, even in the most ordinary of American rural communities, were set apart and recognized by at least some members of the community as having supernatural powers.[26] They were, if we may be permitted the term, a kind of folk-clergy, recognized as having "God-given" powers of healing. From my own researches into Pennsylvania's powwowing tradition, I have found that there was a kind of hierarchy of personnel, all of whom were powwowers of different sorts and status. The commonest type was the completely respectable "unprofessional" powwower—the grandmother, for example, who could "blow burns" and "stop blood" and powwow for a few ailments, along with being an expert brewer of folk teas and stirrer of folk salves and embrocations. The professional powwower, while recognized by the community, was in a sense withdrawn from it, not a completely respectable member of society. In fact he often lived apart literally—in Europe as a shepherd, in Pennsylvania as a hermit or hill country healer on the back roads. Professional powwowers, especially those who achieved the status of "witch doctors" *(Hexedokter),* who specialized in counter-charms against witchcraft that in their elaboration and in their claims approached witchcraft itself, were actually feared and avoided by the community, resorted to only for healing or countering the spells of the neighborhood witch. Among southern Negroes, Puckett observes that "in almost all cases the conjure-doctor is a peculiar individual, set aside because of his very peculiarity for dealings with the supernatural."[27] Sometimes he was physically marked, queer, misshapen. In all of this we see the "outsider" character of the charismatic leader whose charisma disturbs as well as integrates the believing community.

In recent years much has been written on the role of the magico-religious leader, the shaman, the medicine-man, the powwower—as primitive psychiatrist. In his paper on the effectiveness of folk medicine, cited above in connection with natural medicine, Lauri Honko deals at length with the folk healer as a psychotherapist.

> One cannot doubt that the primitive doctor has equally good, if not better qualifications to act as a psychotherapeutic practitioner than the modern psychiatrist. No scientific criticism shakes his visionary confidence in the effectivity of his actions. He is not content only to activate the faith of the patient, but also instills into the whole group a certain conviction of the success of his treatment, awakens the collective faith and promotes the integration of the group. The system of social values as a whole supports his activities, the myths, the religious dogmas, the group feeling of solidarity and the patterns of role-behavior. The modern doctor can nowhere near satisfy the primitive need for motivation of the modern man, or in other words answer the question: why must I be the one to suffer?

In a sense the primitive healer is successful because he treats the community along with the patient. The patient is an integral part of the folk community; the loss of life and the loss of work at crucial times during the year are losses to the community—a disturbance of the normal rhythm of life. The community enterprise, the community itself, is endangered, and the practitioner must reunite the broken community. However permanent the recovery of the patient, "the ritual-mechanism was more or less infallible in dispersing the clouds of uncertainty and fear of the mystery of disease. With the aid of ritual, the crisis which had overtaken the group was overcome and normal order was restored.... This social reintegration is in fact one of the most important functions of the healing rites, and it is here that they diverge most sharply from the modern art of medicine."[28]

Practitioners of magico-religious medicine normally learned their trade either directly from older practitioners or indirectly from books. If from older practitioners, the usual system in some cultures was to alternate the sexes, a man teaching a woman, and vice versa. Sometimes in recording folk-medical materials from an informant, this sex alternation stands in the way, the informant refusing to recite a charm or describe a technique to a person of the same sex. "I would lose my power," is the usual explanation.

The printed charm books of Europe and the United States are extensive. Most of those in current circulation arose in the eighteenth century and, like earlier mystical and prophetic literature, following the biblical precedent, were ascribed falsely to earlier authorship. Moses, Solomon, Albertus Magnus, and Romanus were among the most popular pseudepigraphic ascriptions. For example, in France the commonest books are called *Le grand Albert, Le petit Albert, L'Albert moderne, Clavicules de Salomon,* and so on.[29] In German-speaking countries, the most popular folk-medical book was *Romanus,* the first known edition of which appeared in 1788; others were *Albertus Magnus, or Egyptian Secrets,* and the pseudo-cabalistic *Sixth and Seventh Books of Moses.* All of these German volumes made their way to America, beginning with German editions in Pennsylvania in the nineteenth century. While "powwowing" had been practiced generally in the colonies, the art was standardized and formalized by the Pennsylvania Germans, whose charm corpus was put into print in 1820 by a German emigrant named Johann Georg Hohman in the volume *Der lang verborgene Freund.* Of this curious book, which is the American equivalent of the Romanus book and in fact is pirated in large part from Romanus with some additions from other sources, there are two English translations, both done in Pennsylvania before the Civil War. The first, still in print and available under or over many book counters in the United States, is called *The Long Lost Friend,* and appeared for the first time in Harrisburg, Pennsylvania, in 1846. The second translation, *The Long Hidden Friend,* published at Carlisle, Pennsylvania, in 1863, was reprinted in annotated form in 1904 in the *Journal of American Folklore* and is thus readily available to our readers.[30] This Hohman powwow book is without doubt the most influential conjuring book in the United States; its influence extends to the Negro, the Cajun in Louisiana, the hill man in the Ozarks, and other groups.

Like those used in Europe, the American powwow charms are primitive in text but set in a Christian frame. Most charms, to be effective, must end in the "three highest names"—the trinitarian formula. Christological symbols (the blood of Jesus, the cross of Jesus, the "five wounds" of Jesus, all of which have salvational significance in the official religion) frequently appear. The Virgin Mary and the saints (Peter, Laurence, Caspar, Melchior, Balthasar), the four Evangelists, and the three Archangels make a post-Reformation appearance in many charms. Primitive aspects of the formulae include the fact that to be effective a charm must use the name (usually the baptized name) of the patient. The frequent use of the number three has of course both Christian and primitive undertones. The references to the "three holy drops of blood," "three holy wells," "three lilies on Christ's grave," "three worms," "three false tongues," "three holy tongues," and the poetry of the charms provide living American parallels to the Welsh triads and other medieval folk-poetry of the Middle Ages.

An example is here given from the corpus of Pennsylvania German magic formulae. For the skin inflammation called erysipelas (wildfire) the following charm is used:

> *Wildfeier, flieh, flieh, flieh!*
> *Der rode Fadem jagt dich hie, hie, hie!*
> (Erysipelas, fly, fly, fly!
> The red string chases you away, away, away!)

Note that the disease, conceived animistically, is addressed directly in the charm. While repeating the charm three times, the powwower three times "measures" the patient with a red woolen string (red is the color of the ailment). The disease is symbolically "collected" into the string, which is then "smoked" (lighted to smolder) above the kitchen stove, and slowly turned to ashes. When the string has turned completely to ash, it is brushed into the fire. The belief is that as the string disappears, so the disease disappears. The primitive ideas of transference and vicarious destruction of the disease are clearly seen in this example. The three crosses represent the Christian framework into which the primitive text is set. They signify the Trinitarian formula, since charms normally end with the words: "God the Father, God the Son, and God the Holy Ghost, help to this [here the patient is named]. Amen."

At the present time in the United States a variety of folk-medical practices still exist for study. In most communities there is a kind of hierarchy of medical practice, from scientific medicine to the crudest types of folk practice. Attitudes of the patient toward his illness and toward the various levels of medicine that exist together in many communities are expressed in a recent study made during three months' fieldwork in a Bohemian

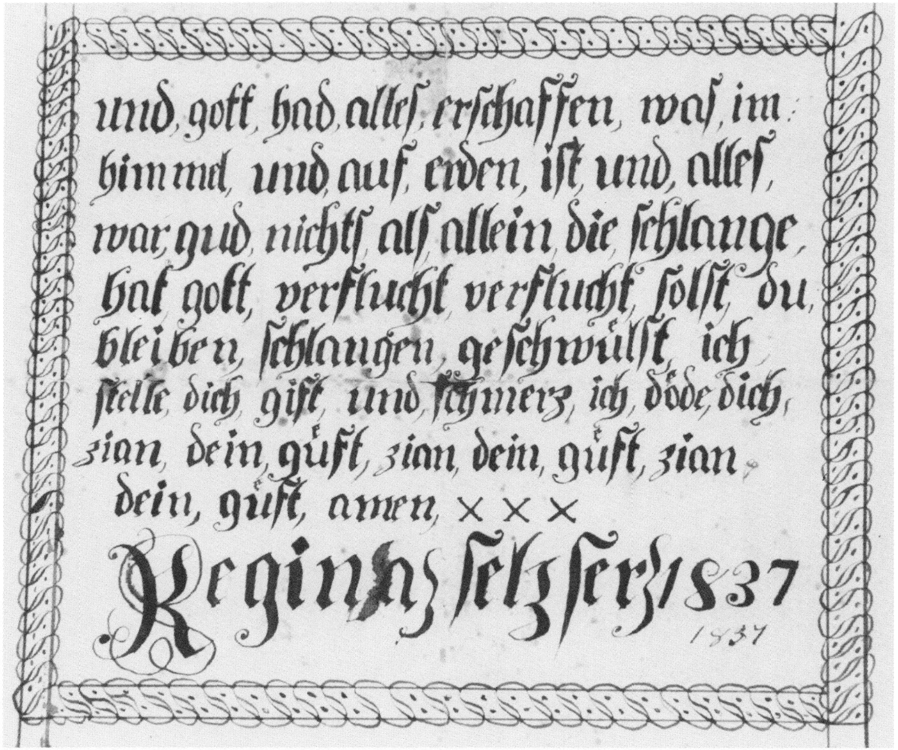

und, gott, had alles, erschaffen, was, im
himmel, und auf erden, ist und, alles,
war, gud, nichts als allein die schlange,
hat gott, verflucht verflucht solst du,
bleiben, schlangen, geschwülst, ich
stelle dich gift, und schmerz, ich, döde, dich,
zian, dein, güft, zian, dein, güft, zian
dein, güft, amen, × × ×
Regina Selzser 1837
1837

Figure 4.2. Powwow charm for snakebite, Pennsylvania German, 1837. The text reads: "and God created everything that is in heaven and on earth, and everything was good, except that God cursed the snake. Cursed shalt thou remain, snake! Swelling, I still thee; poison and pain, I kill thee! Draw back thy poison, draw back thy poison, draw back thy poison. In the name of the Father, the Son, and the Holy Ghost." *(Courtesy Roughwood Collection)*

speech community in Iowa.[31] "Older Bouhimis (at least) are likely to take pain as the result of some minor injury. They do not consider themselves to be ill until they are unable to walk around." When one is sick, the treatment followed is likely to be as follows:

1. Ignore it—it may get better.
2. Try some home remedy or a patent medicine.
3. Make an appointment for chiropractic treatment.
4. Consult a medical doctor, all else having failed.

In rural Iowa the chiropractor seems now to be filling the role of folk practitioner. There are several reasons for this change of roles. Home remedies, while still used by some people, are now too difficult to make for oneself; medical doctors are too expensive; hence one turns to the chiropractor who charges more modest fees. Second, rural Iowans prefer chiropractors because they rarely advise bed rest. Third, the farmer likes the chiropractor's "simple, mechanistic theory of disease and therapy," for they believe that pain is normally the result of some injury rather than "disease," although some still feel that accidental injuries are punishments for wrongdoing. Hence chiropractors are consulted "not only in cases involving muscular and other aches and pains, but also for the treatment of respiratory troubles and conditions described as 'nervousness,' a category that may include psychiatric disorders."

The same claims were made for the Iowa Amish, in a study emanating from the same source.

> Like other rural Iowa populations encountered so far, the Amish exhibit a distinct predilection for availing themselves of chiropractic treatment. Strongly influenced by non-medical health education literature, they make a theoretical distinction between chiropractors, who are used for the treatment of nameless pains and chronic disorders, and who are said to treat the "causes" of illness; and medical doctors, who are said to be pre-eminent in the handling of broken bones and performing surgery, and are said only to treat the "effects."[32]

A similar study of the Pennsylvania Amish, by John A. Hostetler, dealing with the persistence of folk medicine in the Amish community, points out that "certain types of illnesses are taken to the physician and other types to the folk practitioner. The selective principle would appear to operate in this way: critical incapacitating malfunctions are taken to the scientifically trained practitioners, while chronic non-incapacitating ailments are treated by the folk practitioner and by traditional means."[33]

These are some of the areas of investigation in which the folk-cultural scholar obviously needs the help of the medical sociologist.

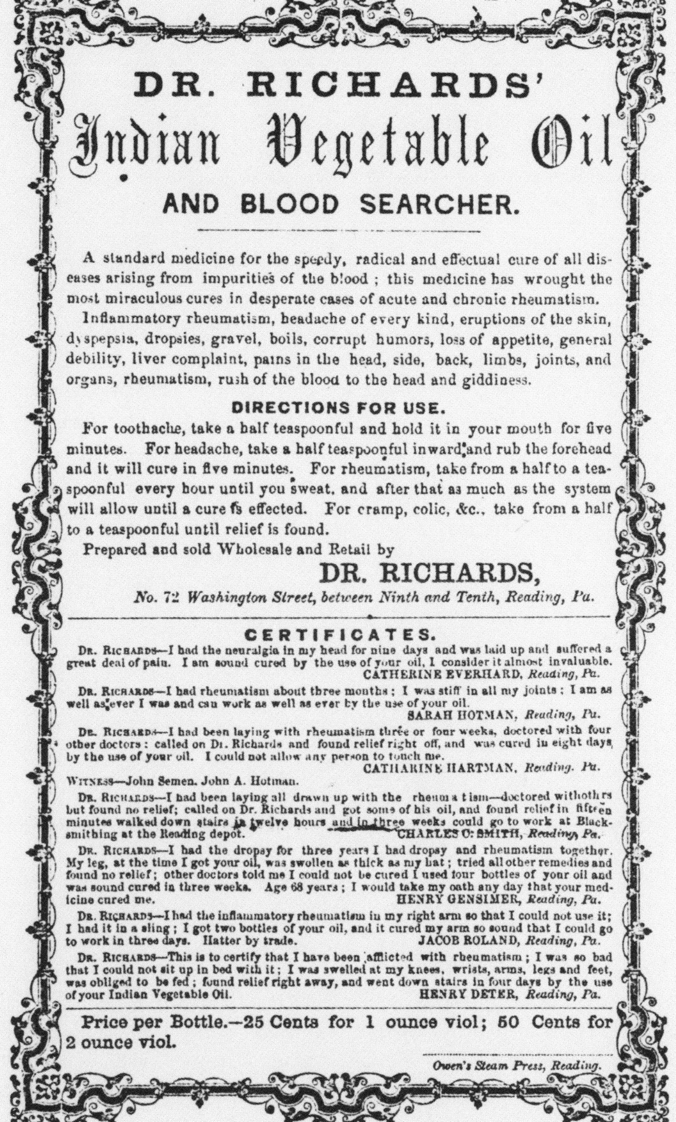

DR. RICHARDS'

Indian Vegetable Oil

AND BLOOD SEARCHER.

A standard medicine for the speedy, radical and effectual cure of all diseases arising from impurities of the blood ; this medicine has wrought the most miraculous cures in desperate cases of acute and chronic rheumatism.

Inflammatory rheumatism, headache of every kind, eruptions of the skin, dyspepsia, dropsies, gravel, boils, corrupt humors, loss of appetite, general debility, liver complaint, pains in the head, side, back, limbs, joints, and organs, rheumatism, rush of the blood to the head and giddiness.

DIRECTIONS FOR USE.

For toothache, take a half teaspoonful and hold it in your mouth for five minutes. For headache, take a half teaspoonful inward and rub the forehead and it will cure in five minutes. For rheumatism, take from a half to a teaspoonful every hour until you sweat, and after that as much as the system will allow until a cure is effected. For cramp, colic, &c., take from a half to a teaspoonful until relief is found.

Prepared and sold Wholesale and Retail by

DR. RICHARDS,

No. 72 Washington Street, between Ninth and Tenth, Reading, Pa.

CERTIFICATES.

Dr. Richards—I had the neuralgia in my head for nine days and was laid up and suffered a great deal of pain. I am sound cured by the use of your oil, I consider it almost invaluable.
CATHERINE EVERHARD, *Reading, Pa.*

Dr. Richards—I had rheumatism about three months ; I was stiff in all my joints ; I am as well as ever I was and can work as well as ever by the use of your oil.
SARAH HOTMAN, *Reading, Pa.*

Dr. Richards—I had been laying with rheumatism three or four weeks, doctored with four other doctors : called on Dr. Richards and found relief right off, and was cured in eight days, by the use of your oil. I could not allow any person to touch me.
CATHARINE HARTMAN, *Reading. Pa.*

Witness—John Semen. John A. Hotman.

Dr. Richards—I had been laying all drawn up with the rheumatism—doctored with others but found no relief; called on Dr. Richards and got some of his oil, and found relief in fifteen minutes walked down stairs in twelve hours and in three weeks could go to work at Blacksmithing at the Reading depot.
CHARLES O. SMITH, *Reading, Pa.*

Dr. Richards—I had the dropsy for three years I had dropsy and rheumatism together. My leg, at the time I got your oil, was swollen as thick as my hat ; tried all other remedies and found no relief ; other doctors told me I could not be cured I used four bottles of your oil and was sound cured in three weeks. Age 68 years ; I would take my oath any day that your medicine cured me.
HENRY GENSIMER, *Reading, Pa.*

Dr. Richards—I had the inflammatory rheumatism in my right arm so that I could not use it; I had it in a sling ; I got two bottles of your oil, and it cured my arm so sound that I could go to work in three days. Hatter by trade.
JACOB ROLAND, *Reading, Pa.*

Dr. Richards—This is to certify that I have been afflicted with rheumatism ; I was so bad that I could not sit up in bed with it ; I was swelled at my knees, wrists, arms, legs and feet, was obliged to be fed ; found relief right away, and went down stairs in four days by the use of your Indian Vegetable Oil.
HENRY DETER, *Reading, Pa.*

Price per Bottle.—25 Cents for 1 ounce viol; 50 Cents for 2 ounce viol.

Owen's Steam Press, Reading.

Figure 4.3. Patent medicine broadside, Reading, Pennsylvania, second half of the nineteenth century. Dr. Richards' "Indian Vegetable Oil and Blood Searcher" was evidently good for almost everything. *(Courtesy Roughwood Collection)*

Figure 4.4. Nineteenth-century American patent medicines used the American Indian as a symbol of health and healing. This illustration is from a booklet advertising "Sagwa Indian Oil." *(Courtesy Roughwood Collection)*

Folk Medicine in the Twentieth Century

It always comes as a shock to learn that folk medicine, like witchcraft, astrology, and other ancient aspects of folk belief, is actually still very much around. With the great advances of modern science in the seventeenth century and the basic shift in worldview brought by the Enlightenment, the educated classes tended to drop these aspects of culture, but they continued on popular and folk levels. As European scholarship has been pointing out for decades, "folk" attitudes often persist in an individual alongside "modern" educated attitudes.

In the twentieth century, in fact, there would seem to have been an increase in irrational medical attitudes and practice, particularly on the popular level of middle-class and mass levels of culture, where astrology, horoscopes, health food fads, Indian healers, blessed handkerchiefs, chain letters, faith healers, rub doctors, blow doctors, and other related phenomena assault us from newspaper, radio, and TV screen. Undoubtedly, as in the Hellenistic era, the breakup of the standard religions and the resultant "loss of nerve," to use Gilbert Murray's phrase, have caused a backwash of parareligious activities and institutions to flow back into Western civilization as substitutes for organized religion. One of the oldest of these substitutes is astrology, which as "Chaldean science" had invaded the Hellenistic world 2,500 years ago and has been waiting in the wings ever since.[34] The astrological worldview, that the heavens and earth are intimately connected in mutual influences, has always been an important ingredient in most European folk worldviews. Today it is seized upon by culturally and spiritually rootless urbanites, without the folk-cultural matrix in which it was once functional, as one version of our century's widespread fatalism.

Another sign of the times is the stepping up of the "fortune teller" as medical practitioner, especially in the pseudo-folk forms of "Indian healer" and "Indian reader." In the post-World War II era these have spread into many areas, mostly within and on the fringes of urban settlement. A recent study of this type of healer pointed out that the same persons who normally form the clientele of native magical healers are turning also to Indian healers. The background of the Indian healers, despite their appeal to the American Indian as symbol, appears to be Mediterranean, and is probably related to the Puerto Rican invasion of the eastern United States since 1950.[35]

Since World War II, also, there has been significant growth of "faith healing" under the aegis of the established, organized religions of the United States. No longer leaving it to the Pentecostal and other healing sects, such groups as the Episcopalians and the United Church of Christ have become concerned to bring religious healing "back to where it be-

MRS. DELLA

Reader & Advisor

Tarot Cards, Also Pow Wow

— Don't Consider Her Just Another Reader — God Sent —
— Guaranteed To Help — God's Messenger —
— DON'T FAIL TO SEE HER TODAY —

I guarantee success where all other advisors fail. I give never failing advice upon matters of life such as love, courtship, marriage, divorce, business, lawsuits, speculations and transactions of all kinds. I never fail to unite the separated, cause speedy and happy marriages, overcome enemies, rivals, lover's quarrels, evil habits (stumbling blocks and bad luck of all kinds).

The Religious Holy Woman healer. God's messenger who guarantees to heal the sick and ailing, to remove all suffering and bad luck. Tell you who to keep away from. She is a religious and holy woman who will show you with your own eyes how she will remove sorrow, sickness and pain, and all bad luck. What your eyes see your heart must believe. Has the God-given Power to Heal by Prayer. Are you suffering? Are you sick? Do you need help? Do you have bad luck?

½ Price With This Ad

Figure 4.5. **Advertisement by contemporary healer who evidently combines tarot readings with powwow medicine. From Eastern Pennsylvania.**
(Courtesy Roughwood Collection)

WHY WORRY SEE

SISTER NANCY

RELIGIOUS WOMAN – HEALER and ADVISOR

Religious Holy woman healer, God's messenger who guarantees to heal the sick and the ailing, to remove all suffering and bad luck from your body. She will call your enemies by name and tell you who to keep away from. She is a religious and holy woman who will show you with your own eyes how to remove sorrow, sickness and pain, and all bad luck. What your eyes see your heart must believe, and then your heart will be convinced that this is the religious holy woman you have been looking for. The touch of her hand will heal you. She has the God-given Power to Heal by Prayer. Everyone welcome at her home. Are you suffering? Do you have bad luck? Bring your problems to see her today and be rid of them tomorrow. She is in this vicinity for the first time. She guarantees to reunite the separated and solemnly swears to heal the sick, and help all who come to her, and remove all evil spells. She has devoted a lifetime to this religious work. She guarantees to cure you where others have failed. Why go on suffering – When just one visit to this woman will take the sickness and pain away from you. One visit will convince you that she is God's messenger on earth. With God's help on this earth she'll show it to you. She has helped thousands and guaranteed to help you too. She removes all pain. This religious healer will help you where others have failed. If you suffer from alcoholism and cannot find a cure, don't fail to see this gifted woman who will help you. She also guarantees her work.

Figure 4.6. Sister Nancy, "Religious Woman, Healer and Advisor," guarantees bodily healing and relief from suffering and personal problems. Contemporary, from Eastern Pennsylvania.
(Courtesy Roughwood Collection)

longs," i.e., into the hands of the ordained clergy and under the control of the institutional church. The Episcopal Church has been the leader in this movement, with weekly "healing missions" in selected churches in American metropolitan areas (for example, Saint Stephen's Episcopal Church in Philadelphia) and the Order of Saint Luke the Physician, which is a national organization involving those Episcopalian priests who are practicing religious healing. At the same time, seminary education is including studies of the relation of religion to medicine, and offering widened programs in pastoral counseling, the inhouse ecclesiastical form of psychotherapy. The significance of these movements is that they are attempting to return religious healing, for those who want it, to organized religion, where it had existed as a normal and permitted phase of religion until Protestantism exscinded it from its world of possibilities, driving it underground in the European Protestant cultures.

Certain new trends in science are also, at last, recognizing the serious study of folk medicine. It is no longer viewed as the "curiosity show" of peasant credulity, smeared with the Enlightenment labels of "superstition" and "quack medicine," but is now taken seriously, and placed, not against the background of bourgeois culture, but in its own proper folk-cultural matrix where its functions and reciprocal relations with the entire culture are obvious. If the religious values in occult folk medicine are being absorbed in the ecclesiastical movements discussed above, its psychological value is being recognized in psychosomatic medicine, community medicine, and psychiatry. In the newer field of parapsychology, European scholars are also investigating a great many subjects of interest to folk-cultural scholars, including extrasensory perception, telekinesis, witchcraft, stigmaticism, and religious healing, and American parapsychologists are beginning to follow their example.[36]

It is strange how wider cultural movements have always determined a generation's academic approach to folk-cultural phenomena. Enlightenment "rationalism" and its nineteenth-century offspring "scientism" made mock of folk medicine. Even the biblical healing episodes, which were both analogues to and in some cases precedents for folk-medical healings, were discarded in the eighteenth and nineteenth centuries, then cautiously taken back in the twentieth century, to be explained by psychological, anthropological, psychiatric, and Jungian approaches.[37] Even the Mesmers, the Swedenborgs, and the Jung-Stillings—Enlightenment Age antiheroes, so to speak, whose ideas formed counter-currents to the dominant rationalism of the era—are receiving respectful attention at the present time.

Folk medicine, especially when labeled "superstition," is one of those areas of folk culture on which ingroup attitudes can be touchy. Vance

Randolph includes the cautionary statement: "Many of the civic boosters in the Ozark area are sensitive about their hillbilly background and regard anybody who mentions the old customs or folk beliefs in the light of a public enemy. This sentiment is reflected in the Ozark newspapers, particularly in the smaller cities."[38] Andrew Pearce, writing in the first volume of the *Caribbean Quarterly,* is equally frank about Caribbean sensitivities:

> We are most grateful to our contributors, and it is fitting to remind them that the dominant theme of these articles may be regretted by considerable numbers of West Indians who may feel that they have illuminated those dark corners of West Indian life which were best forgotten, i.e., "bad" English and French, crude superstitions, a past linked with Africa, and charismatic leadership. These doubters pose the question whether an attempt to reassess the achievements of the "common man" in the West Indies during the past 120 years is compatible with a relentless drive towards enlightenment and progress in science, technique and politics. To this we must answer that progress is not merely compatible with a study of the backward past, but that our thinking and planning for tomorrow will lead us astray if it is not based on a realistic study of yesterday. Enlightenment is not the process of "keeping things dark."[39]

The signs everywhere seem to be pointing to the need for reexamining our folk-medical heritage. We can profitably close with a favorite statement of mine. Ruth Benedict makes clear the value of investigating folk belief and folk custom in these words: "More than any other body of material it makes vivid the recency and the precariousness of those rationalistic attitudes of the modern urban educated groups which are often identified with human nature."[40]

Notes

1. Ludwig Büttner, *Fränkische Volksmedizin: Ein Beitrag zur Volkskunde Ostfrankens* (Erlangen, 1935), 14.
2. Wayland D. Hand, ed., *Popular Beliefs and Superstitions from North Carolina.* The Frank C. Brown Collection of North Carolina Folklore 6 (Durham, N.C., 1961). Introduction, xix–xx.
3. Eugen Mogk, "Wesen und Aufgaben der Volkskunde," *Mitteldeutsche Blätter für Volkskunde* 1 (1926): 17–24.
4. Richard Weiss, *Volkskunde der Schweiz* (Erlenbach-Zurich, 1946), 6–9.
5. Hanns O. Münsterer, "Grundlagen, Gültigkeit und Grenzen der volksmedizinischen Heilverfahren," *Bayerisches Jahrbuch für Volkskunde* 1 (1950): 9–20; reprinted in Elfriede Grabner, ed., *Volksmedizin: Probleme und Forschungsgeschichte* (Darmstadt, 1967), 289–314.
6. Oswald A. Erich and Richard Beitl, eds., *Wörterbuch der deutschen Volkskunde,* 2d ed. (Stuttgart, 1955), "Volksmedizin," 823.

7. See the report of the holdings of the Institut für deutsche Volkskunde, by Johanna Jaenecke-Nickel, in *Current Anthropology* 4 (October 1963): 370–71.

8. Hand, *Popular Beliefs,* xxxiv.

9. Vance Randolph, *Ozark Superstitions* (New York, 1964), 93. See his entire chapter, "Mountain Medicine," 92–120.

10. Ibid., 98–99. See also Katharine T. Kell, "Tobacco in Folk Cures in Western Society," *Journal of American Folklore* 78 (April-June, 1965): 99–114.

11. For his ideas, called "Paullinism" in medical history, see Erich-Beitl, *Wörterbuch,* 142.

12. Åke Hultkrantz, "The Healing Methods of the Lapps: Some Aspects from the Point of View of Comparative Religion," in *Papers on Folk-Medicine,* Carl-Herman Tillhagen, ed. (Stockholm, 1963), 168.

13. Randolph, *Ozark Superstitions,* 95.

14. Lauri Honko, "On the Effectivity of Folk-Medicine," in Tillhagen, *Papers,* 132–42.

15. For Stoy see David E. Lick and Thomas R. Brendle, *Plant Names and Plant Lore among the Pennsylvania Germans.* The Pennsylvania German Society, Proceedings and Addresses 33 (3) (1923): 189–92.

16. Olav Bø, "Rational Folk-Medicine," in Tillhagen, *Papers,* 143–53.

17. A vast literature has appeared on healing shrines and healing saints in Europe. Among the foremost tillers of this field is Rudolf Kriss, whose *Volkskundliches aus altbayrischen Gnadenstätten* (Augsburg, 1930) has been followed by a distinguished series of volumes dealing with the pilgrimage system and the folk-cultural practices associated with it for eastern as well as western Europe; for comparative materials on Islamic cultures see Rudolf Kriss and Hubert Kriss-Heinrich, *Volksglaube im Bereich des Islam,* 2 vols. (Wiesbaden, 1960, 1962).

18. Adolph Franz, *Die kirchlichen Benediktionen im Mittelalter,* 2 vols. (Freiburg im Breisgau, 1909), is essential as background for understanding the medieval prayers and blessings for healing and protection that were sanctioned by the Roman Catholic Church.

19. See Randolph, *Ozark Superstitions,* chap. 7, "The Power Doctors," 121–61, one of the best American analyses of the work and context of the magic healer studied in a regional setting.

20. The description is based on my own researches into Pennsylvania German powwowing or *Braucherei.* On this subject see the standard volume, Thomas R. Brendle and Claude W. Unger, *Folk Medicine of the Pennsylvania Germans: The Non-Occult Cures.* Proceedings of the Pennsylvania German Society 45 (1935); also Don Yoder, "Official Religion versus Folk Religion," *Pennsylvania Folklife* 15 (Winter 1965–66): 36–52; and Don Yoder, "Twenty Questions on Powwowing," *Pennsylvania Folklife* 15 (Summer 1966): 38–40.

21. Wayland D. Hand, "The Magical Transference of Disease," *Folklore Studies in Honor of Arthur Palmer Hudson. North Carolina Folklore* 13 (1965): 83–109.

22. Büttner, *Fränkische Volksmedizin,* 39.

23. Newbell Niles Puckett, *Folk Beliefs of the Southern Negro* (Chapel Hill, N.C., 1926), 207.

24. Walther Zimmermann, *Badische Volksheilkunde* (Karlsruhe, 1927), 94.

25. For the *Alpsegen, Betruf, Alpruf* and related practices see Weiss, *Volkskunde der Schweiz,* 223, 228, 231, 274–75.

26. In addition to the works on shamanism by Eliade and others, and basic anthropological analyses such as A. Irving Hallowell's *The Conjuror in Salteaux Society* (Philadelphia, 1944), the principal work on the role of the magic healer in folk culture would appear to have been done in Scandinavia in the twentieth century. Carl-Herman Tillhagen's *Folklig Läkekonst* (Stockholm, 1958) contains detailed analysis of the role of the folk healer in European society. A thorough treatment using American materials is William Madsen, *The Mexican-Americans of South Texas* (New York, 1964), especially chaps. 10–11, "Cures and Physicians" and "Folk Psychotherapy." Other volumes in the same series, the Holt, Rinehart and Winston Case Studies in Cultural Anthropology, also have useful materials on traditional medical practices and practitioners.

27. Puckett, *Folk Beliefs,* 206.

28. Honko, "Folk Medicine," 140–41. On this subject see also Ari Kiev, *Magic, Faith, and Healing: Studies in Primitive Psychiatry Today* (Glencoe, Illinois, 1964); and Jerome D. Frank, *Persuasion and Healing: A Comparative Study of Psychotherapy* (New York, 1963).

29. Arnold van Gennep, *Manuel de folklore français contemporain* 4:560 ff.

30. Carleton F. Brown, "The Long Hidden Friend," *Journal of American Folklore* 17 (April-June, 1904): 89–152.

31. Edward Kibbe and Thomas McCorkle, *Culture and Medical Behavior in a Bohemian Speech Community in Iowa,* 3d ed. (Iowa City, 1959), 26–27. I have also used Thomas McCorkle, *An Abbreviated Statement on Folk Practices in Rural Iowa* (Iowa City, Iowa, 1960), 4–5.

32. Jochem von Heeringen and Thomas McCorkle, *Culture and Medical Behavior of the Old Order Amish of Johnson County, Iowa* (Iowa City, Iowa, 1958), 27–28.

33. John A. Hostetler, "Folk and Scientific Medicine in Amish Society," *Human Organization* 22 (Winter 1963–64): 269–75.

34. See Franz Cumont, *Astrology and Religion among the Greeks and Romans* (New York, 1960), originally published in 1912; see also Louis MacNeice, *Astrology* (Garden City, N.Y., 1964).

35. George Peterson, III, "Indian Readers and Healers by Prayer: A Field Report," *Pennsylvania Folklife* 16 (Fall 1966): 2–7.

36. Utrecht and Zurich have been European centers for parapsychological studies. Cf. especially the work of Professor W. H. C. Tenhaeff, professor of parapsychology and director of the Parapsychological Institute at the University of Utrecht, *Aussergewöhnliche Heilkräfte: Magnetiseure, Sensitive, Gesundbeter* (Olten and Freiburg in Breisgau, 1957).

37. Cf. Don Hargrave Gross, "A Jungian Analysis of New Testament Exorcism," Ph.D. diss., Harvard University, 1963.

38. Randolph, *Ozark Superstitions,* 7.

39. Andrew Pearce, Editorial Note, *Caribbean Quarterly* 1:3.

40. Ruth Benedict, "Folklore," *Encyclopedia of the Social Sciences* 6:288.

Selected Bibliography

Blum, Richard H. and Eva Blum. *Health and Healing in Rural Greece.* Stanford, California: Stanford University Press; London: Oxford University Press, 1965. Chaps. 11 and 12 deal with folk healing and folk healers.

Bouteillier, Marcelle. *Médicine populaire d'hier et d'aujourdhui.* Paris: Editions G.-P. Maisonneuve et Larose, 1966. The most basic recent study of French traditional medical practices and ideas, by the director of the section of folk belief at the Musée de l'Homme. Particularly good are the materials on the range of healers in French society, based on years of fieldwork and questionnaire analysis.

Brendle, Thomas R., and Claude W. Unger. *Folk Medicine of the Pennsylvania Germans: The Non-Occult Cures.* Proceedings of the Pennsylvania German Society 45. Norristown, Pennsylvania, 1935. So far this is the most detailed analysis of the theory of disease and the charm corpus of any of the older ethnic cultures of the United States.

Clark, Margaret. *Health in the Mexican-American Culture: A Community Study.* Berkeley and Los Angeles: University of California Press, 1959. This is a study based on intensive fieldwork in the Mexican-American community of San Jose, California.

Cockayne, Oswald. *Leechdoms, Wortcunning, and Starcraft of Early England.* 3 vols. London, 1864–66. Chronicles and Memorials of Great Britain and Ireland During the Middle Ages 35. Textual studies of the magical charm corpus and related aspects of folk belief from Anglo-Saxon England.

Davidson, Thomas. "Animal Treatment in Eighteenth-Century Scotland." *Scottish Studies* 4 (1960): 134–49. Discusses the full range of folk-medical veterinary practice from charms to curing-stones.

Frank, Jerome D. *Persuasion and Healing: A Comparative Study of Psychotherapy.* Baltimore: Johns Hopkins Press, 1961; New York: Schocken Books, 1963. Provides comparative treatment of modern psychotherapy, primitive healing, religious healing of the Lourdes type, religious revivalism, and Communist thought reform.

Hand, Wayland D. *Popular Beliefs and Superstitions from North Carolina.* The Frank C. Brown Collection of North Carolina Folklore, vols. 6–7. Durham, North Carolina: Duke University Press, 1961, 1964. The best American regional collection of traditional beliefs, including those dealing with medicine, carefully annotated from a wide variety of collections of similar materials from every ethnic and regional culture of the United States.

Howells, William. *The Heathens: Primitive Man and His Religion.* Garden City, New York: Doubleday Anchor Books, 1962. Despite its unfortunate title, this is an extremely useful introduction to concepts of magical healing. See especially chap. 5, "Magic, Black and White," and chap. 6, "Disease and Medicine." A volume in the Natural History Library, sponsored by the American Museum of Natural History.

Jones, Glyn Penrhyn. "Folk Medicine in Eighteenth-Century Wales." *Folk Life* 7 (1969): 60–74. Offers a full discussion of the range of practitioners of community medicine from apothecaries and apothecary-surgeons through magicians, wizards, and medical astrologers, to country parsons who practiced medicine in their parishes. Also treated are the use of healing stones, herbal medicine, cupping, and household remedies in general.

Kemp, Patience. *Healing Ritual: The Technique and Tradition of the Southern Slavs.* London: Faber and Faber, 1935. One of the few good treatments in English of traditional medicine in the Slavic cultures, based on fieldwork in Yugoslavia.

Kiev, Ari, ed. *Magic, Faith and Healing: Studies in Primitive Psychiatry Today.* New York: The Free Press of Glencoe, 1964. Anthropological symposium with materials from many cultures. See particularly the editor's introductory essay, "The Study of Folk Psychiatry," 3–35.

Lessa, William A., and Evon Z. Vogt. *Reader in Comparative Religion: An Anthropological Approach.* Evanston, Ill.: Row, Peterson and Company, 1958; 2d ed., enlarged and revised, New York: Harper and Row, 1965. A useful collection of essays by the key contributors to the development of comparative religion studies on the subject of magic and related beliefs. See especially chap. 6, "Magic, Witchcraft, and Divination," and chap. 7, "The Magical Transference of Disease."

Madsen, William. *The Mexican-Americans of South Texas.* New York: Holt, Rinehart and Winston, 1964. This volume, in the series Case Studies in Cultural Anthropology, is the most concise analysis of the theory and practice of traditional medicine among the southwest Spanish groups yet available. See especially chap. 7, "Religion"; chap. 8, "Sickness and Health"; chap. 9, "Witchcraft"; chap. 10, "Curers and Physicians"; and chap. 11, "Folk Psychotherapy."

Middleton, John, ed. *Magic, Witchcraft, and Curing.* Garden City, New York: The Natural History Press, 1967. This volume, in the series American Museum Sourcebooks in Anthropology, gathers together a variety of ethnographic reports and theoretical discussions on magic, sorcery, shamanism, and their relation to healing, mostly in primitive settings.

Preisendanz, Karl L. *Papyri Graecae Magicae.* Leipzig/Berlin: Trubner, 1928–31. The standard textual study of the basic body of magical formulae from the Hellenistic world, echoes and analogues of which appear everywhere in the folk-medical practice of medieval and modern Europe.

Sigerist, Henry E. *A History of Medicine.* 1. *Primitive and Archaic Medicine.* New York: Oxford University Press, 1951. Among the many histories of medicine in English, this work is the best introduction to the initial stages of medical belief and practice, with examples from many cultures.

Tillhagen, Carl-Herman, ed. *Papers on Folk-Medicine Given at an Inter-Nordic Symposium at Nordiska Museet, Stockholm 8–10 May 1961.* Stockholm, 1963. Reprinted from *Arv: Journal of Scandinavian Folklore* 18–19 (1962–63): 159–362. The best regional approach in English to research problems, typology, and theory of traditional medicine.

Tillich, Paul. "The Relation of Religion and Healing." *The Review of Religion* 10 (May 1946): 348–84. The basic theological approach, starting with the fundamental connection in all the ancient religions between religion and health. Religion (essentially salvation) symbolically restores the broken unity of both cosmos and individual.

Wallace, Anthony F. C. *Religion: An Anthropological View.* New York: Random House, 1966. Contains several theoretical sections on religion and magic; see especially "Ritual as Therapy and Anti-Therapy," 113–26.

Weatherhead, Leslie D. *Psychology, Religion and Healing.* 2d ed. London: Hodder and Stoughton, Ltd., 1952. Discusses all the "non-physical methods of healing" and the principles underlying them. Includes detailed analysis of the healing practices of the organized healing cults within Protestantism.

Williams, Phyllis H. *South Italian Folkways in Europe and America.* New Haven: Yale University Press, 1938. Reissued New York: Russell and Russell, 1969. Especially good on the evil eye and the magical remedies used to counteract its spell.

5

Historical Sources for American Traditional Cookery

The Pennsylvania German culture is one of the early American colonial period cultures, with wide influence on other ethnic groups in Pennsylvania, and, through migration, upon other areas of the United States and Canada. While the average American insists on looking at Pennsylvania German culture as something German and European and essentially foreign, the culture actually is a highly acculturated, hybridized system of elements combined on American soil from two principal sources: the Continental European, essentially Germanic culture of the immigrant generations, and the British Isles cultures of their neighbors in Southeastern Pennsylvania. This indigenous American culture began to take shape in the first half of the eighteenth century and has continued to develop to the present time.[1]

In looking at Pennsylvania German cookery today we have to press our way past the undergrowth of tourist menus at the pseudo-"Dutch" restaurants in Eastern Pennsylvania, which include, in atrocious dialect forms, a mixture of a few regional specialties with a full range of general American dishes.[2] In attempting to determine what the Pennsylvania Germans ate traditionally, on the farms and in the small towns of Eastern Pennsylvania, we can approach the problem in two ways. First, we can use the ethnographic approach of interview and questionnaire, so successfully used in European food research, to determine the geographical diffusion of certain dishes and food customs in the present. At the same time, of course, from the memories of our informants, we can get a good idea of the changes in Pennsylvania German foods and foodways roughly over the past seventy-five to one hundred years, from the era of the grandparents of our present informants down to the present time.

Linked with the ethnographic approach, and a necessary supplement

---

This article originally appeared in *Pennsylvania Folklife* 20 (3) (Spring 1971): 16–29.

to it, is the historical approach, used much more extensively in European scholarship than in American regional research. Here the total range of historical documentation on the Pennsylvania Germans needs to be combed and sifted for references to cookery and foodways. This can take us farther into the past and can sketch in the background of our ethnographic materials, as well as providing a guide to what to ask for on our questionnaires.

Roughly we can divide historical sources into the three categories of printed texts, manuscript materials, and iconographic sources.

Printed Texts

Printed source materials on the Pennsylvania Germans include: travelers' accounts of the eighteenth and nineteenth centuries; cookbooks[3] in German and English; government reports, such as those of the national and state departments of agriculture, which deal with farm crops, food preparation, and the material culture of cookery; laws, particularly state and borough regulations dealing with marketing; newspapers, which include advertisements involving foods; periodicals, particularly the agricultural journals which were concerned with progress in farm life and therefore came to report constantly on "bad" traditional regional ways of doing things; the nineteenth century literary monthlies which include many accounts of life among the Pennsylvania Germans; the women's magazines which contain recipes and household hints about cookery; almanacs, which include recipes and household hints; broadsides,[4] some of which deal with medicine and nutrition; biographies and autobiographies of Pennsylvanians; local histories, particularly the county histories which appeared in the last third of the nineteenth century in the wake of the Centennial; and finally novels, particularly the regional, local-color works which record ethnic and regional patterns of life.

Manuscript Sources

The best sources for cookery in the manuscript category are those personal legal documents which are found by the thousands in all of our early courthouses: (a) the wills (last will and testament) of individuals, which often give detailed instructions on the yearly food outlay that the estate is to provide for the widow; and (b) estate inventories and sale accounts, which list foods and food-preparation tools and implements in the estate of the decedent. These have not been studied for foodways in detail as yet in any area of the United States. They are extremely valuable for terminology and vocabulary, and will have to be used eventually to enlarge the dictionaries of American English for American terms, which are thus far based only upon printed sources. In addition there are, of course, by the hundreds in libraries, historical societies, and private collections, manuscript autobiographies, travel accounts, and cookbooks which have not been studied. Personal letters are another important source, particularly *Amerikabriefe* of the eighteenth century, recording the emigrant's reaction to the foodways of the "New Land," and letters from Pennsylvanians who moved westward in the nineteenth century, comparing Pennsylvanian foods and life styles with those on the prairies. Finally, records of agricultural improvement societies are a prime source for food and foodways; one important example is the manuscript records, beginning in 1785, of the Pennsylvania Society for Improving Agriculture, which are on deposit in the Van Pelt Library of the University of Pennsylvania.

Iconographic Sources

These, too, are legion, and turn up in unexpected places. Book and periodical illustrations are an excellent source. Children's books and the illustrated weekly of the *Harper's Weekly* and *Gleason's Pictorial* type provide a wide record of nineteenth-century American rural life, including food preparation. Manuscript drawings are found in various collections; one example is the Charles Lesueur Collection in the Museum of Natural History at Le-Havre, France. Lesueur, a French naturalist, spent much time in Pennsylvania in the first quarter of the nineteenth century, and his manuscript drawings of a walking trip through the Pennsylvania German country in 1825 provide us with valuable dated and geographically pinpointed pictures of Pennsylvania houses, barns, inns, wagons, and bakeovens.[5] Photographs, including stereopticon views, are also legion, and there are now enough good collections of photographic Americana in libraries and museums to make it profitable to use them for foodways research. Of unusual value are the products of the local Pennsylvania photographers of the late nineteenth and early twentieth centuries, who traveled through the farm areas taking group pictures of farm families at work and at recreation.[6] Many of these are still in private hands and deserve archiving. Finally there are prints and cartoons and newspaper illustrations, all of which provide insight into food and foodways; the newspaper advertisements in particular give us many dated pictorial evidences of the material culture of food preparation.

Instead of arranging my paper on the basis of types of historical source materials, it will be more useful to focus on six problems in Pennsylvania German cookery research to see what help the historical approach can give us toward their solution. These are:

Figure 5.1. Cider-making in nineteenth-century America. Illustration from *Gleason's Pictorial* (Boston), October 1853. Note horse-powered cider mill at right, used for grinding the apples into pomace, which was then pressed into cider and barreled (*left*). The curiously designed scorpion used with the name of the month is the leading sign of the zodiac for October. *(Courtesy Roughwood Collection)*

1. Determining the Dietary Profile of Pennsylvania German Culture.
2. The Acculturation of Ethnic Cuisines in Eastern Pennsylvania.
3. The Diet of the Emigrant Generations.
4. General American Influences on Pennsylvania German Cookery.
5. Pennsylvania German Reactions to Changes in Food Technology.
6. The Relation of Urban and Rural Foods in Eastern Pennsylvania.

Determining the Dietary Profile of Pennsylvania German Culture

Until we can survey the culture with interview and questionnaire, the only way we have of determining the dietary profile, which I define as the major dishes and food complexes in order of their importance in Pennsylvania German cuisine, is to use the historical sources.

Let us begin our discussion with the "Germanic" elements in Pennsylvania German cuisine, since most of the travelers' and outsiders' accounts of the culture accented these. They include such staple dishes as sauerkraut, identified universally as a Pennsylvanian food; less-known regional specialties such as *Panhaas* (scrapple) and *Schnitz un Gnepp* (dried apples stewed with ham and dumplings); a great many noodle and dumpling dishes which link Pennsylvania German with the *Mehlspeisen* cuisine of South Germany; an elaborate *Wurstkultur,* if I may be permitted the term, involving a variety of smoked *(Brodwarscht)* and sour sausages *(Summerwarscht* and *Rollitsch);* a strong soup tradition, mostly flour and potato soups *(gereeschdi Mehlsupp, Grumbieresupp);* the tradition of the hot salad of dandelion or other spring greens with sweet-sour bacon dressing; and a tradition of dessert baked goods in which both the *Kuchen* and the pie have rivaled for first place.

The traditional festival cookery of the Pennsylvania Germans involves New Year's, pre-Lenten *(Fastnacht),* Easter, Pentecost, and Christmas specialties.[7] New Year's Day was a day for feasting on sauerkraut. The lore accompanying the dish in this case claims good luck throughout the coming year for the eater. Turkey is the general American festival dish, particularly for Thanksgiving and Christmas and secondarily for New Year's Day. Sauerkraut is normally served with pork; a curious folk rationale for eating pork rather than fowl on New Year's is that barnyard fowl scratch backwards, while the pig roots forward. There is, however, one geographical area in Central Pennsylvania and Western Maryland where it is traditional to eat sauerkraut *with* turkey for New Year's dinner—this is the area west of Harrisburg and extending into the German counties of Western Maryland.

Let us look in some detail at the historical documentation on the Pennsylvania German hot salad. A Scottish traveler in post-Revolutionary America provides us with our first dated documentation on this distinctive

Pennsylvania German dish, describing the dish as served to him at an inn in the mountains of Central Pennsylvania:

> Salad was produced to us at one of the Dutch hotels in the Alleghanies, with a hot, sweet, and acid sauce, but as this was not relished, the ladies of our party made the usual salad sauce, substituting for oil the liquor from a boiled ham just cut, which is in the United States to be preferred to oil wherever it can be had.[8]

Another eighteenth-century reference is provided by a New Jersey farmer on his way to settle in Lycoming County, Pennsylvania, in 1799. Passing through Eastern Pennsylvania, he remarks, "This country has been settled with Germans about fifty years, I hope to be soon through them." He objected principally to their food. "My breakfast this morning two cups of coffee without sugar, and 3 eggs; bread baked hard, and crust wet." For another meal: "Salad with milk, oil, vinegar, bonny clabber and bread; good God! how can they work so hard on such food! A fine lesson (he admits): I was determined to eat as they did, but was forced to take a piece of dried venison." When finally he comes into the Quaker settlement of Roaring Creek in Columbia County, he writes of the food he got there as follows: "They live pretty well, ham, eggs, lettuce, plain; much better than the German warm salads."[9]

There is of course a long history of the hot salad in German cuisine, nor was it unknown among some other ethnic groups in the United States. Professor Günter Wiegelmann has suggested that the hot salads of South Germany are a peasant-level adaptation to the olive oil and vinegar salad of Italy which made its way north of the Alps in the Middle Ages, finding acceptance first in the cloisters, then in the upper classes, and finally in the peasantry. The "folk" substituted hot meat drippings for olive oil, which was not always available or was too expensive for peasant budgets.[10]

The function of the hot salads—particularly the earliest spring salad, dandelion greens—to balance and counteract the dough and meat dishes on which a family subsisted through the long winter—is borne out by dietetic studies. The New York historian Jared van Wagenen has a lengthy passage in which he describes the function of "greens" in country diet:

> There is a class of plants that the housewife designates by the generic word "greens," and which the economic botanist refers to by the descriptive term "pot herbs." Of these the best known and most commonly used is the dandelion. This plant, while now naturalized everywhere, is of European origin and was not available on the front line of settlement. Purslane, or colloquially "pussly" of old gardens, is also (as very many other plants are) a European migrant. The common nettle, cowslip, or marsh marigold, and milkweed are American species that have gained a good repute as pot herbs. My own mother, within my memory but before every country store had fresh vegetables all

winter, used to speak of the "six-weeks' want," meaning the early spring period when the old vegetables and apples were gone and nothing new was available. No wonder the housewife scoured the spring fields for something green to cook. Pot herbs were a change and probably they corrected certain vitamin deficiencies, but after all they were mainly water and their caloric values low. Again, these familiar greens were commonly plants of old fields and gardens and probably would not be available to the pioneer homemaker.[11]

The Acculturation of Ethnic Cuisines in Eastern Pennsylvania

Historical sources make clear the early acculturation, the cultural trading and sharing of the distinct ethnic cuisines of Eastern Pennsylvania. Eastern Pennsylvania was settled principally by three groups: the English and Welsh Quakers and others from England proper, the Scotch-Irish Presbyterians from Ulster, and the Pennsylvania Germans. While there were distinct settlement areas where each of these ethnic groups predominated, there were enough enclaves of the other groups scattered through them to bring about early acculturation in food and foodways as well as other aspects of culture. In cookery, sauerkraut and apple butter and panhaas and other Pennsylvania German specialty foods came to be served on Quaker and Scotch-Irish farm tables, while certain British Isles specialties were early adapted to German tastes.

Chief among the latter is the round fruit pie, which in its apple version was long America's "favorite dessert" and whose universality has led to the phrase "as American as apple pie." There is linguistic as well as historical evidence that the pie is a borrowing from the British Isles cultures into the Pennsylvania German world. *Pie* is an English word, meaning a mixture, as, according to some authorities, in "piebald" and "pied." The Pennsylvania German hausfrau came to make numerous pies, so many, in fact, that one Pennsylvania scholar has suggested that the Pennsylvania German country is the center of the American pie belt.[12] We find, however, that the Pennsylvania Germans have no Germanic word for pie. Rather they call pie *"boi,"* as in *"Schnitzboi,"* dried apple pie, *"Kaerscheboi,"* cherry pie, *"Boigraut,"* pie plant, i.e., rhubarb, etc. Why *"boi"*? Probably because "poy" was the commonest English-Irish pronunciation of "pie" in the eighteenth century, when the borrowing first began to register in the culture.

However, there are many analogues to the English "pie" on the continent of Europe, from the *Wähe* to the *pizza*.[13] The Pennsylvania Germans, from their German and Swiss background, were accustomed to making the square or rectangular *Kuchen*—flat pieces of dough into which slices of plums or other fruit, or onions, are literally stuck—the whole baked in the outdoor bakeoven. In the nineteenth century such *Kuchen,* as for example, *Zwiwwelkuche,* onion pie (or onion cake?), were favorite foods for the

Figure 5.2. Making apple butter. Two Pennsylvania Dutch farm women dressed in work aprons and sunbonnets are busy stirring the apple butter in the huge kettle. It took many hours and was hot work, hence the long pole to work the paddle in the kettle. The illustration shows the value of historic photography for analyzing American folklife. *(Courtesy Fegley Collection, Schwenkfelder Library, Pennsburg, Pa.)*

Zehnuhrstück, the ten-o'clock piece which was carried to the men in the harvest fields.

Throughout the nineteenth century the "Kuchen" and the "pie" continued to be made by Pennsylvania German cooks. Toward the turn of the century the pie had gradually won first place and the *Kuchen* was then old-fashioned and fading out of the picture. Older informants still recall the *Kuchen* from the late nineteenth century, but I do not have evidence as yet of its use in Pennsylvania after the First World War period. The term "Kuchen" is still used by some cooks interchangeably with "pie" for the curious hybrid cake-pie called "shoofly pie" or "shoofly cake," a molasses-flavored crumb cake baked on a round pie shell without a top crust. But that is another story.[14]

The ethnic conflict in Pennsylvania was always rather sharp. Prejudice between "Dutchman" and Irishman, or between "Dutchman" and Yankee (New Englander) was very common, and often expressed in the historical documentation of the nineteenth century. As the travel accounts we have cited show, the groups at first disliked each other's standard foods—a universal human trait, it would seem. But gradually the cuisines were acculturated to each other, so that by the end of the nineteenth century one can speak with justification of a *regional* Pennsylvanian farm cuisine shared by most of the groups.

By the end of the century the Pennsylvania Dutch, the Scotch-Irish and the Quakers had largely forgotten their old rivalries and name-calling. They now could turn their attention to the "new immigration" which was bringing Central European and Mediterranean ethnic groups to the Pennsylvania cities. Good Quaker Wilmer Atkinson's *Farm Journal* opened a blast against these newer immigrants in October, 1897. The reason—again, a universal human one involving ethnic food habits:

> The farmer, the gardener and the dairyman load up their wagons with choice supplies, and drive to the city week after week, and wonder why they cannot sell their produce as they once did. Let him look around carefully and this is what he will see: A three-room house kept by a Hungarian boarding mistress, with ten Italians with no families; blocks of houses filled with Slavs and Poles, nearly all men—hundreds of them in every manufacturing city, each man taking a place that should be held by some loyal American supporting a family.

"What do these foreigners consume?" the editorial demanded. The answer: "Rye bread, noodles, refuse meat, bologna and beer." The complaint continues: "Do our farmers ever sell them any butter, any eggs, any fruit, and choice vegetables? Do their milk wagons stop at their doors?" Obviously the answer is No, and the indignant farmer calls for restriction of immigration.[15]

Figure 5.3. Hominy was a widespread American dish North and South, East and West, long into the nineteenth century. Today it is considered a Southern dish. This commercial example is made by a Pennsylvania Dutch firm in Pennsylvania.
(Courtesy Snyder Packing Co., Delta, Pa.)

Figure 5.4. Hominy block, a primitive hand-operated mill for pounding corn into hominy or grits. The pestle is attached to a strong, supple branch of a tree which supports some of its weight. The hominy block was probably an American Indian innovation. *(Courtesy Roughwood Collection)*

If the polemicist and his editor could only come back today, they might find their own rural progeny relishing the very foods that those "foreigners" brought to the American city—spaghetti and pizza, stuffed cabbage and borscht, pepperoni and pastrami.

The Diet of the Emigrant Generations

It is evident that the cuisine of the Pennsylvania Germans developed in stages, and is in fact an extremely complex historical development. Let us look in more detail at the source materials on the food and foodways of the emigrant generations in the eighteenth century.

America is a nation of immigrants, and each new immigrant group and each new immigrant generation has had to react to what American historians refer to as the "American experience" and the "American environment." The *Amerikabriefe* sent back home to Europe by German and Swiss emigrants of the eighteenth century, reporting as they did their astonished reaction to the plenty of staples such as white bread and meat in America, are one of our best sources on the diet of the immigrant generation. One such letter was sent back to Franconia from Pennsylvania in 1753:

> Grains are as dear here as in Germany, but one can earn five loaves of bread sooner in this country than one in Germany, for the day's wages are very good. In the winter a man gets 18 pence, that is in German money 7 (27?) kreuzer; in summer 11 batzen, but rich board along with it—meat two to three times a day, and a good drink made of apples.[16]

The "Newlander" Mittelberger echoed hundreds of *Amerikabriefe* when he wrote in his little account of his trip to Pennsylvania:

> Even in the humblest and poorest houses in this country there is no meal without meat, and no one eats the bread without butter or cheese, although the bread is as good as with us. It is very annoying, however, that nothing but salt meat is eaten in summer, and rarely fresh meat in winter.

He reinforces his statement by adding, "I don't think that there is any country in which more meat is eaten and consumed than in Pennsylvania." And he gives us some comparative notes on English and German diet. "The English know little or nothing of soup eating; bread and butter and cheese are always their dessert, and because sugar, tea and coffee are very cheap, they drink coffee and the like 2 or 3 times daily."[17]

For the diet of the emigrant generation one might think the shipping contracts signed by the emigrants with the Rotterdam shipping firms which brought them to Philadelphia an unlikely source. While they spell out the

Figure 5.5. Gristmills ground grain for rural customers. This very English-looking example, Pennock's Mill on the Pennepack Creek, was built in 1697. Drawing by Breton, engraved by Gilbert. *(Courtesy Roughwood Collection)*

food available to the emigrants during the long Atlantic crossing, a supposedly atypical period in the emigrant's life, actually the contracts do very probably reflect some standard foods. One such "Agreement for Transport from Rotterdam to Philadelphia," dated February 16, 1756,[18] promises that the ship shall be fitted out

> with good and proper provisions, namely: good bread, meat, bacon, flour, rice, barley, peas, syrup, butter, cheese, beer, good fresh water, and whatever else is necessary; likewise the ship shall be twice daily cleansed with vinegar and juniper berries, to purify the air; and daily there shall be given out to each whole freight the following:
>
> Sunday—one pound of beef cooked with rice
> Monday—barley and syrup
> Tuesday—one pound of white wheat flour
> Wednesday—one pound of beef cooked with rice
> Thursday—one pound of beef cooked with rice
> Friday—one pound of white wheat flour and one pound of butter
> Saturday—one pound of bacon, one pound of cheese, and six pounds of bread for the entire week.
>
> Besides, every day, one quart of beer (as long as it remains good), and two quarts of water daily. Lovers of tobacco, however, shall receive one pound to take along on the journey.

The undersigned passengers (71½ "freights" in number) "want to have freedom (as God's weather permits) to cook a few victuals for ourselves and the little children, and to make use of the fire from six o'clock in the morning till the same time in the evening." The ship owners (Isaac and Zacharias Hope of Rotterdam) made some attempt to adapt their provisions to the dietary standards of their "High German" clients:

> Inasmuch as we, as experienced merchants, who have been transporting people twenty or more years already, have found that bacon and meat are very heavily salted, from which salted provisions scurvy and other complaints arise, and moreover the High Germans are brought up more on fresh than salted provisions, we are ready to give two or three fresh meals weekly, which they will judge more fit for them.

Immigrant German reaction to the increased use of meat and other "American" tendencies in cuisine continued with the nineteenth-century emigration to Pennsylvania. A letter from the Birkenauer Johannes Klein, from "Grinwilitsch" (Greenvillage), Franklin County, Pennsylvania, October 8, 1831, sounds the familiar note once again:

> If they don't have meat three times every day, they can't stand it. Meat consumption here is really astounding. My neighbor, a shoemaker, in three months devoured four pigs and has to earn it all with shoemaking.

And thinking of his "Freundschaft" still living under the old cuisine in Germany, he writes:

> I just wish my old infirm mother was with me in freedom and could enjoy the white bread and the good apples. Astonishing amounts of molasses, syrup, honey and butter are consumed. Meat and white bread are smeared with butter and eaten together. This style of life is quite different than in Birkenau. For the womenfolk it is an outstandingly good country. Washing and baking is their work. They act like noblewomen, whether they are poor or rich, it's all the same. They have leghorn summer hats for the price of 3 to 18 dollars with veils on them. They have great rights in this country. Their husbands are not allowed to beat them, or they get the worst of the deal. If a woman wants to go visiting two miles away, they ride there on horseback. They all smoke tobacco.[19]

Additional light is shed on this problem and a different conclusion reached in a recent study by James Lemon, based on the wills and inventories of Eastern Pennsylvania.[20] Lemon makes the suggestion that since grains are usually mentioned first in eighteenth-century wills, bread was still considered the "staff of life" by the European settlers, English and German, where meat was scarce and potatoes had not emerged by 1750 as a significant part of the diet. Certainly, he says, bread and porridge remained important items of diet; perhaps three times as much grain was used per person then as now. He argues against the common idea that the frugal Germans ate more rye bread than wheat bread, in fact suggesting that the Germans, once settled in Pennsylvania, satisfied their preference for wheat bread and seemed to have consumed less maize than New Englanders and Southerners. Certainly Southeastern Pennsylvania was one of the prime grain producing areas of colonial America. It was also, for that reason, the biggest distilling center.[21]

The widow's arrangements of the farmers' wills are a prime source for our knowledge of what Pennsylvania farm families considered basic as everyday food. A sample is the will of Georg Remely, Whitehall Township, Northampton (now Lehigh) County, Pennsylvania, dated 1801, the original of which is in the author's possession.[22] By this document the decedent transfers to his "dear wife Elisabetha" a tract of eighty-five acres with all of its buildings "as her widow's residence as long as she shall bear my name," further ordering his executors to build for widow Elisabetha "a roomy one-story dwellinghouse, 26 by 22 feet, with a [knee]-wall and a cellar, as also a stable with an entry for her cattle." For her animals the executors were to clear a one-acre meadow and fence it well, and were to provide her with "a garden with a clapboard fence and a bake-oven with a shed-roof," all to be kept for her in top condition. They were to cut and haul her yearly supply of firewood, and provide her with ten bushels of rye out of the estate and sixty pounds Pennsylvania currency, and the "choice of two

Holiday Treats!!!

Salami (Genoa), Capicola, Prosciutto, Pepperoni
Provolone Cheese (Sharp), Mozzarella
Hot Cheese, Romano Cheese (Imp.)
Olives (Largest Selection In Town)
Frozen, Ravioli, Manicotti, Gnocchi
Cavetelli, Noodles, Fresh Ricotta Daily
Assortment of Italian Cookies
Ass't. of Italian Torrone Candy
Baccala (Cod Fish), Lupini Beans
Electric Pizzelle Iron, Noodle Machines
Expresso Coffee Pots, Spaghetti Dishes

ORDER NOW!!

Ricotta, Christmas Fish
Italian Sausage (All Pork Our Own Made)

LaJo

Genuine Italian Sausage

1101 8th Avenue — Across from Mt. Carmel Church

Figure 5.6. Newspapers are an important source for food history. This advertisement from a Central Pennsylvania newspaper, *The Altoona Mirror,* is obviously aimed at the Italian ethnic population in the town. Note that the ethnic food store is opposite the Mt. Carmel Church, the Italian Catholic parish. The advertisement offers not only Italian food specialties for the Christmas holidays but pizzelle irons, noodle machines, and expresso coffee pots.

cows, two sheep, and two pigs, as also whatever she needs of household furniture and kitchen utensils." If she were to remarry, Elisabetha was instructed to take with her "one cow and all the household goods and kitchen utensils which she brought to me" (i.e., as dowry at the time of the first wedding).

General American Influences on Pennsylvania German Cookery

In addition to the acculturation of ethnic specialties in colonial Pennsylvania, there was the influence on Pennsylvania German cuisine of what one must term general American food habits and taboos, i.e., foodways which were more general in their extent and not limited to one ethnic group. There are two examples: (a) the general American, standard food known as "mush"; and (b) the widespread American taboo on alcoholic beverages known as the "temperance movement." Both were to influence the everyday life of the Pennsylvania Germans deeply and permanently.

Mush[23] is cornmeal porridge, eaten with milk or molasses in its fluid form, and fried, usually as a breakfast food, in its solidified state. As a general American dish, widespread from New England to the South in the colonial period, it became also a staple in Pennsylvania German cuisine. While cornculture and corn dishes were in a sense borrowings from Indian cultures, mush is more directly an American adaptation of European porridge dishes which were staples of European peasant cuisine, and actually, substitutes for bread or even primitive forms of bread. The Scotch subsisted on oatmeal, the English on porridge of various sorts, the Germans and the Netherlanders on *Brei* and *pap,* both of which words are used in Pennsylvania. American cornmeal mush came to supplant the European porridges and became what was perhaps the most widespread American everyday dish of the colonial period. The dish went under various names in early America, from "hasty pudding" in New England, "suppawn" (an Indian word) in New York State, "stirabout" among displaced Yankees in "New Connecticut" (the Wyoming Valley of Pennsylvania), and "mush" in most of Pennsylvania and the South. The standard word today is simply "mush."

One of our earliest historical references to mush among Pennsylvania Germans comes from a Moravian missionary diary of 1753, when after arrival at Bethabara, North Carolina, the Pennsylvania missionaries wrote: "We began to build a bake-oven, so that we can again eat bread, which for a time has been pretty rare for us. Our principal fare is now pumpkin sauce *(Kürbis-Brey)* and mush *(Sapan),* and we are quite well with it."[24]

As a cornmeal dish served with milk, mush is also related to "hominy" and "samp." The Swedish historian Acrelius writes of the diet of the Delaware Swedes in 1759: "The arrangement of meals among country people is usually this: for breakfast in summer cold milk and bread, rice, milk pudding, cheese and butter, cold meat. In winter, mush and milk and milk porridge, hominy and milk. The same served for supper if so desired."[25]

The earliest reference to "mush and milk" among the Pennsylvania Germans dates from 1787, in a humorous article by "Stoffel Ehrlich" in a Lancaster newspaper: "In the morning I drink neither tea nor coffee, but eat my mush and milk or sour milk soup, and a piece of bacon with it, like my late father, and then end with a sip of brandy."[26] According to his biographer, Johannes Helffrich (1795–1852), Reformed minister of Eastern Pennsylvania, had two favorite dishes. One was the old-fashioned Dutch potato soup, the other—naturally—was mush.[27]

Although mush was a universal American pioneer dish, the Pennsylvania Germans have added their own flavor and technique to its preparation. They used yellow field corn *(gehl Welschkarn)* for their "mushmeal" but before taking it to mill for grinding they roasted the ears in the oven which imparted a toasted, nutty flavor to the meal. This roasting of corn before milling appears to be limited to the Pennsylvania German culture and the Brandywine Valley in Delaware. As reason for this geographical limitation Dr. Alfred L. Shoemaker has suggested that the Pennsylvania Germans consistently had large outdoor bakeovens while some of the other early ethnic groups did not. Large quantities of corn could not practically be roasted over the fireplaces where cooking was done in most pioneer homes. It seems probable that the Pennsylvania German settlers, with their outdoor bakeoven tradition (part of their continental heritage) developed the added refinement of roasted cornmeal as their contribution to early American corn-culture.

There was a time in the twentieth century when mush, for city dwellers, was looked down upon as a kind of old-fashioned, poverty dish. Today, now that cornmeal is an "in" food again, one finds rows of commercial bags of cornmeal in American supermarkets. But alas, most of it is white unroasted cornmeal shipped up from southern mills. It is only in the smaller country stores and specialty shops that the Pennsylvania German roasted yellow cornmeal can be bought.

The effects of the temperance movement upon Pennsylvania German housekeeping and mores were widespread. The temperance movement, one of the most curious examples of religious taboo in history, invaded most of the American Protestant churches in the nineteenth century. Temperance was one of the major thrusts of the Evangelical-Revivalist-Reform movement (partially derivative from continental Pietism) which radically changed the life-style of large groups of the population of the British Isles and of the United States. Actually, as recent scholarship has pointed out, temperance was a middle-class wedge separating the upper and lower classes, both of which of course continued the earlier general drinking habits of colonial America.

In the colonial era, hard liquor flowed freely as part of family entertaining as well as those social events where the folk community gathered, e.g., baptisms, weddings, funerals, militia musterings, tavern dances, harvest frolics.[28] Liquor was served to the men working in the harvest fields, it was dispensed at the country store to customers, and it was part of tavern meals from breakfast to supper. After the temperance reform, drinking, like some of the older folk-cultural amusements and recreations, was made into a sin. As I have pointed out elsewhere,[29] Evangelicalism (in America: Revivalism) broke up not only the old historic sense of the church with its socially celebrated rites of passage, but at the same time destroyed the folk-cultural concomitants of many of these social events. In individualizing Protestantism and centering it in the conversion experience, revivalism divided families and broke up both historic church and folk culture.

Because of the widespread influence of the temperance movement upon various American groups, churches, and sects, one has to speak of "pre-temperance" and "post-temperance" eras in their history. The drinking habits of the Pennsylvania Germans before the temperance movement came to Pennsylvania are easily documentable. Eastern Pennsylvania had the heaviest concentration of distilleries in early America. The Scotch-Irish developed rye and corn whiskey as a substitute for the universal drink of the colonial era, rum. Of Eastern Pennsylvanian counties, it was Lancaster County, with its heavy concentration of Scotch-Irish Presbyterians and Swiss Mennonites, that led in the production of whiskey in the early Republic. Today, curiously enough, Pennsylvania's Mennonites have adopted the temperance stance and it is very difficult to find them expressing interest in their ancestral distilling prowess. One of Pennsylvania's finest whiskeys, known earlier as "Old Monongahela" Whiskey, from Western Pennsylvania, is today known commercially as "Old Overholt," named for the Mennonite farmer of Westmoreland County who first opened the distillery.

Nowhere is the post-temperance view of the pre-temperance era expressed more pointedly than in a Pennsylvania genealogy of 1876. The author was thirty years old, a Pennsylvania German farm boy who had just graduated from college and theological seminary of a denomination whose upper echelons had accepted the temperance reform. His accepting of temperance as normative for religion led him to rationalize the everyday use of liquor by his ancestors. He found it especially hard to understand the will of his emigrant ancestor, dated 1775, which provided many gallons of the best whiskey per annum to the widow. His comments show how Americanized in religion the young preacher was, for he shared the pietistic moralism and temperance mind-set which nineteenth-century Revivalism had fastened upon Protestant America. In commenting on the provision he writes:

> This seemed very strange to us, and no doubt will to the reader; and we could not become reconciled as to the meaning of this clause until we made inquiry of some old persons, when we were informed that at that time there were but few practising physicians, and every family had to be prepared for any emergency; they had different kinds of roots and herbs in bottles of whiskey; which was then used as medicine. We do not sanction this mode of doctoring, yet at that time, when whiskey was pure and unadulterated, it was probably the best method to be had.[30]

In other words, the temperance-minded nineteenth-century American Protestant outlook, so typically and stubbornly American, was entirely different from the pre-temperance eighteenth-century culture, where whiskey had not only medicinal purposes but was used widely in entertaining, in the harvest, and at community gatherings as well. Maybe the old lady even liked her schnapps, but of this we get no hint from the young preacher. He is teetotally opposed to whiskey in *any* form, and his misunderstanding of its commonness in the eighteenth-century world, when it was accepted by most Pennsylvanians without protest, makes him distort his description of his forefathers' world.

Pennsylvania German Reactions to Changes in Food Technology

The greatest change in cooking technology in Pennsylvania until the twentieth century was undoubtedly the shift from the open hearth style of cooking of the pioneer period to the kitchen range (stove) in the 1840s to the 1870s.

The Pennsylvania Germans had essentially two cooking areas, the open hearth in their kitchen, and a freestanding outdoor bakeoven in the yard. Sometimes also there was a summer kitchen or butcher- and wash-house where water could be heated and large operations of food preparation, as for example the making of meat products at butchering time, could be taken care of. In addition, on the Pennsylvania German farm there were springhouses (dairy buildings) and smokehouses (for curing meats) and dryhouses (for drying fruits and vegetables), which were connected with cookery in the largest sense of the word.

The commonest dishes of the Pennsylvania German farmers—sauerkraut, schnitz un gnepp, potpie, mush, potato soup, browned flour soup, rivvel soup, etc.—undoubtedly reflect the open hearth cookery that existed everywhere before the introduction of the wood or coal range in the 1840s. This was "pot cookery"—it was simply more practical to cook a stew-like meal for the whole family in an iron pot that could be left to simmer over the open fire.

For example, the meat and dough stew known universally in Pennsylvania as "potpie" (Pennsylvania German: *Bottboi*) is documented in the colonial period and early nineteenth century. It was a favorite family dish, and is also reported as being served for larger crowds, as for example, to General Washington and his soldiers on the way to the "Whiskey Rebellion" in Western Pennsylvania in 1794,[31] and to a gathering of frontier Methodists in the Susquehanna Valley in 1807 at their "quarterly meeting," where a "barrel of potpie" was consumed.[32] A local historian of the frontier areas of Northwestern Pennsylvania calls potpie the standard dish for every logrolling, house-raising, and harvest day.[33]

In addition the Pennsylvania Germans had what other Americans came to call the "Dutch oven," a large covered skillet standing on a tripod which could be placed conveniently over or near the fire to fry or bake meats, and other dishes.

The outdoor bakeoven was the solution to the problem of large family bakings that usually took place once a week. Outdoor bakeovens are found in North America principally among Pennsylvania Germans, French Canadians, Louisiana "Cajuns," and the southwestern Indian tribes.[34] The British Isles settlers normally baked bread in ovens attached to their kitchen fireplaces. Some, like the Irish, baked primitive breads like "johnny cake" on flat stones in front of the fireplace.[35] The large outdoor bakeoven not only enabled one to manage a larger baking, but was important practically because it removed the clutter of the actual baking operation out of the busy kitchen where meals were being prepared even on baking day. Also, the large space under the bakeoven dome or *Hut* could be used for drying vegetables and fruits, and even, as we have mentioned in the section on mush, for parching corn ears before the corn was sent to the mill to make cornmeal, or "mushmeal," as the Pennsylvania Germans called it.

In my preliminary remarks on historical documentation I refer to local-color novels as a source for our understanding of regional cookery. One of my favorite examples of the value of this type of source material comes from the novel *Norwood* by Henry Ward Beecher. In the story a New England soldier, wounded at Gettysburg, was billeted on a Pennsylvania Quaker farm. While the soldier lies recuperating in the farmhouse his New England girlfriend, who has come to nurse him, is shown the farm by the farmer's daughter Martha.

> "What is that?" said Rose, pointing to a queer stack of bricks under a tile shed close by the house.
> "That is our oven," said Martha.
> "What—out of doors? We build ours into the kitchen chimney."
> "It is the way of our fathers. The other perhaps is more convenient."[36]

Which accents the fact that in the nineteenth century Pennsylvania farmers were familiar with the outdoor bakeoven as part of their cultural landscape, the New England Yankee was not.

When the range replaced the open hearth, the range was at first set into the fireplace hole and the original chimney used. After the Civil War, when houses were built without fireplaces, the kitchen stove-pipe was often inserted up through one of the bedrooms to provide a little warmth to the frigid sleeping quarters in winter. But more important, the wood or coal ranges, which were in use from the 1840s into the twentieth century, when coal oil, gas, and electric ranges took their place, displaced both open hearth and bakeoven as cooking areas. In fact, the ranges attempted to combine for the housewife all of the tasks once performed in the fireplace and bakeoven. Frying and stewing could be accomplished on top of the iron stove, water could be heated in a special water compartment, and best of all, a relatively large baking space was available for bread and pies and other baked dishes. For this and other reasons, including the smaller size of families in the twentieth century, the large outdoor bakeovens, so much a distinctive feature of the Pennsylvania German cultural landscape, came into disuse largely by the period of the First World War. My own grandmother, for example, transferred her baking from the outdoor bakeoven to the kitchen range in 1910.

The Relation of Urban and Rural Foods in Eastern Pennsylvania

One of the pressing historical problems in Pennsylvania foodways research is the historical relation of the food specialties of Philadelphia to the foods of the upcountry ethnic groups, particularly the Pennsylvania Germans. The cuisine of cities, particularly our older maritime cities like Boston, New York, Philadelphia, Baltimore, Charleston, and New Orleans, have through the years absorbed dishes from the upstate areas which they serve as market centers. Philadelphia is one of these, an important marketing center for the Pennsylvania German and Quaker settlements in Eastern Pennsylvania. For example, because of its market network, Philadelphia became famous in the nineteenth century for its butter, cheese, ice cream, and other dairy products. In the farm periodicals, "Philadelphia butter" had the highest reputation on the Eastern seaboard. It was the product largely of the nearby Quaker dairy farms of Chester and Delaware and Bucks Counties, Pennsylvania, where an elaborate butter technology was worked out, with improvements in the churn, butter tub, springhouse and other aids to dairying.

To the tourist and the nation at large today, Philadelphia cuisine is identified by two unusual dishes, "scrapple" and "pepperpot." Pepperpot is tripe and potato chowder, and is documented back into the early nineteenth century. Its origins have not fully been worked out, but the term "pepperpot" is a West Indian term, and the dish undoubtedly came into use in the wake of Philadelphia's wide shipping interests in the Caribbean.

Philadelphia scrapple is even more renowned as a Philadelphia food. As with many distinctive regional foods, visitors (and graduate students at the university from outside the state) usually take either violent dislike to it or become incurable scrapple addicts, forcing it on family and unwary visitor alike. As the name suggests, it is manufactured of "scraps," in this case meat scraps from butchering, plus broth, plus flour. Poured into deep rectangular pans to solidify into cakes, it is then fried in slices as a breakfast dish. When we look for its lineage, we find the nineteenth-century historical sources our best help. Wilmer Atkinson's *Farm Journal* describes it as follows: "This is a compound of meats that seems indigenous to Eastern Pennsylvania, and is quite unknown in many sections of the country." And the Editor adds, "No family in this part of the country thinks of going into winter quarters without having their larders well filled with scrapple."[37] In an article in the same journal in 1881, we are told that "our Dutch, who introduced it (scrapple), call it *pan haus* (pan hash)."[38] These references imply that scrapple was a generally made food on the farms of Eastern Pennsylvania, but was originally of Pennsylvania German origin. The dialect term *Panhaas* (literally, pan rabbit) is documented in the Rhineland from which many settlers came to Eastern Pennsylvania in the seventeenth and eighteenth centuries.[39]

Further evidence of the folk-cultural transit of scrapple is found in the manuscript diaries of a Quaker woman named Rebecca Rhoads, of Green Street Meeting, Philadelphia.[40] Although she lived in the city of Philadelphia from the 1820s to the 1850s, Rebecca Rhoads prepared much of her own food in country ways, butchering a pig each winter to make, among other things, a dish which she called "pon horse." (In this case the "rabbit" became a "horse.") Today the term "ponhoss" is documentable in Eastern and Central Pennsylvania, along with "scrapple." The balance between the words is uneven, however, and the word "ponhoss" appears to be losing ground in favor of scrapple.

Philadelphia scrapple is now made commercially by several butchering firms in the area, and is available in most supermarket meat departments. One firm, Habbersett's, of Media, boasts that it has been making scrapple since 1863. Country "ponhoss," homemade by country butchers, is still manufactured upstate, and very often can be purchased, along with Pennsylvania German *Brodwarscht* (farmer's sausage) and *Summerwarscht* (summer sausage, the country ancestor of commercial "Lebanon Bologna") at country stores in the Pennsylvania German counties.[41]

In the case of scrapple we have a good example of a regional dish which, through its connection with the major city of the area, has become a symbol of Philadelphia's urban cuisine to the country at large, while its country cousin remains in the shadow. In the same way, "Boston baked beans" and "New England clam chowder," now identified with Boston, were originally regional dishes from the Yankee farm lands.

Today the influence is reversed. Prepared urban foods are remolding the rural cuisine as part of the general urbanizing of rural life in the twentieth century.

Notes

1. For the Pennsylvania German culture, see Martin Lohmann, *Die Bedeutung der deutschen Ansiedlungen in Pennsylvanien* (Stuttgart, 1923); Emil Meynen, *Bibliographie des Deutschtums der kolonialzeitlichen Einwanderung in Nordamerika Insbesondere der Pennsylvanien-Deutschen und ihrer Nachkommen 1683–1933* (Leipzig, 1937); Frederic Klees, *The Pennsylvania Dutch* (New York, 1950); and the publications of the Pennsylvania German Society, the Pennsylvania German Folklore Society, and the Pennsylvania Folklife Society (*The Pennsylvania Dutchman,* 1949–1956, *Pennsylvania Folklife,* 1956–).
2. Susan Ginsberg, member of my seminar in "Material Aspects of Folk Culture," Spring Semester 1970, wrote her seminar paper on regional foods of Eastern Pennsylvania as reflected in restaurant cuisine and menus. It is strange that with the wide tourist interest in things Pennsylvania Dutch, there is as yet no Pennsylvania Dutch restaurant in Philadelphia.
3. Some of the nationally circulated Philadelphia cookbooks of the nineteenth century show important evidence of Pennsylvania German foods. Cf. for example, *The National Cook Book, By a Lady of Philadelphia, A Practical Housewife,* 5th ed. (Philadelphia, 1855), which offers recipes not only of local Philadelphia specialties such as "Pepperpot" and "shad" oysters, but in addition the Pennsylvania German dishes: "Soused Pig's Feet," Scrapple, German Hot Potato Salad, "Sour Krout," Dandelion, "Dutch Salad" (hot lettuce, with ham vinegar dressing), "Dutch Loaf" (a coffee cake), Pickled Beets (with hard-boiled eggs), and Apple Butter. The earliest German cookbook in Eastern Pennsylvania, *Die Geschickte Hausfrau: Eine Sammlung von Guter Rezepte und Vorschriften zum Kochen, Braten, Kuchen-Backen, und Einmachen von Früchten* (Harrisburg, 1851), 38 pp., contains the following: *Aepfelschnitz-Pei* (Dried Apple Pie), *Getrockneter Kirschen-Pei* (Dried Cherry Pie), *Kürbiss-Pei* (Pumpkin Pie), *Johnny-Kuchen* (Johnny Cake), *Kornmehl-Muffins* (Indian Meal Muffins), *Weiche Lebkuchen* (Soft Gingerbread), *Schwamm-Kuchen* (Sponge Cake), *Kalbfuss-Gallerte* (Calf's Foot Jelly), *Guter Kraut-Sallat* (Cold Slaw), *Sprossen-Bier* (Spruce Beer), *Kuttelfleck* (To souse tripe), *Gepökelte Schweins-Füsse* (Pigs Feet Soused), and *Bratwürste.*
4. One such broadside in my collection, the "Diet" prescriptions by Dr. W. Williamson of Philadelphia, dating from the 1830s or 1840s, seems to list most regional foods among the "forbidden" dietary items: salads, vinegar, pigs' feet, hogs' head cheese, scrapple, sausages, mince pies, smoked meat, smoked fish, oyster soup, and buckwheat cakes. Among the "allowed" items were, however: buttermilk, cottage cheese, hot corn, hominy, Indian or rye mush, groats, and pearl barley.

5. "The Pennsylvania Sketchbooks of Charles Lesueur," Don Yoder, ed., *Pennsylvania Folklife* 16 (2) (Winter 1966–1967): 30–37. The sketchbooks of Lewis Miller (1795–1880), the York folk artist, have been published in selection recently; for Pennsylvania cookery they are the richest iconographic source from the first part of the nineteenth century. See *Lewis Miller: Sketches and Chronicles* (York, Pa.: The Historical Society of York County, 1966).

6. For an example, see *The Countryman's Family Album* (Pennsburg, Pa.: The Schwenkfelder Library, 1954), based on the H. Winslow Fegley Collection of Eastern Pennsylvania photographs.

7. For Christmas and Easter cookery, with the related festivals in Advent, Lent and Pentecost, see Alfred L. Shoemaker, *Christmas in Pennsylvania: A Folk-Cultural Study* (Kutztown, Pennsylvania, 1959), and *Eastertide in Pennsylvania* (Kutztown, Pa., 1961).

8. James Stuart, *Three Years in North America* (Edinburgh, 1783).

9. Thomas Hill, "A Journey on Horseback from New Brunswick, N.J. to Lycoming County, Pennsylvania, in 1799," *Now and Then: A Quarterly Magazine of History and Biography* (Muncy, Pa.), 4 (6) (January–February–March 1931): 176–79.

10. Günter Wiegelmann, *Alltags- und Festspeisen: Wandel und Gegenwärtige Stellung* (Marburg, 1967), Atlas der Deutschen Volkskunde, Neue Folge, Beiheft 1.

11. Jared van Wagenen, Jr., *The Golden Age of Homespun* (New York: Hill and Wang, 1963), 98–99.

12. Preston A. Barba: "The eastern counties of Pennsylvania constitute the piebelt of America. In this area more and better pies are eaten in greater variety than anywhere else on this terrestrial globe. We Pennsylvania Germans eat pie at breakfast, at dinner, at supper." Ann Hark and Preston A. Barba, *Pennsylvania German Cookery: A Regional Cookbook* (Allentown, Pa., 1950), 191.

13. Cf. O. Rhiner, *Dünne, Wähe, Kuchen, Fladen, Zelten. Die Wortgeographie des Flachkuchens mit Belag und ihre volkskundlichen Hintergründe in der deutschen Schweiz* (Frauenfeld, 1958); and A. Wurmbach, *"Kuchen—Fladen—Torte," Zeitschrift für Volkskunde* 56 (1960): 20–40.

14. Shoofly pie is now considered a "typical" Pennsylvania German specialty. It is essentially molasses crumb pie. Central Pennsylvanians in my background called it "granger pie," Eastern Pennsylvanians "shoofly pie." I have no documentation on it before 1900. There was a popular song in the Civil War period, "Shoofly, don't bodder me," which may or may not have a connection. An original etymology was developed by one Pennsylvania German scholar (Preston A. Barba) tracing it from the French word "choufleur," since the baked crumb topping resembles the texture of cauliflower! The essential thing is that it is a moist cake topping baked in a round pie shell. There are other similar pies (Montgomery pie, funny pie, etc.,) listed in the Pennsylvania German cookbooks, but until much more research is done on American pie typology it is unsafe to attribute this type exclusively to Pennsylvania German cookery.

15. "Let Immigration Be Restricted," *The Farm Journal* (Philadelphia, Pa.), October 1897.

16. Otto Langguth, "Pennsylvania German Pioneers from the County of Wertheim," translated and edited by Don Yoder, *The Pennsylvania German Folklore Society* 12 (1947), Appendix 2: The Johannes Schlessmann Letters, 262–66.

17. *Gottlieb Mittelberger's Journey to Pennsylvania in the Year 1750, and Return to Germany in the Year 1754,* Carl Theo. Eben, trans. (Philadelphia, 1898), 64–65.
18. Langguth, "Pennsylvania German Pioneers," Appendix 1, 259–62.
19. Wilhelm Diehl, ed., "Brief eines nach Amerika ausgewanderten Ehepaars aus Birkenau (1831)," *Hessische Chronik* 17 (1930): 83–86.
20. James T. Lemon, "Household Consumption in Eighteenth Century America and Its Relationship to Production and Trade: The Situation among Farmers in Southeastern Pennsylvania," *Agricultural History* 41 (1) (January 1969): 59–70.
21. Carlton O. Wittlinger, "Early Manufacturing in Lancaster County, Pennsylvania, 1710–1840," Ph.D. diss., University of Pennsylvania, 1953.
22. Original German will in the author's collection; the recorded will can be found in the Register of Wills Office, Northampton County Courthouse, Easton, Pennsylvania.
23. Digested from Don Yoder, "Pennsylvanians Called It Mush," *Pennsylvania Folklife* 13 (2) (Winter 1962–1963): 27-49.
24. "Diarium einer Reise von Bethlehem, Pa., nach Bethabara, N.C.," ed. William J. Hinke, *German-American Annals,* 3 (8).
25. Israel Acrelius, *Description of the Former and Present Condition of New Sweden* (Philadelphia, 1874), 158–59, original edition Stockholm, 1759.
26. *Neue Unpartheyische Lancaster Zeitung,* September 12, 1787.
27. William A. Helffrich, *Lebensbild aus dem Pennsylvanisch-Deutschen Predigerstand: Oder Wahrheit in Licht und Schatten* (Allentown, Pa., 1906), 9.
28. For the consumption of liquor in early America in general, see the chapter on the temperance movement in Alice Felt Tyler, *Freedom's Ferment* (Minneapolis, 1944).
29. Don Yoder, "Official Religion versus Folk Religion," *Pennsylvania Folklife* 15 (2) (Winter 1965–1966): 36–52; also *Pennsylvania Spirituals* (Lancaster, Pa., 1961), especially chapter 3.
30. D. B. Shuey, *History of the Shuey Family in America, from 1732 to 1876* (Lancaster, Pa., 1876), 51. A full description of the book's value for folk-cultural scholarship can be found in the article "Genealogy and Folk-Culture," *Pennsylvania Folklife* 15 (1) (Autumn 1965): 24–29.
31. *History of Franklin County, Pennsylvania* (Chambersburg, 1894).
32. George Peck, *Early Methodism within the Bounds of the Old Genesee Conference* (New York, 1860), 167.
33. J. T. Stewart, *Indiana County, Pennsylvania: Her People, Past and Present.* 2 vols. (Chicago, 1913), 1:21.
34. The only decent overall study of the bakeoven in America is included in Fred Kniffen, "The Outdoor Oven in Louisiana," *Louisiana History* 1 (1) (1960): 25–35.
35. The johnny cake is naturally not, as so many Americans naively suppose, a direct borrowing from the American Indian, but an American adaptation of the widespread European hearth-baked bread. For the hearth-bread tradition in the British Isles, see E. Estyn Evans, *Irish Heritage* (Dundalk, 1946); also Caoimhin O Danachair, "Bread," *Ulster Folklife* 4 (1958): 29–32.

36. Henry Ward Beecher, *Norwood: or, Village Life in New England* (New York, 1868), 533.

37. "Butchering Time," *The Farm Journal* 3 (3) (December 1878): 33.

38. *The Farm Journal* 5 (13) (December 1881): 249.

39. See Hark-Barba, *Pennsylvania German Cookery,* 43–44. Pennsylvania German *Panhaas* (ponhoss) is related to the German terms *Pannhase, Pannasch,* and *Pannharst.* For details from the Rhineland dialects, see Preston A. Barba, *'S Pennsylvaanisch Deitsch Eck, The Morning Call* (Allentown, Pa.), December 28, 1935, and April 9, 1938.

40. In the author's collection. Unlike most Quaker diaries and journals, which, like the Puritan diaries, are heavily mystical and introspective, the Rhoads Diaries are domestic, reporting frequently what the diarist served for breakfast, dinner, and supper. The family also had country connections, and Rebecca reports the weekly visits of Cousin "Zekiel" who brings market goods to the Philadelphia Market every Saturday.

41. "Lebanon Bologna" is the only Pennsylvania German sausage specialty which has come into wide commercial sale outside the state.

6

Sectarian Costume Research in the United States

The study of sectarian costume in the United States is important not only because of its wide geographical spread but also because of its curious relation to the American pluralist ethos—examples can be found in Protestantism, Catholicism, and Judaism—and the fact that at the present day, our sectarian costumes are the most vivid living, functional analogues to Europe's peasant costumes.

European costume research has concentrated principally on peasant costume, the regionally varying costumes of village and valley communities, which developed out of historic fashion styles via cultural lag, and which were worn as badges of group identity as well as to signify status of various sorts within the folk community itself.[1] Peasant costumes are "religious" costumes in the sense that they relate their wearers to the sacred turning points in life, the rites of passage, symbolizing in outward forms these community-determined changes in individual status. In some cases, as in Germany, where Protestant and Catholic villages, following archaic political boundaries of pre-1871 Germany, adjoin each other in the countryside, there are sometimes conscious efforts to differentiate Protestants from Catholics by costume. This confessional differentiation, self-conscious and proud, is a European analogue to America's Protestant sectarian costumes which express in outward ways, to the world outside, the sectarian individuality of the sect wearing them.

By sectarian costume we mean of course the standardized dress of a religious sect, sub-group, or order, which serves as a badge of group identity, both to the group itself and to the outside world. I use the word "sectarian" here to cover Hasidic Jewish costume and certain Roman Catho-

---

This article originally appeared in *Forms upon the Frontier: Folklife and Folk Arts in the United States,* Austin and Alta Fife and Henry H. Glassie, eds. (Logan, Utah: Utah State University Press, 1969), 41–75.

lic habits, as well as the great variety of Protestant sectarian dress, since the word "sect" implies conscious differentiation from the outside world, and all of these groups have reasons for symbolizing their religious microcosm against the secular macrocosm of the outside world. As we have stated, aspects of sectarian dress can be found for study within all three of the major religious traditions of America—Protestantism, Roman Catholicism, and Judaism.

The Hasidic Costume

Within the Jewish spectrum the dress of the Hasidic Jews, rather recently imported from Eastern Europe, involves "frozen" or arrested nineteenth-century Eastern European costume, with a few elements from earlier periods among the most conservative—the fur wheel hat or *shtreimel,* for example—just as the most archaic Protestant dress in America, that of the Old Order Amish and the Old Order Mennonites, represents a freezing or arresting of eighteenth- and nineteenth-century costume elements which are continued in use, for religious reasons, into the twentieth century.

Solomon Poll's recent study of the Hungarian Hasidic community of Williamsburg[2] gives details on the use of differentiating costume in Judaism. In Hungary the non-Hasidic orthodox Jews (*Ashkenazishe Yiden,* in the Hasidic terminology) were more acculturated to Hungarian culture—normally speaking Hungarian and dressing like their Hungarian neighbors—than the *Hasidishe Yiden* or Hasidic Jews.

> The external appearance of the Hasidic Jews differed from that of the contemporary Hungarians. They wore full beards that were never cut; such Jews were known as *Yiden mit bord und payes.* Some of them wore black overcoats, the *kaftan;* such Jews were known as *Yiden mit a bekecher.* Some wore round black hats, *biberhet,* and were known as *Yiden mit a biberhet.* Some wore fur hats called *shtreimel* on the Sabbath and holidays and were known as *Yiden mit a shtreimel.* Some wore special low shoes with white socks over their trousers or breeches, and these were known as *Yiden mit shich und zoken.* There were many other requirements for one to become known as, or to be considered, a *Hasidisher Yid.* The many limitations that the larger society puts upon persons of different external appearance who conform to the numerous internal controls associated with Hasidic behavior made such Jews readily identifiable as *Hasidische Yiden,* Hasidic Jews, or Hasidim.

The stratification of the Hasidic community is based not upon such factors as wealth, occupation, lineage, or education, but rather upon "high frequency and intensity of ritualistic observance." "Social and economic characteristics are important determinants of position," Poll continues, "only if they are connected with ritualistic observances." A wealthy person may display his wealth "only through luxuries that are Hasidic in character." Wealth may allow its possessor to "have two sinks, two stoves, or even two separate kitchens—one for meat and one for dairy products—so that he can observe the dietary laws more intensely. Or a wealthy man may have a more beautiful *shtreimel,* which is again an intensification of Hasidic observances."

> The Hasidic garments vary from *zehr Hasidish* (extremely Hasidic) to *modernish* (modern). The less Hasidic men, that is, the persons whose religious performances are of less frequency and less intensity, wear *modernish* clothing. Though still recognizable as "Hasidic," these garments resemble those of western societies. Or these men wear western clothing that is turned into Hasidic clothing by Hasidic overtones; for instance, long-outmoded, double-breasted dark suits that button from right to left. The most observant wear *zehr Hasidish* clothing, and through this they are identified as persons of high rank. Their clothing alone indicates that the frequency and intensity of their observances have secured them high status. A person who wears *zehr Hasidish* clothing would be ridiculed if his behavior were not consistent with his appearance.

This range of adherence to Hasidic standards of dress reminds one strikingly of the present situation in some Mennonite or Brethren congregations, where a double standard of dress adherence exists, the ministry being "plainer" than the laity; and in the case of the women, more conservative styles are worn by the older women, more modern styles by the younger.

> One of the most significant status symbols among men in the Hasidic community is the *shtreimel,* made of sable, the average price of it is one hundred dollars. Anyone who wears such a hat is known as a *"Yid mit a shtreimel."* When a Hasidic man puts on a *shtreimel* for the first time (usually at his wedding), it is an indication that he commits himself to a Hasidic way of life, appropriate to one who wears this hat. The wearing of the *shtreimel* and the behavior expected of a person wearing it are simultaneous reinforcements of the Hasidic norms. A person is expected to behave in a certain manner. When he does, the community permits him to wear a *shtreimel.* Then, because he has a *shtreimel,* he will not commit a breach of trust by not living up to those norms that govern behavior of a person wearing a *shtreimel.* Thus, wearing such a fur hat may identify a person as belonging to a certain status category; but it is not the fur hat itself that puts him there, it is his Hasidic behavior, with which he constantly justifies the wearing of the *shtreimel.*

These are valuable comments, giving us insight into the rationale of Hasidic dress, which in some respects is quite different from the rationale of Amish or Mennonite dress, and in other respects quite similar. Missing is the Protestant sectarian (Puritan and Anabaptist) insistence on "plainness," but present are the same ideas of costume-reinforcing-morality, costume-shielding-from-temptation. More about this later.

The outward elements of Hasidic dress, like the outward elements of

Amish or Mennonite, or European peasant dress, can be traced historically to general fashion sources in earlier historic eras. Even the *shtreimel,* now identified with Hasidic Judaism, was once a generally worn Russian and Polish type of headgear. It originated in the East, and with the kaftan replaced Byzantine costume in Russia in the late Middle Ages, and in the sixteenth century diffused to Poland where it became the national costume.[3] "Frozen" into Hasidic dress in the eighteenth century, it has continued to the twentieth century and is still observable in the Hasidic settlements of the United States.

Roman Catholic Religious Costume

Catholicism has fewer such elements, and these are found, except for such things as the "first communion" dress and parochial school jumpers, only within the monastic orders and congregations. The Catholic monk or nun does not of course wear a "folk" costume. His costume is not so much traditional as it is a rigidly prescribed uniform, in some cases dating from the Middle Ages. But in costume history, monastic costume has often been related to or adapted from the folk or general costume of earlier periods. One such example from the United States is the costume of Mother Seton's congregation, the Sisters of Charity, founded in 1809, which rather faithfully reproduces the common elements of the average American woman's dress of that period—translated into monastic (or Victorian?) black—long skirt and blouse, black shoulder shawl, black chip bonnet, and amazingly enough, the black apron—in this case worn, as is the case with Mennonites and other Protestant "plain" sects, as part of the public dress. In fact the whole costume looks so similar to the more conservative versions of Pennsylvania German "plain" dress that once in Europe I temporarily mistook two nuns of Mother Seton's congregation for Conservative Mennonites. We laughed when they told me that they *were* from Pennsylvania, and that the mistake had happened to them many times before.

Actually there are several branches of Mother Seton's original congregation, which was an American version of the French Sisters of Charity founded by St. Vincent de Paul in 1633. In the United States the two main branches are known—or, as one has to say in this age, when traditional monastic habits are so rapidly being reformed—*were* known as the "Black Cap Sisters" and the "White Cap Sisters."[4] The former, now represented in such branches as that at Greensburg, Pennsylvania, and at Mount St. Vincent-on-Hudson, wore the black habit, the mourning dress of Mother Seton herself, consisting of "a black dress with a shoulder cape, set off by a simple white cap which tied under the chin."[5] There were two additional elements in this habit—the black bonnet which went over the white cap, and a black apron—not a work apron but the apron that was once part of the European and American woman's public dress. Despite the fact that some sources call this original costume an "Italian mourning dress," it is obviously a pre-Civil War ensemble representing, in black, the common elements of European and American women's costume in the era of the bonnet, cape, and apron, a costume which—like the Mennonite costume so similar to it—was "frozen" in time to become the habit of the congregation.

The "White Cap" Sisters are distinguished by the French "cornette" headdress which was part of the original costume of St. Vincent de Paul's Sisters of Charity. Actually this habit "is that of peasant women of the neighborhood of Paris at the date of the foundation, a grey habit with wide sleeves and a long grey apron. The head-dress was at first a small linen cap, but to this was added in the early days the white linen cornette."[6] It was this "cornette" costume which the sisters of the mother house of Mother Seton's congregation, that at Emmittsburg, Maryland, adopted in 1850, while several of the other branches (listed above) continued the "black cap" habit into the twentieth century.

In this age of Catholic renewal, when activist elements are winning out over the strictly contemplative elements, monastic costume is being radically questioned and in many cases reforms have resulted.[7] Outward identification as a religious by means of such exterior elements as costume is no longer seen as important to the dedicated monk, friar, or nun. As one recent Catholic voice has put it, it becomes increasingly difficult for contemporary Catholic sisters to see how "dressing like a European peasant woman of the seventeenth century or a widow of the nineteenth century is intrinsically connected with the fulfillment of the Christian vocation of a religious"[8]

This is essentially the same reasoning through which American Quakers (with the exception of a small sect called Conservative Friends) have finally given up all plain costume. The bonnets and broadbrims have gone into the attics, and today Quakers dress like their non-Quaker neighbors. Like the Catholic sister wrestling with the problem of outward and inward witness, they have not given up the ideals which led to the "plainness" in the earlier stages of Quakerism. In the case of their belief in the equality of man—which they tried to express outwardly in uniform costume—they have simply translated it into contemporary forms, as for example, the civil rights movement. The silent symbol of human equality may have worked in the nineteenth century, but in the twentieth century Quakers, like most religious groups, are finding that direct action serves the present crisis better.

Sectarian Costumes in Protestantism

Within Protestant sectarianism, costume research has the widest area for expansion. At one end of the Protestant denominational spectrum there are two types of organization, both classical sectarian approaches which in some degree or other "flee the world." There are, first of all, the communitarian groups, the nearest Protestant equivalent to the monastic order. America from the seventeenth to the nineteenth centuries was sprinkled with utopian or millenarian experiments, which set up closed communities apart from the "world." For most of these, geographic isolation from the world was strengthened by symbolic isolation through costume. Examples range from Plockhoy's Delaware community of the 1660s through the Shakers. Many of these communities wore identifiable costumes as outward badges of group identity.[9]

The largest number of American sectarian groups, however, are the sectarians proper, who live "in" the world without conforming to the world's ways. These sects in America are the product of the European Anabaptist, Pietist, Puritan, and Evangelical movements, all of which drew lines of demarcation between proper sect behavior and the worldly life beyond. As determined and defined by Weber, Troeltsch, Niebuhr, and other scholars, the sect is a small, voluntary, exclusive group opposing both the state and the state church (as in the case of the Anabaptists), or attempting to transform both (as in the case of Puritans and Evangelicals).[10] At any rate, these groups, for various reasons, produced the costume sects of Protestantism, which today provide the student with the most striking examples of sectarian costume in the United States. Let us look at some of the problems the scholar faces when he studies these American sectarian costumes.

American Quakerism was once the best known as well as the most widely spread "plain" Protestant sect, recognized everywhere for its outward costume. "Quaker bonnets," "Quaker caps," "Quaker broadbrims," and Quaker greys and browns were identifiable in the nineteenth century from Maine to the Carolinas and from Pennsylvania westward to Kansas and northward to Ontario.[11] Quaker "plainness" was of course derived from Puritan plainness, and for a time also other sects which were tinged with the Puritan ethos, like Baptists and Methodists, were almost as "plain" as the Quakers.[12] Quaker plainness existed for many reasons—some positive, some negative—positively to express Quaker ideals such as equality and humility, negatively to express Quaker quietism and symbolize the Quaker's partial flight from the "world," never as complete as the Anabaptist retreat from the world, its politics, and its culture.[13] As we have said, Quakerism in the twentieth century opted for activism in place of the older

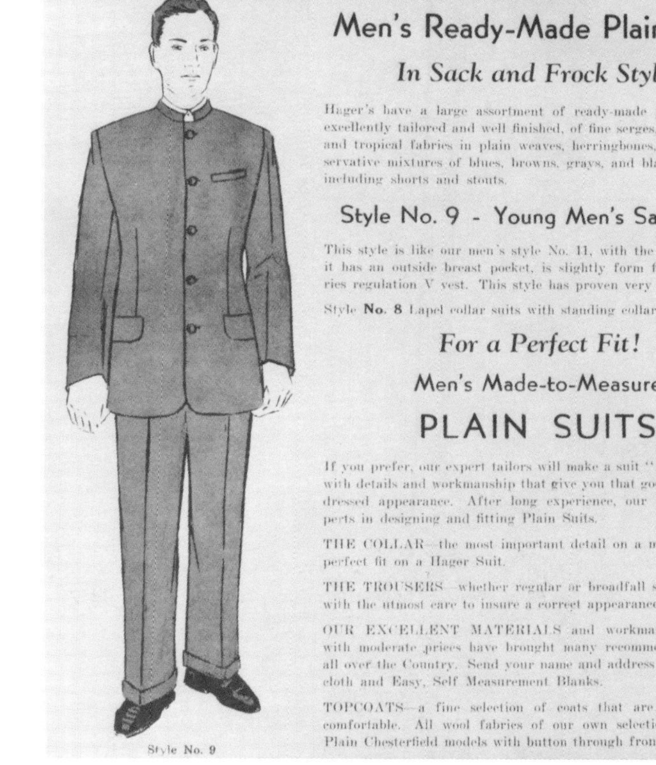

Figure 6.1. Advertisement for "plain suits," Hager's Department Store, Lancaster, Pennsylvania, from the 1950s. The plain clothes department of the store catered to the local sectarian population—Mennonites and Brethren in particular—at least those who were willing to purchase ready-made plain outfits rather than depending on the community seamstresses and tailors. *(Courtesy Roughwood Collection)*

quietism, and found outward costume elements unnecessary for the Quaker witness. Today, therefore, "plain" Quakerism is available for analysis only through historical documentation and in the memories of older Friends who still recall the "plain Friends" of the pre-World War I era—except for one small Quaker sect, the Conservative Friends of the Midwest, with headquarters at Barnesville, Ohio, a rapidly decreasing number of whom still wear the nineteenth-century bonnets, shawls, and long dresses.

In recent decades the incidence of plain dress among Conservative Friends in Ohio has rapidly declined. I am indebted to William P. Taber, Jr., Rural Route 1, Barnesville, Ohio, for the following statement on the subject, in a letter dated August 29, 1968, at the time of the Conservative Friends Yearly Meeting:

> It is now rare to see more than three bonnets at a local conservative meeting—and there are several meetings where no resident member wears one. By and large, dress styles, colors, and patterns—especially for older women—are more conservative and simple than would be found in the general population. Here and there an older man wears a plain hat, black suit, and no tie. Some of these men now wear summer weight and light colored suits in the summer, but still without a tie. Otherwise our men dress formally and informally much like the general population, except that middle-aged and older men are careful to avoid extremes in color and style. As one might expect, almost all people who wear some form of plain dress are over sixty years old, though there are a few exceptions.

A postscript to the letter adds this extremely important statistical statement: "My wife and I just counted that 12 women and 10 men in the membership of our yearly meeting (856 last year) wear 'plain dress.'" An article on the Conservative Friends Yearly Meeting sessions for 1968, in the *Barnesville Enterprise,* August 29, 1968, notes that "the old broadbrim hats of the men and Quaker bonnets on the women were almost missing this year, but mini-skirts, although not in evidence, were not overlooked." One of the "plain" members attending the yearly meeting, in broadbrim hat and full beard, "expressed concern over the trend to the mini-skirt," and added, "Modesty is still a Christian virtue although it has gone out of style."[14]

The largest and most spectacular area in the United States where Protestant sectarian costume can still be observed covers the so-called Pennsylvania Dutch or Pennsylvania German Country of Southeastern, Central, and Western Pennsylvania, plus the areas settled by the Pennsylvania Dutch Diaspora—Western Maryland, the Shenandoah Valley of Virginia, the Kitchener-Waterloo sector and other areas of Ontario, and large settlements of the Midwest, as for example, Holmes County, Ohio, Goshen and Elkhart

Counties, Indiana, and Johnson County, Iowa. In all of these areas Pennsylvania Dutch plain sects (Mennonites, Amish, Brethren, and others) have settled.[15]

The Pennsylvania German "plain" sects form a distinct subculture within the larger Pennsylvania German culture which was originally dominated by the continental churches, Lutheran and Reformed.[16] Today, through cultural lag, the "plain" Pennsylvanian is preserving many elements of the wider Pennsylvania German culture once generally practiced—as for instance horse and buggy transportation, general rather than specialized farming, and such highly Pennsylvanian aspects of material culture as the outdoor bakeoven. With his archaism, symbolized in his striking costume and flowing beard, the Old Order Amishman has strangely enough become the symbol of Pennsylvania, so that the tourist no longer thinks of the "Quaker State" but rather of the "Amish State."

This identification of "Amish" with "Pennsylvania" has led to some unfortunate simplifications which confuse even Pennsylvanians at times, although the tourist is quite happy with them, as he is with the "hex signs" and the "seven sweets and seven sours" and the "blue gate" and the other myths of the Dutch Country.[17] The scholar, who unfortunately cannot live on myth alone, points out that there is not one but several "Old Order" Amish groups, each with a separate and identifiable costume.

C. Henry Smith, in *The Story of the Mennonites,* gives us a good idea of the diversification among the Amish, taking one settlement, the Big Valley (Kishacoquillas Valley) of Mifflin County in Central Pennsylvania, as an example:

> There are seven grades of Amish in this beautiful valley, including the Amish Mennonites; and five of these at least might be classed as Old Order with beard, long hair, hooks and eyes, and without meeting houses. They range in order on the basis of conservative practice all the way from the *Nebraskas,* who observe all the usual taboos of the Amish, and besides are distinguished by white shirts, and white dearborns, hair falling to the shoulders, no suspenders, the old fashioned homemade shaker hat tied under the chin for women, and whose chief dish at the Sunday dinners given after the services by the host is bean soup; through the *Old School* who may wear colored shirts, with hair a bit shorter than the above, driving yellow topped dearborns, and whose women wear small bonnets; then the *Yost Yoder* church whose members may cut their hair to the tip of the ear, are permitted one suspender if non-elastic, and no bean soup at the common Sunday dinner, a stipulation however, that may have no religious significance; then fourth, the *Peachey* church, a little more liberal still, which permits hair cut as far as the middle of the ear, dearborns black or brown, and women permitted to wear the pasteboard or "slat" bonnet; and so on through several other advancing grades until we reach the *Amish-Mennonites,* who have meeting houses, and, with the exception of hats for the women and musical instruments in worship, have no objection to modern forms of dress or up to date conveniences. Each of these groups believes its own brand the best.

Figure 6.2. Anabaptist couple pictured selling milk in Basel, Switzerland. They are wearing typical Swiss peasant costumes, which formed the basis for some of Pennsylvania's plain sectarian ensembles of the nineteenth century. This hand-colored print was published in Basel in 1815.
(Courtesy Roughwood Collection)

And each group, says one who grew up in a Big Valley Amish family, "looks at the church above with suspicion, and the church below with compassion."[18]

In addition to the "Old Order" Amish costumes there is the distinct costume of the "Church Amish" or "Beachy Amish" who have meeting-houses, trim their beards, and drive automobiles. There is also a Mennonite costume family, with several sub-sects each with an identifiable costume—"Old" Mennonite, "New" Mennonite, and "Old Order" Mennonite.[19] And there is a Brethren or "Dunkard" family of sects, each with identifiable costumes, including the conservative congregations of the Church of the Brethren itself, and such sub-sects as the German Baptist Brethren. Finally, there are the River Brethren, whose Old Order wear a distinct costume. Each of these can be distinguished from the others—although I admit it takes years of practice.

In addition to the Pennsylvania German plain sects, who today form the largest bloc of practicing costume sects in the United States and Canada, there is in the western provinces of Canada and the adjoining states of the United States a group called the Hutterites, a communitarian group stemming like the Mennonites from the sixteenth-century Anabaptist Reformation. They originated in the Tyrol, and spread to Czechoslovakia and Russia, whence they came to Canada in the 1870s. They wear a peasant-type costume which expresses both humility and equality.[20]

In the Mormon world of Utah and adjoining states there are some comparable aspects of religious costume. First there are the "temple garments," or "garments" as they are familiarly called, worn by practicing Mormons as both a sign and reminder of devotion to the Mormon faith—like the *shtreimel* among the Hasidic Jews. The following analysis of the Mormon garments is from the pen of a Mormon correspondent of mine, whom I am happy to thank anonymously for his careful description. Religious dress is always a delicate matter to discuss, no matter what group one is dealing with,[21] and we appreciate the frank yet sympathetic description we are given here:

> As you no doubt know, members of the faith who by philosophic and behavior pattern are accepted as "worthy" are permitted to enter one of the temples and receive their "endowments," which are certain sacred rites or ordinances which lead toward acceptance in the Celestial Glory of God's kingdom. At this time they receive the "garment" that is worn the remainder of one's life if one is faithful and true to the covenants made in the temple ceremony. The garment is underwear of the union suit variety. It originally had long sleeves to the wrist and long legs to the ankle. It has been altered since to meet social demands. The wearing of the garment is deeply founded in religious symbolism. The garment becomes sacred in that symbolism because of certain markings and is worn by both men and women (different cuts and styles of course) with the markings.

> Vows to secrecy in the temple as to the meanings involved are faithfully kept by nearly everyone. Four specific and different types of marks are on each garment: one at each nipple, one at the navel and one on the right knee (this latter has gradually crept up, especially on women). If your students of religious costume and symbolism want to examine the garments, they could call an LDS Church official in your vicinity and ask for information on where the Temple garments are dispensed and then go there and examine them. There would be a dispensary in Philadelphia.
>
> As one goes through the Temple ceremony, he wears special robes as well as the under garments. The style, symbolism and religious significance of these garments are also held sacred and revealed only by those who are more unfaithful than I. Again try anti-Mormon writings. The student reading these sources, however, should be aware of the prejudice of the writer and that he may poke fun at what to the faithful person is meaningful, beautiful and sacred in its religious symbolism.
>
> Any student of this area of folklife might do well to look through the many volumed set of *Brigham Young's Discourses*, and read everything he has to say about temples and temple work, the temple endowment, and work for the dead. Brigham Young gives more specific information in this area than most loyal Mormon writers.

Since the Mormon "garments" are not visible to the outside world, but are worn under outer clothing, they resemble some of the Roman Catholic "scapulars," and have in their usage perhaps even more of a suggestion of asceticism than the more common sectarian costumes which are worn outside for all the world to see.

On the fringes of the Mormon world there is also the small offshoot group known officially as the "Order of Aaron," and unofficially as "Levites," founded by the ex-Mormon Dr. Maurice Lerrie Glendenning.[22] He joined the Latter-Day Saints at Provo, Utah, in 1929, but after claiming to receive revelations through the Angel Elias, he was condemned by the Mormons in 1931. In 1938, in Utah, according to the terminology of the group, he "restored the Keys of the Aaronic Priesthood" and in 1943 incorporated his following as the "Order of Aaron." In 1948 the organization became one of America's costume sects when the women of the order adopted a uniform garb—"as an outward evidence of their inward desire to be one in all things." The garb consists of a blue jumper, white blouse, and a religious cap or "covering" similar to the Mennonite covering except for a raised crescent from side to side over the top of the crown, lettered with the word "AARON." According to the historian of the group, "a notable distinguishing feature of the dress is the line of blue-grey fringe on a blue ribbon worn over the heart in obedience to the commandment found in Numbers 15:37–40." In 1952 a white dress of the same pattern was prescribed for the widows of the Order.

The motivation for uniform dress appears not only to have been to promote group solidarity, but also positively to symbolize the group's Puritan-like desire for plainness.

Figure 6.3. Three Alsatian women in regional costume, 1870s. This photograph shows the similarity of European peasant costume to American "plain" religious costumes, except for the unusual, distinctively Alsatian, headdress. *(Courtesy Roughwood Collection)*

Figure 6.4. Three generations, ca. 1900. The Mennonite grandmother is dressed in the extreme plain costume; the daughter and granddaughter wear worldly dress. *(Courtesy Roughwood Collection)*

> Though subtle in nature, the wearing of the uniform dress did much to dim the vanity, show, and false aura of pride in dress common to women. They were all dressed alike, and there was no occasion for vain comparison, no matter how seemingly unconscious such comparisons may have been before wearing the uniform dress. Once rid of these blinding shackles, their eyes were open to see the true beauty of the soul of their sister companions.

The sources of the plainness of the Order of Aaron can be traced to Glendenning's *Book of Elias,* which is a record of the revelations he claims to have received from the Angel Elias. According to Glendenning, the revelations "were spoken by an unseen personage to the writer in a voice with a slight accent, as audible as if two people were conversing together." A revelation of 1930, "Unto the Daughters of Zion," inveighs against style, with the strong words, "You are drunken with the wine of fashion. . . ." Another dated 1944 deals with "The House of Aaron and the Garments of Ephraim." But Glendenning, who called himself the Servant, also was an admirer of the Hutterites, whom he visited as "brothers," and in the official history of the movement a curious chapter entitled "Levitical Shadows in the Middle Ages" points proudly to Wycliffe, the Waldensians, and the Mennonites as pre-Aaronic Order examples.[23] It appears, then, that the group adopted plain dress for much the same reasons as the Quakers and Mennonites.

The Rationale of Protestant Plainness

We are interested, of course, in why certain Protestant sects persist in remaining "plain" in the twentieth century. If one seeks the rationale of plain dress within the Pennsylvania German sectarian population, one gets several answers. For instance, if you ask a "plain" Mennonite woman why she wears the little white net cap while at work and at meeting and indeed everywhere in public, she will cite the Bible, St. Paul, I Corinthians 11:2–16: "Women must keep their heads covered when praying and prophesying," the same verse that traditionalists in other Protestant churches (or Catholics) may cite for the explanation of why women "wear hats in church." Mennonites are biblicists, seeking the source of their life in the Bible and attempting to draw all of their practices from Bible sanctions. Like other "restorationist" groups within Protestantism, they have attempted to "restore" the apostolic church. This is of course an ingroup rationalization for wearing the "prayer covering" or "prayer veiling,"[24] as contemporary Mennonites now call the "cap." Such a reason makes no attempt to relate the present use of the cap to costume history, or costume origin—that is not its purpose.

If the Bible command explanation is one common ingroup explanation, the identification theory is another. I once asked a member of one of the smaller plain sects in Pennsylvania, the Old Order River Brethren,[25] who wear a distinct costume by which (after years of practice) one can tell that a person is a member of that sect, why they wore the plain dress. Her answer was (with a Dutch accent): "So that we can know our own," meaning of course that wherever she was she could always recognize a fellow sectarian by the costume. This would be one of the tangential reasons also for the differing costumes of the Catholic orders and congregations, as well as for the peasant costumes of Europe—they are "uniforms" or symbols of group identity. This offers a partial explanation for the uniformity of dress within the sect, and the development of identifiable sectarian "badge" costumes. They are "uniforms" or symbols of group identity.

The Hasidic Jews, Solomon Poll found in his intensive study of the Williamsburg community, also found "Hasidic garments" "essential for group identification but not identification as 'Europeans,' which could have had the effect of reducing their status in the community into which they had immigrated." On the reason for wearing the full Hasidic uniform, one Hasid said: "One can, I gladly concede, be just as Orthodox and know more Gemorah, without them [the articles of clothing]. Yet the genuine type of independent Jewish life, proud of its traditions and customs, needs them as a safeguard for the future. Any form of compromise is dangerous because it breaches the inner discipline." But not only is such costume considered important for group identification, and as a symbol of one's total adherence to the Jewish tradition, it also, as another Hasid expressed it, shields the wearer from temptation: "With my appearance I cannot attend a theater or movie or any other places where a religious Jew is not supposed to go. Thus, my beard and my sidelocks and my Hasidic clothing serve as a guard and shield from sin and obscenity."[26]

Likewise, American Quakers, who basically understood their wearing of plain costume as a symbol of their testimony in favor of human equality, also expressed the ingroup "shield" or "hedge" theory of plain costume. Plainness is to be, the Baltimore Discipline put it, "as a hedge about us, which, though it does not make the ground enclosed rich and fruitful, yet it frequently prevents those intrusions by which the labor of the husbandman is injured or destroyed."[27]

Another ingroup statement on plain dress relates to what the historians of European peasant costume have written about peasant rural practicality in the selection of just which parts of fashionable dress the farmer chooses to wear.[28] The plainest of Plain Pennsylvanian sectarians wear no ties. One sees them on the streets of the neighboring cities (Lancaster, Pennsylvania, or Kitchener, Ontario, or Elkhart, Indiana, for examples) wearing dress suits and white shirts, but no tie. They haven't forgotten ties, they just do not

Figure 6.5. American Quaker costume. This print, from a volume of poetry by the Pennsylvania poet Bayard Taylor, is an accurate portrayal of the dress of Quaker women in the 1870s, with shawls (instead of coats), caps, and bonnets. *(Courtesy Roughwood Collection)*

Figure 6.6. Fashionable costume of the 1840s, from a Paris fashion plate. Note the similarity to the plainer version of it in the Quaker costume, complete to the bonnets and shawl. *(Courtesy Roughwood Collection)*

believe in wearing them. There is a plain proverb which expresses this selectivity in regard to neckwear: "A tie is neither for hot nor cold—it won't keep you warm in winter, or cool in the summer." Hence why wear it? A similar proverb which used to circulate among the plain sects suggests that "fashion is never too hot or too cold," that is, the fashion-oriented person will wear anything to be in style, despite the physical discomfort it may cause. The plain sects with their practical spirit attempt to avoid blind conformity to changing styles and fashion.

Theories of the Origin of "Plain" Costume

When we turn to objective historical research on the historical origins of the present plain costumes of the Mennonite, Amish, and Brethren groups in the North American areas of settlement, three principal theories have been offered, the survival theory, the borrowing theory, and the crisis theory.

1. The survival theory is found in two forms, the earlier regarding the costumes as essentially European sectarian costumes which were brought to America by the emigrants and simply continued here. This is a popular theory which used to come to the surface even in Quaker costume pageants which had William Penn dressed in nineteenth-century Quaker costume, or early seventeenth-century emigrant Quakeresses peering out of nineteenth-century bonnets. This theory does not take into account the general fluidity and change which is apparent in all folk costume as well as sectarian costume. Because the costumes stand out today as radically different from the dress of the average "worldly" American, they were considered to have always been different, and therefore essentially European transplants.

The danger in this version of the survival theory is that it blinds the person who holds it to the easily attestable fact that very few plain costumes have had an actual duration of more than a century—four generations. What we call the "Quaker costume" is essentially a nineteenth-century ensemble—from the same period as the Mother Seton ensemble of bonnet, shoulder cape, long dress, and apron. The eighteenth-century Quaker woman dressed somewhat differently—the "hood" or the "flat hat" was worn instead of the nineteenth-century bonnet, and colors were different—we read in Pennsylvania Quaker inventories of "green aprons." And when we get back to the formative century of the Quaker movement, the seventeenth century, the Quaker ensemble then included, strangely enough, the "Halloween witch" pointed hat. In other words, there has been no consistent, continuing "Quaker costume" through the three centuries, but plainness has varied according to the outlook of Quakers in various times, and at least three different identifiable Quaker ensembles have developed in the three centuries.[29]

The same is undoubtedly true of the Pennsylvania German plain sects. A great deal of the tourist-level literature about the Amish supposes that they both live and dress as their ancestors did in the seventeenth century. One way in which this is often stated is that "the Amishman dresses now just as his forefathers did when they stepped off the emigrant boats in the eighteenth century." While there are some elements of Amish costume which undoubtedly link present-day American Amish dress with the dress of the European Amish forefathers—the broad-brimmed hat of the men is one such element—the Amish costume of today is just as much an American hybrid costume as was the nineteenth-century Quaker costume. That the emigrant generation of Amish did not dress as the Amishman did even in the nineteenth century is clear from the statement of the careful observer Redmond Conyngham, whose close contacts with the Amish of Lancaster County produced the following statement on Amish emigrant dress:

> The long Beards of the Men and the short petticoats of the Females just covering the knee attracted the attention of the English Settlers. The Men wore long red caps on their heads; the women had neither bonnets, hats or caps but merely a string passing around the head to keep the hair from the face. The dress both of the Female and Male was domestic [,] quite plain [and] made of a coarse material after an old fashion of their own.[30]

The second version of the survival theory, that held by scholars, is that plain dress as worn today is essentially a survival, or retention, of once-general costume elements which were continued in service to express the sect's nonconformity with the world. That is, the "plain" costume was just that, it was a "plain" version of the general costume of the times, worn without fashionable frills and decoration.[31] However, this theory does not explain why and just when the identifiable costume ensembles of the present-day plain sects came into being and why the sects insisted on their retention, i.e., the change from "plain" adjustment of general costume to rigid "plain" uniform. Or to put it more graphically, it does not explain when and why the costume ensembles were "frozen" in their present forms.

2. The borrowing theory places the German plain sects in secondary position to the Quakers, who in colonial Pennsylvania were admittedly the aristocrats, the movers and shapers of the plain world politically as well as socially. Since from the standpoint of successful adjustment to the American scene, the Quakers were in advance of the German groups, there was a natural tendency for the German sectarians to copy Quaker adjustment. This theory suggests that, since the plain sects linked arms politically with the Quakers in the colonial period, and since there are distinct similarities between such culture elements as Quaker meetinghouse patterns and the

early nineteenth-century meetinghouse styles of the German plain sects, there must also have been a borrowing of costume from Quakerism to the Pennsylvania German plain sects.[32] The "plain" bonnet, which seems to have been adopted in the American Quaker world from Britain around 1800, is one of the key exhibits in this argument,[33] as the bonnet seems to appear among the German plain sects a bit later, the country Mennonites and Dunkards holding on to the eighteenth-century "flat hat" (a predecessor of the bonnet in fashion history) for at least a generation longer than the Quakers.[34] However, this obvious similarity (striking in the case of some conservative Mennonite and Dunkard ensembles) may have come not from borrowing but from independent adjustments to the same styles of general dress. Also, this theory involves principally the women's costumes, but does not explain certain archaic portions of the ultra-conservative Old Order Amish dress, which may, after all, have been imported with the Amish sect from Europe.[35]

3. The crisis theory can be offered along with these other approaches. This is essentially the sociological theory that when a group faces crisis, from without or within, it rigidifies, stiffens its structure and doctrine, and defines or insists upon its symbolism. Certainly in mid-nineteenth century the plain sects were plagued with crisis, both from within and from without. Within, there was the tension between the "Old Order" and "Progressive" movements, which eventually split Mennonites and Dunkards and Amish into several sub-sects. From without, there was (1) the all-penetrating crisis of the Civil War and (2) the introduction—the intrusion one can say—of revivalism as a recruiting technique into the plain community from the Evangelical churches of the outside world, beginning in the South, and then spreading back to the conservative heartland of plain sectarianism, Southeastern Pennsylvania.[36]

There seems to be increasing evidence that the uniformity of plain costume was stepped up *after* the Civil War, when "becoming plain" or "going plain" was made a test of membership, thus linking (1) plainness as a symbol of rejecting the world with (2) plainness as an outward sign of the inward conversion experience. The Civil War tested and sharpened the nonconformity of the plain sects, while revivalism made a plain "uniform" a test of membership, an outward symbol of one's conversion as well as of one's devotion to sectarian ideals.

As the peasant complex of cap, cape and apron began to yield to fashionable dress in the 1870s, there was much correspondence in Mennonite and Brethren periodicals on the rationale of these costume elements. For example, in the Mennonite *Herald of Truth* for June, 1873, there appeared an article entitled "On the Covering of the Head," from the Brethren *Vindicator*:

> A bonnet or a 'kerchief, it seems, will not answer for they are worn for other purposes, and hence would not be a proper token of their subjection to their husbands. Consequently we see at once the propriety of a special covering—one that speaks for itself, that the beholder will understand as soon as he sees it, and will know for what it is worn. So the brotherhood have adopted a plain cap to constitute this covering: and by looking into history, we find that a cap has been worn in the case of marriages for a great many centuries until within the last thirty-five or forty years. A great many of our old friends remember when it was a universal practice. It no doubt became a practice from the command of the gospel, and the bride, when she united herself to her husband, wore this cap as *visible sign* of her intention of becoming a *subject to her husband.*

This is an important reference in that it tells us that the "universal practice" of wearing the cap was only a memory in the 1870s, and that "plain" sectarians were concerned to put specific *religious* meaning into the once universal peasant custom of the *Haube.*[37]

Another article on "Woman's Sphere and the Covering Question" appeared in the *Herald of Truth,* October, 1873, from the Brethren *Christian Family Companion:*

> Some understand Paul to refer only to married women; and that they should wear a covering as token of their subjection to their husbands. Who invented this theory we do not know; and why any one who can read for himself should accept it, we cannot tell.

He uses the sun and moon theory to explain the equal necessity of the sexes each in its own sphere. The author comes to several conclusions, (1) that the covering, as a token, should be "worn by the women whenever they expect to be seen," i.e., constantly; (2) unmarried women should also wear it; (3) the covering of the unmarried women should be differentiated from that of the married women; (4) the "proper covering" is a "plain cap," and finally (5) "Would not plain bonnets, such as are generally worn by our sisters, answer the purpose? Bonnets are not worn for that purpose; and we cannot see how they could answer a purpose for which they are not worn. Bonnets are worn for the same purpose that men wear hats—to protect them from the sun's heat and the inclemency of the weather."

Another example of this type of debate, in the face of costume change, comes from the Brethren or Dunkard world, in a petition to the Annual Meeting of the German Baptist Brethren in 1886:

> Inasmuch as necessity required a specification in the order of dress to be worn by the brethren, we therefore petition Annual Meeting, through District Meeting, to make the time-honored custom of wearing the plain cape or kerchief, in connection with a plain skirt dress, a specification for the order or uniform to be worn by the sisters, as many of them are departing from Gospel plainness as interpreted by our fathers and the church, thus destroying that oneness and admitting in its stead the popular fashions of a proud world.

Figure 6.7. Magdalena Maurer (1784–1876) of the Mahantongo Valley, a great great-grandmother of the author. She was a Lutheran, but her formal costume bears resemblance both to European peasant dress and to the sectarian garb of the Pennsylvania Dutch plain sects. *(Courtesy Roughwood Collection)*

Figure 6.8. Two plain couples from Lancaster County, ca. 1890. Note that the wives are wearing plain garb, while the husbands are dressed in worldly fashion. The women's plainness includes plain hairdo, cap tied under the chin, capes, aprons, and floor-length dresses. The costume of the "sister" on the left is a bit more fashionably cut than that of the sister on the right.
(Courtesy Roughwood Collection)

The Annual Meeting gave answer:

> We decide that Gospel plainness requires our sisters to attire themselves in plainly-made garments, free from ornaments, ruffles, and all unnecessary appendages, and that it is the duty of all housekeepers to see that our sisters are properly instructed concerning the necessity of this Gospel plainness, and it is also their duty to see that the order of the church, respecting plainness, is properly carried out in their respective congregations, both upon the part of the brethren as well as the sisters.[38]

The struggle to regulate sectarian dress and to give it religious meaning continued into the twentieth century. A Mennonite historian tells us that it was not until 1912 that the "Pennsylvania bonnet" was made a test of membership in the Franconia Conference—"everyone then in those congregations where the bonnet had not been worn universally had to purchase and wear a bonnet or withdraw from the fellowship of the Franconia Conference."[39]

Further research in the late nineteenth century source materials will, it appears almost certain, turn up additional evidence that the double crisis of Civil War and Revivalism fastened a "frozen" plain uniform upon both the Mennonites and the Brethren. The reactivated peasant plainness, made into a religious symbol, became the outward symbol of the inward conversion experience. Before, the Mennonites and Brethren wore "plain" versions of general dress. Now, having submitted to the pietistic conversion system of Revivalism, they wore a "frozen" plain uniform, an archaic nineteenth-century ensemble.

The crisis theory might be developed to explain the relative uniformity of plain costume among certain of the sects from about 1875 to the present day, for example, the ritual insistence on the white "cap," now dignified and sanctified with the religious term "prayer covering" or "prayer veiling" in the larger groups (Mennonites, Brethren) which came under revivalist influence. It would not explain the adherence to nineteenth-century dress synthesis of the Old Order Amish or Old Order Mennonites, neither of which has as yet submitted to nineteenth-century Evangelical Revivalism and its chain of institutions including the Sunday School, the Missionary Society, and the Youth Group. The theory does, I feel, throw a light on the vexed question of why the present-day costumes represent a nineteenth-century "plain" synthesis, a frozen or arrested ensemble of nineteenth-century style elements.

When the future American costume specialists have exhausted the study of the structure and history of the sectarian costumes, there is still a fourth viewpoint by which we can begin to understand why plain costumes are still worn in the sectarian world. This is the functional analysis which has proved so fruitful in understanding the European peasant costumes.[40] The functionalist or folk-community theory still makes most sense as explanation of why plain costumes continue in use. Firstly, the sect, as a community[41] operates similarly to the costume villages of Europe in developing and wearing a distinct and identifiable costume to identify itself both to itself and to the outside world. Secondly, the individual within the plain community (as in a folk community) wears plain costume to de-individualize himself and thus dramatize his adherence, his submission to the community. Whether rationalized, ingroup fashion, as Biblical nonconformity to the "world," or as a "hedge" or "shield" to protect the wearer, this explains sufficiently, in terms of function, all plain costume. It does not explain why particular nineteenth-century costume syntheses continue to be worn, via cultural lag, long after the time they were in general use among the general population. But then, European scholarship on peasant costume has not really come up with a completely satisfactory answer to that question either.

Notes

1. A detailed summary of European folk costume research can be found in my chapter on "Folk Costume," in Richard M. Dorson, ed., *Folklore and Folklife: An Introduction* (Chicago: University of Chicago Press, 1969).

2. Solomon Poll, *The Hasidic Community of Williamsburg* (New York: The Free Press of Glencoe, 1962). The quotations in the following paragraphs are from pp. 16–17, 60–61, 65–66, 219. For the Hasidic look in contemporary dress, see the photographs in Jerome R. Mintz, *Legends of the Hasidim: An Introduction to Hasidic Culture and Oral Tradition in the New World* (Chicago: University of Chicago Press, 1968).

3. Raphael Straus, "The 'Jewish Hat' as an Aspect of Social History," *Jewish Social Studies* 4 (1942): 59–72.

4. *The Catholic Encyclopedia,* 3:607.

5. Annabelle M. Melville, *Elizabeth Bayley Seton, 1774–1821* (New York: Charles Scribner's Sons, 1951), 151. For photographs and descriptions of the habits of the various branches of Mother Seton's congregation, see Thomas P. McCarthy, C.S.V., compiler, *Guide to the Catholic Sisterhoods in the United States* (Washington, D.C.: The Catholic University of America Press, 1955), especially p. 30 (Sisters of Charity, Seton Hill, Greensburg, Pennsylvania), and p. 45 (Sisters of Charity of St. Vincent de Paul, Mount St. Vincent-on-Hudson, New York). The habit of the former group is described as follows: "The dress is the black cap of Mother Seton with an inner white cap; a simply made black habit with a white collar and white inner sleeves; black apron and cape."

6. *The Catholic Encyclopedia,* 3:607; for the habits of Mother Seton's groups, see also Charles I. White, *Life of Mrs. Eliza A. Seton, Foundress and First Superior of the Sisters or Daughters of Charity in the United States of America* (Baltimore: John Murphy and Co., 1856), especially pp. 240, 296–97.

7. For present-day debate on continuance of monastic habits, see Gerard Huyghe, et al., *Religious Orders in the Modern World: A Symposium* (Westminster, Md.: The Newman Press, 1966), especially pp. 157–59; Thomas E. Clarke, "Religious Dress and Renewal," *America* (April 6, 1968): 417; Horton Davies, "From Penguins to Personalities," *Sisters Today* (October 1967): 41–45; Sister M. Claudelle Miller, S.C.L., "Attitudes towards Religious Garb and Its Adaptation," *Review for Religious* (May 1966): 438–46; and Sister Judith Tate, O.S.B., "Religious Habits and the Psychology of Dress," *Sisters Today* (April 1967): 276–79.

8. William P. Roberts, S.J., "The Religious Habit and Contemporary Witness," *Sisters Today* (April 1967): 273. I am indebted to Gaye Weinstock, a member of my Fall 1968 class in Folk Religion, for this quotation, from her detailed paper on "Nuns' Habits in the Post-Vatican II Era."

9. One of the best descriptions of the costume world represented by the communitarian experiments is Charles Nordhoff, *The Communistic Societies of the United States* (New York, 1875), now available in facsimile edition with the original illustrations (New York: Schocken Books, 1965). Nordhoff is particularly good on the costumes of the Amana Community, the Harmony Society, and the Shakers.

10. The most recent summary of the sectarian stance in relation to the world is the excellent chapter by A. Leland Jamison, "Religions on the Christian Perimeter," in James Ward Smith and A. Leland Jamison, eds., *The Shaping of American Religion* (Princeton, N.J.: Princeton University Press, 1961), 162–231, vol. 1, "Religion in American Life" Series.

11. The best history of Quaker dress is Amelia Mott Gummere, *The Quaker: A Study in Costume* (Philadelphia: Ferris and Leach, 1901).

12. For Methodist plainness, see John Wesley, "Advice to the People Called Methodists, with Regard to Dress," *The Works of the Rev. John Wesley, A.M.* (London, n.d.), 11: also "Sermon 93—On Dress," in *Sermons on Several Occasions* (New York: Carlton & Phillips, 1856), 2: 258–65.

13. For an extremely lucid analysis of the difference between the Anabaptist (Mennonite) and Quaker positions in regard to the "world," see Thomas G. Sanders, *Protestant Concepts of Church and State* (Garden City, N. Y.: Doubleday Anchor Books, 1965), 83–178.

14. In light of this rapid adjustment from plain dress among Conservative Friends, it seems important to suggest the undertaking of a study to interview members on why this change is coming about, half a century after Pennsylvania Quakers gave up plainness. Such a project would record much valuable Quaker data on individual and group attitudes toward dress in general and plain dress in particular.

15. For the geographical expansion of the Pennsylvania German plain sects to other areas in the United States, the authority is Emil Meynen, *Bibliography on German Settlements in Colonial North America, Especially on the Pennsylvania Germans and Their Descendants, 1683–1933* (Leipzig: Otto Harrassowitz, 1937). Several dissertations are at present in progress in the Department of Geography at the Pennsylvania State University dealing with the settlement patterns of several of the "plain" sects in Eastern Pennsylvania and elsewhere.

16. For the relation of the sub-culture to the dominant culture, see Don Yoder, "Plain Dutch and Gay Dutch: Two Worlds in the Dutch Country," *The Pennsylvania Dutchman* 8 (1) (Summer 1956): 34–55.

17. A rational approach to the tourist and journalist myths of the Dutch Country is provided in the valuable essay by Alfred L. Shoemaker, *Three Myths about the Pennsylvania Dutch Country* (Lancaster, Pa.: Pennsylvania Dutch Folklore Center, 1951).

18. C. Henry Smith, *The Story of the Mennonites* (Berne, Ind.: Mennonite Book Concern, 1941), 636–37.

19. In addition to the Amish, who are the best known of the plain groups, having captured the imagination and interest of the tourist as well as the twentieth-century scholar, Old Order Mennonites and one or two other plain groups still prohibit automobiles, continuing the pre-automobile type of horse-drawn transportation. In fact, the common dialect name for Old Order Mennonites is *Fuhr-Mennischte* or "Team Mennonites." A faction of the Old Order Mennonites in the 1920s adopted the automobile but kept conservative costume elements. The catch is that they must buy only black cars, and paint the "flashy" chrome fenders and other chrome elements black. These are known in the Lancaster County area as "Black Bumper Mennonites." For Amish and Mennonite groups, their beliefs and practices, the handiest reference work is *The Mennonite Encyclopedia*, 4 vols. (Scottdale, Pa., 1955–59).

    The Mennonite Quarterly Review, 1927 ff., also offers scholarly articles on Amish as well as Mennonite patterns of religion. See also John A. Hostetler, *Annotated Bibliography of the Amish* (Scottdale, Pa.: Mennonite Publishing House, 1951), an invaluable work which is at present being brought up to date.

20. The handiest introduction to the Hutterites is the recent anthropological study of John A. Hostetler and Gertrude Enders Huntington, *The Hutterites in North America* (New York: Holt, Rinehart & Winston, 1967), 115 pp. For additional works, see Robert Friedmann, "Recent Hutterite Studies (1965–1967)," in *The Mennonite Quarterly Review* 42 (4) (October 1968): 318–22.

21. On the problems involved in getting frank information about Hasidic dress and practices, see Poll, *Hasidic Community,* Appendix, 267–78.

22. The printed literature available on the Order of Aaron includes *The Book of Elias or The Record of John: Book of Instructions to the Aaronic Order, a Corporation of Utah, the House of Levi, and to All Who Would Be in Their Fullness before God.* Published by the Aaronic Order (Salt Lake City, Utah, 1944), 101 pp. Two histories by Blanche W. Beeston are also extremely useful: (1) *Now My Servant: A Brief Biography of a Firstborn Son of Aaron* (Caldwell, Idaho: The Caxton Printers, 1957), 216 pp.; and (2) *Purified as Gold and Silver* (Idaho Falls, Idaho, 1966), 315 pp. In addition, the Order publishes the periodical *Aaron's Star.* My thanks to Professor Jan Brunvand of the University of Utah, Salt Lake City, and to the Curator of the Western History Collection at the University of Utah, for making available information on the Order of Aaron. The quotations in the following two paragraphs are from *Now My Servant,* 137–38.

23. Blanche W. Beeston, *Purified as Gold and Silver* (Idaho Falls, Idaho, 1966), chap. 7, "Levitical Shadows in the Middle Ages," and chap. 8, "The Hutterites."

24. For the present-day Mennonite rationale on the "covering," attempting to give it religious sanction, see the following pamphlets: Richard C. Detweiler, *The Christian Woman's Head-Veiling: A Study of I Corinthians 11:2–16* (Scottdale, Pa.: Herald Press, 1959); Paul M. Miller, *The Prayer Veiling: An Expository Study of I Corinthians 11:2–16* (Scottdale, Pa.: Herald Press, 1956); and J. C. Wenger, *The Prayer Veil in Scripture and History: The New Testament Symbol of Woman as the Glory of the Race* (Scottdale, Pa.: Herald Press, 1964).

25. The River Brethren are one of the least known of the Pennsylvania German groups, and one of the most interesting from the standpoint of costume. They are divided into two main branches, the conservatives or Old Order River Brethren, also known as "Yorkers" because one of their settlements is York County, Pennsylvania; and the progressives or Brethren in Christ, who were heavily influenced by the Holiness Movement in the post-Civil War era. It is the Brethren in Christ to which the Eisenhower family belonged, as was reported in several of the campaign biographies at the time of President Eisenhower's election. For the River Brethren and offshoot groups, see A. W. Climenhaga, *History of the Brethren in Christ Church* (Nappanee, Ind.: E. V. Publishing House, 1942).

26. Poll, *Hasidic Community,* 35, 65.

27. *Rules of Discipline, and Advices of Baltimore Yearly Meeting of Friends, Held on Lombard Street* (Baltimore: John W. Woods, Printer, 1881), 99.

28. Richard Weiss points out that Swiss farmers in the twentieth century, even though they wear store-bought clothing, adapt it to their own folk-cultural ideas, omitting cuffs on the trousers as "dirt-catchers," supporting trousers with suspenders rather than the more usual belt, and wearing their hats, literally wearing them everywhere but in church and in bed (*Volkskunde der Schweiz* [Erlenbach-Zurich: Eugen Rentsch Verlag, 1946], 140, 147–48).

29. Gummere, *The Quaker,* Introduction, iii-vi.

30. Redmond Conyngham, "History of the Mennonites and Aymenists" (1830), Manuscript Collections, Historical Society of Pennsylvania; published in *Hazard's Register of Pennsylvania* 7 (1831): 128–32, 150–53.

31. Gummere, *The Quaker,* 8–9, 14–17, 20–22, 26–27.

32. See John C. Wenger, "Dress (Costume)," *The Mennonite Encyclopedia* 2:99–104; also Don Yoder, "The Costumes of the 'Plain People,'" *The Pennsylvania Dutchman* 4 (13) (March 1, 1953): 6–7, 8, 9; and "Plain Dutch and Gay Dutch: Two Worlds in the Dutch Country." One of the earliest ascriptions of Pennsylvania German plain costume to Quakerism appears in the rare Canadian novel by Clyde Smith, *The Amishman* (Toronto: William Briggs, 1912), 132 pp., the original dust jacket of which tells us that "This is the first story by a Canadian writer dealing with the trek of the Pennsylvania Germans into Ontario. It racily describes the dress, customs, and beliefs of the Amish, an interesting sect of Mennonites who are among Canada's best settlers. Incidentally the story touches upon such problems as Non-resistance, War, Bilingual Schools and the Home of the Retired Farmer." For an analysis of the contents, see Alfred L. Shoemaker, "The Amishman," *The Pennsylvania Dutchman* 5 (5) (September 1953): 2.

33. It was Gummere (*The Quaker,* 190) who first pointed out that the "technical" Quaker bonnet—called by the irreverent the "coal-scuttle" or "sugar-scoop" or "stiff-pleat" bonnet—was adopted in Pennsylvania about 1800 in imitation of the plain bonnet worn by Martha Routh (1743–1817), a Quaker minister from England visiting in America in 1798. The evidence she cites is from the Memorandum Book of Schoolmaster Ennion Cook, Birmingham, Pennsylvania: "Martha Routh, a Minister of the Gospel from Old England, was at Goshen (Pennsylvania) Meeting the 11th. day of 11th. mo. 1798; was a means (if I mistake not) of bringing bonnets in fashion for our leading Frd's, and hoods or Caps on the Cloaks in the Galleries, which of Latter time the Hoods on the Cloaks of our overseers and other active members have increased to an alarming height or size:—how unlike the dress of their grandmothers!"

34. For some new information on the use of the "flat hat" in eighteenth-century Maryland, see Julian Ursyn Niemcewicz, *Under Their Vine and Fig Tree: Travels through America in 1797–1799, 1805 with Some Further Account of Life in New Jersey,* Metchie J. E. Budka, trans. and ed. (Elizabeth, N.J.: The Grassmann Publishing Company, 1965), Collections of the New Jersey Historical Society at Newark, 15:112, fig. 48.

35. John A. Hostetler, "The Amish Use of Symbols and Their Function in Bounding the Community," *Journal of the Royal Anthropological Institute* (London) 94 (1) (1963): 11–22.

36. For the crisis that the Pennsylvania German sects faced in revivalism, see Don Yoder, *Pennsylvania Spirituals* (Lancaster, Pa.: Pennsylvania Folklife Society, 1961), 95–118; also "The Bench versus the Catechism: Revivalism and Pennsylvania's Lutheran and Reformed Churches," *Pennsylvania Folklife* 10 (2) (Fall 1959): 14–23.

37. The cap, sometimes called the "day cap" to distinguish it from its nocturnal counterpart, was in common usage among European and American women in the eighteenth and early nineteenth centuries. As late as 1850 an American household manual tells us that "day caps are worn by many married ladies, and by some also that are single" (*The American Ladies' Memorial: An Indispensable Home Book for the Wife, Mother, Daughter; In Fact, Useful to Every Lady throughout the United States* [Boston, 1850], 53 ff.). For comparative data and bibliography on the European *Haube* and related headgear, see Robert Wildhaber, *Kopfbedeckungen aus Europa* (Basel, 1963), 1–15.

38. *Revised Minutes of the Annual Meetings of the German Baptist Brethren.* Revised by D. L. Miller, D. E. Price and Daniel Hays, Committee Appointed by Annual Conference, 1898. Designed for the Use of the Churches (Mount Morris, Ill.: Brethren Publishing House, 1899), 132–33. This from the long section on "Nonconformity."

39. John Christian Wenger, *Separated unto God: A Plea for Christian Simplicity of Life and for a Scriptural Nonconformity to the World* (Scottdale, Pa.: Herald Press, 1955), 83–84.

40. The model treatment here is Mathilde Hain, *Das Lebensbild eines oberhessischen Trachtendorfes. Von bäuerlicher Tracht und Gemeinschaft* (Marburg, 1936); see also her essay which I consider the best single short introduction to folk costume research in Europe, "Die Volkstrachten," in Wolfgang Stammler, ed., *Deutsche Philologie im Aufriss,* 2d ed., vol. 3, columns 2885–2900.

41. A model study of a religious group, viewing its traditional elements folk-culturally, is Irmgard Simon, *Die Gemeinschaft der Siebenten-Tags-Adventisten in volkskundlicher Sicht* (Münster/Westfalen: Verlag Aschendorff, 1965).

7

Another Look at George Pullen Jackson

It has been almost thirty years since George Pullen Jackson's final work, *Another Sheaf of White Spirituals* (Gainesville, Florida: University of Florida Press, 1952) made its welcome appearance in the scholarly world. Since his *White Spirituals in the Southern Uplands* had appeared in 1933 he had worked constantly in the research field that he had marked out especially for his own—the religious folksongs of the American people. Three solid volumes—*Spiritual Folk-Songs of Early America* (1937), *Down East Spirituals and Others* (1939), and *White and Negro Spirituals* (1943)—and a host of articles preceded his last sheaf. As I pointed out in my introduction to the reprint edition of his first book, his life's work was a major achievement and his conclusions and theories stirred up widespread controversy and forced an almost total rewriting of the early history of America's music.[1]

Another Sheaf of White Spirituals rounded out Jackson's search by further refining his typology of spiritual folksong and his theory of tune families; by using more recorded songs as evidence of differing singing styles; by comparison of northern with southern sources in several key chapters; his addition of a map of the "receding shores" of the "inland sea of spiritual song" (p. xiii); and his greater coverage of the Middle State area (building on the work of Samuel P. Bayard and myself), which in Jackson's opinion "shows the early religious folksong scene to have had complete national unity" (p. xvii).

On its publication in 1952 the book was well received. The *United States Quarterly Book Review* referred to the author as "the Francis J. Child of the white spiritual," and Irving Lowens in the *Music Library Association*

This article originally appeared as the Foreword to a reprint of George Pullen Jackson's *Another Sheaf of White Spirituals*, No. 1 in the Series, Folklorica Publications in Folksong and Balladry, Kenneth S. Goldstein, ed. (New York and Philadelphia: Folklorica Press, 1981), i–vi.

Notes described Jackson as maintaining "his position as folk hymnody's pre-eminent authority and most eloquent exponent."[2] A review by John W. Work praised the book as revealing "the same devotion to the cause of white American folk music and the same contagious affection for his material shown in his earlier history-making volumes." However, he found it "striking" that the call-and-response chant, which Work considered "the prevailing form in the Negro spiritual—was encountered in not one of the songs in this sheaf."[3]

Charles Haywood's lengthy review in the *Journal of American Folklore* refers to the compiler as "the indefatigable George Pullen Jackson" and his compilation as a "remarkable testimony to our rich heritage of sacred folksongs."[4] Professor Haywood went over the book section by section commenting on Jackson's typology and some individual songs. Bertrand H. Bronson in *Western Folklore* concentrated largely on criticism of Jackson's tune-family typology, which was not refined enough for him. "Since neither Barry nor Bayard nor Jackson has objectified his identifications in any abstract characterizations, matters are still, obviously, in a very amorphous and amateurish stage. We can only long for the arrival of some Linnaeus to tell us what defines the Lazarus-Hallelujah-Babe of Bethlehem family, distinguishing it from other tune families."[5]

Since Jackson's death in 1953 his life work has, of course, been subject to constant revaluation. His most controversial theory, that of white-to-black influence in the spiritual, has apparently reached a draw, although the recent upswing in black studies has carried the opposite view to the extreme position. Like the historiography of other American ethnic groups in early stages of its development, when individuals within the group are forging a new sense of personal and ethnic identity, some of the anti-Jackson opinions expressed have been intemperate and one-sided. These need to be rebalanced against the total picture of acculturation in American life, through which ongoing process American culture can be seen as the product of the reaction of European and Asian immigrants, Native Americans, and Afro-Americans to each other and to the American environment. The canvas is broad indeed. I personally recommend the compromise position illustrated by Gilbert Chase, D. K. Wilgus, and H. Wiley Hitchcock.[6]

Apart from the white-to-black formula, Jackson's pioneer work on the white spiritual stands after fifty years as a monumental, creative, and necessary contribution to the understanding of what we are as Americans. The "songways" of the revival folk, as he liked to call them, are still with us in manifold ways. Like a constant refrain, the choruses, the fasola songs, and the religious ballads are still around. Proof of their vitality is seen in their inclusion in the standard hymnals of the major denominations, their adoption by sacred harp groups on our university campuses, as well as their transmutation into gospel songs, radio choruses, and songs of the Jesus generation.

In tracing the hymnological currents of the revival and camp-meeting movement in early America, from New England through the Middle States to the Upland South, Jackson presented a unified tradition in folk hymnody that is still alive and among us. But in this present day when American society is being re-ethnicized, there is a broader canvas on which to portray religious folk music in our culture. In my own seminars in American Religious Folk Music, for example, I include not only the "spiritual" in the received sense of the word ("white" and/or "black"), but Anabaptist (Mennonite, Amish, Brethren) hymnody, Shaker dances and chants, Mormon religious song, Doukhobor psalmody, Hasidic and other traditional Jewish music, Quaker singsong preaching, the chants of the Hari Krishnas and other oriental syncretistic cults in our midst. The canvas is as broad in fact as the religious map of America. The recording possibilities for creative fieldwork—which Jackson, who worked mostly from songbooks, relatively neglected—are immense and of the highest scholarly priority. For as has been found with dialect and folklore in general, the periphery of a national culture formed by emigrant groups in another context across the ocean often preserves earlier forms of religious folksong which may no longer be in circulation in the homeland.

Not only are older traditional forms of hymnody abundantly alive among us, but the evolution of religious folksong continues apace in the United States. The evangelical and fundamentalist progeny of the camp-meeting revivalists are today producing new songs for new contexts. We see a steady cranking out of commercialized gospel productions, radio choruses, child evangelism jingles, and now the songs of the Jesus People. Paul Baker's book, *Why Should the Devil Have All the Good Music? Jesus Music—Where It Began, Where It Is, and Where It Is Going* (Waco, Texas: Word Books, 1979), with "Prelude" by Pat Boone and Foreword by Larry Norman, gives elaborate lineage charts of Gospel Music from Appalachian Folk and Spirituals, through Country and Western, to Southern Gospel and eventually to the Jesus Music. We learn of Jesus Festivals, Love Song Festivals at Knott's Berry Farm, Jesus Rock Concerts, and the event known as the "Christian Hootenanny." The keynote song appears to be Larry Norman's "I feel good every day 'cause Jesus is the rock and he rolled my blues away." Despite the contemporary style one nevertheless feels the pull of the earlier tradition.

In recent years even Roman Catholicism has been swept into the folk music camp. In the freer ecclesiastical atmosphere following Vatican II, new hymns have been written, some of them in folk idioms, and folk masses have made their appearance in some churches. Among the highly critical treatments of this movement was that of Father Richard Wojcik, Director of Music of St. Mary of the Lake Seminary in the Archdiocese of Chicago. Although he credited the introduction of folk music into church liturgy with giving many people "the first inkling they have had that the liturgy could be truly exciting, truly expressive, truly involving," he maintained that "most of the folk music in use today is inappropriate for weekly use." Its popularity reflects the generation gap. "The young people 'dig' it; the older people, for the most part, either tolerate or abhor it," was his conclusion.[7]

Somewhat earlier a Texan bishop had banned such innovations in the Dallas-Ft. Worth diocese. "The use of guitars, drums and other percussion instruments commonly associated with secular music," he ruled, "is strictly forbidden during all religious services." "Spirituals and similar songs, including popular hit tunes, religious parodies on folk tunes, jazz and the like do not conform to the requirements for liturgical music laid down in recent official documents, and hence will not be tolerated."[8] One wonders what George Pullen Jackson would have said to this, or indeed those medieval hymnists and experts in contrafaction who fashioned new spiritual songs out of the popular tunes of their day.[9]

If the field of spiritual song is continuing to expand, the scholarly study of it is also expanding. Following Jackson's last sheaf, other scholars have both deepened and widened the field of American folk hymnody. In the study of the hymnody of the Upland South, Jackson's successor appears to be Richard H. Hulan, whose solid work on the Disciples-Christian hymn traditions and on the Methodist camp-meeting poet John Adam Granade (1763–1807) have enlarged Jackson's canvas considerably.[10] The excellent theoretical analysis of the camp-meeting songs by Dickson D. Bruce, Jr., *And They All Sang Hallelujah: Plain-Folk Camp-Meeting Religion, 1800–1845* (Knoxville: The University of Tennessee Press, 1974), gives anthropological depth to the meaning both of the conversion experience and the camp-meeting spiritual, with original conclusions on the function of the chorus in relation to text. Daniel W. Patterson's beautifully researched work on Shaker music, *The Shaker Spiritual* (Princeton, N.J.: Princeton University Press, 1979), can serve as a model for historical treatment of the folk-hymnodic expression of any American ethnic group or sectarian movement. On Mormon songs, the work of Austin E. and Alta S. Fife[11] and Thomas E. Cheney[12] is also exemplary. And finally, my own work, *Pennsylvania Spirituals* (Lancaster, Pa.: Pennsylvania Folklife Society, 1961) was aided in its preliminary stages by the support and encouragement of Dr. Jackson, who transcribed many of the tunes I recorded in the Pennsylvania German valleys of Eastern Pennsylvania, and commented on them. My correspondence with Dr. Jackson on these subjects as well as his transcriptions of the tunes are now part of the Don Yoder Collection of American Hymnody at the University of North Carolina.[13]

Several symposia on folk hymnody have been called in recent years, to expand and criticize Jackson's work. The first major symposium was that projected and chaired by William H. Tallmadge, then of the State University College at Buffalo, at the annual session of the American Folklore Society at Atlanta in 1969. It included the following papers: Joe Dan Boyd, "Judge Jackson: Black Giant of the 'White Spirituals'"; William H. Tallmadge, "The Baptist Lining-Hymn: An Unexplored Area of Study"; Philip H. Kennedy, "One Half Century of the *Christian Harmony* and Harmony, N.C. Camp Hill Sings"; Hilda Adam Kring, "The Hymns of the Harmonists"; Alan Buechner, "The Origins of Contrapuntal Style in Three Voice Shape-Note Hymns"; and Don Yoder, "European Analogues to American Spirituals."

A more extensive gathering of scholars was the Symposium on Rural Hymnody held at Berea College, Berea, Kentucky, April 27–29, 1979. The sessions were supported by the National Endowment for the Humanities and planned by a committee composed of Daniel W. Patterson, Archie Green, William H. Tallmadge, and Loyal Jones. The program included the following papers: Nicholas Temperley, "The Old Way of Singing: Its Origins and Development"; Terry Miller, "Thoughts on the Growth of the Old Baptist Song Repertory"; Jeff Todd Titon, "Hymnody of the Fellowship Independent Baptist Church of Stanley, Virginia"; Arthur F. Schrader, "Songs in Vogue with the Vulgar"; Doris Dyen, "Black Shape-Note Singing in Southern Alabama"; Alan Buechner, "Joshua Leavitt's *Christian Lyre* and Other Developments of Revival Hymnody in the North"; Dorothy D. Horn, "Jackson's White and Negro Spirituals: Thirty-Six Years Later"; Portia K. Maultsby, "Black Spirituals: A Manifestation of the Black Aesthetic Concept"; William H. Tallmadge, "The Black in Jackson's White Spirituals"; James C. Downey, "The White and/or Black Spiritual and Rural Revivalist Religion: A Study of Origins"; Richard H. Hulan, "Wyeth's Wellsprings"; and Harlan Daniel, "Peripheral American Hymnody: A View of History from the Back of the Brush Arbor." The symposium included performances and demonstrations of lining-out and spiritual singing by various groups, and visits to local spiritual-singing congregations.

The discological deposit of Jackson's spiritual repertory also continues to grow. Following the pioneer Library of Congress recording by John and Alan Lomax of Sacred Harp Singing, for which Jackson made the arrangements and wrote the commentary, hundreds of disks of religious folk music have been published. Music from the South abounds, with Sacred Harp Singings, Old Harp Singings, Harmonia Sacra Singings, Southern Journeys, Southern Folk Heritage, to cite a few album titles. Black Gospel from the Urban North, Spanish Religious Songs and Dances from the Southwest,

Cajun Religious Songs, Songs from the Iroquois Longhouse, Jewish Liturgical Music, Mormon and Doukhobor and Shaker tunes—all are (or were) on the record racks thanks to the increasing taste for religious folk music sparked by the work of George Pullen Jackson. Ethnographic films featuring religious folk music are also increasingly available. For one example, the work of William Ferris of the University of Mississippi, whose Center for Southern Folklore has produced two such exemplary contributions, "Delta Religion" and "Fanny Bell Chapman: Gospel Singer."

A few suggestions for further research may be in order here. The major need is fieldwork, to record examples of every genre of religious folksong and every singing style in every American ethnic and sectarian group. Continued analysis and dissemination of selections from earlier commercial disk recordings of spiritual and gospel traditions are needed as well. This can add historical depth, providing sounds and singing styles from the recorded past. An excellent commentary on this procedure in folk hymnodic scholarship is offered in Archie Green's article, "Hear These Beautiful Sacred Selections," in the *1970 Yearbook of the International Folk Music Council,* edited by Alexander L. Ringer (Urbana: University of Illinois Press, 1971), pp. 28–50. This concentrates on the "beautiful sacred selections" issued by the Okeh Record Company in the 1920s, discusses the relation of George Pullen Jackson to field recording scholarship, and ends with the call: "Disk collectors, church historians, record-company executives, and folklorists have a collective responsibility not only to continue, but to extend George Pullen Jackson's work into the talking-machine land where he strayed, but did not tarry."

Another research need is the examination of the relation of the religious folksong to the chanted sermon of the revival groups. Indeed, the entire context of the worship service of revivalism, with the theory of worship it involves, deserves more attention. The work of such scholars as Bruce Rosenberg, Jeff T. Titon, and Servalia Levels can be expanded here into other religious groups. And finally, even though the spirituals as we know them today grew up in an American matrix, more work now needs to be done on European (as well as African) backgrounds and analogues. The European spiritual song—*geistliches Lied, chanson spirituelle* and other terms—needs attention from American scholars both in its lengthy history and development, and in its oral and broadside dissemination. The printed evidence of both Catholic and Protestant spiritual song from Europe, in broadside and chapbook form, is immense and deserves wider acquaintance in American scholarship.

In conclusion, George Pullen Jackson was and remains the principal discoverer and analyst of the white spiritual. His sociological insights into the longstanding conflict between fasola folk and urban elite with their robed choirs and literary hymns, the conflict between the spiritual and the literary hymn, revealed a cleavage in American Protestantism which still plagues most denominations. In its wider context it involves country versus city, individualist conservative revivalism versus social gospel, isolationism versus interdependency in culture and politics. Louis F. Benson, whose history of Christian hymnody was the best treatment before Jackson's work illuminated the area of folk hymnody, also saw the two forces in dialectic opposition to one another.

> The movement to elevate the literary and musical tone of church worship leaves indifferent a large class both in and beyond the Church whose taste is for light music and emotional verse. It thus invites, and, in the opinion of many earnest Christian workers, justifies a counter-movement to reach that element upon the plane of their own taste and accomplishment. Hence the Evangelistic Hymn, the Camp Meeting and Revival Song, and in our own day the Gospel Hymn.[14]

Isaac Watts, whose textual influence on the American spiritual tradition is profound, said it differently and perhaps more sympathetically: "Strange that a harp of a thousand strings should keep in tune so long."

Notes

1. "George Pullen Jackson (1874–1953)," in George Pullen Jackson, *White Spirituals in the Southern Uplands: The Story of the Fasola Folk, Their Songs, Singings, and "Buckwheat Notes"* (Hatboro, Pa.: Folklore Associates, 1964), i-xv.
2. Mertice M. James and Dorothy Brown, eds., *The Book Review Digest: Forty-Ninth Annual Cumulation, March 1953 to February 1954 Inclusive* (New York: The H. W. Wilson Co., 1954), 472.
3. *Southern Folklore Quarterly* 17 (1953): 195–96.
4. *Journal of American Folklore* 66 (1953): 276–78.
5. *Western Folklore* 13 (1954): 73–75.
6. Gilbert Chase, *America's Music from the Pilgrims to the Present,* rev. 2d ed. (New York: McGraw-Hill Book Co., 1966); D. K. Wilgus, *Anglo-American Folksong Research since 1898* (New Brunswick, N.J.: Rutgers University Press, 1959); and H. Wiley Hitchcock, *Music in the United States: A Historical Introduction* (Englewood Cliffs, N.J.: Prentice-Hall, 1969, Prentice-Hall History of Music Series).
7. "Many Folk Masses Don't Make It, Magazine Finds," *The Catholic Standard and Times* (Philadelphia), December 11, 1969, citing and commenting on an article in *Church Music.*
8. *The New York Times,* 22 February 1966, UPI release from Dallas.
9. See Walter Wiora, "The Origins of German Spiritual Folk Song: Comparative Methods in a Historical Study," *Ethnomusicology* 8 (1964): 1–13.

10. "John Adam Granade: The 'Wild Man' of Goose Creek," in "Symposium on Folk Religion," Don Yoder, ed., *Western Folklore* 33 (1) (January 1974): 77–87.

11. See "Folksongs of Mormon Inspiration," *Western Folklore* 6 (1) (January 1947): 42–52; *Saints of Sage and Saddle: Folklore among the Mormons* (Bloomington: Indiana University Press, 1956).

12. *Mormon Songs from the Rocky Mountains: A Compilation of Mormon Folksong* (Austin: University of Texas Press, 1968).

13. Jackson's major correspondence was given after his death to Vanderbilt University, Nashville, Tennessee; and his songbook collection to U.C.L.A. For the latter, see Paul J. Revitt, *The George Pullen Jackson Collection of Southern Hymnody: A Bibliography* (1964), UCLA Library Occasional Papers 13.

14. Louis F. Benson, *The English Hymn: Its Development and Use in Worship* (Richmond, Va.: The John Knox Press, [1915], reprinted 1962).

Explorations in a Region

Explorations in a Region

The first essay in this section recounts my own very personal discovery of Central Pennsylvania, my home country, as a distinct cultural region. This was an address given March 8, 1986, at the annual meeting of the Pennsylvania Folklore Society, held at Bucknell University, Lewisburg, Pennsylvania, on that lovely nineteenth-century campus overlooking the Susquehanna River and its valley. A more formal paper which readers may wish to look up on the wider subject of the discovery of the traditional culture of Pennsylvania as a whole is "Folklife in Pennsylvania: An Historical Survey," which appeared in *Keystone Folklore: The Journal of the Pennsylvania Folklore Society,* n.s. 1:2 (1982): 8–20. It was read as a paper at the meeting of the society held in International House at the University of Pennsylvania in 1981.

Two additional papers offered in this section are examples of my historical ethnography approach to a "folklore" topic—the saint's legend, and a "folklife" topic—harvest home. The paper "The Saint's Legend in the Pennsylvania German Folk Culture" was read at Wayland D. Hand's U.C.L.A. Conference on American Folk Legend, held June 19–22, 1969, and appeared first in his conference volume, *American Folk Legend: A Symposium.* The lengthy article on the relations of the Pennsylvania German Harvest Home and the New England Thanksgiving appeared under the title of "Harvest Home" in *Pennsylvania Folklife* 9 (4) (Fall 1958).

Both as an example of my extensive fieldwork and to introduce readers to my delightful informant and old, old friend Frank Eckert (1871–1960), I have included here the article "Witch Tales from Adams County," with its transcription of my interview tape of June 7, 1958. It appeared in *Pennsylvania Folklife* 12 (4) (1962). In 1963, at the annual meeting of the Society for Folklife Studies at the University of Leeds in England, I gave a copy of the article to Richard Dorson. With his characteristic "tale" orientation he found Frank Eckert's stories so intriguing that he used several of them, including "The Bewitched Automobile," in his book *Buying the Wind.*

The diminutive piece, "Fraktur: An Introduction," dealing with Pennsylvania Dutch manuscript art, appeared as the introduction to *Pennsylvania German Fraktur and Color Drawings* (Lancaster, Pa.: Pennsylvania Farm Museum of Landis Valley, Pennsylvania Historical and Museum Commission, 1969). It represents my continuing interest in unraveling the religious symbolism displayed visually in the folk arts. My most recent production in this field bears the same title but has a different text, and introduces the volume *Pennsylvania German Fraktur and Printed Broadsides: A Guide to the Collections in the Library of Congress,* compiled by Paul Connor and Jill Roberts for the American Folklife Center (Washington, D.C.: Library of Congress, 1988).

The final offering is an article I wrote for the popular press, unfootnoted but completely documented in the text, "Sauerkraut for New Year's." This deals with New Year's customs among the Pennsylvania Dutch past and present, from the sacred rite of eating sauerkraut for good luck throughout the coming year, through the ancient practice of "shooting in" the New Year, to the folk-religious ritual of "wishing in" the New Year. The article appeared in *The World & I* 4 (1) (January 1989).

8

The Discovery of Central Pennsylvania

As my students and colleagues know, I have always been convinced of the value of studying one's own culture. When I came to prepare this paper on the culture of my own backyard, so to speak, I was pleased to find the following statement in the preface to the two-volume *Commemorative Biographical Encyclopedia of the Juniata Valley* (1897):

> Every neighborhood is a world in miniature. As the natural phenomena which may be observed within any limited area furnish abundant illustration of the grand laws that govern the physical universe, so the virtues that build up nations and the passions that wreck them are all exemplified, in even the smallest community.

And again, "The annals of the quietest neighborhood are as attractive, in their way, and as profitable a study, as the history of a nation."

Pennsylvania, like Gaul, is divided into three parts, Eastern Pennsylvania, Western Pennsylvania, and Central Pennsylvania. If Pennsylvania has the dubious reputation of being relatively neglected historiographically in comparison with New England and other more self-conscious American areas, of these three parts of Pennsylvania, Central Pennsylvania has in my opinion been less written about than Eastern or Western Pennsylvania.

As a Central Pennsylvanian by birth and upbringing and long family backgrounds in many counties, it is a pleasure for me to say something about the discovery of and the basic cultural personality of Central Pennsylvania. If I may, I will describe first my own discovery of Central Pennsylvania, and then comment on the perception of it by native writers and the outside world.

This article is taken from an address given at the March 8, 1986 meeting of the Pennsylvania Folklore Society.

I must begin by confessing that I was born in a place called Altoona, a town built by and for the Pennsylvania Railroad. In its great days the "system," as the railroad network was called, connected those three parts of Pennsylvania east and west, but also had numerous north-south branches that connected Pennsylvania with New York State—the ride from Williamsport to Buffalo was one of the great train rides in the U.S.—and with Maryland, Virginia, and West Virginia.

When I was a boy there were dozens of trains east and west that stopped daily under the great train shed at Altoona, some going only as far as Pittsburgh, others on to Chicago and St. Louis. If I recall the schedules, one fascinating train, the "Lehigh Express," left the train shed at 8 A.M., and touched at Tyrone, Milesburg, Bellefonte, Lock Haven, Williamsport, Sunbury, and up the North Branch of the Susquehanna to Wilkes-Barre. It returned the same day, backing into Bellefonte whistle blowing, continued west through Milesburg, passing my grandfather's farm at Martha Furnace about 4 o'clock, giving my grandmother the signal to start the preparation of supper for the family, the hired hands, and any visitors who happened to be there.

When I was a boy growing up in Altoona, the railroad age was in the forefront of our thinking. The shops there were the largest in the country. The 12 o'clock and the 3:30 whistles sounding from them gave us part of our time-sense as we moved through the day. Many of the institutions of the city had been founded by the "Company," as it was always called, for the citizenry of the town, like the Mechanics Library which is now the Altoona Public Library, and the Cricket Club.

Those great railroading days of the nineteenth and twentieth centuries in Central Pennsylvania, when the Allegheny Mountains were threaded with roads of iron, form an important chapter in our history. My own interest in them led to my discovery of the travel literature about Central Pennsylvania. When I first began searching for descriptions of my home country, I came upon Dickens' *American Notes* (1842) with his vivid chronicle of a trip over the Allegheny Mountains via the Allegheny Portage Railway that connected Hollidaysburg with Johnstown through an ingenious system of inclined planes and level stretches between them. This made me aware of the importance of travelers' accounts of a region as part of what the British call "topographic literature." I have continued to assemble similar evidence from a host of travelers, and certainly have enough of them for a volume called *Pen Pictures of Central Pennsylvania*, to match John Harpster's volume on Western Pennsylvania. One of my favorites, I must admit, is a tiny volume that appeared in Philadelphia in 1836 with the title, *A Pleasant Peregrination through the Prettiest Parts of Pennsylvania, by Peregrine Prolix*, which is all one needs to say about that.

Figure 8.1. Cedar Spring Farm in Fermanagh Township, Juniata County, Central Pennsylvania. Christian Stouffer (1773–1850), a Mennonite farmer from Lancaster County, settled here in 1812 and erected all of the buildings. Ancestral farm of the author.
(Courtesy Roughwood Collection)

Figure 8.2. The Gingrich homestead in Juniata County, an ancestral farm of the author. Note the so-called "grandfather's house" to the right, customarily built for the parents when the youngest son married and took over the farm. An outdoor bakeoven can be seen to the right of the smaller house.
(Courtesy Roughwood Collection)

But in my growing consciousness of Central Pennsylvania's past there were other, older strands than the railroad story. There was of course the American history track—the first World War that my parents' generation remembered, the Civil War—I interviewed all the Civil War veterans in my family and its circle of neighbors—and the Revolution, from which there were still family legends to record. But there was an even more basic strand in our past. When my family visited aunts and uncles and cousins and old friends here and there in those valleys in Blair, Huntingdon, Centre, Clearfield, Mifflin, Juniata and other counties, I became aware of the local history—especially the settlement history—of the area. I discovered the county histories, those thick old books bound in red and stamped in gold, with their steel engravings and colored maps and their reminiscences of the pioneers dating from the days of the very settlement of the Allegheny Mountain counties. These books, all of them the product of the new wave of pride in America that emanated from the Centennial of the American Revolution in 1876, took me back to the founding of the towns, the county seats in particular—Huntingdon, Bedford, Hollidaysburg, Bellefonte, Clearfield, Lock Haven and others. Among them Altoona was a brash newcomer, dating only from 1849 when the first railroad shops were built.

As I grew older I came to see that historical time in America is very different from that in Western Europe, where towns celebrate their 1000th or 1200th anniversaries without batting an eye. Two centuries, or two and a half, is as far as we can look back in Central Pennsylvania. And when we do look closely at that period we find that Central Pennsylvania in the eighteenth and nineteenth centuries was a true frontier, an area in process of settlement. One of the books that influenced me greatly when I was a boy was U. J. Jones' *History of the Juniata Valley,* published in 1856. I read it from cover to cover. It was important to me because it dealt with *my* part of the world.

The story of the Indian wars in the area as retold in this book was a thrilling chapter, and I pictured the events as I visited relatives in some of the valleys where skirmishes had taken place. The map of Central Pennsylvania took on new meaning for me when I realized the underlying contribution of the Indian culture to the successive white settlements. The Indian trails became our highways, Indian clearings became town space. For example, Standing Stone became Huntingdon, and the Bald Eagle's Nest became Milesburg. Above all the map instructed me—the names of mountains and streams called to one their Indian origin—Juniata itself, Susquehanna, Lycoming, Moshannon, Sinnemahoning, Muncy Mountain, Tuscarora Valley, Bald Eagle Valley, Snow Shoe, Warriors Mark—the map was covered with Indian names, or names associated with Indian legends.

The pioneer days were also very near the surface in people's memories when I was growing up in Central Pennsylvania. I was born in Logan Township, Blair County, and Chief Logan and his Indian eloquence were in all the old school readers I had inherited from older members of my family who had gone to country schools. Family traditions and identity became important to me as I talked with older members of my family, some of whom told me Indian stories and tales of the first settlers; this happened long before I had ever heard of oral history or folklore. I like to tell my students that when I was a boy I filled a notebook with the stories my grandfather told me. He was born in 1861, and his grandfather was born in 1776.

So from my longtime observation of the culture of Central Pennsylvania—I suppose I will have to say participant observation—I came to several conclusions about the basic nature of that culture. Firstly, the cultural blend achieved in Central Pennsylvania was the direct product of the mingling of various ethnic and regional groups who came from all over the map to settle the area. They came from several directions. Eastern Pennsylvania furnished most of the earliest settlers—Pennsylvania Germans, Scotch-Irish, English Quakers, and others. New Jersey and New York furnished some settlers, New England others. After the Civil War there was a migration of Nova Scotian lumbermen into the West Branch area, when Lock Haven and Williamsport were humming with sawmills and the river was full of rafts.

But I am always impressed with the large migration of Marylanders into Central Pennsylvania, a subject that I am working on at present. Central Pennsylvania faces south, toward Baltimore, and in the pioneer era had closer trade and cultural connections with Baltimore than with Philadelphia. In the days before the railroad, it was easier to ship goods down the Susquehanna to the Chesapeake ports than overland to Philadelphia.

If this was true of trade, it was also true of culture. For example, many of Central Pennsylvania's religious patterns showed closer ties to Baltimore than to Philadelphia. Our Catholic settlements were part of the Baltimore Catholic network. The Quakers of Central Pennsylvania belonged historically to Baltimore Yearly Meeting, and Friends used to ride horseback from the meetings in Centre, Clearfield, and Bedford Counties to attend the yearly meeting in Maryland's main city. Central Pennsylvania's Methodists were also tied to Maryland and Virginia, and were in fact part of the Baltimore and East Baltimore Annual Conferences until 1868, when the Central Pennsylvania Conference was set off. The earliest Methodist churches in Centre County, Pennsylvania, for example, and the adjacent parts of Huntingdon, were planted in the 1780s and 1790s by families who had migrated from Maryland—the Penningtons, Benns, and Beckwiths of Penns Valley in the eastern part of Centre County, who came from the Eastern Shore, and in the western part of the county the Grays, Matterns, Hartsocks, Hyskells and others—Pennsylvania Dutch or Maryland Dutch families who had migrated north from the Hagerstown area.

Secondly, the dominant cultural patterns of the area in the earlier stages of its development were shaped principally by two groups of the earliest settlers. Geographers speak of the pattern-setting that the first occupants of any area perform which combine to influence succeeding settlements. That is still true of much of Central Pennsylvania, even though many other later ethnic groups settled over the area, particularly in the cities, forming ethnic enclaves and influencing the culture in new ways.

What I am dealing with of course is the overarching regional culture of Central Pennsylvania which was created and more or less set in the eighteenth and nineteenth centuries. Still through much of the area the mark of two early cultures is quite visible—that of the Pennsylvania Dutch and the Scotch-Irish. The Pennsylvania Dutchman contributed basic architectural patterns—it seems that everybody in the rural areas copied the practical Pennsylvania Dutch bank barn. The Dutchman's wife contributed many basic food patterns and food customs that are still evident in the area. When I was a boy in Altoona the newspapers were filled every year after Christmas with advertisements for local butcher shops, urging Altoonans and Blair Countians to buy their pork for New Year's day dinner, and some of them even sold the sauerkraut to go with it. As you all know, a Pennsylvania Dutchman wouldn't think of beginning a new year without feasting on sauerkraut and pork, for good luck throughout the year. For a second example, farmers all over the area, whether they were Pennsylvania Dutch or not, made the Eastern Pennsylvania delicacy called "scrapple" in Philadelphia. But in Altoona the people still knew its original Rhineland name—"ponhoss."

The Scotch-Irish, the second formative element, contributed other elements to the common culture of Central Pennsylvania. Their linguistic patterns and vocabulary have impressed the folkspeech of the area in many ways. When I was a boy people still used the word "flit"—not for butterflies but for the move a farmer makes from one farm to another. The wagonload of household goods that is moved on flitting day is called in fact the "flitting," or more properly, the "flittin." I looked up "flit" in the English dialect dictionaries and found that it came from Scotland to Northern Ireland, and thence to North America. But it got to Scotland from Scandinavia. The Norse word *flitta* means to move from place to place.

My Centre County grandmother, the one who used to start supper when she saw the Lehigh Express pass by on the railway at Martha Furnace, came from a background that consisted mostly of Pennsylvania Dutch families who had originated in Switzerland, but she spoke the common Scotch-

Irish English of the area. She pronounced *early* "airly" and *are you* "air ye?" and she didn't even use the word "ain't"—she pronounced it "haint" as in the completely Central Pennsylvanian sentence, "Haint youns comin' over today?" The "youns" is our Central Pennsylvania plural of the singular "you" (even though that is really plural) and it does make sense, like "y'all" in the South, or "yous" among the Pennsylvania Dutch. It is even used in the written language there. A schoolteacher cousin of mine in Centre County wrote us a letter one time with the sentence, "When are you ones coming up to see us?" And she could have added, "We ones would like a visit from you ones." A last example of Scotch-Irish influence on folkspeech. When I was a boy we called a rounded stone, heavy but throwable, that one could hold in the hand, a "gooney." Hence, years later, when I was formally studying the common speech of my home area, I was pleased to see "gooney" in a word list from the Allegheny Mountain counties that had appeared in *American Speech.* I also seem to recall from my boyhood days the phrase, "whale a gooney at him," but that is another matter.

This little discourse on regional language leads me to a third observation about the culture of Central Pennsylvania—its influence on the rest of the United States. Central Pennsylvania is in fact geographically and culturally the upper fourth or fifth of Appalachia. The culture of the upland South or mountain South—the western parts of Maryland, Virginia, West Virginia, North Carolina, etc., and the adjoining parts of Eastern Kentucky and Tennessee, and their extension culturally into the Ozarks—shows the impress of Central Pennsylvanian cultural patterns. I recognized Central Pennsylvania's kinship with Appalachia when as a boy I discovered Raines' *The Land of Saddlebags* and Eaton's *Handicrafts of the Southern Highlands.* And more recently, Henry Glassie's book, *Pattern in the Material Folk Culture of the Eastern United States* (1968), contains a striking map showing a great arrow pointing south from Central Pennsylvania, designating the Pennsylvanian diaspora and its cultural impress on the South.

The same blend of early ethnic cultures of Central Pennsylvania—Scotch-Irish and Pennsylvania Dutch in particular—was found in the middle and lower parts of Appalachia. In fact Pennsylvanian patterns of religion, folk belief, architecture, cookery, and speech can still be found in large areas south of the Mason and Dixon Line. The religious institution known as the camp-meeting was once thought to be an original Southern creation which moved North to Pennsylvania. Actually it was in a sense returning home, for the American camp-meeting grew out of the "sacramental occasion" of Pennsylvania's Scotch-Irish Presbyterians, when communion and preaching services were held in the open air, with a preaching platform which Appalachians came to call a "brush arbor."

Lastly, the early Central Pennsylvanian culture seems to have been extremely ecumenical in its spirit. It is always pleasant to read of the Irish emigrant Patrick Cassidy, a devout Roman Catholic who founded and named the town of Newry in Blair County for his birthplace in Ireland, who gave land for a Protestant church. And Aaron Levy, Jewish merchant of Philadelphia, who founded Aaronsburg in what is now Centre County in 1787, gave land for a Lutheran and Reformed church for the Pennsylvania Dutch families who purchased his town lots. In my travels about Central Pennsylvania, visiting kinfolk and friends here and there, I have always been impressed with the friendly, open, neighborly, welcoming spirit of the people. Denominations and ethnic groups seem more cooperative with each other there than in some areas of Eastern Pennsylvania, possibly because of the more widespread acculturation of these groups to each other. For one example, Central Pennsylvania Lutheranism has historically been friendlier and more accommodating to Anglo-American religious bodies than has Eastern Pennsylvania Lutheranism. Central Pennsylvanians certainly have no monopoly on these pleasant characteristics, but they certainly have them. And to express hospitality some of us still use that pioneer saying from the days of the unlocked log cabin, "The latch string is on the outside."

How has all this been recorded in literature, or has it? Certainly local historians began in the nineteenth century to extol the uniqueness of the area. As with Eastern and Western Pennsylvania, local schools of novelists captured some of the flavor of Central Pennsylvania. If you will forgive me for mentioning Centre County again, there is an excellent portrayal of life among the Pennsylvania Dutch of the Seven Mountains in a novel called *The House of the Black Ring.* It is full of good descriptions of Dutch folk beliefs, particularly powwowing and witchcraft. It was written by a professor at the (then) Pennsylvania State College named Fred Lewis Pattee, for whom the Pattee Library was named. A Bellefonte Quaker named Edward Uffington Valentine, at least a part-time Bellefonter, wrote a novel called *Hecla Sandwith,* which deals with families on different social levels involved with the iron industry in the Bald Eagle country. And in more recent times Martha Barnhart, a native of the area, wrote a series of novels about life among Centre Countians, which, like the two works already cited, were issued by national publishers. Similar examples could be given from other areas in Central Pennsylvania, although one must add that the area does not yet have a John Updike or a John O'Hara or even a Bayard Taylor, whose novels about Eastern Pennsylvania characters, as for example *The Story of Kennett,* achieved wide circulation in the nineteenth century.

One cannot discuss Central Pennsylvania's literature without mentioning Henry W. Shoemaker, whom I knew and liked, but about whose work I have mixed feelings. He had two positive effects on Pennsylvania scholarship. He certainly drew attention to what he called the "Pennsylvania mountaineers," and, in doing so, came close to what I have pointed to as the Appalachian connection. Secondly, he did gather and publish some folksongs, as for example, in his book *North Mountain Minstrelsy.* His books of stories are attractive, but I never know in what category to place them. They are neither history nor folklore; in fact his tales are local-color fiction. His book, *Tales of the Bald Eagle Mountains,* deals with Centre County and purports to record traditional tales from the area. But knowing the area so well, I have always found more of Colonel Shoemaker than of Centre County tradition in his stories. Classic is his "legend" of Penns Cave. This he claims was told to him by an "aged Seneca Indian" who returned to Central Pennsylvania in 1892—rather late for that, I should judge. As some of you know, the story involves the hot love affair of a white man with the Indian "princess," Nita-Nee, for whom the Colonel said Nittany Mountain and Nittany Valley were named. Need I say more, except to add that the "legend" of Nita-Nee used to be taught in the State College public schools, and I have clippings from the *Centre Democrat* to prove it.

On this same level of "forced lore," fakelore, or whatever else one wants to call it, is the creation of the Indian maiden "Bright Alfarata" (typical Amerindian name, of course) who, according to a sentimental Victorian song, roved the Blue Juniata. This had one positive result on the Central Pennsylvania culture—it led to the wide use of the girl's name Alfarata or Alfaretta. I think sometimes there were more Alfaratas or Alfarettas in some Central Pennsylvania counties than there were Filomenas in Naples, at least before the Vatican Council removed St. Filomena's credentials.

Seriously, we are all happy that new generations of scholars, local historians, folklorists, folklife researchers and anthropologists, novelists, artists and filmmakers are turning their attention to Central Pennsylvania themes. Two film projects that deserve mention out of many are Jay Ruby's team project from Temple University that studied Juniata County, and Kenneth Thigpen's filming project, based at Penn State, on various aspects of Central Pennsylvania life. The work of Mac Barrick has enlightened us on both the lore and life of the Cumberland Valley, and we are all in the debt of Jeannette Lasansky for her solid historical and ethnographical studies of the crafts of Central Pennsylvania. Simon Bronner at the Penn State Capitol Campus, which faces into Central Pennsylvania from across the river and attracts many students from the trans-Susquehanna counties, has directed many research projects in the area. And Shalom Staub is tying it all together, as only Shalom can tie it together. This to mention only a few of those working in this wide and rewarding field of Central Pennsylvania culture.

And now my conclusion. The Chinese-American geographer Yi-Fu Tuan discusses "attachment to homeland," which he calls a common human

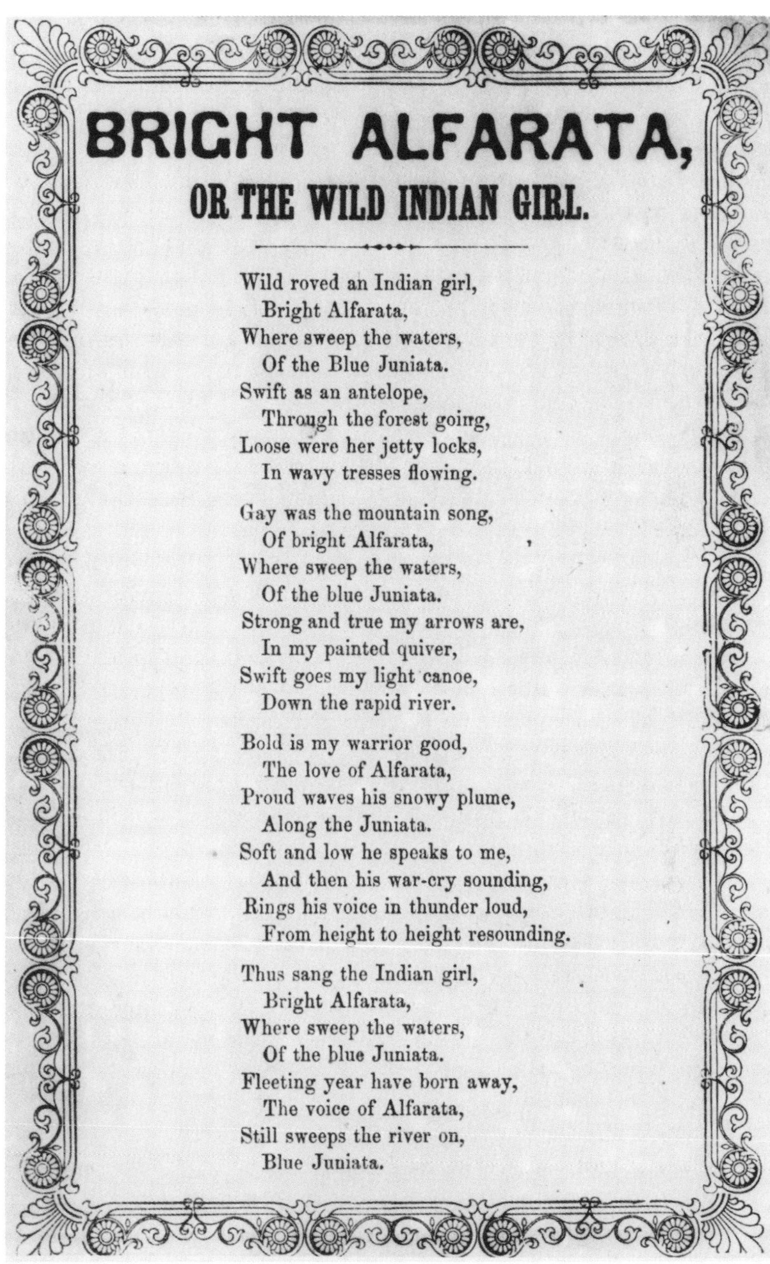

BRIGHT ALFARATA,

OR THE WILD INDIAN GIRL.

Wild roved an Indian girl,
Bright Alfarata,
Where sweep the waters,
Of the Blue Juniata.
Swift as an antelope,
Through the forest going,
Loose were her jetty locks,
In wavy tresses flowing.

Gay was the mountain song,
Of bright Alfarata,
Where sweep the waters,
Of the blue Juniata.
Strong and true my arrows are,
In my painted quiver,
Swift goes my light canoe,
Down the rapid river.

Bold is my warrior good,
The love of Alfarata,
Proud waves his snowy plume,
Along the Juniata.
Soft and low he speaks to me,
And then his war-cry sounding,
Rings his voice in thunder loud,
From height to height resounding.

Thus sang the Indian girl,
Bright Alfarata,
Where sweep the waters,
Of the blue Juniata.
Fleeting year have born away,
The voice of Alfarata,
Still sweeps the river on,
Blue Juniata.

Figure 8.3. Song broadside, "Bright Alfarata, or The Wild Indian Girl." Philadelphia, ca. 1870. *(Courtesy Roughwood Collection)*

Figure 8.4. View of the Lewistown Narrows on the Pennsylvania Railroad. The river is Alfarata's favorite roving ground, the Juniata. From a volume of lithographs from the age of railroad tourism in the decades following the Civil War, when Americans were seeing their mountains and valleys with new eyes.
(Courtesy Roughwood Collection)

emotion, in his books *Topophilia* (love of place) and *Space and Place.* In the latter he asks the question, What is a place? What gives a place its identity, its aura? He describes a visit paid by the physicists Bohr and Heisenberg to Kronberg Castle in Denmark, where they asked the same questions. As scientists they first perceived the castle as a composite of stones, and admired the way the architect had put them together. And then they admitted that their overall perception of the castle changed entirely when they shifted their focus to the castle's connection with the story of Hamlet.

In this brief, reminiscent paper I have attempted to point out some of the complex and multi-layered character or personality of that part of the human world known as Central Pennsylvania. These traits grow out of a working together, or combination of:

1. *natural environment,* with its overlay of
2. *cultural or manmade environment,* plus
3. *the social network of settlement groups.*

Together these factors make up the "spirit of place"—as in the title of Lawrence Durrell's book, *Spirit of Place.*

Let me close with a statement from one of those county histories that I referred to earlier—H. H. Hain's *History of Perry County, Pennsylvania Including Descriptions of Indian and Pioneer Life from the Time of the Earliest Settlement* (Harrisburg, 1922). The dedication of the book reads as follows:

> To all those Perry Countians who first saw the beautiful rays of the morning sun as it came up o'er the Blue Ridge Mountains, who cherish fond memories of the land of their birth, and to those other citizens of the Republic who have chosen to make their abiding place within the borders of the Best Little County in the Commonwealth, this book is respectfully dedicated.

Professor Tuan would call such expressed feelings "Heimat sentimentality." Well, what can I say?

9

The Saint's Legend in the Pennsylvania German Folk Culture

The Pennsylvania German folk culture, which was built up in the acculturation process between the emigrant cultures from the continent of Europe and the British Isles, was a mixed bag, a very mixed bag, a hybrid affair in which the elements that came into the culture from the "outside" were equally important with the elements that came with the German-speaking immigrants of the eighteenth century to colonial Pennsylvania. I have dealt at length with these aspects of hybridization in other papers,[1] and I am delighted to have the opportunity to present here my conclusions on one element in Pennsylvania German culture that can be almost wholly traced to the continent of Europe and to the German-language belt of central Europe.

By saints' legends, I mean the specific knowledge of the legends of certain saints in and out of the traditional church year. Apart from specific legends, however, there was a partial survival and widespread reminiscence of the European saint system among the Pennsylvania Germans, in which names and days and functions of at least some of the European folk-saints continued in operation on American soil and, strangely enough, in a Protestant environment.

The cult of the saints had developed in ancient Christianity from the human need to have tangible, visible, human-scale patterns embodying the values central to one's society. When the saint system flowered into full classic proportions in the Middle Ages, not only were the saints individuals in which the values of medieval society were embodied, but they represented, especially for the peasantry and lower strata of society, a manageable humanized version of divinity. In the construction of the Christian plan

This article first appeared in *American Folk Legend: A Symposium,* Wayland D. Hand, ed. (Berkeley: University of California Press, 1971), 157–83.

of salvation by the early theologians, "the logic of popular piety," as Mecklin puts it, "insisted that theology make central in its scheme the work of the Savior-God Jesus, but the intellectuals demanded that Jesus be raised to the level of the God of the universe, for otherwise the Christian plan of salvation would lose its authoritativeness and its universal appeal."[2] The masses, however, were unable to comprehend the Christian myth as formulated by Augustine, preferring and eventually getting a syncretistic "Christianity of the second rank." Hence they "gradually built their faith around the cult of the saints. The cult of the Virgin in time came to fill the gap left by Jesus, now remote and incomprehensible as a member of the Trinity." This syncretism between theology, sacramentarian cult, popular piety, and pagan survivals led to the universal popularity of the saint figure in the Middle Ages.

While the legendry of medieval sainthood was a creation largely of the "Christianity of the second rank," it was legitimized and used by the official Church. For the masses it expressed the aristocratic ideals of asceticism and world-denial and pointed here and now to the paradisiacal world that was open to the common man only after death. Also for the masses, the saints, as did the shrines and holy places of pilgrimage and the church building itself, represented both a localization of divinity into tangible forms and a concretizing of the divine and the holy which, according to Richard Weiss, is one of the marks of Catholic folk piety.[3] Where the official Church could not keep pace with the human drive to create usable local saint figures, the phenomenon of "folk-canonization" operated.

At the time of the Protestant Reformation, the very nerve of the cult of the saints was cut by the reformers, and with it the veneration of the chief of saints, the kingpin of the system, the Virgin Mary. This retrenchment varied according to denomination, the Lutherans keeping much more of the official Catholic church year and its saints' days than the other Protestant groups, the Reformed churches and the Anabaptist sectarians. The canon for the purification of the church year of the Catholic saints' days was, according to Albrecht Jobst, a pioneer German analyst of the relation between Protestantism and folk culture, that "all specifically Catholic saints' days and festivals were set aside, because their pedigrees were not 'pure.' On the other hand, the festivals of the biblical saints, the apostles and the Virgin Mary were retained, in so far as they possessed 'pure' pedigrees, that is, the gospel pericopes."[4]

This protestantizing of the church year was sharpened in the seventeenth century when an additional retrenchment came—in that period, for example, the Saint Nicholas cult of gift-bringer at Christmas was transferred to the *Christkind*. In the eighteenth century there was another cutback, when both Pietists and Rationalists, for different reasons, dropped other continuing aspects of medieval church life.

The Pennsylvania German folk culture, which was built up in the eighteenth and early nineteenth century, reflects the passive continuance of much of the medieval Catholic world view and saint lore that marked the earlier European Protestantism, that is, the "Old" Protestantism before it was retreaded in the eighteenth century by Pietism and Rationalism. In the twentieth century, the specific knowledge of the saints' legends is of smaller consequence in Pennsylvania German culture than the general survival of bits and pieces of the European medieval saint complex that was so large a part of the pre-Reformation folk-mind. I shall organize my paper into three sections: (1) The Saint in Folk Medicine and Magic; (2) Transplanted European Saints' Legends; and (3) Native Analogues to the Saint's Legend.[5]

The Saint in Folk Medicine and Magic

In "powwowing" *(Brauchen, Braucherei),* Pennsylvania's continuing brand of occult folk-medicine, which uses charms in the attempt to heal the ills of man and beast, to quote the title of the principal powwow book still in use,[6] the saints make a brief post-Reformation appearance, occasionally trailing parts of their legends behind them.

Chief among the dramatis personae of the charm literature is Saint Mary—*unsere liebe Jungfrau* or *die Mutter Gottes*—who makes many appearances, sometimes alone, sometimes in company with other New Testament figures. Principal among the latter is Saint Peter, who seems to keep up a running conversation with Mary in many of the formulas. Other biblical personages who serve as saints in the folk-medical literature are Tobit, Job, Pontius Pilate, *"unsere liebe Sara,"* the *drey heilige Männer,* Shadrach, Meshach and Abednego, *der liebe heilige Daniel*, Annania, Azaria, and Misael, the four archangels, Michael, Gabriel, Raphael, and Uriel, and last but not least, Judas, the anti-saint. Above all stands the Blessed Trinity, *"die drei höchste Namen"* as the Pennsylvania powwower calls them, the Trinitarian formula, without which terminal blessing the powwow charm is incomplete.

From the use of the saints, angels, archangels, Mary, and the Trinity in the world of the folk-medical incantations and charms, one gets a reminiscence, in Pennsylvania, across the Atlantic and four centuries after the Reformation, of the medieval *Weltbild* of the heavenly hierarchies so frequently portrayed in Catholic art—academic, popular, and folk.

Occasionally, too, bits of the saints' legends are embedded within the charm. For example, among the legends of Mary that are remembered, at least in charm form, is that of the attempt to steal the baby Jesus. In a charm manuscript in my own collection,[7] dated 1816, from Berks County, Pennsylvania, appears the formula:

> Maria lay in childbed when two Jews came who wanted to steal the Baby Jesus. Maria said to Saint Peter, "Child." Peter said, "I have bound them. Whoever comes to me to steal my property must stand like a sack and look around like a buck and count all the stars that are in heaven and rain drops and all the snowflakes and stumps and sticks and must stand until daybreak." In the name of God the Father, the Son, and the Holy Ghost, Amen.

To release the thief, in case one needs that detail of the procedure, one repeats the words:

> Thief, lay down what is mine and [keep?] what is thine and go forth in the name of God the Father, the Son, and the Holy Ghost, Amen.

Saint Peter, with his keys and powers of binding and loosing, was obviously a favorite saint in the charms relating to thieves and thievery. Another goes like this:

> A formula for making thieves, male or female, to stand still, and not to be able to move forwards or backwards. ***
>
> O Peter, O Peter! Take the power from God: What I bind with the band of the Christian hand, all thieves, male or female, large or small, young or old, thus shall they be stationed by God, and none shall move a single step further forward or backward, etc.[8]

To loose the thief after this charm, two alternate methods are listed, the first of which is: *"heiss ihm in Sanct Johannis Namen fortgehen"*—"bid him depart in Saint John's name." So Saint John has the power to loose what Peter binds.

One of the several postbiblical Catholic saints who appears in the charm literature is Saint Laurence, appropriately on his grill.

> For burns.
>
> Our dear Lord Jesus Christ went out walking, when he saw a fire burning; there lay St. Laurence on a fire-grate. Came to help and comfort him; He lifted up his divine hand and blessed it, the fire; He signified that it must dig no deeper and eat no further round about. So blessed be the fire in the name of God the Father, the Son, and the Holy Ghost. Amen.[9]

The biblical figure Job appears in a charm versus sore mouth:

> When a person has a mouth and throat infection, say the following, it will surely help. Job went out walking, with his staff in his hand, when God the Lord met him, and said

to him: Job, why are you mourning so? He said: O God, why should I not mourn? My mouth and my throat are rotting away. Then God said to Job: There in that valley flows a spring which heals you (here name the name of the patient) your mouth and your throat in the name of God the Father, the Son, and the Holy Ghost. Amen.[10]

For burns and gangrene *(heissen und kalten Brand),* there is the curious formula that invokes *"Sanct Itorius."*

A very good remedy for burns and gangrene.

St. Itorius, res, call the plague. Then the Mother of God came to comfort him; she offered him her snow-white hand, for burns and gangrene (literally, for the hot and the cold burning). In the name of God the Father, the Son, and the Holy Ghost. Amen.[11]

The anonymous "three holy men," probably Shadrach, Meshach, and Abednego of the fiery furnace incident in the book of Daniel, appear in a charm to stop burns:

A cure to quiet a burn.

Three holy man went out walking. They blessed the heat and the burning. They blessed it to keep it from eating further. They blessed it that it would be consumed. In the name of God the Father, the Son, and the Holy Ghost. Amen.[12]

A curious picture is presented in the charm that contains the reference to "Sara": *Unsere liebe Sara zieht durch das land; sie hat einen feurigen, hitzigen Brand in ihrer Hand*[13] [Our dear Sara goes through the land; she has a glowing, fiery coal in her hand].

Saint Cyprian is invoked in a charm against witchcraft:

When man or beast is bewitched, how to help him.

Three false tongues have locked you, three holy tongues have spoken for you. (These are of course the Trinity.) ***

If a man has ridden over you, bless you God and St. Cyprian; if a woman has stepped over you, bless you God and Mary's womb; if a hired man has given you trouble, I bless you by God and the law of Heaven; if a hired girl or maid has led you astray, bless you God and the constellations of Heaven etc.[14]

And finally all the supernatural powers are invoked in a charm against thieves, and we get a Pennsylvania version of the medieval hierarchical universe. This is the charm: to charm a thief, so that he has to stand still. This charm, which is valid only on Thursday, invokes the power of the Trinity, and for good measure, thirty-three angels, Maria, "dear Saint Daniel," Saint Peter, and finally "all angelic hosts and all God's saints." Again, to release the unfortunate thief, who has just been ordered "to count all the stones that are on earth, and all the stars that are in heaven," is relatively simple—tell him to be on his way, in Saint John's name.[15]

Transplanted European Saints' Legends

Of the medieval saints' legends that have been transplanted intact, none is more widespread nor more popular among the Pennsylvania Germans than the story of *die heilige Genoveva* (Saint Genoveva of Brabant).[16]

Although her hagiographical authentication is not so sure as that of her namesake, Saint Geneviève (Genoveva) of Paris, and although German scholars are constantly in opposition to one another, in attempting to determine to which genre of folk literature the medieval story of Genoveva belongs, there appears to have been a cult of Saint Genoveva in the lower Rhineland, whence the story and possibly the devotion spread to the areas from which came the seventeenth- and eighteenth-century German and Swiss immigrants to Pennsylvania.[17]

The essential legend of the "Pfaltzgravine Genoveva" is that of the innocent wife, accused by her nobleman husband of infidelity and condemned to the forest, but vindicated at last. A version collected from oral tradition in Pennsylvania will give us the details; it calls the heroine "Genoeva":

> Genoeva was a beautiful and a good woman, who was married to a prince, and who lived happily with him. The prince had many servants and among them was one—either the jester *(Hofnarr)* or the butler—who wanted to lead Genoeva into the path of sin. He tempted her, but she would not in the slightest way yield to his evil designs.
>
> Then the butler—I know now, it was the butler and not the jester—became full of hatred toward Genoeva, and he went to her husband and told him that Genoeva was an unfaithful and a deceitful wife.
>
> The husband believed the butler, and became infuriated at Genoeva. He drove her and her baby boy out of the palace into the dark forest.
>
> Genoeva, carrying her baby in her arms, walked on and on through the forest, not knowing where to go for there were no homes among the dark trees.
>
> Finally, she came to a bear cliff *(Beregliffs)* in which there was a bear den. Here she sought refuge, and here she made her home.
>
> She lived on berries, herbs, bark, and roots, and every day there came to the cliff a doe from whom she got milk for her baby.
>
> Thus she lived for many years. Her baby boy grew up into manhood and then he supplied her with food and clothing. She had often told him how she had been falsely accused by the butler and had been unjustly driven from the palace. When the boy was grown up and strong, he determined to go to his father, to defend his mother and to accuse the false butler.
>
> After the father heard the son's story, he sent for the butler, who, when brought face to face with the son and hearing the accusation, broke down and confessed the evil which he had done.
>
> Then, straightway, the prince went into the forest for Genoeva. He brought her back to the palace, where she lived happily with him the rest of her life.
>
> As for the butler, the prince took four wild oxen and chained the butler to the oxen, one limb to each ox; and as the oxen sprang apart they tore the body of the butler to the four winds *(ausnanner grisse noch di vier Wind).*[18]

While the story is still obtainable in Pennsylvania in oral tradition, it was principally circulated in printed form and *nacherzählt* or told according to a printed original.[19] The earliest known American edition of the little *Volksbuch* or chapbook on Genoveva is: *Geschichte von der Pfaltz-Gräfin Genovefa* (Lancaster: Gedruckt bey F. Bailey, 1774), listed in *The American Bibliography of Charles Evans* (Worcester, Mass.: American Antiquarian Society, 1959) as No. 13297. A more elaborate edition appeared from the same press in 1790: *Historie von der unschuldigen Heiligen Pfalz-gräfin Genoveva* (Lancaster: Gedruckt bey Jacob Bailey, 1790), Evans, No. 22524.[20]

The nineteenth-century editions are many. The most wide-spread, which turn up at country auctions and antique shops and book stores, are those published in the 1830s and later by Gustav S. Peters[21] of Harrisburg, Pennsylvania's first color printer, and his successor, Theo. F. Scheffer. Typically, Peters and Scheffer issued and advertised together the Pennsylvania German chapbooks both of magic and of piety—*The Long Lost Friend, The Sixth and Seventh Books of Moses, The Heart of Man ('s Haerz-Buch,* as the Pennsylvania Germans called it), and the two medieval saints' legends, those of Saint Helena and of Saint Genoveva. The Peters and Scheffer presses were bilingual, and the English edition was entitled: *The thrilling history of Genovefa who by a villain was doomed to be executed* (Harrisburg: printed and sold by Theo. F. Scheffer [1850?]), 38 pp., cover-title, illustrations, and advertisements. The advertisements are of value for the light they shed on the popularity of other items in the German chapbook repertoire among the Pennsylvania Germans. An undated German copy of *Die Leidens-Geschichte der unschuldigen Genovefa, Welche sich 7 Jahre in einer Wildniss von Wurzeln und Kräutern ernährte, und wie ihr Kind durch einen Hirsch wunderbar am Leben erhalten wurde* (Harrisburg: Gedruckt und zu haben bei Theo. F. Scheffer, n.d.), 38 pp., advertises on the back cover: *Heinrich von Eichenfels, Oder das von einer Zigeunerin geraubte Kind; Die Leidens-Geschichte der Genovefa;* and *Die Trübsale der schönen Helena.*

The cover illustrations occasionally show Genoveva, as naked as her babe, seated at the entrance of her cave, with the friendly doe in attendance, as the wicked husband rides up on horseback. The nudity aspect has made Genoveva one of the three most popular motifs in "nude" or "topless" folk art, along with Sebastian and, of course, Adam and Eve. Like these worthies, she gave the folk artist a unique chance to try his or her hand at a nude, which was otherwise forbidden in "Christian" art. This freedom of artistic expression reached even the closed world of the cloister, according to Robert Wildhaber, who recently sent me pictorial evidence in the form of three-dimensional wax figures of Genoveva and the other cast of characters, done as *Klosterarbeit* in the nunneries of the Catholic cantons of Switzerland.[22]

In fact it was the folk art produced by the Genoveva cult in Europe that first alerted me to the possibility of studying our homely old Genoveva comparatively. Reverse glass paintings in Czechoslovakia[23] and Sicilian cart panels[24] of the Genoveva story first showed me the wide influence of the Genoveva legend in Europe.

On higher cultural levels, too, Genoveva was a popular subject in the eighteenth and nineteenth centuries. There were several long poetic versions of her legend, several plays, and at least two operas.[25] And Richard Weiss refers to the countrified dramas that were played on rural Swiss stages in the eighteenth and nineteenth centuries, created from the chapbooks of Genoveva, Griselda of Saluzzo, and other heroines whose unchanging loyalty is put to the test by suspicious husbands.[26]

In addition to the legend books, the folk art, and the rural plays about Genoveva, there were also songs, as for example the *Cantique de Ste Geneviève de Brabant* (Paris, 1766), which became part of the Épinal repertoire in the nineteenth century as the *Cantique spirituel sur l'innocence de Geneviève, reconnue par son mari* (Épinal, 1874).[27]

The most recent German scholarship on the background of the Genoveva legend locates the beginnings of the cult in the middle Rhineland, at Frauenkirch (Fraukirch) near Andernach. At Andernach there was a church dedicated to Saint Geneviève (Genoveva) of Paris, from which her cult may have spread to the country regions adjacent. From this historical saint, the writer of the legend of Genoveva of Brabant may have taken the name of his heroine.

At any rate, the legend is late medieval, and exists in two versions, which differ only in inconsequential details. It is worthy of note that the two copyists whose versions are the sources of the modern legend both came from Andernach. The one version was copied around 1500 by Johannes of Andernach from an older Latin original, whose editor is unknown. The other version, part of the collections of the Stadtbibliothek in Trier (Hs 1353) was produced by Matthias von Emiych, also of Andernach, from an older version, around 1472. Matthias von Emiych was later prior of the Carmelite cloister at Boppard and died after being consecrated bishop of Mainz. From these medieval versions, the first printed version was drawn up; it was compiled by the French Jesuit Cerizier and appeared in 1638 as *L'innocence reconnue ou vie de Saint Geneviève de Brabant,* which was translated into German by 1685.[28] It is from the Cologne version of 1750 that the first American edition, that of Lancaster, Pennsylvania, in 1774, is derived.

In dealing with Genoveva of Brabant, Hermann Bausinger relates the legend on the one hand to the *Märchen,* and on the other to the *Schwank:*

> As a tale of many episodes of wondrous occurrences, the legend is above all close to the Märchen; a story like that of Genoveva of Brabant is related to the Märchen not only in individual motifs, but also in its entire course. This legend, composed in the late 15th Century by a Rhenish monk with reference to the Paris saint of the same name, received its characteristic form in the 17th Century at the hands of a French Jesuit and was then disseminated in Germany as a chapbook. Tieck produced a new version of it, Görres called attention to the chapbook, Christoph von Schmid wrote the popular sentimental version, and even to our own time the material has remained extraordinarily popular. To this popularity the Märchen-like character may have contributed; but it is especially in the oral narrative that the differences over against the Märchen clearly stand out. A short time ago an old woman in the Franconian area told me a variety of legends and Märchen. The only Märchen she told were those of the Grimm brothers. These she narrated matter-of-factly, almost indifferently, and even remarked on the inadequacies in the narrative, since Märchen are of course only for children. But the legend she took very seriously. In telling this latter her narration was directed toward the central miraculous events: these are accented, proved, attested; the story is true, and the miraculous events are immediate interventions of God. And there was still a second difference: while good fortune is the normal reward of the figures in the Märchen, in the legend the moral performance of the characters, their action, their perseverance, their patience are emphasized.
>
> Of course, this concern with the deeper aspects of man's nature is in constant tension with the cheerful certainty, indeed the triumphant certainty, which characterizes the frame of the legend. In this frame the legend can even approach the Schwank. The intimate connection between foolishness and sanctity (fool-ness and saint-ness, *Narrheit und Heiligkeit*) in the devaluation of worldly systems has already been pointed out in different ways; so it is no surprise when in the legend of St. Symeon of Emesa, for example, we encounter definite Eulenspiegel elements, and even the cunning deceits of Stricker's Pfaffe Amis must be viewed in this light.[29]

In a sense the material involved is best approached via the chapbook, which after all is our immediate introduction to Genoveva. Since the publication of the Cologne edition of 1750, Genoveva's story has spread even more widely in western Europe, until it has become common knowledge among the masses. The Dutch author Bilderdijk in a letter to a friend in 1786 mentions having seen old women sitting by their market wagons absorbed in the stories of Helena of Constantinople, Griselda of Saluzzo, and the like, books that were made out of traditions from the span of time from the last centuries of the Hellenistic period to the establishment of the Frankish kingdom.[30]

In conclusion, I make no attempt at this point to analyze further the reasons for the popularity of the story of Genoveva, or (heaven forbid!) to psychoanalyze it, preferring to listen someday to Professor Dundes's version of that. Apart from its being a good story, to rural Pennsylvanian audiences its didactic and moral character kept it alive, with its pointed and simple message—virtue will be rewarded, murder will out.

While the Genoveva legend is no longer read by the majority of the Pennsylvania Germans (although it is still passively known and occasionally told by older folk), among one segment of the culture it is very much alive. The Old Order Amish of Lancaster County, Pennsylvania, have recently established a press, and one of the first items issued from it is a pamphlet, a modern-day chapbook, entitled *Genevieve: Or, God Does Not Forsake His Own* (Gordonville, Pa.: A. S. Kinsinger, 1964), 44 pp. True to the aniconic character of Amish culture, there are no pictures, nude or otherwise. But even the publisher's pitch in the brief preface reflects the older chapbook tradition:

> Generations come and go. Many books have been written and printed, thrown on the book market and then become a thing of the past; but not so with "Genevieve"—it was written to stay. Its contents are healthful, interesting and instructive, for children as well as their elders, and it is suited for all generations. It shows that also in the ancient times good and bad people lived, and that man, trusting in God, could, with perseverance, overcome privations, where otherwise in his misery he would have gone to ruin.
>
> This is a popular edition, and the price is such that even the poorest are able to buy it. This publication contains a great deal of reading matter, and good printing. May this little booklet find a welcome in every family.[31]

Native Analogues to the Saint's Legend

The Christian saint's legend proper belongs to the Middle Ages and to Catholic or Orthodox environments and cultures. It is difficult to deny the human drive to create saints, however, so even within the Protestant cultures we have native analogues to the saint's legend.

If the saint as ecclesiastically permitted mediator was exscinded from the Protestant realm of possibility by the reformers, the saint as model—of virtue, charity, forbearance, and universal love—has continued to appear, if somewhat sporadically, within the Protestant world. Protestant biography, especially the lives produced during the Puritan and Pietist centuries in Europe and America, bear the vestigial marks of at least the virtue aspects of the earlier saints' legends.[32] Full-length studies of the various sectarian varieties of spiritual biography—the Puritan lives, the Quaker journals, and the Methodist circuit-rider autobiographies—reveal a striking resemblance in motif to the earlier saint's legend—resistance to the temptations of the "world," a radical conversion, which enables the subject to keep on a radarlike track direct toward salvation, in some cases the triumph of forbearance amid almost insurmountable difficulties, the detachment from personal love to universal charity, and detailed descriptions of the "holy dying" as well as the "holy living" of the saint.

Of the two foci, virtue and miracle, suggested by Professor Bausinger for the medieval saint's legend,[33] the Protestant versions normally accent virtue. The wondrous elements of the saint's legend are there, however, in some biographical cycles, although to a sharply decreased degree.[34] The Quaker journals, for instance, are full of guidance through dreams, visions, psychic leadings toward persons in need of spiritual counsel, and other hints of extrasensory phenomena.[35]

The Pennsylvania German materials are of interest in this connection. One form of charisma in the Dutch Country involves a reputation achieved as a folk-medical practitioner. While most of the healers were laymen, occasionally a minister was connected with healing practices. One such case involves the story told of a very famous early Pennsylvania Lutheran minister, Dr. John George Schmucker (1771–1854) of York, Pennsylvania. His biographer tells of an incident where he almost became a charismatic healer:

> Though not superstitious, he was not entirely free from belief in supernatural influences. If his mind had not been well balanced, he was just the man to be wrought on by the presumed revelations of modern Spiritualism. I believe this infirmity was fostered by his high admiration of, and thorough acquaintance with, some of the mystic theologians of the last century, especially Jung Stilling.
>
> Quite unintentionally, and to his great annoyance, he once acquired the reputation of being a semi-miraculous healer of wens, warts, and similar ugly excrescences. On one occasion a plain countryman came to his study and complained of a wen on his head. "Let me see it," said the Doctor. He examined it, as a matter of curiosity, and touched it. The man declared that, from that moment, it began to diminish until it disappeared altogether. His neighbors heard of it, and, for miles around, all who were affected with similar unnatural protuberances, hastened to the "Pastor" to be healed by the magic touch; and it required some effort to convince the simple people that he possessed no supernatural powers, and he dismissed them to their deep chagrin.[36]

In this case the minister, whose education and world view differed from those of his parishioners, scotched the layman's drive to promote him into the role of charismatic healer.[37]

The principal Pennsylvania analogue to the European saint's legend that I wish to discuss is the story of Mountain Mary *(Die Berg-Maria),* a local Pennsylvania German hermitess who died in 1819 and about whom legends have arisen. So persistent are they that Mountain Mary is today one of the best-known characters from early Pennsylvania history.[38]

Hermits, saintly and secular, abound in early American society. I am always amazed at the amount of material one comes upon in early American

Figure 9.1. Maria Jung, called "Mountain Mary," was a local Pennsylvania Dutch good neighbor and healer who was looked upon as a saint in the early nineteenth century. This is the cover of a recent book about her.

documentation on the nonconformists of this sort, whether voluntary or forced rejects of society. If our roads were crowded with offbeat "hawkers and walkers," tramps, religious itinerants, self-appointed messiahs, and utopia builders, Penn's woods seem to have had more than their share of hermits and hermitages. I recommend these as a special area of legend scholarship in America.

The life of Mountain Mary—whose name was Maria Jung (Young)—is today so shrouded in legend that it is difficult to cut back to what must have been her historical profile. A German immigrant of 1830 named Ludwig A. Wollenweber (1807–1888) published in 1880 a romanticized version of the life of Mary Young entitled *Treu bis in den Tod: Die Berg-Maria, oder Wer nur den lieben Gott lässt walten. Eine Geschichtliche Erzählung aus Pennsylvanien* (Philadelphia: Verlag von Ig.[natius] Kohler, 1880), which appears to be responsible for some of the legendary framework of Mountain Mary's life. Long a resident of Mary Young's home county of Berks, and with an interest in his adopted culture, which helped to stimulate its flowering into dialect literature,[39] Wollenweber may have gathered some of the legendary details in the neighborhood, but recast them into an historical novella, centering on the Revolutionary War period. The story as it appears on his pages is a highly romantic and sentimental one, a Dutch tearjerker from an era long before the television soap opera.

According to Wollenweber, Maria Jung emigrated with her parents and two brothers from a village (he names it Feuerbach) in Württemberg shortly before the Revolution. Parents and brothers died of plague and were buried at sea, and Maria was left alone. Love came to the rescue, however, in the form of a young fellow passenger named Theodore Benz, from the city of Lahr in Baden. When they landed in Philadelphia after a voyage of ninety-two days, Maria generously paid Theodore's passage to avoid his being sold as a redemptioner, and the young orphans were befriended by Pastor Muhlenberg, Lutheran minister of Philadelphia, who got Maria a kitchen job at the Golden Swan Inn under a charitable (Lutheran) widow named Mrs. Kreuder, while Theodore the farm boy was sent to Oley to work on the Frederick Leinbach farm. After a year's work, Frederick Leinbach, who was growing old, gave Theodore a 175-acre farm in the Oley Hills, and Theodore hastened to Philadelphia to tell his prospective bride the good news. By this time the outbreak of the Revolution had Philadelphia in turmoil, and Theodore was prevailed upon to join the Berks County volunteers in Captain Hiester's company, and also finally to marry Maria. Pastor Muhlenberg tied the knot and Frau Kreuder gave a Swabian wedding party at the Golden Swan, but alas, Theodore was forced to leave his bride that very night, as his company was ordered across the Delaware to Trenton.

Treu bis in den Tod.

Die Berg=Maria,

oder

Wer nur den lieben Gott läßt walten.

Eine

Geschichtliche Erzählung

aus

Pennsylvanien.

Von

L. A. Wollenweber.

[Der Alte vom Berge.]

Mit Illustrationen von F. Schlitte.

Philadelphia:

Verlag von Ig. Kohler, No. 911 Archstraße.

1880.

(2)

Figure 9.2. The life and legends of "Mountain Mary" are enshrined in a considerable number of printed books and articles. This is the title page of Ludwig Wollenweber's novella, *Die Berg-Maria* (Mountain Mary), published in Philadelphia in 1880. Wollenweber was a German immigrant (1830) who edited the *Philadelphia Demokrat* before retiring to the Pennsylvania Dutch country which he came to love as his second home. In his later years he wrote travel articles for German-language newspapers under the name "Der Alte vom Berge" (The Old Man of the Mountain). *(Courtesy Roughwood Collection)*

Figure 9.3. "Mountain Mary," from Wollenweber's book of 1880. The artist, a European immigrant, pictures her in a German *Einsiedler* (hermit) setting. *(Courtesy Roughwood Collection)*

They were never to see each other again. Theodore and his Berks County buddies were taken prisoner at the battle of Long Island and put on board the prison ship Jersey where they finally died of starvation. Heartbroken, Maria settled as a hermitess on the farm in the Oley Hills, where as a good neighbor and herbal healer she achieved a reputation for sanctity. When she died in 1819, Wollenweber tells us, her funeral was the largest that had ever taken place in Pike Township. There was no house in Oley and the adjoining townships which had not sent its representative, and from far and wide the mourners came by wagon and on horseback to pay Maria their last respects.[40]

Fortunately there is some historical documentation preserved about Mary Young from which we can determine that she never married, and that while she lived as a hermitess for at least thirty years in the Oley Hills, she had first settled there at least a decade previously, evidently during the Revolution, with her widowed mother and two sisters, who preceded her in death and are said to be buried in the private burial ground on Mary's farm. Mary's will, dated March 13, 1813, is on record at the courthouse in Reading—in it she describes herself as a spinster, left legacies to two brothers-in-law, Matthias Motz and John George Schneider, and a niece, Maria Elizabeth Schneider, and names as executors her neighbors Daniel Joder and Thomas Lee. Mary died November 16, 1819, her will was probated November 20, and her forty-two-acre mountain farm sold to Martin Joder.[41]

Between the full-blown romance and this historical skeleton of fact, there was a body of legendry about Mountain Mary. As was the case with the classical European saint, her legend began to take shape while she was yet alive. Benjamin M. Hollinshead, a young Philadelphia Quaker, visited Mary Young in her mountain hermitage in the summer of 1819. The account is a lengthy one, hence we shall digest it here.[42]

Upon his arrival in Oley Valley, Hollinshead's hosts proposed an ascent of the Oley Hills. Above all, they suggested paying "a visit to Mary Young, commonly known in the neighborhood as 'Mountain Mary.'" She received them with kindness, and "after an interchange of inquiries on the part of her and our friends, she commenced speaking in a religious strain, informing us through a lady of our party who acted as interpreter, that on serious subjects she was obliged to speak in her native language, the German." After a hike around the mountain farm they returned to say good-bye, and found "a table spread with delicious bread, butter, cream, milk and preserved fruits: and we were invited to partake in a manner so sincere and courteous, that we did not distrust our kind hostess when she assured us we were welcome."

The account accents her unshaken faith and bright hope "that nothing would be permitted to happen to her that was not for her good." From her neighbors in Oley and acquaintances in Reading and Philadelphia, Hollinshead collected anecdotes revealing her character, and all his informants "concurred in bearing testimony to her great worth." Her industry, they reported, was prodigious. Living alone, she kept several cows and did all her haying; she marketed butter; she kept bees. The paths on the mountain she graded to make the ascent easier. Her benevolence extended even to "animals of a noxious kind." When marmots invaded her walled garden, she set traps and caught them, but "instead of putting them to death, which she might have done as sole lady of the garden, she took them to the neighboring hills, telling them to go and trespass no more."[43]

From the period immediately after her death, there came two tributes in verse which increased the veneration. In 1822 there appeared in Philadelphia a small volume of verse entitled *The Phantom Barge, and other Poems,* by an unidentified poet (possibly Hollinshead himself), who called himself "The Limner." The book contains a poem called "Mary Young," who according to the author was "an old German lady, of a remarkably pious character, residing among the Oley Hills, near Reading, in the State of Pennsylvania."[44] While Mary had died in 1819, it is clear from the poem that she was living when the verses were written.

The second poetic tribute to Mountain Mary was written in 1819, a poem that John Joseph Stoudt in his recent collection of Pennsylvania German verse calls "Mountain Mary's Epitaph" and ascribed to "A Gentleman of Oley."[45]

Mountain Mary's Epitaph

Hier unter diesem Steine
   Sanft ruhen die Gebeine,
   Der frommen Maria:
Ihr Herz und ganzes Leben
   War ihrem Gott ergeben,
   Dass man's an ihrem Wandel sah.

Sie hat ganz unverdrossen,
   Bis dreis[s]ig Jahr verflossen,
   In Einsamkeit gewohnt:
Ihr Angesichtes Zügen
   Verriethen Gottes Lieb,
   Damit der Herr sie hat belohnt.

Nachdem sie schon verschieden,
   Sah man den Süssen Frieden
   In ihrem Angesicht;
Es war voll Lieb und Wonn
   Als zur Gnaden-sonn,
   Noch immer hingericht.

Nun ist sie weggenommen;
  Gott hies[s] sie zu sich kommen,
  Aus diesem Jammerthal:
Wo auf den Himmels-Auen,
  Sie Jesum wird anschauen,
  Mit seiner auserwählten Zahl.

[Here under this stone rest in peace the remains of the pious Maria, her heart and her entire life were dedicated to God, as any could see from her conduct. In solitude she lived without complaint for thirty years, the lines of her face betraying God's love with which the Lord rewarded her. Even after death sweet peace was visible in her countenance, it was full of love and bliss, as if still directed toward the sun of grace. Now she is taken away, God bade her come to Him out of this vale of tears, where on the meadows of Heaven she will look upon Jesus amid his elect number.]

The poem actually was written by a neighbor of Mary's, Daniel Bertolet (1781–1868), poet, hymnist, farmer, and local preacher whose work in folk hymnody I have described in detail elsewhere.[46] In his German journal for 1819 he describes his neighbor's death and funeral, and includes as a tribute the lines above.[47]

The legend of Mountain Mary continued to grow in the nineteenth century. At the end of the century, a Reading newspaperman named Frank Brown, one of the first active folklorists to deal with Berks County's own traditions, wrote a sketch of Mountain Mary for the *Sunday Eagle,* based principally upon Wollenweber, but to which he appended materials he gathered by interview in the Oley Valley.[48] Among the information that he collected is that she grafted apples, known among her neighbors as the "Mammy," "Weiss," and "Good Mary" apples, that she carried her cheese to the huckster's down the mountain on a tray on her head, and that she made her own paths over the mountain in every direction, lightening the grade in some spots to enable her to move with ease even at all hours of the night, since her services as a healer were required as much at night as in the daytime. But we are also enlightened by this writer about Mary's belief in and use of occult powers:

She was a great believer in witchcraft. She frequently related that for a time an owl came and drank out of her milk pail every evening while she was milking. She could not prevent the bird from getting near the pail except by catching it, since it was so tame that it couldn't be scared away. So one night she caught the owl and burned its feet by slightly holding it over her fire. The next morning a neighboring woman, whom she took to be the witch, couldn't put on her shoes on account of burned feet. "Die Berg Maria" was known not only in every corner of this county, but all over Eastern Pennsylvania. She was sometimes called as far as Philadelphia to practice medicine in her novel way.

The importance of this evidence is that while the contemporary accounts accented the virtue and holiness of the mountain recluse, these later traditions, gathered from old folk who remembered seeing Mary sixty or more years previously, accent Mary the apple-grafter, Mary the road-grading engineer, and what is more significant, Mary the healer. Even, it appears, Mary the powwower, the practitioner not of the rational herbal medicine encouraged, according to Wollenweber, by Pastor Muhlenberg, but what is much more likely, a healer by traditional means in which religion, prayer, and even magico-religious charms played a great part.[49]

Actually the best historical account of Mountain Mary was Daniel Miller's "Maria Young, the Mountain Recluse of Oley," a paper read before the Historical Society of Berks County, December 10, 1912. Miller noted that "all the older people are familiar with the story and love to recite it, but these are rapidly passing away. For the benefit of the younger people and future generations it has been thought well to put into proper form and on record a sketch of the life of this interesting character, before the flight of time shall bury her in oblivion." He thought it especially urgent to get the story straight since Wollenweber's booklet of 1880—"an interesting and touching story written in fascinating style"—unfortunately "contains many errors, and is therefore unreliable. It is evidently far more legendary and imaginary than authentic."[50] Miller's account, drawn from Hollinshead, Rupp, and other early sources, emphasized Mary's industry (a Pennsylvania Dutch virtue), her role in the community as spiritual adviser, and her work as healer. He mentions nothing of an occult side to her practice.

> Mary Young was also a physician, of course not in the modern sense. She gathered many kinds of medicinal herbs and prepared remedies for various ailments. In this employment she was successful. Her intelligence served her well in this line of usefulness. People came to her from near and far for help in sickness, and in this way she came to be widely known as "Mountain Mary." She used mostly so-called household remedies in the treatment of the sick and rendered the community a great service in the absence of regular physicians. She not only relieved the sick, but gave Christian comfort to the dying. It is said that she spent much time at the bedside of those departing this life and gave them such instruction and comfort as were at her disposal.

In the twentieth century a kind of local cult of Mountain Mary developed. In 1934 the Berks County chapter of the D.A.R. erected a marker to her memory which described her as "a pioneer nurse, comforter of body and soul, benevolent, pious, brave and charitable," closing its tribute with the biblical verse, "She hath done what she could."[51]

From 1945 until 1962 pilgrimages to Mountain Mary's grave were annual affairs in November. Responsible for this development was a local dialect poet, Ralph W. Berky. Among the speakers on one of these cold, shivering occasions in the November woods that I myself remember attending were Dr. Preston A. Barba of Muhlenberg College and Dr. Elmer E. S. Johnson, Schwenkfelder historian and retired Hartford Theological Foundation professor.[52] Also involved in stimulation of contemporary interest in Mountain Mary is Dr. Barba, who republished earlier accounts of the mountain saint in his column in the Allentown *Morning Call.*

In conclusion, the legend of Mountain Mary has some of the same general appeal as the legends of the classic medieval saints. To her neighbors as well as to a wider circle of admirers including some representatives of Philadelphia Quakerdom, Mary's renunciation of the world showed an inward strength that most of them admired, even envied in their dealing with everyday interpersonal crises. Her saintliness had an appeal in the early stages of Pennsylvania German culture when frontier crudities were found everywhere—it offered a glimpse of the unworldly in a world of confusion. But with all her high and holy qualities that make this Protestant saint different from and yet a model for her common neighbors, she was obviously one of them in her human sympathies and in her folk-medical beliefs.

Where does it go from here? Mountain Mary is of course not a saint complete with cult, either ecclesiastical or folk-religious, in the European sense of the word. But somehow through the century and a half since her death, her story and her memory, complete with minimal but significant legendary framework, have continued to minister to some need in the local culture of Berks and adjoining counties and to a certain extent to the entire Pennsylvania German area.

Conclusion

Our brief study of the saint's legend in the Pennsylvania German folk culture points to the following conclusions.

1. American legendry must be studied in relation to the stratigraphy of the cultures that produced and used it. In addition to the obvious values of comparative legend studies, we need more and not fewer historical studies, more documentation on the shifts and trends in the use of myths and legend in our American regional folk-cultures as well as our national culture. Applying Professor Dorson's three-century framework[53] to such regional folk-cultures as the Pennsylvania German culture, we can ask, what types of stories were dominant in the culture of the eighteenth, the nineteenth, and the twentieth century? Since the myths and legends of one epoch are never completely replaced by those of the new, what happened, for instance, to the oldest stratum of legend in the culture, the European

saint's legend, in the American experience? Old materials inherited from earlier stages of a culture are often reshaped, retreaded, combined, syncretized with the new. When an earlier form does disappear (or is relegated to an ultra-conservative or sectarian remnant culture, for example, the retention of the Genoveva legend among the Amish), what substitutes has the majority culture found for the lost trait?

2. Cross-genre and cross-media studies of American legendry are also called for. As in European settings, American legendry was presented in multigenre and multimedia approaches. Iconography (folk and popular prints, for example) as well as balladry and popular imprints (chapbook and broadside materials), have to be studied together for American legend subjects, to see whether the same values are not expressed in all the media. When the fraktur symbols of the eighteenth century, the Lilies and Tulips and Flat Dutch Hearts, were replaced by the popular culture symbol of the American Eagle,[54] what happened at the same time to the legends of the Genovevas and the Mountain Marys? Pictorial evidence is particularly important. In some cultures, portraits of holy men—paintings of Zen masters in Japanese Zen Buddhism, framed portraits of favorite preachers in Protestant areas—served as foci of lay devotion, a kind of devotional shorthand, a substitute for the biography or the legend, but calling forth the same emotional reaction.[55] This is even more apparent in European Catholic cultures, where the simplest peasant recognizes his favorite saints by the crude almanac woodcut, or the starkest *ex voto* on the walls of a healing chapel.

3. Shifts or trends in the concept of sainthood itself need study in the United States.[56] We have mentioned the obvious difference between Roman Catholic and Protestant attitudes toward the "saint," and the development of Protestant substitutes for the forbidden items after the Reformation, as for example the substitution of Old Testament stories for earlier saints' legends. The ethos of American Catholicism also has produced a new syncretism in regard to traditional saints. Not all the favorite saints of all the ethnic groups that make up the American Catholic church were portable. Flying nuns, for example, who have recently made an appalling reappearance in television, belong in places like Calabria, where the folk culture provides a rationale for them.[57]

If there has been an obvious shift from the miraculous to the virtue pole of the saint's legend, there are some other questions that need to be studied. What is the reason, for instance, for the continuance in popularity of so many of the traditional women saints in the twentieth century, while the number of favorite male saints has sharply dwindled? What effect will the downgrading of so many of the popular saints in the wake of Vatican II have on everyday Catholic piety? Will there be Catholic substitutes, intellectual or biblical, for the Philomenas and the Christophers? These are some of the many questions that can and should be asked about the concept of the saint, as one studies the surviving legends of the saints in our twentieth-century world.

One closing thought. Perhaps we can remind ourselves, after looking over the vast range of human personality represented in the saints' legends, that as one of the great students of medieval sainthood put it, "goodness admits more variety in type than wickedness, and produces more interesting characters."[58]

Notes

1. "Pennsylvania German Folklore Research: An Historical Analysis," in Glenn G. Gilbert, ed., *The History of the German Language in America* (Austin: University of Texas Press, 1971). "Plain Dutch and Gay Dutch: Two Worlds in the Dutch Country," *The Pennsylvania Dutchman* 8 (1) (Summer, 1956): 34–55.

2. John M. Mecklin, *The Passing of the Saint: A Study of a Cultural Type* (Chicago: University of Chicago Press, 1941), 15. The following quotation in this paragraph is from pp. 13–15. For the ultimate origins of the saint in ancient Christianity, see also the old standard works by the Bollandist Father Delehaye, *Les Origines du culte des martyrs* (1912), *Les Légendes hagiographiques* (1927), and *Sanctus* (1927).

3. Richard Weiss, *Volkskunde der Schweiz: Grundriss* (Erlenbach-Zürich: Eugen Rentsch Verlag, 1946), 303–11.

4. Albrecht Jobst, *Evangelische Kirche und Volkstum: Ein Beitrag zur Geschichte der Volkskunde* (Stuttgart: Alfred Kröner Verlag, 1938), 64.

5. Because of space limitations, I have omitted two additional sections of the original paper, (1) The Saint in the Pennsylvania German Calendar, which deals with the profusion of days, times, and customs associated with saint-lore in the Pennsylvania German folk culture, and (2) The Saint in Pennsylvania German Onomastics, in which I discuss survivals of the European saint-complex in family names, personal names, place names, and church names. Both sections will be published as papers elsewhere.

6. John George Hohman, a Catholic immigrant who arrived in Philadelphia in 1802, published in 1819–20 the single most influential volume of occult charms in America, *Der Lang Verborgene Freund* (Reading, Pa., 1820). Translated into English in two separate translations as *The Long Lost Friend* (Harrisburg, 1846) and *The Long Hidden Friend* (Carlisle, 1863), the book has gone through many editions in both English and German and has been used in occult folk-medical practice far beyond the borders of the Pennsylvania German counties. In my quotations from the book in this paper, I have used the third German edition, published at Harrisburg, Pa., in 1840. The translations are my own.

7. This document, one of two purchased in Berks County in 1967, is signed by Peter Schles[s]man. The Schlessman family were immigrants of 1752, 1753, and 1773, from the county of Löwenstein-Wertheim in the Main valley up from Frankfurt. See Otto Langguth, "Pennsylvania German Pioneers from the County of Wertheim," Don Yoder, trans. and ed., *Pennsylvania German Folklore Society* 12 (1947): 241–44, 262–66.

8. Hohman, *Der Lang Verborgene Freund* (1840), 29.

9. Ibid., 53.
10. Ibid., 38.
11. Ibid., 15.
12. Ibid., 26.
13. Ibid., 46.
14. Ibid., 47.
15. Ibid., 50–51.
16. I am informed by Professor Américo Paredes of the University of Texas that the story of "Genoveva de Brabante" is also popular among the Mexican-Americans in the Southwest.
17. The literature on the legend of Genoveva of Brabant is extensive. In addition to the works cited in our notes (28–29), see F. Görres, "Neue Forschungen zur Genovefa Sage," *Annalen des Historischen Vereins für den Niederrhein* 66 (1898): 1–39; *Die Religion in Geschichte und Gegenwart,* vol. 2, cols. 1389–1390; *Lexikon für Theologie und Kirche,* vol. 4, cols. 384–85; and finally, Agnes B. C. Dunbar, *A Dictionary of Saintly Women* (London: George Bell & Sons, 1904–5), 1:336–38, which retells the story in charming fashion, gives the saint's day as April 2, and at the end of her account admits that, as Cahier says, "Geneviève has no business among the saints [i.e., because she was never really canonized]. Local belief has it that she is still sitting spinning behind the altar in the church of Frauenkirchen, on the site of the famous Abbey of Lach, and that the hum of her wheel is heard there."
18. Thomas R. Brendle and William S. Troxell, *Pennsylvania German Folk Tales, Legends, Once-Upon-a-Time Stories, Maxims and Sayings Spoken in the Dialect Popularly Known as Pennsylvania Dutch* (Norristown, Pa., 1944), Pennsylvania German Society, vol. 50. The story was recorded from Mrs. Kate Moyer of Egypt, Lehigh County, Pa. In the late 1940s when Professors Boyer and Buffington and I were gathering materials for *Songs Along the Mahantongo,* one of our informants, Mrs. William Beissel of Leck Kill, Northumberland County, Pa., recited a spirited version of the story of Genoveva, but unfortunately since we were at the time genre-oriented and interested only in folk songs, we failed to record it. I have in the past year begun to sound out my present informants on the Genoveva tradition and will report my findings on Genoveva in oral tradition in a subsequent paper.
19. On the relation of printed text to oral transmission of folk legend material, see Linda Dégh, *Folktales and Society: Story-Telling in a Hungarian Peasant Community* (Bloomington: Indiana University Press, 1969), 146–63. For the Genoveva legend in Hungary, see p. 159.
20. An additional eighteenth-century edition is entitled *Unschuldige Genovefa, Wie sie durch Verleumdung zum Tod verurtheilet, und nachdem sie 7 Jahr von Kräuter und Hirsch-milch gelebt hatte, wunderbarlich errettet worden* (Ephrata: Gedruckt bey Benjamin Meyer, 1796), 48 pp.
21. Gustav Sigismund Peters was born in Langebrück, Germany, in 1793, and died at Harrisburg, Pa., March 22, 1847. His name appears on Carlisle imprints from 1823 to 1827, after which he printed in Harrisburg. See Alfred L. Shoemaker, "Biographical Sketches of the Dauphin County Publishers," *The Pennsylvania Dutchman* 3 (21) (April 1, 1952): 8.
22. Thus far I have, unfortunately, found no similar development of the Genoveva cult into folk art forms in Pennsylvania, except for the crude woodcuts that embellished the chapbooks.

23. Josef Vydra, *Die Hinterglasmalerei: Volkskunst aus tschechoslowakischen Sammlungen* (Prague: Artia, 1957), plates 23, 59–64, and 85.

24. Noted on an autumn visit to Sicily during my 1961 sabbatical. For examples, see the plates in the book, Salvatore Lo Presti, *Il Carretto: Monografia sul Carretto Sicìliano* (Palermo: S. F. Flaccovio, 1959).

25. On the literary and artistic use of the Genoveva legend, see B. Golz, *Pfalzgräfin Genoveva in der deutschen Dichtung* (1897); A. Müller, *Die dramatische Bearbeitung der Genovefa-Legende* (1902); and Albert Schneider, *Geneviève de Brabant dans la littérature allemande* ([1957]). The two operas were those of Schumann (1848) and Scholz (1875).

26. Weiss, *Volkskunde der Schweiz,* 205–6.

27. For parallel versions of these two editions of the French song, see Pierre Brochon, *Le Livre de colportage en France depuis le XVIe siècle: Sa Littérature—Ses Lecteurs* (Paris: Librairie Gründ, 1954), 113–16. For an eight-verse German *Moritat* with the Genoveva theme, published at Hamburg in 1867 in the chapbook *Genoveva, der frommen Pfalzgräfin Leiden und Errettung,* see facsimile reproduction in L. Petzoldt, ed., *Graue Thaten sind Geschehen: 31 Moritaten* (München: Heimeran, 1968). Dr. Petzoldt's notes on the text refer to the earlier German version, *Eine erschröckliche Geschicht, welche sich hat zugetragen mit einem Grafen* ([Oedenburg?], 1767), as well as to a Dutch ballad entitled *Nieuw Liedeken van de deugdelyke Palsgravinne Genoveva,* published in Antwerp in the first half of the nineteenth century by the printer, J. Thys (1783–1854). For the texts and tunes of several of the ballads about Genoveva, see Wilhelm Heiske, ed., with collaboration of Erich Seemann, Rolf Wilhelm Brednich, and Wolfgang Suppan, *Deutsche Volkslieder mit ihren Melodien: Balladen* 5 (5) (Freiburg/Breisgau: Deutsches Volksliedarchiv, 1967), 163–80, with bibliography on p. 180.

28. Nikolaus Kyll and Josef Räder, "Die Fraukirch in der Pellenz im Rheinlande und die Genovefalegende," *Rheinisches Jahrbuch für Volkskunde* 1 (1950): 81ff.; Heinrich Günter, *Psychologie der Legende: Studien zu einer wissenschaftlichen Heiligen-Geschichte* (Freiburg: Verlag Herder, 1949), 58. The latter work discusses the Genoveva legend's universal motifs of innocent-rejecting-seduction and animal-aiding-human (pp. 46, 58).

29. Hermann Bausinger, *Formen der "Volkspoesie"* (Berlin: Erich Schmidt Verlag, 1968), 195–96.

30. C. Kruyskamp, *Nederlandsche Volksboeken* (Leiden, 1942), 52.

31. The Preface contains also a P.S. signed by Ray S. Kinsinger, Springs, Pa., Star Route, representing the Amish community of Somerset Co., Pa., and Grant Co., Md. It reads as follows: "Having read this book over a few times I found it very interesting and impressive. I decided to get some more printed (as they are not to be gotten anymore) and believe most of them have passed through lots of hands to be read, as is the case with the one that I am rewriting this story from, which is getting very shabby. I do believe whoever reads it cannot help but take a liking to it." From the Kinsinger Press at Gordonville there also appeared, in 1966, *The Stolen Child: Or How Henry von Eichenfels Came to the Knowledge of God. A Narrative for Children and Children's Friends, Designed for Reading Classes in Sabbath schools, Etc.,* as translated from German by J. Bachman and J. Miller and published by I. D. Rupp in 1836. This from my unpublished paper entitled, "Cultural Lag in Amish Reading Matter."

32. For the rationale of Protestant biography, see Kenneth B. Murdock, "Clio in the Wilderness: History and Biography in Puritan New England," *Church History* (Sept. 1955): 221–38, which makes use of the theories in Romein's *De Biografie: Een Inleiding* (Amsterdam, 1946). Also useful is Daniel B. Shea, *Spiritual Autobiography in Early America* (Princeton, N.J.: Princeton University Press, 1968).

33. Bausinger, *Formen der "Volkspoesie,"* 186.

34. See the discussion of American Puritan biography in Richard M. Dorson, *American Folklore* (Chicago: University of Chicago Press, 1959), chap 1.

35. Rufus M. Jones, *The Later Periods of Quakerism* (London, 1921), 1, 92–103.

36. John G. Morris, *Fifty Years in the Lutheran Ministry* (Baltimore, 1878), 13–14. Letter written April 14, 1861, for Sprague's *Annals of the American Pulpit*. The reference to the influence of Jung-Stilling is valuable. His *Theorie der Geisterkunde,* with its pioneer analysis of extrasensory perception, was so popular among the educated Germans in this country that it was reprinted here in 1816.

37. For a different assignation of charisma to a preacher, see Harry H. Hiller, "The Sleeping Preachers: An Historical Study of the Role of Charisma in Amish Society," *Pennsylvania Folklife*, 18 (2) (Winter, 1968–69): 19–31; see also Don Yoder, "Trance-Preaching in the United States," ibid., 12–18.

38. Bibliography on Mountain Mary, in addition to the items cited in the following notes, include Rupp, *History of the Counties of Berks and Lebanon* (Lancaster, Pa., 1844); and Morton L. Montgomery, *History of Berks County in Pennsylvania* (Philadelphia, 1886). My editorial introduction to Frank Brown, "New Light on 'Mountain Mary,'" *Pennsylvania Folklife*, 15 (3) (Spring, 1966): 10, contains the basic general bibliography. The Sunday supplement versions of Mary's story, important for pictorial representation, include "Romances of Pennsylvania History 15—The Hermit Saint of Oley Valley," *The North American* (Philadelphia), May 31, 1914, showing a strong young Mary ax in hand, having just felled a tree in front of her one-story log hut. Wayne Homan's "Pennsylvania Heritage: Mountain Mary," *The Philadelphia Inquirer Magazine* (July 15, 1962), includes photographs of the Hill Lutheran Church, organized 1747, which Mary attended, and Mary's bakeoven and springhouse, which many of the travelers' accounts mention. Some additional documentation on the Jung family appeared in the *Historical Review of Berks County* (Jan. 1939), and *The Pennsylvania Dutchman* 3 (12) (Nov. 15, 1952).

39. Ludwig A. Wollenweber's little book, *Gemälde aus dem Pennsylvanischen Volksleben. Schilderungen und Aufsätze in poetischer und prosaischer Form, in Mundart und Ausdrucksweise der Deutsch-Pennsylvanier.* Cyklus I. (Philadelphia und Leipzig: Verlag von Schäfer und Koradi, 1869), 140 pp., is actually the first volume of Pennsylvania German dialect prose published—as nearly as his acculturated *Pfälzisch* dialect could be called Pennsylvania German.

40. Wollenweber's *Gemälde* contains a short sketch of Die Berg Maria (pp. 125–27). Since he assigns her here a different European origin than in his novella of 1880, I quote his text in full: "In Pike Township, Berks County, hot vor Johre z'rick e wunnerbar Weibsmensch sich ufgehalte, ihr Name war *Maria Jung,* un sie hot über dreissig Johre lang ganz allenig in ener Art Hütt nächst zu Motz Mühl gewohnt. Sie hot während der lange Zeit bei Niemand gebettelt, Niemand nix böses, aber dorch ihre Kräuter un Medizin den Kranken arg viel Gutes gethan.—Mir ischt gesagt worre, in ihren Papieren hät gestande, sie wäre in Deux-ponts (Zweibrücken) in der Pfalz geboren, un sei anno 1769 in's

Land komme mit em junge Mann, der sie gege ihr Vaters Wille fortgenomme. Wie sie e Zeitlang in dem Land gewese wärre, hät ihr Liebhaber sie verlosse in Philadelphia, un sie hät ihn dann lang gesucht, sei noch Reading kumme, un wie ihr Müh all umsonst wor, hot sie in die Berge verkroche, un e armselig Lebe geführt bis an ihr End. Sie isch im Johr 1819 gestorbe, un e Freund, der die Tugenden des armseligen verstossene Menschenkindes gekannt, un sie mit Leut oft besucht, die viele Meil geträwelt sind, for die *Berg Maria* zu sehne, hat folgende Verse uf sie gemacht" (here follows the four-verse tribute by Daniel Bertolet, reproduced later in our text).

41. Daniel Miller, "Maria Young, the Mountain Recluse of Oley," *Transactions of the Historical Society of Berks County* 3 (1910–1916) (Reading, Pa., 1923): 209–20.

42. Benjamin M. Hollinshead, "Mountain Mary (Die Berg Maria)," *The Pennsylvania German* 3 (1902): 133–42. The account was made available to the present generation of readers by Dr. Preston A. Barba in his column, "'S Pennsylvaanisch Deitsch Eck," *The Morning Call* (Allentown, Pa.), Nov. 20 and 27, 1965.

43. Mrs. Mayer Sprague of Germantown, Pa., in connection with the publication of the Hollinshead account in 1902, added to the Mountain Mary legend the following extrasensory incident from family tradition: "The friend spoken of by Mr. Hollinshead was an ancestor of mine (Mrs. Susanna de Benneville Keim, wife of John Keim, and daughter of Dr. George de Benneville), who, upon awakening from a vivid dream, in which she saw Mountain Mary in dire distress, was so impressed that she made immediate preparations to see Mary. The lady's son tried to dissuade her from going, saying the distance was great, through roads almost impassable, the weather inclement, and the lady herself neither young nor robust. 'My son' said she, 'Mary needs me. My Master has bidden me seek her. I dare not disobey His call.' With the early morning light the old lady, with her grandson, started, taking such comforts as she thought might be needed. Upon arriving there she found her vision confirmed—Mary confined to her bed, and the creatures dependent upon her care in bad need. Great-grandmother stayed with Mary until the end. Mrs. Keim was frequently heard to say, that she counted among her earthly blessings the privilege of being with this sainted woman in her last hour, to witness her loving faith and confidence in her Heavenly Father, who has promised He will never leave or forsake His children who seek Him in spirit and in truth."

44. The poem was republished in Barba, "'S Pennsylvaanisch Deitsch Eck," *The Morning Call,* Nov. 27, 1965.

45. John Joseph Stoudt, *Pennsylvania German Poetry, 1685–1830* (Allentown, Pa., 1956), Pennsylvania German Folklore Society 20 (1956): 266. The poem had earlier appeared in print in Rupp, *History of the Counties of Berks and Lebanon,* 260; and Wollenweber, *Gemälde,* 126–27.

46. *Pennsylvania Spirituals* (Lancaster: Pennsylvania Folklife Society, 1961), 356–57, *passim.* For translations of his German poetry, see Raymond W. Albright, "Daniel Bertolet of Oley," *Historical Review of Berks County* (April 1945), 74–79.

47. The German Journals of Daniel Bertolet for 1819–1820, Bertolet Collection, Pennsylvania Folklife Society, contain three references to Mountain Mary: (1) "Sam Feb 6 1819 Heute war ich bey der Berg Maria" [Saturday, Feb. 6, 1819: Today I was at Mountain Mary's]; (2) "Den 18 November 1819 Heute war die Maria auf dem Berge begraben—'Hilf Herr die Heiligen haben abgenommen' Der tode Leuchnam sehe gans liebreich und schön und ohn Zweifel ist sie in die Ruhe eingegangen" [Nov. 18, 1819: Today Mary of

the Mountain was buried—"Help, Lord, the saints have decreased." The dead corpse looked quite lovely and beautiful and without doubt she has entered into rest]; (3) On Tuesday, Jan. 25, 1820, he inscribed in his journal the four-verse poem and headed it with the words: "Grab-Schrift vor Maria Jungin die am 18ten Novem 1819 begraben siehe Blad 719" [Epitaph for Maria Jung who was buried Nov. 18, 1819, see p. 719].

48. I republished these materials, with an introduction on sources of the life and legend of Mountain Mary, in Frank Brown, "New Light on 'Mountain Mary,'" *Pennsylvania Folklife*, 15 (3) (Spring 1966): 10–15. The materials quoted in this paper are found on pp. 14–15.

49. I am here interpreting the folktale of the owl-witch, which of course involved counter-witchcraft rather than folk medicine proper, to mean that by this period Mary's reputation as healer involved the occult as well as the herbal approach. In nineteenth-century Pennsylvania, belief in both witchcraft and the efficacy of powwowing were part of the common folk religion of the layman, and Mary's reputation may have been based on her actual use of magico-religious formulas in her comfort and care of the sick and dying. On the negative side, of course, is the fact that none of the earlier accounts mention the occult element.

50. Miller, "Maria Young," p. 209. Miller (1834–1913) was a native of Lebanon County who established the *Republikaner von Berks* in Reading in 1869 and also published and helped to edit the *Reformirter Hausfreund.* He was himself a well-known dialect writer and published two volumes of Pennsylvania German dialect poetry and prose. For his biography, see Harry Hess Reichard, *Pennsylvania-German Dialect Writings and Their Writers* (Lancaster, Pa., 1918), Pennsylvania German Society 26 (1915): 158–61.

51. Cited in Barba, "'S Pennsylvaanisch Deitsch Eck," *The Morning Call,* Nov. 27, 1965.

52. The memorial meeting described was on Nov. 16, 1946. See ibid., for John Birmelin's dialect poem, *"An der Baerrig Maria Ihrm Grab"* [At Mountain Mary's Grave], which was read on the occasion.

53. See Richard M. Dorson, "How Shall We Rewrite Charles M. Skinner Today?" *American Folk Legend: A Symposium,* Wayland D. Hand, ed. (Berkeley: University of California Press, 1971), 69–95.

54. See Don Yoder, Introduction, *Pennsylvania German Fraktur and Color Drawings* (Lancaster: Pennsylvania Farm Museum of Landis Valley, 1969).

55. Martin Scharfe's valuable book, *Evangelische Andachtsbilder: Studien zur Intention und Funktion des Bildes in der Frömmigkeitsgeschichte vornehmlich des schwäbischen Raumes* (Stuttgart: Verlag Müller und Gräff, 1968), suggests the relationship of the icon and portrait to devotional literature.

56. Here again I recommend to my folklorist colleagues Mecklin's book, *The Passing of the Saint.*

57. For some of the more unusual aspects of South Italian folk religiosity, see Ernesto de Martino, *Sud e Magia* (Milano: Feltrinelli Editore, 1959); also Phyllis Williams, *South Italian Folkways in Italy and America* (New Haven: Yale University Press, 1934), especially chaps. 7–8.

58. Vida Scudder, trans. and ed., *Saint Catherine of Siena as Seen in Her Letters* (London: J. M. Dent, 1906). 2.

10

Harvest Home

New England had its Thanksgiving, Pennsylvania its Harvest Home. The New England festival, which has become the national Thanksgiving on the last Thursday of November, celebrated the Pilgrim Fathers' gratitude for deliverance in the new homeland. Because New Englanders, following the Puritan tradition, refused to celebrate Christmas, Thanksgiving became for them a social festival, with family reunions and turkey dinners, which took the place of the forbidden Christmas festival. Harvest Home, on the other hand, was a summer or early autumn festival, held by Pennsylvania's Lutheran and Reformed churches in celebration of God's goodness to them at harvest time.

While the New England Thanksgiving was a harvest festival too, its historical framework has made it appropriate as a national festival, using New England history, as we have done in so many cases, as symbolic of the history of the entire nation.[1]

Pennsylvania's Harvest Home was once—in the farming valleys west of the Delaware—more important to Pennsylvania farmers of Dutch tongue than the November Thanksgiving Day, which was looked upon as a dubious and unnecessary, almost resented, Yankee gift. Lutherans and Reformed celebrated Christmas and gave their private and public thanks to God for their summer's harvest at the summer Harvest Home. Hence for many years they felt no need of celebrating the Yankee Thanksgiving.

Let us look at the history of this Pennsylvania festival which was long the rival of Thanksgiving Day, and even after the absorption of Thanksgiving into Pennsylvania's calendar, is still celebrated in Lutheran and Reformed churches, even in the cities, and has been borrowed by Mennonites, Methodists, and other church groups in Pennsylvania and areas where Pennsylvanians settled in North, South, and West.

The comparative study of folklore and primitive religion has shown the

---

This article originally appeared in *Pennsylvania Folklife* 9 (4) (Fall 1958): 2–11.

universality of harvest festivals throughout the world. To show his gratitude to the gods the farmer celebrated harvest variously with a harvest supper, a blessing of the fields and the produce of the fields, harvest dances and merry-making, harvest songs, harvest fertility rites, harvest services in temple and meetinghouse. The Palestinian harvest festivals described in the Old Testament are only one example of primitive harvest festivals with a religious motivation.[2] Roman Catholicism with its multitude of holy days had no special harvest thanksgiving festival, but in Germany the Autumn Ember Days (*Quatemberfasten*) and the beating of the bounds (*Flurprozessionen* or *Bittgänge*) served the purpose. In the Protestant churches of Germany, as witnessed by the oldest church liturgies from the Reformation period, there were special Protestant services (Lutheran and Reformed) for harvest thanksgiving. Many of these, we are told, were held in September, on the Sunday nearest to St. Michael's Day (September 29).[3] This was known as the *Erntedankfest* or *Erntefest,* and the sermon preached on the day was the *Erntepredigt* or *Ernterede.*[4]

In the British Isles ancient Celtic and Saxon rituals united to give us the time of summer or autumn merrymaking known as "Harvest Home." Brand's charming chapter on "Harvest Home, alias Mell Supper, Kern, or Churn Supper, or Feast of Ingathering" tells us of the British customs in their variations from Cornwall to Scotland, with the Harvest Doll or Kern (Corn) Baby, or as the Scots called it, the "Maiden" (the last sheaf dressed and paraded through the fields), Harvest Dinners, Harvest Suppers, Harvest Dances.[5] These rites were part of the "Merry England" tradition and for the most part were pagan survivals. The Church gave its blessing on Lammas Day (August 1) to the first loaves made from the harvest wheat, which were offered at mass. In more recent times in Protestant England the "harvest thanksgiving" has become an unofficial religious festival, on a Sunday in September or October. In both the Church of England and the Free Churches it has become customary to "decorate the church with fruit, flowers, and vegetables which are later devoted to charity; special hymns are sung; and there is frequently a visiting preacher."[6] There seems to have been no provision for such a service in the Book of Common Prayer, as there was in the continental German liturgies, but special forms do exist from the end of the eighteenth century.

Pennsylvania's Harvest Home

The Pennsylvania "Harvest Home" as celebrated by Lutherans and Reformed, consisted originally of a service, with harvest sermon, in the church, usually during the week, either in the midst of harvest or at the close of harvest. It could be held anywhere from the first week of July till

Figure 10.1. Harvest Home display in a Pennsylvania Dutch church, ca. 1910, with pastor posing in pulpit. Note tall corn stalks and garden vegetables.
(Courtesy Roughwood Collection)

Figure 10.2. Typical Harvest Home display in a Pennsylvania German church, Strasburg Lutheran Church, Lancaster County, 1908.
(Courtesy Roughwood Collection)

mid-October, depending upon the decision of pastor or congregation. Sometimes the Harvest Home service was combined with the Fall Communion and the ingathering of fall catechumens. In the period after the Civil War we begin to read of churches decorated with the fruits and vegetables and grains of harvest, and the gradual centering of the festival on a Sunday rather than on a weekday. The service had its hymns and its liturgy and was one of the joyous festivals of the church year as conceived by rural Pennsylvanians.

A special feature of Pennsylvania's Harvest Home was the special collections—"harvest thank offerings"—that were usually a part of it. The early editorials on Harvest Home in the Lutheran and Reformed press begin to mention this offering in the 1830s and are happy to report that while a few congregations devoted it to parish needs (the earlier custom?), generally it was shared by the church boards and given to missions, education, and other benevolent causes.

As the churches came to be decorated with the fruits of the harvest, it became customary to give the display either to the minister and his family, or to the church orphanages or homes for the aged. The custom of giving the fruits and vegetables to the minister is related, of course, to the old American custom of the "Donation" or "Pound Party" which in most cases came to be centered in the Advent and New Year season.[7]

Before looking at the historical evidence, let us study the words used for Harvest Home in Pennsylvania.

While the present name (Harvest Home) derives from the British Isles tradition, the older terms "harvest service" and "harvest sermon" were in use throughout the nineteenth century and are the American adaptations of the dialect terms *Aernkarrich* and *Aernbreddich.* Variants occasionally reported are "harvest festival" and "harvest thanksgiving." Gradually, however, "harvest home" has absorbed all of these terms and has become fixed in usage.[8]

Early References to Harvest Home

By 1820 we find Harvest Home in full operation in Pennsylvania as a church festival. Since it was not a general American custom, references by travelers through the Dutch Country tell us something of the practice in the early nineteenth century. The earliest of these is a blast from the eccentric Methodist circuit-rider, Jacob Gruber (1778–1850), who lost no opportunities to point up what he considered the lack of "religion" among Pennsylvania's Lutheran and Reformed people. Describing his travels on Dauphin Circuit in German Pennsylvania about 1820, he writes: "I found they had an old custom. On Sunday after harvest their parson preached a harvest sermon, as it was called; but this year there were very few to hear it; most of the congregation were gone to the mountain to gather whortleberries. It would be hard if the poor parson should have to preach another thanksgiving sermon when the berries were all gathered; then when all is safe take a week-day for it. That would hinder any from visiting on Sunday, and having their play and amusements."[9]

This early reference by an outsider—if the Pennsylvanian Jacob Gruber can be called an "outsider"—can be paired with the reference made by John W. Richards, grandson of Henry Melchior Muhlenberg, in 1825, when pastor of the New Holland Lutheran charge in Lancaster County, to preaching "harvest sermons."[10]

The nation learned of the custom in August, 1847, when the *Union Magazine* commented on Pennsylvania's distinctive harvest festival. "In Pennsylvania, where perhaps a preponderance of settlers from the continent of Europe—a less absorbingly ambitious people than the Yankees—has infused a more genial spirit; they hold what they call a harvest service—a general meeting for thanksgiving and prayer. This is a graceful and interesting custom, and one which might be adopted wherever the plough opens the soil."[11]

Harvest Home in the Church Papers

Our best source for Harvest Home is the weekly press of the Lutheran and Reformed Churches. This reflected the customs and interests of pastor and people from generation to generation. One of the first references to the custom to appear in print dates from 1837. A "country minister," writing in the Reformed Church *Messenger,* notes that "it is usual, in most of our churches, to preach a Thanksgiving Sermon at this time of the year [August]." This he conceived to be "very appropriate, in order to fix the minds of our people to that gratitude, which we should feel for the many blessings which God has been pleased to bestow upon the labors of the husbandman." He notes also that "it is the practice of many of the churches at this time to take up collections for missions, education, the synod's fund, and other similar objects" (*Weekly Messenger of the German Reformed Church,* August 2, 1837).

"From time immemorial," states the editor of the *Messenger* in 1846, "it has been customary in our German churches, to preach what is technically called a harvest sermon, at the close of the season for the ingathering of the grain, which custom is still regularly observed wherever the German spirit is retained in our churches." The editor liked the custom "exceedingly well," and expressed the hope "that our German churches will ever cleave to the good old custom, handed down to them as a heritage from

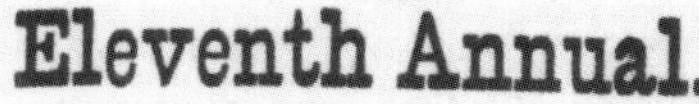

Figure 10.3. The secular use of the term "Harvest Home" has roots in English tradition and involved a farmers' picnic. This badge from 1870 illustrates the secular Harvest Home. *(Courtesy Roughwood Collection)*

their forefathers, of annually assembling themselves in the house of God, for the special purpose of acknowledging the goodness of God and in furnishing us with the necessaries of life, and of making to him appropriate returns of thankfulness" (*Weekly Messenger of the German Reformed Church,* July 22, 1846).

And again in 1859—"This is the season of the year at which harvest festivals are observed and harvest sermons preached. . . . The harvest festival is observed in the old country; harvest sermons are very common in Germany. The observance of this festival was also introduced into our own country by our German forefathers. It is a beautiful and appropriate custom." In the same issue a correspondent calling himself "Matthias" found it also a beautiful old custom "to take up a collection for Missions and other objects of benevolence immediately after harvest, when the Harvest Sermon is preached," as the "thank offering of the people for a plentiful harvest" (*German Reformed Messenger,* August 3, 1859). And in 1860: "We hope this year, more than ever, the good old custom will be observed, to preach harvest sermons, and take up special collections for benevolent objects" (*German Reformed Messenger,* August 15, 1860).

One of the finest general descriptions of Harvest Home comes from the pen of George B. Russell, editor of a Reformed periodical in Pittsburgh, in August of 1873: "At this season of the year, our churches usually hold a Harvest Festival. In some it is marked by a Harvest Sermon. In others, a regular Harvest Home celebration is observed by all the people in a social and religious gathering; where, besides the special sermon and other religious services, the joyful thanksgiving is expressed also in a general festival. Young and old unite together in a round of common social religious intercourse; every family contributes something to the general bounty of the long table, laden with substantial evidences of plenty; and the gathered pledges for the supply of the current wants of the people for the year, makes the glad hearts as full as the well-stored barns.

"Before the invention and general observance of the New England Thanksgiving day, these Harvest Home celebrations were the chief thanksgiving among our ancestors. They had their own peculiar habits and customs; and the sons of the sires are not entirely forgetful of these old ways to which they were trained" (*Our Church Paper,* August 1, 1873).

With the social changes that came about through urbanization in the 1870s and 1880s the custom showed some signs of senescence. "We have heard persons speak unfavorably of special harvest sermons and services," reports a Reformed source in 1882. "They say, the daily and weekly offerings of praise to God for temporal and spiritual blessings are sufficient; and of far more account than any special service once a year. We answer—*do both,* and then be more sure of being right; or rather, do both as a privilege you would not be deprived of." There is, to be sure, a biblical warrant for an annual harvest festival. "We suppose their pastors may have told them about it, but some of them may have forgotten it" (*The Messenger,* July 19, 1882). In 1885 our editor praises the churches for celebrating "this time-honored festival," but noted that "there are congregations which are inclined to imitate the Baptists, Presbyterians, etc., and ignore the customs of their German fathers. Others say that it is all very well for the country congregations to observe the harvest thanksgiving but pretend to see no propriety in city or town churches keeping up the custom" (*The Messenger,* September 16, 1885).

The end of the century brought a plea for "The Harvest Festival in City Churches" by S. R. Bridenbaugh (1899): "But why should every city congregation not engage in a similar service? We rejoice that many do. The custom of holding Harvest Festivals is by no means confined to the country and village churches, but is coming to be quite generally observed in towns and cities as well. Not all, however, recognize the fitness or acknowledge the obligation to render such special service of thanksgiving. City people are engaged in other than agricultural pursuits. Many of them rarely see a harvest field, and can scarcely distinguish wheat from rye, or barley from oats. All the stronger is the reason, therefore, why they should be reminded of the Giver of our daily bread." Another point in favor of a city Harvest Home was the fact that "members of city churches need to be reminded that they are all children of the soil; that, with few exceptions, they are the descendants of farmers; that their fathers, if not themselves, came from country homes . . ."—which should have been an obvious fact to the membership of urban Lutheran and Reformed churches in Pennsylvania in the year it was written (*Reformed Church Messenger,* August 31, 1899).

The Ministers Describe It

The ministers themselves, naturally, of both Lutheran and Reformed Churches, provide us with important evidence. From the large body of clerical journals and memoirs from Pennsylvania we select two witnesses.

We step into the study of Henry Harbaugh in the Reformed parsonage at Lewisburg in the Susquehanna Valley. His diary is open to 1844. "Sunday, July 28 . . . Preached at 10 a harvest sermon. 'The harvest is past etc.' . . . Thursday, August 1[.] Was principally engaged in writing a harvest sermon—Friday, August 2[.] Wrote still at the harvest sermon—" "Sunday, August 17, [1845]—preached a harvest sermon." "Friday, July 31, [1846]—Br. Fisher preached the harvest sermon." "Thursday, August 19, [1847]—Rev. Kieffer came. He preached the Harvest Sermon—." "Sunday, July 23, [1848] . . . Preached a Harvest Sermon at 10, German . . ." "Sunday, August

12, [1849]. Preached in Milton in English. Harvest Sermon on 'Oh that men would praise the Lord' 118 Ps. (I think)— . . ."[12] Which tells us that Harvest Home was held both on Sunday and on weekdays and that Harbaugh occasionally let his Dutch influence his English.

In Eastern Pennsylvania the great German preacher of the Reformed Church of the nineteenth century was William A. Helffrich. Let us allow Pastor Helffrich to tell us something of his Harvest Sermons: 1851: "At my harvest sermons I laid more weight on the matter of missions. In the Ziegel, Heidelberg, and Longswamp congregation it began slowly to go better. In the whole parish I collected about ninety dollars, where earlier twenty dollars was given. Nothing is more difficult than to give our members a conception of the importance of the missionary cause. Although I preached missionary sermons in all five congregations shortly before the harvest festival (*Erntefest*), it still progresses only slowly." 1858: "This summer I had seven Harvest Sermons (*Erntepredigten*) to give. These were formerly all conducted during the week. The people left all work in the field and came in great numbers to the house of God. The harvest collections ran to $115. But how difficult it continues, to bring the people the conception of giving!" 1859: "My Harvest Sermons (*Erntepredigten*), of which there were eight, I conducted in the month of August, and those all on weekdays, and collected $132."[13]

Church Decoration

The distinctive feature of the Pennsylvania Lutheran and Reformed Harvest Home is the decoration of the church with the fruit and grain of the harvest. Christmas and Harvest were the two occasions when the country churches were decked in the green and color of the natural world—when, so to speak, the farm and the forest came to church. And unforgettable to Pennsylvanians are those childhood memories of tall cornstalks, pumpkins, huge loaves of bread, and sheaves of wheat camouflaging the pulpit and almost hiding the minister.

It seems as if the members competed with one another to bring the finest products of the summer's harvest—the largest pumpkins, the tallest cornstalks, the most grotesque squashes, the reddest apples. And church vied with church through the years—all unofficially, of course—to see which congregation could put on the finest display.

While this feature of our festival undoubtedly had ancient and pre-Christian roots—the bringing of the finest products of the field to the temple not only as thanks to the deity for an accomplished harvest but as insurance in advance of a good harvest next year—our printed references to Pennsylvanians decorating their churches at Harvest Home do not begin until the Civil War period and later. For example, in 1878 the Reformed home missionary, A. C. Whitmer, spent "four days among the hills of Somerset County," visiting the Beam Charge, centering in Stoystown, in an area "noted for its pasture land, rich butter, pure honey, long hills, and very many Reformed people." "I attended," he tells us, "the harvest home services in the four congregations of said charge, and so passed over a wide range of 'hill country.' The churches were nicely decorated with the fruits of the season—wheat, rye, oats, corn, apples, grapes, peaches, pears, potatoes, even down to peppers, hops, pop corn and sunflowers. Wreaths and beautiful crosses, made of grasses, grain, and trailing moss, adorned the pulpits, baptismal fonts and reading desks. Part of each service was, of course, the special thank-offering of the people for their abundant harvest" (*The Messenger,* September 11, 1878).

Whitmer's own church in Buffalo Valley celebrated Harvest Festival on Sunday, August 6, 1882: "The Church was beautifully decorated for the occasion. The harvest fields had been made to contribute their beautiful and well-grown sheaves, and the still growing grain stood among these with promises for the future. The floral kingdom had contributed an abundance in the form of living plants. A beautiful sickle formed of white petunias, geraniums and other flowers, adorned the front of the pulpit" (*The Messenger,* August 16, 1882).

Several additional descriptions, all from the year 1885, enable us to picture decoration styles at the time—before the invasion of canned goods and cereal cartons.

Elk Lick, Paradise Charge—"The last of the harvest services were held in this charge August 23rd. The attendance was large and the interest was such as to gratify pastor and people. The decorations were extensive and consisted of evergreens, cut flowers and blooming plants, grains and all manner of fruits, beautifully arranged on and around the altar. On the walls were sentences and emblems that were suggestive" (*The Messenger,* September 16, 1885).

Lock Haven—"September 6th, harvest home was celebrated in St. Luke's Reformed Church at Lock Haven, Pa. The church was tastefully decorated with flowers, vines, fruit, vegetables and grain. It was a memorable Sabbath both for the congregation and pastor.... Besides harvest home, it was the pastor's birthday and the first Sabbath of his third year's pastorate" (*The Messenger,* September 23, 1885).

Carlisle—"Seldom, if ever, has the Reformed Church in this place held a more delighted audience, or looked grander, than on Sunday. This day had been set apart for the Annual Harvest Home Thanksgiving Service, which is looked forward to with much interest.... The pulpit and altar was handsomely decorated. Around the altar were potted plants, such as palms, ferns, etc., handsomely arranged, and on either side of the pulpit was a sheaf of grain, together with a number of vegetables. A beautiful pyramid of fruit set in the baptismal font. The reading desk was also handsomely decorated with smilax, which, taken as a whole, made one of the prettiest sights we have ever seen. Mr. Henry Keller did the decorating, and to him must be given all the praise" (*The Messenger,* October 21, 1885, quoting the *Carlisle Herald).*

Lebanon—"October 11th would, no doubt, seem to many persons to be a late date for holding a 'Harvest Home Festival,' but this date was chosen by St. John's of Lebanon, of which Rev. George B. Resser is pastor, for the reason, among others, that it would afford the opportunity of including every variety of the fruits of the earth in symbolizing the opening of God's beneficent hand; and the service at this time was a joyous, beneficial one to all the participants. The decorations of the church were very profuse, and very beautiful. Under the skillful management of a committee of ladies, and some gentlemen helpers, appropriate mottoes, arches, Gothic and various other styles, pyramids of fruits, and well-selected plants were so arranged in and about the chancel as to produce a very pleasing effect" (*The Messenger,* October 21, 1885).

Ashland—" . . . celebrated their annual harvest festival on Sunday, October 11. The church was elaborately decorated for the occasion; on the altar rested a pyramid of choice fruit, with vases of beautiful flowers on either side; the chancel was surmounted by an arch trimmed artistically with vines and the cereal grains; on either side of the pulpit platform were immense pyramids of vegetables and fruits of every description tastefully arranged, the whole being not only pleasing to the eye but conveying an idea of the rich bounty of God" (*The Messenger,* October 21, 1885).

Of the eighteen Reformed parishes which reported Harvest Home celebrations in the *Reformed Church Messenger* for September 13, 1900, all held their services on a Sunday, September 2 and 9, except Muddy Creek (26 August). The accounts are proud to mention "liberal" or "generous" offerings. At Danville "the entire lot of decorations was donated to the pastor, for which he is sincerely thankful." The displays were "elaborate," "artistic," "profuse," "beautiful," "tasty," "appropriate." It seems that our minister friends, who vied with each other in describing the displays that banked their pulpits and altars, were running out of adjectives. Hence we will stop, before becoming monotonous, with the year 1900.[14]

The Harvest Festival among the Plain People

Harvest Home, as we have described it, was a Lutheran and Reformed institution. But a word needs to be said about the observance of harvest festivals by the other Pennsylvania churches of German origin. Both the

Dunkards (Brethren) and the Mennonites had harvest services, but whether or not they were indigenous in the plain tradition, or—as J. Winfield Fretz suggests in a recent study[15]—borrowed from the Lutheran and Reformed environment, cannot be definitely stated at this time.

First, the Dunkard practice of "harvest meetings," evidence of which comes from the Shenandoah Valley of Virginia. Elder John Kline, the Dunkard evangelist, mentions "harvest meetings" yearly in his journal, as for instance: "Friday, August 11, [1843]. Attend harvest meeting at the Flat Rock.... Saturday, August 12. Harvest meeting at our meeting-house." And again in 1844: "Saturday, July 27. Harvest meeting at Copp's schoolhouse in Shenandoah County, Virginia. Wednesday, July 31. Harvest meeting at the Brush meetinghouse. Thursday, August 1. Go to harvest meeting at Daniel Garber's meetinghouse...." At a harvest meeting on Friday, July 25, 1845, Luke 16 was read, and the elder's meditation was on "how best to help the poor...." And at the "harvest thanksgiving" at the elder's home meetinghouse on Friday, August 8, 1851, a baptism took place, suggesting the connection between the spiritual and the material harvest.[16]

The Mennonites had a similar practice. "One inspiring custom of the Franconia Mennonites, hallowed by long observance" writes John C. Wenger, "is the observance of 'Harvest-Home' services. These meetings are held in all the meetinghouses in the fall of each year to commemorate the ingathering of the harvest and 'to remember the Lord of harvest in thanksgiving.' Texts are usually selected from the Old Testament and considerable attention is devoted to the promises of material prosperity given to the Israelites in Canaan if they would truly serve the Lord. Warnings are sounded against apostasy and the example of the apostate Hebrews is pointed out. The meetings are usually held on Saturday afternoon, and ordained men from many congregations are present at all the Harvest-Home meetings. In general the members are very conscientious about attending at least one such service each year."[17]

If it is true that the festival—at least in the form of decorated sanctuaries—spread from the Lutheran-Reformed groups to some of our plain cultures, it also spread to the revivalist groups—the Methodists and their Pennsylvania Dutch stepchildren, the United Brethren, Evangelicals, and other conversionist sects. The Methodist festival is known both as "Harvest Home" and "Booth Festival," the churches are decorated, and the produce goes to the church homes, according to conference direction.[18]

Pennsylvania Variants of Harvest Home

Connected with the Harvest Home service—which was a festival *in* the churches—there were in the nineteenth century four additional institutions that made use of the term "harvest home." These were the Sunday School Harvest Home, the Harvest Home Children's Service, the Harvest Home Picnic (a church affair), and the Harvest Home Picnic (secular affair).

1. *The Sunday School Harvest Home.* In the early 1840s, reports of Sunday School Harvest Home celebrations begin to appear in the church papers. These were of a picnic nature, with sermons and picnic meal, Sunday School processions and recitations.

Here is an example from 1841. On July 26, 1841, the Boehm's, Whitemarsh and adjoining Reformed Sunday Schools held a "Harvest Home Celebration" in the woods, "where the necessary arrangements of seats, &c. had been made by the committee appointed for the purpose." The "concourse of children" and others numbered between seven and eight hundred. German and Dutch Reformed, Baptist and Lutheran clergymen gave the children plenty of sermonic material to digest before and after their brief intermission for lunch, of which the clerical reporter notes with satisfaction that "few or none during the interval left the ground; & the afternoon of the day was pleasantly, and we hope not without profit spent in singing and prayer and mutual exhortation" (*Weekly Messenger,* August 11, 1841).

2. *The Harvest Home Children's Service.* Children's Day, now generally fixed in the spring or early summer, is an American contribution to the unofficial church year. While Pennsylvania churches now generally hold it on a Sunday in May or June, when the church can be decorated with roses and early summer flowers, in the last quarter of the nineteenth century it was customary for Lutheran and Reformed churches to combine "Children's Day" with "Harvest Home." The decorated church seemed an appropriate frame for a display of juvenile elocution.

One account must suffice, that of St. Paul's Reformed Church, Butler, Pennsylvania, which celebrated its first Children's Day, September 13, 1885:

> The church was filled with smiling faces and eager little hearts at an early hour. The decorations, though not elaborate, were very neat and tasteful. At the rear end of the pulpit platform was a very beautiful arch made of autumn leaves, tinged with autumnal hue, with a picture of the cross in the centre. Under each end of the arch stood stalks of corn trimmed with vines and fruit; under the picture a flower-stand with an arch, handsomely decorated, in which hung a canary that mingled its sweet warblings with the songs of the children. In the centre of the platform was a beautiful floral cross and crown, and on each side stood a stand filled with fruit; in front of these were seen two sheaves of wheat with sickles in them; and between the sheaves, two halves of a luscious watermelon. In front of the platform, on each chandelier, hung another cage with a canary in it. Bouquets, baskets, and banks of flowers helped greatly to beautify the scene.

> The whole presented a unique appearance, and was beautiful indeed. But the eager little faces in front presented the loveliest sight of all. (*The Messenger,* September 30, 1885)

3. *The Harvest Home Picnic*—the church affair—is revealed in the "Harvest Home Pic-Nic" that was reported in the *Lutheran Observer* for September 26, 1884, from the Greensburg *Evening Press.* This was an annual affair, bringing together the Lutherans of Ligonier, Greensburg, Derry, Latrobe, and Youngstown in Western Pennsylvania. It was held Thursday, September 11, at Idlewild, on the Ligonier Valley Railroad. There was no lack of provisions, "the good Lutheran housewives having a reputation to sustain in that direction."

4. *The Harvest Home Picnic* (secular) is a Central Pennsylvania affair. We read, for instance, in the *Democratic Watchman* (Bellefonte), for 1882, of the Huntingdon Furnace Harvest Home Picnic, an annual community affair. The Grangers' Picnic or Grange Fair, at Centre Hall in Centre County, was originally also called Grangers' Picnic and Harvest Home. The Harvest Home "member's badge," which we reproduce among our illustrations, is a product of the secular Harvest Home.

Pennsylvania versus Thanksgiving

The New England Thanksgiving—like other Yankee gifts to American culture—was not originally welcomed by Pennsylvanians. For many years Lutherans and Reformed paid only grudging attention to it. Editorials in the church papers commented, almost with an I-told-New-England-so feeling, on the sparse attendance in the churches on the day of National Thanksgiving and clucked editorial tongues at the too relaxed character of the diversions to which the rest of the day was devoted.

The editor of the *Lutheran Observer* (Baltimore), December 2, 1853, made no attempt to conceal his dislike for the day. "Thursday last we celebrated as thanksgiving-day, in the usual way; the churches were thinly attended; places of amusement, grogshops, oyster-cellars, &c., were crowded; the surrounding country abounded with shooting-parties, who, in the absence of game, shot at what they might. Many a tame pigeon and 'barn-yard pheasant' was popped over and bagged. More stragglers and drunken men were seen than on any other day in the year, except perhaps Christmas.

"Thanksgiving-days may operate favorably in New England," he continues, "but we don't think they suit our latitude, and incline to the opinion that there would be more virtue in the *breach* than in the *observance* of them."

"Our readers may recollect that when the move was first made to induce the Governor of Maryland to recommend such a day, we opposed it, and some of our friends were amazed that a *religious* paper should pursue such a course. But we knew what we were about; we had our painful apprehensions, and regret to find them now fully verified. The religious portion of our community were not anxious for the appointment of a thanksgiving-day; many of them resisted it, and very justly too. It was mostly those who make no pretentions to religion, and are by no means remarkable for their attendance at public worship, who were most clamorous for such a festival. They have accomplished their purpose, and to us it is evident that the cause of good morals has greatly suffered by the measure."

The editor of the *Reformed Church Messenger* reported December 2, 1868, in an article entitled "National Thanksgiving," that "the day was generally observed. The accounts published, would indicate, that the occasion was one of more than usual interest. In our city [Philadelphia], the places of business generally were closed and the most of the churches open. As far as we can learn, the religious services were well attended. As is mostly the case, perhaps to too great an extent, there was no lack of public amusements, at least during a portion of the day. The community will now move on again in the usual routine, until the holidays arrive, when, we trust, the religious aspect which the observance of such occasions should wear, will not be forgotten."

A correspondent in the *Messenger* the following year was not so enthusiastic about the national Thanksgiving. "How different are the feelings of the people on Christmas, from what they are on our Puritan Thanksgiving day, which comes on the 26th of November, at a time when it is neither winter, summer, spring, nor fall; at a time when the weather is usually the most disagreeable and depressing, rainy, muddy and foggy; in fact generally too much so to half digest the usual Thanksgiving turkey. Then go listen to the unedifying political pulpit discourses, as delivered in the majority of cases on that day; the dozen or two of people who attend church, the eagerness with which they rush from church to the post-office, in hope of finding something with which to drive away their ennui and kill the day; and the laggard manner in which the people close their places of business; and the general perplexity to know what to do with themselves, so as not to offend against the proclamation of the President—and you will wonder no longer why it is, that Christmas is being more and more restored in the affections of the people." The reason, he felt, was that Christmas had an inner vitality, "a power mysterious and inexplicable as the mystery of godliness itself . . . while the Thanksgiving proclamations of Governors and Presidents fall, for the most part, dead upon the ears of the people, and leave them dead as the turkeys upon which they feast, and empty as the plates from which they have eaten" (F. Wall, in *Reformed Church Messenger,* January 13, 1869).

The Lutherans continued their opposition into the 1880s, and also made the logical proposal—logical, that is, to Pennsylvania farmers—that the National Thanksgiving be moved forward into early October, so that it might become a National Harvest-Home Festival. The *Lutheran Observer* for September 5, 1884, came out with the proposal that Thanksgiving be moved—this year—to October 12th. The last Thursday in November having no special meaning (to Pennsylvanians), October 12th, the anniversary of the discovery of America, would fulfil the patriotic motivation and the end of harvest would connect it with the traditional Harvest-Home festivals of Pennsylvania's churches. The editor's description of a Pennsylvanian's view of Thanksgiving is a classic:

"On the shivering edge of winter, long after harvests and autumn fruits have been gathered in, a paltry few mechanically meet in their places of worship and go through the barren form of a sermon and a song, so that many feel the custom would be 'more honored in the breach than in the observance.' In the utter want of fitness as to time, as well as utter lack of any significance, our Thanksgiving day has become a ghostly, funeral relic of something past, rather than the living, vital expression of grateful hearts for present mercies."

A celebration at the end of harvest, in October, would be a different matter: "What a grand thanksgiving day it would make! Every consideration urges that the change be made this year. The month, too, is pre-eminently fitting. The results of the year have all been garnered. Hearts are swelling with thankfulness, as the barns are bursting with plenty. Just then, when all hearts are full and all harvests are housed, a call on the part of our executive to make some formal expression of our grateful feelings, would turn our thanksgiving day into a real national harvest-home festival."

When its campaign failed, the *Observer* on December 5, 1884, gave space to a long editorial with the title "Wrong Time for Thanksgiving," which calls it pure and simple a New England custom, at the beginning of winter, whose purpose (in New England) was to provide a substitute for Christmas, which was forbidden by the Puritans. The implication in all this is that Pennsylvania, in celebrating both Harvest Home and Christmas—needed no extraneous and unhappily scheduled New England Thanksgiving Day.

The *Observer* represented the "New Lutheran" or revivalist viewpoint on holidays. The more high-church *Lutheran* of Philadelphia, with its emphasis on the ecclesiastical year, countered by exclaiming how good it is to have Thanksgiving Day on the last Thursday of the church year, because (as it somewhat over-optimistically estimated) the vast majority of Christians in the United States observe the church year (*The Lutheran,* November 30, 1882).

It is true, of course, that beginning with the Mercersburg Movement, the Oxford Movement and its American parallels in the Protestant Episcopal Church, and the stiffening up of Lutheran confessionalism in the latter half of the nineteenth century, the church year was given more attention, but in 1884 certainly the Puritan and revivalist groups were still dominant and set the tone for American Protestantism.

By 1900 Pennsylvanians and Yankees had reached a truce on the matter. Thanksgiving Day—turkey and all—had become part and parcel of the Pennsylvanian's year—ecclesiastical as well as secular. But Harvest Home lingered on in the rural and small-town churches. Although each year more and more cans of Campbell's Soups came to be displayed around the pulpit, the decorating committees did not forget the tall corn-stalks, the pumpkins, the loaves of bread, and the sheaves of wheat.

Notes

1. For the New England Thanksgiving, see Horatio Smith, *Festivals, Games, and Amusements, Ancient and Modern* (New York, 1847); George W. Douglas, *The American Book of Days* (New York, 1940); H. S. J. Sickel, *Thanksgiving, Its Source, Philosophy, and History* (Philadelphia, 1940); *Thanksgiving and Harvest Festivals* (New York, 1942).

2. In a Protestant, Bible-based culture such as the Pennsylvania Dutch community of the nineteenth century, all that was needed to justify Harvest Home was to point to the Hebrew example, as for instance, in Exodus 34:22: "And thou shalt observe the feast of weeks, of the first fruits of wheat harvest, and the feast of the ingathering at the year's end" (*German Reformed Messenger,* August 3, 1859). For the biblical harvest festivals, see Hastings, *Encyclopedia of Religion and Ethics.*

3. *Die Religion in Geschichte und Gegenwart* 2 (Tübingen, 1928), col. 289, article on *"Erntedankfest."* See also J. G. Frazer, *The Golden Bough,* 1 (New York, 1914): "Spirits of the Corn and of the Wild"; and "Harvest Festivals" in Hastings, *Encyclopedia of Religion and Ethics.*

4. Grimm, *Deutsches Wörterbuch* 3 (Leipzig, 1862).

5. John Brand, *Observations on Popular Antiquities,* 1 (London, 1813), 439–52.

6. F. L. Cross, *The Oxford Dictionary of the Christian Church* (London: Oxford University Press, 1957), 611.

7. For example, see the description of the "pound party" as it existed in the lumbering country of the Sinnemahoning Valley in North Central Pennsylvania in the 1870s: "That winter the Dent's Run community had a 'pound party' for the preacher at Benezette. There was a regularly stationed Methodist preacher at that place and Dent's Run was one of his appointments. The preacher received for regular salary a small cash stipend and a furnished parsonage. Nevertheless, his parishioners saw that he was also well supplied with provisions and fuel. It was an old custom for the brethren to hold parties in which

each person presented the preacher with one pound of provisions. Hence it was called a 'pound party,' but the Dent's Run quota did not confine its gifts to only one pound each. They were more generous. A ham, slab of bacon, sack of flour, bag of potatoes, a squash, head of cabbage, fruits and the like, made quite a sled load, which kept the preacher and his family from going hungry until the similar party again replenished his larder. The Dent's Run people made a sleigh ride of this occasion. At the parsonage an oyster supper and play party were indulged in before returning home" (George William Huntley, Jr., *A Story of the Sinnemahone* [Williamsport, Pa., 1936], 471).

8. For the British Isles term "harvest home" and its long background, see the *Oxford English Dictionary,* vol. 5. For the Pennsylvania dialect terms it is instructive to check the recent dialect dictionaries. Edwin R. Danner's *Pennsylvania Dutch Dictionary* (York, 1951) gives *"Aiirn Bredich"* (Harvest Home). *A Pennsylvania-Dutch Dictionary* (Quakertown: Meredith Publishing Company, n.d.), based on Prof. A. R. Horne's earlier word-lists of the nineteenth century, gives *"arnkarch"* (harvest home service). Here we have the two principal dialect terms. Howard Snader, *Glossary of 6167 English Words and Expressions and Their Berks County Pennsylvania Dutch Equivalents* (Reading, Pa., 1948) gives for "harvest festival" the improbable term *"Harribscht fescht."* Of the older word-books, James C. Lins' *Common Sense Pennsylvania German Dictionary* (Kempton, Pa., 1887), gives *Arnkarich* (harvest home service).

9. W. P. Strickland, *The Life of Jacob Gruber* (New York: Carlton & Porter, 1860), 276–77.

10. John W. Richards, *Diarium,* 1 (1824–1830), Ministerium of Pennsylvania Archives, Philadelphia Lutheran Seminary, Mt. Airy. His first reference to the custom is September 18, 1825: "Today I preached a harvest sermon I Thess. 5, 18, at Allegheny." In 1826 he "preached Harvest Sermon" three times, all on Sundays in July and August, at Muddy Creek, Bergstrasse, and New Holland. On Sunday, August 6, 1826, having no service of his own, he attended Mr. Hertz's church—St. Stephen's Reformed Church, New Holland—"to hear his harvest Sermon—Text Matt. 6, 11. Gib uns heute unser täglich Brod. . . ." In a later volume of the *Diarium,* that for 1834, he tells us of a somewhat ecumenical service at the Trappe in Montgomery County, his grandfather Muhlenberg's old headquarters, on August 13, 1834: "Preached a Harvest Sermon in German, to a full church at the Trapp, from Ps[alm] 147, 12. 'Eine feierliche Aufforderung zum Preise Gottes für seine Wohltaten.' I got Mr. Wack [Reformed minister] to give out the lines of the first hymn, & as Mr. Hunzicker, the Mennonist preacher was present I got him to line the second hymn, & Mr. Wack the latest [hymn] & the concluding prayer."

11. [Mrs. C. M. Kirkland], "Harvest," in *The Union Magazine of Literature and Art* (New York, 1847), 91.

12. *The Diary of Rev. Henry Harbaugh, D.D.,* [1], 1844–1849, bound typescript in Historical Society of the Evangelical and Reformed Church, Schaff Library, Lancaster Theological Seminary, Lancaster, Pa.

13. William A. Helffrich, *Lebensbild aus dem Pennsylvanisch-Deutschen Predigerstand: oder Wahrheit in Licht und Schatten* (Allentown, Pa., 1906), 187, 245, 256.

14. The most important development in the history of Pennsylvania's Harvest Home since 1900 has been the attempt to extend it into a national and inter-denominational festival under the Federal Council of Churches, now the National Council. This movement began in January, 1942, in a meeting of the Federal Council's Home Missions Council. The leaders involved in pressing for an extension of the festival to other rural churches throughout the nation were the Reverend William J. Rupp (Evangelical and Reformed),

Dr. Benson Y. Landis (Moravian), Dr. Mark Rich (Director of Rural Work for the Northern Baptist Convention), Dr. O. O. Arnold (Church of the United Brethren in Christ), and Dr. O. O. Tripp (Director of Rural Work for the Congregational-Christian Churches). The Town and Country Committee of the Federal Council in 1942 published its first Harvest Home Bulletin, of which 18,000 copies were distributed throughout the nation. The bulletin, with outline of a harvest home service, has been an annual affair since then. For this information we are indebted to the Reverend William J. Rupp, Pastor, United Church of Christ, Souderton, Pennsylvania.

15. *The Mennonite Encyclopedia*, 2 (1956): 671: "In some churches the present observance seems to be an outgrowth of an earlier Thanksgiving Day worship service. In other instances Mennonites imitated the pattern established by other Protestant churches. In Eastern Pennsylvania, for instance, the harvest festival is widely observed in Lutheran and Reformed churches by annually placing the best fruits of the harvest on the altar of the church in connection with a worship service." Similar practices in the Mennonite groups of the United States and Canada, says the writer, are "of comparatively recent origin," coming in during the first third of the twentieth century.

16. Benjamin Funk, ed., *Life and Labors of Elder John Kline, The Martyr Missionary* (Elgin, Ill.: Brethren Publishing House, 1900), 147, 157, 191, 295.

17. John C. Wenger, *History of the Mennonites of the Franconia Conference* (Telford, Pa.: Franconia Mennonite Historical Society, 1937), 36: see also 179, reference to the "harvest thank offering" of the Blooming Glen congregation in Bucks County, held Monday, July 24, 1882.

18. The *Lancaster Advertiser*, sometime in the early 1950s, included a description of a Methodist "Harvest-Home Service" in Lancaster: "The Festival of Harvest-Home will be observed in Ross Street Church next Sunday, 10:45 a.m. Donations of canned fruit and vegetables, potatoes, soap, soap powders, cereals, will be on display, together with seasonal decorations. All donations will be divided equally between The Cornwall Methodist Church Home for the Aged and The Crispus Attucks Center, Lancaster. Food donations may be brought to the church all day Saturday, also Sunday morning. Gifts of money will also be received."

Figure 11.1. Charles Franklin Eckert (1871–1960), farmer and butcher of Adams County, who delighted in telling stories from his own and his family's past reflecting belief in the occult powers.
(Photo: Don Yoder)

11

Witch Tales from Adams County

Frank Eckert was an experience to know—one of those persons who in themselves represent an era and a way of life that is now mostly past. Apart from being the best of my informants on the folktale west of the Susquehanna, Frank was a delightful person, with the wisdom and humor that had grown out of a lifetime on the farm.

Born Charles Franklin Eckert in 1871 in Butler Township, Adams County, "down close Bender's Church," as he put it, he spent his lifetime as a farmer and butcher in Adams County, and died in 1960, at the age of 89, at the home of his daughter near Bendersville in the county of his birth. He is buried in the cemetery at Bender's Church.

In the twenty-some years that I knew Frank Eckert I had many opportunities to talk with him of the old days and the old beliefs of the rural Pennsylvania that he represented. In several lengthy recording sessions, first on wire (now re-recorded on tape) and later on tape, I was able to record many of his favorite tales and reminiscences, his versions of English folksongs and some amusing Dutch-English ones, even his recipes for sausage and "ponhoss" and "rolidge" from a lifetime of expert butchering—many things that fill out our knowledge of folklife in an area largely unrecorded.

The folktales in this article were recorded by me on tape, June 7, 1958, at the home of Frank's son-in-law and daughter, Donald F. and Margaret (Eckert) Garretson, Aspers R. D., Adams County, Pennsylvania. As far as I know they are the first recorded folktales from Adams County—a county known to the nation as the location of the Civil War's most important battleground and the retirement home of President Eisenhower. But Adams County (erected in 1800 out of York County) has had an interesting settlement history and a fascinating mixed folk culture as a result. In a sense it is a microcosm of Pennsylvania folklife in that it had all the major ingredi-

This article originally appeared in *Pennsylvania Folklife* 12 (4) (1962): 29–37.

ents that molded early Pennsylvania—Quaker, Scotch-Irish, and Pennsylvania Dutch. In addition there were the important "Low Dutch" (Holland Dutch) settlement at Hunterstown and one of Pennsylvania's few early rural Catholic settlements at Conewago and McSherrystown. Culturally Adams County has a double relation—to South-Central Pennsylvania and to Western Maryland. Adams County was on one of the principal routes westward at the time when the young nation was on the move to its western frontiers, and in the late nineteenth century became one of Pennsylvania's pioneer commercial fruit-growing areas, but it has preserved earlier ways.

Frank Eckert was of Pennsylvania Dutch background. Although he could not speak the dialect, except for a few words and phrases that he used in jest, his parents did speak it and he himself had a Dutch accent, mixing "v's" and "w's" in authentic fashion. In transcribing the recording I have faithfully reproduced both his Dutchisms (as for example "shindle" for "shingle") and his Central Pennsylvania English dialect pronunciations (examples: "nawthing," "cheer" for chair, "skeared," "afeared," "hems" for hymns, "kittle," "childern," and "hanted"). Especially interesting is his occult vocabulary. He uses both the terms "witchcraft" and "devilment," plus four verbs to bewitch: "bewitch," "witch," "charm," and "put a spell on." For countercharms we have to "take a spell off," to "take a witch's power from her," to "work on somebody" (i.e., a witch doctor working a countercharm against a witch), to "fix" doors (against witches), and to "fix somebody's business" (i.e., really getting back at the witch). For a practitioner of countercharms against witchcraft, he uses constantly the term "witch doctor."

Frank Eckert's formal education was limited. Forced to go to work early in life, he had a very meager schooling. He could do the mathematics of huckstering and farm accounts, but he never learned to read. This was once very common in Pennsylvania and in early America in general. However, Frank's lack of formal education undoubtedly made his thought world of folktale and folk belief all the more sharply focused. In his versions we have the folktales direct rather than in secondary and rationalized form; in other words we have them from a believer rather than in the truncated versions we get from the family, to whom they are no longer important. To Frank they were part of his life, to his family they are "those old stories of Pop's."

A lifelong member of the Lutheran Church, Frank's belief was, however, wider than standard Protestantism, for he shared aspects of the once widespread folk religion of the Dutch Country which most Pennsylvanians have by now discarded. Among these were the belief in witchcraft and counter-witchcraft, powwowing as a form of folk healing, and the connection of heaven and earth in the farming process as seen in his dependence

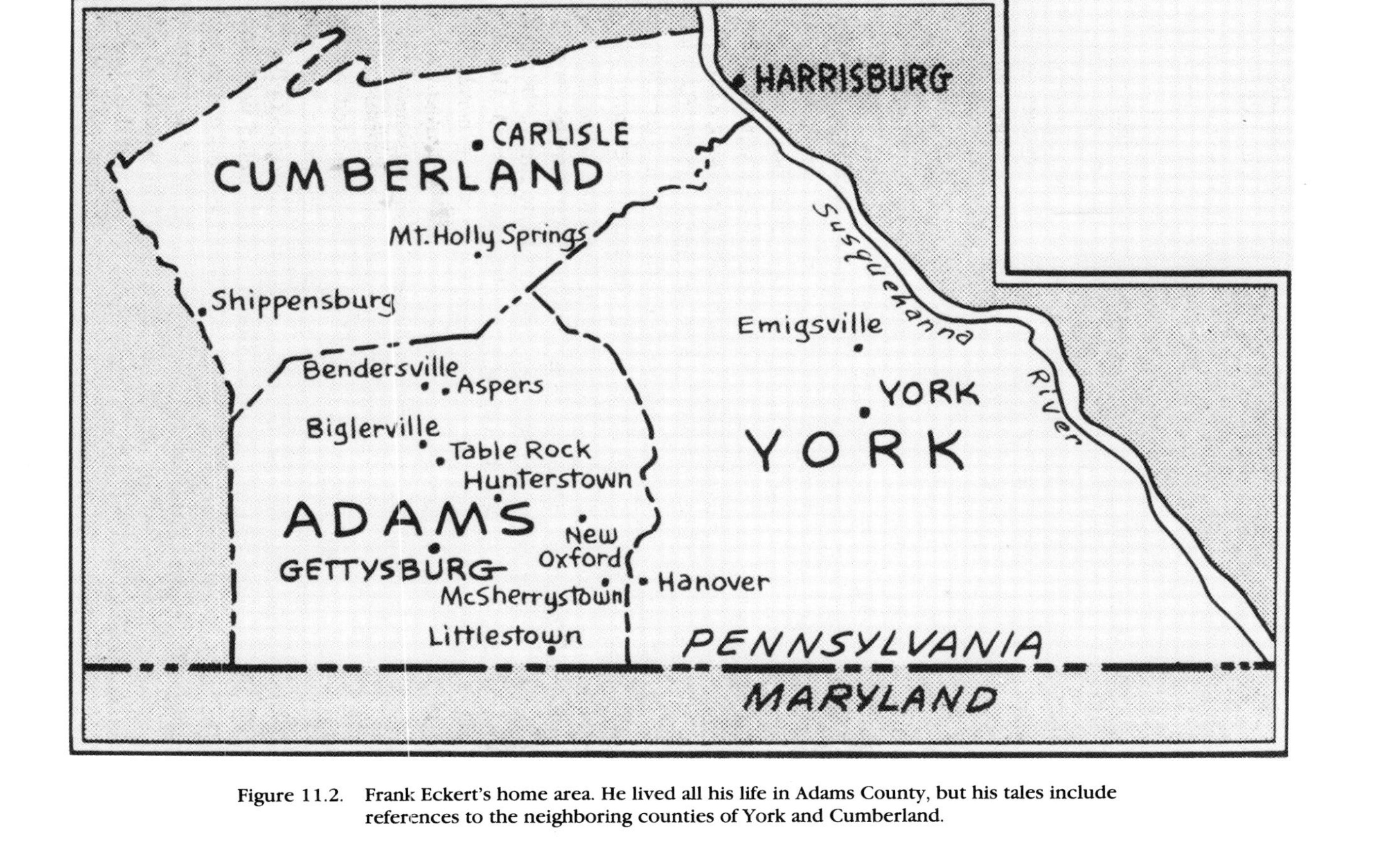

Figure 11.2. Frank Eckert's home area. He lived all his life in Adams County, but his tales include references to the neighboring counties of York and Cumberland.

upon almanac and "up and down signs." For most twentieth-century Pennsylvanians as for most twentieth-century Americans, to borrow a phrase from Thomas Jefferson Wertenbaker, the sense of the invisible world has faded, but for Frank Eckert it was still alive. It is obvious from the tales themselves that these are the tales of a believer.

The boundaries of Frank Eckert's occult world (see our map) include Gettysburg (where "Black Mag" the Fortune-Teller lived), Hanover and York (seats of prominent witch doctors mentioned in the tales), Hunterstown (where the "Irish" witch operated), and to the north, Carlisle, where Frank went to the powwower. Parts of three counties are covered—Adams, Cumberland, and York. Of these, York County came into national notoriety as a "hex county" in 1929 through the most widely publicized "hex" case in Pennsylvania history.

In transcribing the tapes I have set my own questions in brackets, leaving the tales and Frank's answers to my questions in relief, forming the main text of our article. The recording session of several hours' duration is faithfully and completely transcribed. There is only one addition—the titles of the tales are my own, although I have used expressions from the tales themselves, as for example, the "forty-eight-month spell." There is only one deletion—I have abbreviated to initials the names of persons involved in the tales of witchcraft and powwowing. Note also that Frank's "laughter" reported in his telling of the tales does not imply disbelief in them on his part, but rather a kind of nervous tribute to the success of his own tale-telling.

Comparisons of Frank Eckert's tales with the Stith Thompson *Motif-Index of Folk-Literature* (Bloomington, Ind.: Indiana University Press, [1955]), reveal some interesting adaptations. Since some of Frank's tales are twentieth century, the "bewitched wagon" has become the "bewitched automobile" (No. 9), although in No. 15 we still learn the "pole-axe" counter-charm to disenchant the wagon, straight from the witch doctor's mouth. As Witch Doctor Mrs. K. said on another occasion, "That's *true,* Eckert!"

In conclusion, a statement on the importance of this collection of tales. English folktale research is an open field in Pennsylvania. Thus far folktale studies in Pennsylvania have been principally focused upon the Pennsylvania Dutch dialect area, with the unique work of Thomas R. Brendle and William S. Troxell that resulted in their volume of *Pennsylvania German Folk Tales* published in 1944 by the Pennsylvania German Society, and the work of Alfred L. Shoemaker, a small portion of whose extensive recordings have been published from time to time in the publications of the Pennsylvania Folklife Society. From Western Pennsylvania has come the collecting of

Professor Samuel Preston Bayard of the Pennsylvania State University. We trust that this pioneer publication of folktales recorded in South Central Pennsylvania will stimulate research in the English folktale in our state.

[This is a recording made at D. G.'s in Adams County, on the 7th of June, 1958. Now, what is your name?]

Frank Eckert.

[And where were you born?]

I was born in Butler Township, down close Bender's Church.

[And in what year?]

Seventy-one.

[1871. What have you been all your life? What did you do?]

Well, I've worked on a farm all my life, been a farmer all my life. Through the winter I butchered, every winter, for outsiders, neighbors, and through the summer I farmed all my life.

[And always in Adams County?]

Yes. Always lived in Adams County here.

[1] The Hunter and the Witch

[You told me some time ago some stories about your boyhood, about people who had the power to "do harm" to other people. You told the story of a woman who could charm a gun, the gun of a friend of yours. Would you tell me that story?]

That there was an old lady who lived neighbors to us. Her name was Susie H. And if she'd see you in her fields, huntin' rabbits in the Fall of the year, no matter how many rabbits you seen, you couldn't shoot 'em. She'd put a spell on your gun. She'd stand out on the porch and watch you and you could shoot at those rabbits and never git 'em. So one day there was an old man out in the field there huntin'—and he seen a rabbit, and he shot at it and missed it. So wasn't long and they chased up another one. Then she had his gun primed, you know, and [he] shot at the rabbit and missed it. So he drawed a piece of paper out of his pocket, and he drawed a woman's picture on this piece of paper, and tacked it up on the fence and went back for the gun and was gonta shoot into it and she hollered blue murder—this old lady—this old Susie H.—and she run in the house and of course he didn't shoot into it. But that settled her charmin' *his* gun. She never bothered him after that.[1]

[That would stop *her*.]

(Laughter.) Yeah.

[2] The Witch's Butchering

[Do you have any other stories about Susie H.?]

Well, I butchered fer her, me and my son. Went up there one morning. She had an old cow that was 21 years old. And she had a nice big hog to kill. So of course I said to my boy that was with me, I said, "We'll kill the cow first, and hang her up, and then we'll kill the hog." So my boy went out where the old cow was, to the barn. And here the boy was milkin' her—milkin' this cow—and he, my son, went in, and pulled the gun, and he hollered, "Look out, M., I'm gonta shoot her." Old M. said, "Jist wait a minute, till I git out of here." (Laughter.) So we got the old cow out and shot her and when she fell down it sounded like an old barrel fell together. She was 21 years old. And she was that poor she could hardly walk. So we hung this old cow up, then we killed the hog. (Laughter.) And there was snow on the ground, and a neighbor lived right across from 'em. And my boy that was with me was full of the devilment, you know, and tried to git old M. H. excited, or the old woman excited. So we started to cut up this meat, and W. he (that's my boy) hollered that this dog, you know, made like there was a dog draggin' the meat away. Old Susie come out on the porch. She said, "What in the world's goin' on?" "Why," W. said, "that dog over there's draggin' the meat away as fast as we cut it up." W. had throwed a couple of pieces of meat down in the field, in the snow—it didn't hurt it, you know. Oh, she cursed the dog and she cursed them people over there. I laughed more that day than I did any place I ever worked. Had more fun than enough. Well, when we got done, towards evening, why, the old lady said, "Well, God Almighty! We're fixed now." Said, "We've got plenty of meat, and plenty of wood, and plenty of coal." She said, "Let it blow and shnow," she said, "we're fixed." (Laughter.)[2]

[3] The Witch in the Tenant-House

I heard a witch story about a man that I *knowed*—lived in York County. And he had a bunch of cattle, and he had neighbors livin' close to 'im, in a tenant-house on the end of the farm. And his cows began to go *dry,* didn't git 'ny milk from these cattle. And so he went to York, down—he knowed of a witch doctor in York. And he went down to York to this witch doctor, and tol' him about this. "Well," he said, the witch doctor said, "well, it's your neighbor that lives out in that little tenant-house at the end of the farm, that's doin' this." "Well," Frank P. said—that was the man that owned the cattle—said, "what can I do about it?" "Well, now," he said, "listen, don't you try to do anything about it. I'll come *up,* to your place. *I'll* have to do it. I'll have to drive nails in these cow troughs and got to drive 'em a certain way. You might drive 'em in and you might kill her the first time you hit this nail." So this man comes up, drove nails in these troughs, and give him some medicine to put in the troughs, and he left. He said, "Everything'll run all right in a few days," this witch doctor said. So it did. The cows come back to the milk and all right, hadn't any trouble. And this woman they found out was layin' in bed then, helpless. She couldn't get up, she couldn't do nawthin'. The doctors couldn't do nawthin' about it, couldn't help her in any way. This witch doctor had put a spell on her.[3]

[A spell?]

Yes. So that was the end of that story of that witchcraft there.

[Now, how long ago would you say that was? Was that when you were a young man?]

No, it's been—I lived eight years on the Spangler farm—sixteen—about sixteen years back, back, that I heard this about these cattle.[4]

[4] The Forty-Eight-Month Spell

Well, I'll tell you a story of what happened [to] me in my time. I had a neighbor lived neighbors to me—Irish people they were—and they moved on out above Gettysburg. And then they advertised in their paper, the *Times* paper, that they had two hogs to sell—a male hog and a sow that was gonta have pigs—wanted to sell them both. So me and my neighbor went up to see these hogs—and they were all right. She wanted forty-five dollars for the pair. So I bought 'em. I said, "I'll give you a note for three months, with good security, and if you want the money before the note's due, you'll have to pay the discount on it and git the money." So she agreed. Everything was O.K. I bought the hogs and fetched them home and [in] a week or so, the old lady come down to my place—this old Irish lady. She said, "I must have the money for that note." "Well," I said, "you must stand the discount. I told you that when I give you the note: if you wanted the money before the note was due you'd have to pay the discount on it." She said she wouldn't do that. She wanted me to pay the discount or give her a pair of pigs when this sow had pigs. "Well," I said, "I won't do nawthin' of the kind." I said, "Jist let things the way they are and when the note comes due, your money'll be there." She said, "I'll put a spell on you for forty-eight months, if you don't give me the money." "Well," I said, "I won't give you the money." And she went off.

And this thing went on—and I had a good brood mare—as nice a horse as one in the country. And she was to have a mule colt. When this mule colt come, it was marked like a see-bray. And it couldn't suck—it couldn't suck at its mother, [no] matter what you try to do with it. You couldn't get it to drink. His head would jist fly back and for'd and finally the colt died.

Then the sow got pigs—that I got up there—and they were the same as the colt. They couldn't drink. Whenever they'd go to drink, their head would start to fly around and they couldn't take ahold of the nipple. So they all died.

Then I went to Hanover, to a witch doctor, and told her about this. She said, "If I had her picture," she said, "she'd never put a spell on anything else." "Well," I said, "that I can't give you." "Well," she said, "I'll work on her." She worked on this woman. She told me what the woman looked liked—everything. Said she was a big stout husky woman—an Irish lady. I said, "That's right." And I come home, and of course I had nawthin' to do about it. The pigs was dead, the colt was dead, and the mare got that I couldn't go close to her. She wouldn't let me come near her. So I sold her, got rid of her. And when it's all said and done, I was the loser.[5]

[When did that happen, Frank?]

Well, while I lived down here on the last place—on the Lower Farm.

[Table Rock?]

Yes, here at Table Rock. I don't know how many years back that was.

[Thirty years?]

Yes, somewhere around thirty years ago.

[5] The Devil and the Kittle of Money

Well, now, I'll tell you a story. Now I'll tell you a story what happened years back. There was an old gentleman[6] walkin' the road and he came to this farm building and asked to stay over night in the barn. And they turned him down, wouldn't let him stay. And when it got dark, why, he came back and sneaked in the barn and got on the haymow to sleep. Wasn't up there so long till he heard a racket down on the barn floor. So he crawled to the edge of the mow and he looked down. And here this old farmer that he asked to stay all night and the Devil was on the barn floor. Took up some plank, laid 'em back, and went out, fetched a bunch of money, and throwed it down in this kittle that they had. And he fetched a second batch. Said that's all he was gonta put in. So they covered the plank up, and the Devil said to this man, "Now," he said, "there's nobody can take that money out of there, if they find it, unless they throwed pear peelin's around this kittle." All right, then, the old man hung himself, the Devil helped him, and [he] hung himself there on the barn floor. The Devil left and next morning this old man was on the haymow sleeping, and he crawled out there early, and left. So of course the family found the old man out on the barn floor, hangin'—he was dead.

So this went on fer about a year, and this old man that slep' up in the haymow come back, and stopped at this place, and it was in the winter time. Then he said to this old lady, he said, "Could I stay here all night?" "Na," she said, "we couldn't keep you." Said, "We've hardly got stuff enough to live on ourselves. We couldn't keep you." "Well, now," he said, "listen, let me lay back of the stove here in the kitchen and in the morning I'll make you all rich." Well, they thought *that* was fine. So they left the old gentleman stay in the kitchen all night. Next morning, why, they got up and come down and made a bite to eat and he said, "Do you know where you can get any pear peelin's?" "Well," she studied a little while, "yes," she said, "I think I know one of my neighbors had canned some pears whole—didn't peel them." So they went to the place and finally they found pears that had to be peeled and got the peelin's off these pears—and fetched them home. And now, this old man said, "We'll go to the barn." Went out to the barn and pried up these plank, they laid 'em back, and here set the kittle of money. *Then* they all got excited. He said, "Now listen, don't nobody touch that, till I put these pear peelin's around this kittle." So he put the pear peelin's around the kittle. And he said, "Devil," he says, "there's what you asked fer, now the money is mine." And they picked the kettle up, and they took it out, and they were all well fixed. They said that was a *true story.*[7]

[Where did that happen?]

Well, I can't tell you—that must have been in Adams County, somewhere, but I don't know where. I heard my father tell that different times.

[6] The Devil and the Playing-Cards

Well, now, I'll tell you a story that happened to me when I was a boy. I lived on a farm with a man by the name of John Sponseller. And neighbor boys and me, used to go and play cards at night. And I was always told, that where the cards was, the Devil was. So this night we was away playin', over there below a place called Hunterstown, at Mose Gould's, where he kept bachelor's hall there. So we went over there and his sister had baked us some pies and some cakes and we had a nice time all evening, playing euchre, what they called euchre.

So me and my neighbor boy started home, I guess it was about eleven o'clock at night. Come up through the fields and come on down to the end of the road, where I went up to where I lived and he went home to his place.

So I went in, and took my shoes off, went up stairs, and opened the bedroom door where I slept. And when I did, here set a big cat—looked like a cat, but it was twice as big as an ordinary cat—big fiery eyes, settin' right aside of my bed. I opened the door and tried to chase it away and it moved over under my bed. I had no light, so I went and I got a lamp—

searched the room, couldn't find nawthin'. I got in bed, and I just thought, Well, there's the story that my mother told me a many a time. Now I've met it. And that's the last time I'll ever play cards. I'll never play cards no more in my life. And I never did.[8]

[7] The House of the Suicide

Now I'll tell you a story about a place that my parents moved to—called the *Felix* place. This old gentleman and his wife didn't get along together. So she had went to Oxford in to town, to the store, this day. And the old gentleman decided to bury his money and cut his throat. So he buried his money and he went out back of the barn where there was a stream of water. And he laid his hat on the bank, where they found him, with his throat cut from one ear to the other. Well, of course, we moved to this place, and this old gentleman—I guess [the place] was hanted—what they said, he come back there at the place. Then we'd hear him on the porch at night, hear this noise on the porch like someone was cleanin' their shoes to come in. We'd open the door and there was nobody to be seen. We'd close the door, and he'd start this racket again on the porch, cleanin' his shoes and he kep' it up and kep' it up. And my Daddy told the neighbors about it up there. They didn't believe it. They didn't believe there was such a thing. They were Catholics. They didn't believe in this ghost business. Well, Pap said, "Come down some evening." So one evening here come E. and his wife and his mother, down to our place. It was nice and moonlight. Settin' in the kitchen about 8 o'clock every evening, this racket would start. Well, this noise come on the porch. And E. said to my Daddy, "Jake, someone on the porch." "Well," Pap said, "open the door." "No," he said, "I won't *open* the door." So Pap got up and opened the door. There was nobody to be seen. Closed the door and set down, [and this racket] started up, kep' it up. So when these people wanted to go home, they were afeard to go home, afeard to go out. So my Daddy went with them, up through the orchard, straight up, wasn't [far]—we could holler back and for'd together—we was neighbors. So after he got them up home, he looked back down home and old E. said, "Why, there's a light settin' on your garret window, Jake." Blue light, like a big lamp. Blue light. Well, what could you do about it? Come on home, and he never said nawthin' about it to Mother. Mother was a little hard of hearin'. She didn't hear this noise and this racket that was goin' on. You had to be close to her to talk to her. So, this thing kep' up and kep' up so that Daddy was readin' the paper one evening and this noise was on the porch and he jumped up, opened the door and nobody was there, and now he said, "Listen, if there's anything you want, I want you to come and get it, and stop this damn racket on the porch!"

So it stopped on the porch. That's the last we hear it on the *porch*. Then it was above the kitchen. Someone trampin' the spinnin' wheel and you could hear it just as plain as if it had been settin' aside of you. Well, that kep' up. Well, then, the next thing we heard a noise in the cellar. I said to Pap, I wakened my Daddy, "Daddy, there's somebody throwin' the lids off the milk crocks, in the cellar." And he opened the door—and we slept downstairs—and I could see right out on the porch where he opened the cellar door. And he opened the cellar door and something come up, looked just like a big black dog, and he kicked at this and it all disappeared, left. Well, so, in the meantime, then, this racket was goin' on. My mother wanted to know, of course, what [we] was gettin' up, and goin' on about. And they tol' her. And she wanted to leave there. So we moved away.

But in the meantime I had banty chickens—seven little hens—and there was an opening in the wall outside, this out-kitchen, that they could—the chickens could go in and out. I heard them cacklin' under there. And this cellar had no steps down to it, the inside. I said to Daddy, "You let me down the cellar—and I'll look about these banty chickens, they're layin' down there." So he took me by the hand and left me down in there. And I searched the thing all around. Of course I had no light. And there was a place in the wall at the side of the building that wasn't finished diggin' out. So I got up on this bank and crawled back there and there was an opening between the outside wall and this pile of ground. So I poked my head in this place and a man laid his hand on my breast and pushed me back, away from this. And I went back the second time and he pushed me away. Then I hollered for Daddy. And I said "Daddy, get a light and come down here, and see what this is." "Oh," he said, "you're just skeered." Don, I wasn't skeered. But he just made fun of me and [I yelled], "Come and some one git [me] out." Didn't find no eggs, so he took me out, and that was the end of that racket down there.

Well, then, we moved away from there. And after we moved away there was a man owned the place, by the name of Gregg S., and he decided to tear this old out-kitchen away from the other building, and he tore it down and when he tore it down, there where I was pushed away from, in that cellar, they lifted out a pot with 1500 dollars in, that this old man Felix had buried before he cut his throat. So that was the end of that. (Laughter.)[9]

[8] Black Mag, the Fortune-Teller

Well now, I'll tell you a story about an old lady that lived in Gettysburg, an old colored lady. She went by the name of Black Mag. And she could tell you your fortune or she could tell you anything that was taken from your place, that was stole, and go to her and tell her about it and she'd bring it back. So there was a lady that had a woman cleanin' house for her every week, cleanin' up her house. She had worked fer her fer a couple of years. And finally finger rings and earrings and all that stuff disappeared one time. So she couldn't make herself believe that this lady took it, because she had worked fer her fer years. So she went to Old Black Mag, told Old Black Mag about this. And Old Black Mag laughed. She said, "I'll see that it all comes back—every bit of it."

So in a few days here come this woman back. Had all these finger rings and earrings and stuff that she'd taken—and returned it. Well, they thought that couldn't be possible. And she had this woman to excuse her and apologize that she'd never do it again and she'd make everything right. (Laughter.)

So Old Black Mag could bring back anything that was taken. So there was a party had their smokehouse robbed and [they] heard of this old lady. And they went to her, told her about this. "Oh," she said, "it'll all come home. Just go home," she said, "and be satisfied. Your meat will all come back." By God, in a few days one of the neighbors come in—carrying this meat they had taken. So she seemed to be—could git you out of any trouble you could get into.

[You don't know how she got the meat back?]

Why, the party that stole it brought it back.

[No, but you don't know what she said to get it back?]

Oh, no, no, no. But she had a way of doin' these things.[10]

So there was two young fellers—yeah—three young fellers—that I knowed—[that] went to Old Black Mag, and thought they'd git their fortune told. "Well," Old Black Mag said, "I can tell your fortune." "Well," they said, "Now listen, we want to know the good and the bad that we've done." She said, "Are you satisfied for me to tell you what you've done in your time and all the devilment that you've been goin' through?" Yes, they wanted to hear it. So she got to tellin' them and she got down to facts and she said, "Am I tellin' you the truth?" They said, "Yes, you're tellin' me the truth, and that's enough of it, too. I don't want to hear any more of it." (Laughter.)

She could do anything like that. Now why was it, I don't know, but she had the power of doin' these things.

She was a nice friendly, honest old lady, never done *any* body any *harm.* And there was a lotta people went there, and had their fortunes told and she told them the *truth.* And she never told them a story that wasn't true. And as fer as the colored part, my wife often said she was as nice a person as a lot of *our* people were. So she, my wife, never had her fortune told by the old lady. But she often told me about this old lady livin' there in Gettysburg. And a many a one she helped out of their troubles that they had, and never charged 'em anything for doin' it. They'd go to her and explain their trouble and she'd give them satisfaction and everything come true. And she never charged anybody anything for doing it.

[9] The Bewitched Automobile

Well, now, I'll tell you a story what happened to an old lady and her husband down close Hanover. They decided they'd buy themselves a new car—so they did. Well, when Saturday evening come, why, the old gentleman said to his wife, "Now let's take a ride in the new car, this evening." "All right." They started off and they got in as fer as Hanover. And right at the square in Hanover the car stopped. Nobody could start it. They done everything they knowed, got garage fellows there to look at it, nobody could find anything wrong. Car wouldn't move. Somebody said, "Well, you go out to Mrs. K. and tell her about this." Went out to Mrs. K. and told her, and Mrs. K. said, "Well, I'll write you on a piece of paper here and you don't—you're not to read it. You take it back to the car and put it on the starter and put your foot on this paper, on the starter, and," she said, "your car will go." And so they did. Went back, a whole crowd around the car. They put this piece of paper on the starter and he put his foot on it, and the car started right off, and away they went. Didn't have no more trouble that evening with the car.

So the next morning some time, why, they got someone come and said, "Well, the neighbor woman over here is *awful* sick." "Well," they said, "what's wrong with her?" Said, "She's in bed, she's jist that sick she can't be up." And this was the woman that put the spell on the automobile. And Mrs. K. fixed ***her*** business fer her that she didn't bother nobody around there fer awhile.[11]

[10] The Mother Who Bewitched Her Own Daughter

So I'll tell you what happened at this same place, at Mrs. K's. Mrs. K. told me this herself. I didn't hear it from anybody but her. A lady come walkin' in one day and had her daughter with her. And this daughter was nawthin' but a shadow. She was sickly and doctors couldn't help her and nobody could do her any good, so she fetched this child in to Mrs. K. And she said to Mrs. K., said, "Mrs. K., I fetched my daughter over here. I want you to tell me whether you know what's wrong with this child." "Yes," Mrs. K., said, "I can tell you pretty quick." And she said, "If you don't take that spell off of that child," she said, "I'll kill you right where you're settin'." "Oh," this woman jumped up, she said, "what would become of *you?*"

"Well," Mrs. K. said, "nawthin'. The doctors, anybody would pronounce it a stroke." And she said, "I'll give you a *damn* good one. A damn good stroke. If you don't loosen up on that child of yourn. You've made that child all this trouble." And she said, "If you don't take that spell off the child, I'm gonta fix *your* business."

So from that day on the child growed, and no more about it. Now she didn't like that child for some reason or other and she bewitched it, put a spell on it.[12]

[The mother did.]

Yes, the mother of this child. "Well," Mrs. K. said, "That's *true,* Eckert," she said, "I'm not tellin' you a joke," she said, "That's honestly true." And said, "You'd be *surprised* to know what's goin' on in this country."

[11] The Blasphemy of the Flailers

I'll tell you a story what happened one time. Three young fellows, they were flailing rye straw—them times they flailed out rye straw for to tie corn fodder, tie corn shocks, in the fall, when they cut corn and used this straw. And so they got up an argument, these three boys, how strong this rye was. One stalk of rye straw, you could hang yourself with. "Oh," one said to the other, "why," he said, "that couldn't be possible." "Well," he said, "let's try it." Well, they decided they would try it. So they put a big pile of straw underneath of 'em—and they got up above the overhead in the barn—and tied a rye straw around the log right under, right above this pile of straw so's if they'd fall down they wouldn't hurt themselves, you know, if the rye straw would tear. Well, the one went up and fixed himself, and put this rye straw around his neck. And he come down, socked on the barn floor. Well, he got up and the one said to the other, "Why," he said, "Well, the rye straw didn't hold you." "No," he said. "I hung myself in God's name." "Oh." So the other one said, "Well, I'm going up and hang myself in the name of the Devil." So he went up and fixed the rye straw around the log and around his neck and left himself down and there he was—he hung himself. And when they tried to take him down, they said this was a *fact,* there was a *wire* through this rye straw and around his neck. That's the reason the rye straw didn't break. (Laughter.)[13]

[12] The Hanted Hotel

I'll tell you about a story of a hanted house, that happened right here between New Oxford and Brush Run Station. It was a big stone building, as pretty a stone house as you want to look at—was there at the battle of Gettysburg. Was a hotel stand. And it was a rough place. And at this place there was a person killed. Now I don't know whether it was a woman or whether it was a man that was killed at this place, but at this place she was killed and the blood stains was on the wall and couldn't be covered. They were there for people to see. Anybody who wanted to see it could go in and see it. And this place, after this war was over, why, this place was hanted. They seen different things there, they seen men ridin' up the stair case on gray horses, and all such stuff. Well, nobody could stay there and wouldn't stay there. And this M. that owned the place had a boy hired and he kep' his wheat and his oats, after it was thrashed, he put it down there and stored it there, in this building. So he sent this boy down one evening for to get some oats fer the horses and it was a little while before sundown and when he opened the front door he seen a man dressed up without a head on—ridin' up this stair way. And he went back, slammed the door shut, and went up and told M., he said, "I won't go in that place down there," he said, "there was a man rode up the steps, had no head on, ridin' a big gray horse." Old Curt M. said, "If that's the case, be damned if *I*'ll ever go in there after that oats." So I don't know what happened, *with* the oats, or what happened. But a year after that or two, this place was tore down—they tore this building away. Didn't use it no more. M. got skeered—he wouldn't go in it. And it was as pretty a stone house as you ever saw, couldn't be made nicer. So that was the story of that.[14]

And this lady—a neighbor man told me—I knowed him good—he said he went up and down there on Saturday nights, or Sunday nights. He went to see a lady in Oxford—a young fellow—and this girl was settin' in this sycamore tree, out from the porch—and he said that she was as pretty a lady as you ever *looked* at. And she was singin' nice hems [hymns]—church hems. Now he said that's the truth. He seen it with his own eyes. He *told* me this story. So that was the end of that place. They tore it down then and got rid of it.[15]

[13] How to Protect Buildings against Witches

[You mentioned in one of your stories how to protect a barn against witches doing harm to cattle, driving nails, etc. Would you say something about that, Frank?]

Well, now, I want to connect this to a story that I've told, that I missed. About this here story of these cattle that was witched. And this man went to York County for a witch doctor and brought him up there, and fix up that witch story. Now where there's nails, horse shoes nailed above a door no witch can go in, no witch can do anything there, no matter *how* they tried—even in your house. If you have horseshoes hung up above your doors any place, here in the house, and the witch comes in here—she's done, finished. She can't do nawthin'. Her power's taken from her, it seems.

So this place that I'm tellin' you about—this lady that bewitched *my* stuff—down on the farm where I had lived when I bought the *Lower* farm. When I had sale there, after I bought the Lower farm, I made sale and reduced my stock and my machinery to move up on this farm—it was as big a farm—I didn't need this *stuff.* But I should of—before I sent my horses and stuff up to this place, that I was gonta hold over, for up at that place—I had no *horseshoes* above these doors at this barn, and this old witch bewitched the horses. One of the horses that [I] had taken up there, they couldn't hitch her up. After my day of sale the boys went up to bring this horse and stuff home, what was to be brought back, and they couldn't hitch this horse up. And the children had drove this horse day after day haulin' milk to the creamery. And as soon as they taken this horse out of the stable up there—and fetch her out, she'd start kickin'. And they couldn't hitch her to the spring-wagon to bring her home.

So there's where I made *my* mistake—when I sent this stuff up there. I should of had them *doors* fixed. Down below where I lived on this farm—a witch couldn't bother me there—no matter *who* she was, or *where* they come from. I had horseshoes above all the stable doors, hog pen doors, and every place. So there's where I got hung up with this witch, this old Mrs. T. She went up by there the day of my *sale*—they *seen* her goin' up past there—seen her *stop* up there at the barn—and then she bewitched this horse of mine. And from that time on the devilment was started. (Laughter.)[16]

[I asked Frank if he had heard the idea that a broomstick laid across the threshold of a house would keep a witch out.]

To tell you the truth, Don, I've don't—never heard of anybody having any trouble with a witch stepped over a broom, or tried to make any trouble at these places that she'd step in.

[But you know the idea.]

Yes, I know the story that was *told* about them. But I never *seen* any of it.

[That a witch can't step over a broom?]

Yes, that I heard for years and years and years.[17]

[14] The Witch and Her Powers

[What about witches having the power to go through, for instance, keyholes? I think you told me about that once.]

That was an old lady lived here in Hunterstown. She was a witch. She killed two hogs for my grandmother. She had a spite at my grandmother, and she come down there one evening. Wanted to be friendly and nice, and she walked along down to the hog pen, where they had two big heavy hogs to kill that Fall. And she picked up a corn-cob and she stroked them over the back, both of these hogs.

[Did she say anything when she did this?]

Well, Grandmother never [told me]—if she said it, she said it to herself. Anyhow, Grandmother often said, that same night these hogs got sick, both of them, and the next morning they were both dead. She killed both of them, this old Devil. They had her in jail there in Gettysburg, I don't know what she had done, but she was locked up in jail in Gettysburg. And every night she was home with her childern. She said if she had the blood of a calf, she could go through any keyhole, or knothole, no matter where it was. So they had her penned in jail in Gettysburg for some cause. I don't know what. But the old lady was home every night with the childern. And before sunup she was back in jail.

[And that was in your Grandmother's time?]

Yes, that thing happened right down here in Hunterstown.[18]

[15] A Counter-Charm against Witches

Now I'll tell you a story that this Mrs. K. at Hanover told me, the time I had this trouble. She said, "Eckert, if you're out on the road with your team, and anything happens that you get stalled, you say, a team stops on the road and your horses can't pull the wagon away or have trouble—you carry a pole-axe with you, in the wagon. And if anything like that happens [to] you, you get off of the wagon, get your pole-axe and say, "I'm gonta knock a spoke out of the front wheel of this wagon." And you haul off and knock that spoke out and you'll knock Old Mrs. T's arm off—up at her shoulder. And if you don't want to do that—take a spoke out of the hind wheel and knock one of her legs off. And if you want to get rid of her entirely, just go in front of your team, and hit that clevis on the front of the tongue. And she said, "There'd be no more Mrs. T."[19]

[16] A Visit to the Powwower

I'll tell you a little story about [what] I seen done and I couldn't help but believe it. And I *do* believe it. An old gentleman over in Carlisle could cure fer you. No matter what was wrong with you, what your trouble was, if you'd go to him, he'd give a relief. So my grandson come home from the army, and he had adaletic feet, had big sores on his feet, sores as big as a silver dollar, and itch! he said if anything could [have] tore the hide off would feel good. They had him in the hospitals—Hanover, York, Harrisburg—finally they told him in Gettysburg here at the hospital, they could be nawthin' done about it, couldn't heal 'em up. So I took him over to Carlisle to this fellow, this old gentleman, took him in, and told him what the trouble was, and my grandson showed him these sores. And he looked at him, and he said, "Well," he said, "You come back over here in so many days or weeks," I don't know which it was, anyhow, the old man set down to the table and he wrote some stuff on a piece of paper—you couldn't read it—with red ink—and marked it all off—in little, with red ink. Told him, "Now, you put that in your pocket and carry it with you. And you come over here in sich and sich a time." So we went home and that's all that was done about it—and he seemed to get relief right away. This itchin' quit, stopped, and it wasn't but a few weeks his feet looked healin' up nice, smooth, and he's never been bothered to this day.

And then the second time I took him back to this old man—why, after we had went in there, there was three men come in to this same place. Well, two men was carryin' a man—couldn't walk. So after he was through with us, why, we set there. And this old man said to these parties that this man that they fetched in and set on a cheer, "Well, what seems to be *your* trouble?" "Well," this old man said, "I lost my power; I can't *walk*—I got no power to walk. I can't *walk*—and there hadn't been anything done—anything can be done—doctor says nawthin' can be done about it." He said how long he was helpless that he couldn't walk. So this old man give him a piece of paper to stick in his pocket. And when they went to leave, these men went to pick the man up and carry him up in the car. And "Oh, no," this old man said, "he can walk out. Just let him alone, he'll walk out." He got up and walked out to the car. And from that day on he walked.[20]

[And you saw that?]

Yeah. Yeah. And this old man said to me and C., "If these doctors here in York would a dared kill me, if it wouldn't've been found out, I'd have been killed years ago." He said, "I cured cases that they pushed out—that they couldn't do nawthin'—they couldn't help. I *cured* 'em. Today they're"[21]—H.—Old Man H.—C.H.![22]

[Is he the only one around that you know that does this type of healing?]

Yes, I never knowed of any other ones.

[There's no one down around Gettysburg?]

No. No, sir, that was the wonderfullest thing, Don, that I ever seen happen. And he had as pretty a stone house as you want to look at, and he built it himself. This old gentleman. He didn't *charge* anything. He didn't make no charge. If you wanted to give him something, you could give him something.[23] Yes, the poor old fellow's dead and gone too.

[This was after the last war, was it?]

Yeh.

[When your grandson came back from the army.]

Yeh.

[17] The Up and the Down Sign

Well, I'm gonta tell you a little story that happened [to] me. A lot of people don't believe in it, never did believe in it, I guess. And you can't convince them. Anyhow, I was putting a new line fence between me and my neighbor and I had a Catholic man helpin' me to put this fence up. So we put up fence for I don't know how many days we was workin'. And I said to this man in the evening, his name was John C., I said, "John, don't come down tomorrow. It's in the *up* sign, starts tomorrow, and we won't dig in any posts tomorrow. We won't dig in any posts in till sometime towards the last of the week, till it goes in the down sign." Oh, he laughed! He said, "Anybody that believes in that kinda stuff's crazy." I said, "I don't know whether I'm crazy or not, but I believe in it. And to *prove* to you that you don't know, I'm gonta *show* you. So you come down tomorrow morning and we'll dig in eight posts, right out along the public road here, and then we'll quit. And when Spring comes, the winter's over, and Spring comes, I want you to watch these posts, these eight posts, and tell me what you *seen*." "All right," he said. (Laughter.) So we dug in eight posts the next day. It was in the *up* sign then. So this went on. Winter come or passed away, and I didn't look about these posts. Winter was over, Spring come, why, John come down the road one morning. I said, "John," I said, "did you ever look about them *posts* that we dug in, them eight posts, when it was goin' in the up sign?" He looked at me and laughed, and said, "Yes, I did." "Well," I said, "what did you see?" He said, "They are up out of the ground about eight inches, every one of them. The frost raised them." "Well," I said, "now do you believe that?" "No. I don't believe it." "*Why* don't you believe it?" "I'm not supposed to believe it." I said, "O.K., then, don't you believe it," I said, "when you seen it with your own eyes you can't convince yourself that it's true." (Laughter.)[24]

[Would you mention about the shingles?]

I'm gonta tell you about this up sign business that we was talking about a bit ago. You nail a—buy these old-fashioned shindles that they—guess there isn't any to get no more—use to make 'em out of oak and you put that oak roof, shindle roof, on your house or your barn in the *up* sign, and in the course of years them shindles will all raise up and curl up at the ends. I said I've seen it happen time and time again.

And the same people laughs—they used to laugh at me, I wouldn't butcher in the up sign, that is, for myself. Kill my hogs in the up sign, and cut up my hams and shoulders and I wouldn't butcher in the taking off of the moon.

[What would that do, if you would do that, to the meat?]

Why, it would shrink up, shrink it. Yeh. And I wouldn't butcher in the takin' off of the moon. I always butchered in the growin' of the moon, killin' a beef or killin' my own hogs. I said, other people, I'd butcher anytime they'd want it done, but not for myself. And I said that I wouldn't butcher in the takin' off of the moon, because that meat, them hams and shoulders, that you'd cure, fer your own use, would all shrink in a certain—they'd shrink up in a certain amount that they'd lose, it seems. The meat would dry up. And the same way with beef—beef will do the same thing. You take a piece of beef that was killed in the takin' off of the moon and cook it and you'd weigh that piece of meat. Before you'd put it on the stove to roast it or cook it, and put it on the stove. You seen what it looked like when you put it on, and when it was cooked or fried, whatever you done with it, it was shrunk up, pretty near lose one third, in looks, you'd lose. And I said it was *proven,* that I *done* it, and *seen* it done. I say anybody that wants to try it can try it and find out for their own satisfaction. (Laughter.)[25]

[18] The Almanac

Well, I'll tell you a story about the almanac, or the Brownie Calendar. I said she always—my wife always wanted an almanac, either that or the Brownie Calendar. And she'd go there to look on this calendar, about plantin' potatoes or plantin' onions—sowing lettuce or anything that she had any b'lief in, she'd get her this almanac. Well, we generally had a Lancaster Almanac. And we generally had a Brownie Calendar. These Brownie Calendars were put out by some medicine company and we could get them at the store, these Brownie Calendars, and she always had a lot of belief in lookin' about signs, and plantin' stuff.[26] Now she always watched when I planted potatoes. She never said, always said, "Don't plant potatoes in the *up* sign," said, "if you do you'll find in the Fall when you come to take your potatoes out, you'll have a lot of potatoes that's sunburnt." Said they'll push up out of the ground beside of the stalks and get sunburnt. If you plant them in the down sign—you'd have no trouble, never will have any trouble. So that's what we always looked to when I farmed and kep' house. Why, we had these signs to go by and I said it always proved that it was the right thing to do, it was a benefit, by doing it.

[Did you ever use the Hagerstown Almanac?]

Well, I guess we had. I think we used that. I was never particular about getting an almanac just so we had an almanac or a Brownie Calendar. There's a Brownie Calendar hanging out there *now.* M. always believes in getting one of them.

[19] The Faith People and the Doctor

Now I'm gonta tell you a story what I've seen about this faith doctorin'. This faith religion. I lived aside of a party, neighbors, that were faith people and they had a dog that they thought a lot of. And they tried this faith cure on this dog, and it didn't work. So they took the dog to a doctor, and got medicine, and got the dog fixed up. So awhile afterwards, why, this man's wife fell down off of the pear tree and broke her hip. Well, they decided they wouldn't git no doctor. They would try this faith cure on this old lady's hip. It didn't work out, so finally they called a doctor in—old Doc H.—I knowed him. He said, "There's no use for me to come down there," he said, "your faith cure didn't hold out with the dog, and it won't hold out with the Mrs. So you just—I won't bother—I won't come down—you wouldn't believe anything I tell you anyhow." So she hobbled around for years, until her death. And her hip was never right, it never healed, never—so but they still had the faith cure. It didn't prove good to them in the end.

[Are there many of these people, these faith people, around?]

No, and they have a church in Biglerville, where they some of them go, and believe in this doctrine. I said, it's no harm to me, I said, everybody for their own b'lief. Believe what they please. Find out what they please. (Laughter.)[27]

Notes

1. From the *Motif-Index:* Gun bewitched so that it will not hit target—G265.8.3.1.1; Shooting object breaks spell—G271.4.8; Disenchantment by shooting—D712.7; Exorcism by injuring image of witch—G271.4.2.

2. While this is a reminiscence of a practical joke played on the "witch" rather than a folk-tale, I have included it as an example of Frank Eckert's superb tale-telling gift, including his imitation of the witch's Dutch accent and rural profanity. He was obviously proud that he had played a joke on this old neighbor of his who had the reputation of being a witch.

3. Cf. *Motif-Index:* Cattle bewitched—G265.6.2; Exorcism of witch by countercharm—G271.6.

4. In later conversations with Frank this tale was dated earlier, forty or fifty years ago.

5. Cf. *Motif-Index:* Curse by disappointed witch—G269.4; Witch punishes owner for injury or slight by killing his animals—G265.4.0.1; Witch causes pigs to behave unnaturally—

G265.6.1; Witch causes horse to behave unnaturally—G265.6.3. Although not agreeing as to the cause, some of Frank's family told me that they too remembered the farm animals reacting in these ways. The time was between forty and fifty years ago.

6. The phrase "an old gentleman walkin' the road" is a euphemism for tramp. Could it be an apotropaic phrase, the speaker wishing to avoid such a life becoming his lot? Perhaps not, because he does use it in other connections (cf. No. 16).

7. Cf. *Motif-Index:* The Devil teaches man how to hang himself—G303.9.4.2.1; Treasure buried by dying man—N511.1.0.1; Treasure buried in ... kettle—N511.1.8; Treasure found in ... kettle—N525. The "pear peelin's" add a domestic nineteenth-century note to this widespread folktale.

8. Cf. *Motif-Index:* Devil appears when cards are played—G303.6.1.5; Devil in form of cat—G303.3.3.1.2; Devil with glowing eyes—G303.4.1.2.2.

9. This, Frank Eckert's most elaborate tale, comes from his childhood, when he was still at home. We get the impression in this tale as in No. 17 that the Catholic neighbors involved wished to differentiate themselves from their Protestant Dutch neighbors when it came to occult folk beliefs. Cf. *Motif-Index:* Dead person spins—E561; Phantom spinning wheel makes noise—E534; Ghosts protect hidden treasure—E291; Treasure in cellar of ruined house—N511.1.6; Ghost as hand or hands—E422.1.11.3; Revenant as dog—E423.1.1; Ghost laid when living man speaks to it—E451.4; Ghost laid when treasure is unearthed—E451.5; Treasure buried by dying man—N511.1.1; Ghost-like lights—E530.1; Blue lights follow witches—G229.7; Treasure buried in ... kettle—N511.1.8; Treasure found in ... kettle—N525. In a second version of this tale, Frank ended with the words, "Now that was true. I went through with it and seen it and knowed it to be a fact."

10. I got the impression here, from Frank's vehemence in denying that he knew Black Mag's methods or words, that he was either afraid to repeat them, or loath to repeat them even to me.

11. Cf. the "Bewitched Wagon" in the *Motif-Index:* Witch bewitches wagon—G265.8.3.2; Wagon refuses to move—D1654.5; also Exorcism of witch by countercharm—G271.6.

12. Cf. *Motif-Index:* Witch punishes person who incurs her ill will—G269.10. This particular motif, however, of a witch bewitching her own child, is not found in the *Motif-Index.*

13. Cf. *Motif-Index:* Hanging in game or jest accidentally proves fatal—N334.2.

14. Cf. *Motif-Index:* Headless ghost rides horse—E422.1.1.3.1; Ineradicable bloodstains after bloody tragedy—E422.1.11.5.1.

15. The "singing ghost" in the sycamore tree was the ghost of the woman murdered in the "hanted hotel." At least Frank told the stories together and connected them. Cf. *Motif-Index*: Ghost sings—E402.1.1.4

16. The tale Frank refers to in the first paragraph is No. 3. However, the most valuable part of this section is Frank's firmly expressed belief that he left himself open to witchcraft by not "fixing" the stable and pen doors on the barn of his newly bought farm, before moving his cattle into it. The "witch" again is the "Irish witch" mentioned in other tales. She even had a Scotch-Irish name. Cf. *Motif-Index:* Witch causes horse to behave unnaturally—G265.6.3; Horseshoe hung up as protection against witches—G272.11.

17. Cf. *Motif-Index:* Broom across door protects from witch—G272.7.2. This is an extremely common belief in the more active Dutch dialect areas. I have many references to it in my recordings from the Hegins and Mahantongo Valley areas in Schuylkill and Northumberland Counties.

18. Cf. *Motif-Index:* Witch causes death of animals—G265.4.1; Witches go through keyholes—G249.7; Witches vanish from prison—G249.9.

19. The witch referred to in this tale is the "Irish Witch." Cf. *Motif-Index:* Witch bewitches wagon—G265.8.3.2; Exorcism of witch by countercharm—G271.6. A "pole-axe" is an axe with a spike, hook, or hammer opposite the blade.

20. Powwowing is Pennsylvania's version of primitive folk healing—once almost universal in colonial America and based upon the folk religion of medieval Europe. This story is typical of those told by believers in it—when certain ailments gain no relief from regular medicine, powwowers are turned to in desperation and a cure results. Note, however, that Frank does not use the word "powwow" but rather the Dutchism to "cure for," a word found in Western Maryland as well as Pennsylvania.

21. This paragraph reflects the supposed enmity of the M.D. for the powwower. By York Frank here means Carlisle.

22. Here Frank burst out triumphantly with the name of the powwower which he had been trying to think of while telling me of this case.

23. Powwowers naturally know better than to charge a set fee, which can bring them before the courts on the charge of practicing medicine without a license.

24. The "up sign" means in the increase or waxing of the moon, the "down sign" in the waning of the moon. Anything that is to stay down (as for example, fence posts) or grow downwards (as for example, root crops) were planted in the "down sign," and for opposite results the "up sign."

25. Here Frank applies his belief to his trade of butchering. The expression "takin' off" of the moon is a Dutchism for decrease or waning of the moon, from the Dutch dialect *op-nemma (abnehmen),* to decrease.

26. Note that Frank was not particular about the kind of almanac, for he could not read. His wife, who could read, consulted the almanacs and supervised the planting.

27. It is obvious from Frank's negative reaction to the "faith religion" (Pentecostal healing cults) that he saw no relation between it and the more primitive type of faith healing—powwowing—which he definitely believed in. They are both, however, religious forms of healing. The difference is that powwowing is outlawed from organized religion and hence has gone underground; the Pentecostal sects attempt to gear healing into the worship services of the church, basing their example on the charismatic healing of the apostles in the New Testament Church. I like Frank's ending, however—"everybody for their own b'lief. Believe what they please. Find out what they please."

12

Fraktur: An Introduction

When Pennsylvania German *fraktur* was first discovered, in the last decade of the nineteenth century, it was described as "the art of fraktur or illuminative writing" and a lineage was drawn up which stretched from medieval cloister to backwoods schoolhouse in Pennsylvania. As Henry C. Mercer, the discoverer, put it in 1897, "with strange sensations, we rescue from the Pennsylvanian garret evidence indisputable of the passing away in the New World of one of the fairest arts of the cloister, which, meeting its deathblow at the invention of printing, crossed the Atlantic to linger among the pious descendants of the German reformers until recent years."[1]

When the first public exhibit of fraktur was held in Lancaster County, Pennsylvania, in 1902, Professor Joseph Henry Dubbs of Franklin and Marshall College described the pieces as "rustic art," the American analogue to Europe's "peasant art" (*Bauernkunst*).[2] Research since then has alternated between these emphases, or combined them. The two principal authorities on fraktur today—Donald A. Shelley and John Joseph Stoudt—have in differing ways expanded both the Mercer and Dubbs approaches. Shelley's outstanding contribution is his filling in of the lineage of the technique of fraktur, highlighting its sixteenth- and seventeenth-century roots in Europe, as well as his careful analysis of the sectarian "schools" of fraktur.[3] Stoudt's contribution has been to work out the historical, theological, and literary lineage of the symbolism of fraktur.[4] Both have helped us to understand the place of fraktur in the total Pennsylvania German culture.

Looking at fraktur, to make outward sense of it, we must first divide it into its component parts. Fraktur as a totality is a combination of two elements: (1) religious symbolism, as seen in (a) the hymn texts and scripture verses used, as well as (b) the visual illustrations of these texts, plus

This article first appeared as an Introduction to *Pennsylvania German Fraktur and Color Drawings* (Lancaster, Pa.: Pennsylvania Farm Museum of Landis Valley, Pennsylvania Historical and Museum Commission, 1969).

(2) baroque calligraphy. The roots of fraktur lie in Central Europe, where fraktur flowered in the German-speaking lands—Germany, Switzerland, and Austria—in the sixteenth and seventeenth centuries, the period immediately preceding the Atlantic migration. As an art form, fraktur is graphic art, two-thirds calligraphy and one-third drawn symbol. The combination of calligraphic text, abstract borders, and primitive symbolic figures makes up a total that is more than the sum of its parts—a design that has pleased the eye from the day the scrivener put the finishing touches of color upon the paper, to today.

As folk art, even though the artist-craftsman who produced it developed his own repertory of symbols and patterns which he used continually, piece after piece, so that one can recognize his "style," each individual piece of fraktur is unique.[5] In many cases the abstract designs used by the fraktur scrivener are the same as those which appear on other genres of Pennsylvania German folk art from the tombstone to the barn—the six-pointed star with its variations, the tulip-rose-lily, the tree of life design, the whirling swastika, and others. There was a continuity in folk art motifs from the earliest decorated tombstones and stove plates to the latest Berks or Lehigh County "hex sign" barn. This "community of design" links the folk arts of Pennsylvania to those of the peasant worlds of Europe and the Near East.

In analyzing fraktur, the basic discovery that one makes about it is that it is first, essentially religious art, and second, that it is essentially Protestant. European folk art scholarship has normally concentrated on the spectacular developments in Catholic folk art—the ex voto, the santo, the saint's print, the devotional picture. Pennsylvania German folk art is, like the culture that produced it, overwhelmingly Protestant. Catholic art focuses upon the continuing miracles of God's actions among men, as seen in the ex voto, and in the legends of the post-biblical saints, and concentrates on the visual and emotional elements. It is picture-oriented. Protestant art, as Richard Weiss of the University of Zurich points out in his analysis of Protestant as compared with Catholic folk culture, is word-oriented, Bible-centered.[6] Pennsylvania German folk art illustrates this Protestant orientation. While there is a strong undercurrent of Catholic folk practice and folk belief in Pennsylvania folk culture, fraktur, which was so closely associated with institutional religion (the parochial school, and the baptism and confirmation rites of the church) expresses a basic Protestant ethos. Even the Catholic mystical elements in fraktur are mediated through the Protestant mystic Boehme and the Pietist hymnody of the seventeenth and eighteenth centuries. Certainly in our illustrations of Protestant fraktur, "word" dominates over picture. For this reason, the term "manuscript art" is a particularly appropriate term for what we see before us.

Figure 12.1. Fraktur baptismal certificate of Anne Andres of Sussex County, New Jersey, 1783. This is an English-language example of the striking fraktur work of Johannes Spangenberg, Reformed schoolmaster of Easton, Pennsylvania, who produced artworks on both sides of the Delaware.
(Courtesy Garbisch Collection, National Gallery of Art)

Scholars have long debated the meaning of the visual symbols found on fraktur pieces. The most vocal of them have been the symbolists, led by John Joseph Stoudt. His theory, first published in 1937 in *Consider the Lilies,* is that fraktur symbolism represents an American flowering of a peculiar brand of Christian mystical theology leading down from the medieval Catholic mystics to Boehme and the Pietist hymnists of the seventeenth century. Stoudt maintains that the symbols are Christian in substance. A widespread rival theory maintains that the fraktur designs as well as the "hex signs" are essentially pre-Christian and pagan.[7]

If Pennsylvania's fraktur is Protestant in ethos, it can be further subdivided into the two sociological divisions of "church" and "sect," which produced two distinct but related culture worlds in Eastern Pennsylvania. The radical Reformation as represented in the sects (Anabaptist, Mennonite, Schwenkfelder) and the pietistic religious communities of Ephrata and the Moravian settlements, produced more than their share of fraktur. The majority "churches"—the Lutheran and Reformed—with their elaborate systems of religious "rites of passage" from baptism to funeral, however, produced the largest body of fraktur—the *Taufschein* (baptismal certificate), the *Patenbrief* (baptismal letter), the *Confirmationsschein* (confirmation certificate), the *Trauschein* (marriage certificate), and the *Denkmal* (memorial for the dead). Statistically the largest single genre of fraktur in all collections is the *Taufschein.* Next would appear to be the *Vorschrift,* produced in both the church and sect worlds.

Who produced fraktur? What type of individual in the Pennsylvania German culture expressed himself in this form of rustic art? During the period when fraktur as an art was flourishing—approximately from the 1750s to the 1850s—there were several types of individuals who became expert in it. Both church and sect during this period had German-language parochial schools. The country schoolmaster was one of the greatest producers of fraktur. Not only did he produce the *Vorschrift*—the very word means a "set model" of calligraphy to be "copied" by the pupil—but he often became the most frequent designer or filler-in of the baptismal certificates of his community. Many famous scriveners are now recognized by their styles—Brechall, Krebs, Otto, Münch, Portzline, for a few examples—all schoolmasters from the world of the churches, the majority Lutheran and Reformed culture of the Dutch Country. In addition, some ministers of the churches became renowned frakturists—the Lutheran Daniel Schumacher and the Reformed George Geistweit are two examples.[8]

Among the "sects" there was—at least in the pieces that are available for study in collections—more of a popular, democratic participation in frakturing. This is especially the case among the Schwenkfelders, who, true to their Quaker-like mystic theology, believed in the equality of all men. Among them many of the fraktur pieces are drawn, and signed, by women—those remarkable Susanna Kriebels, Schultzes, Jäckels, and others. Among Mennonites, with typical Mennonite modesty and self-depreciation, fraktur was less frequently signed, but it too came out of the schoolmaster's leisure, and we recognize the style of the Deep Run School in Bucks County in a multitude of decorated tunebook title-pages, and the doubleheaded bird that was the trademark of the schoolmaster of the Earl Township School in Lancaster County who gave his Vorschriften to his *"fleissigen Schüler and Schülerinnen,"* whom he affectionately names in one corner of his design.

Fraktur flourished for almost a century because it was needed in the culture that produced it. It was a visual, moral, and religious symbol of the individual's relation to the institutions within the folk culture—the church, the school, and the family—the three institutions that were the individual's triple focus in life. The economic life, the fourth institution in which the individual was involved in folk culture—so important in the rural world—was subsumed under the religious life. As in the Benedictine motto, *Ora et Labora*—reflected in the Ephrata symbol, *Arbeite und hoffe*—work and prayer were equal partners, but work received its meaning in the devotional life of the individual.

The devotional life of the Pennsylvania Germans centered around Bible, hymnbook, and prayerbook, and strangely enough, fraktur. For the devout Protestant of the Dutch Country, these pieces, which were found in every home and connected with every individual's passage through life, were in a very real sense what a recent European scholar has studied as "Protestant devotional pictures."[9] These did not of course draw the sharp focus that Catholic folk art has drawn, but they were part of the individual's devotional life. They were Protestant "aids to devotion," admonishing, comforting, reminding the Dutchman of the limits and the possibilities of his world.

Art produced by a culture both conceptualizes that culture and provides within the culture a communication of its values. As visual communication its symbols provide the beholder with cues, reminders of the ideals, the values of the human group of which the individual is a member. Both the graphic symbols and the texts of Pennsylvania's fraktur provided such cues and reminders to the Pennsylvania Dutch farmer, his *Hausfrau*, and his growing children. To the twentieth-century beholder, the keys are lost, the language is foreign, and if we are to make sense of them for ourselves we are forced to reconstruct them out of the seventeenth- and eighteenth-century background.

The German-language texts of the Vorschriften provide us with the most direct clues to the meaning of fraktur in the culture that produced

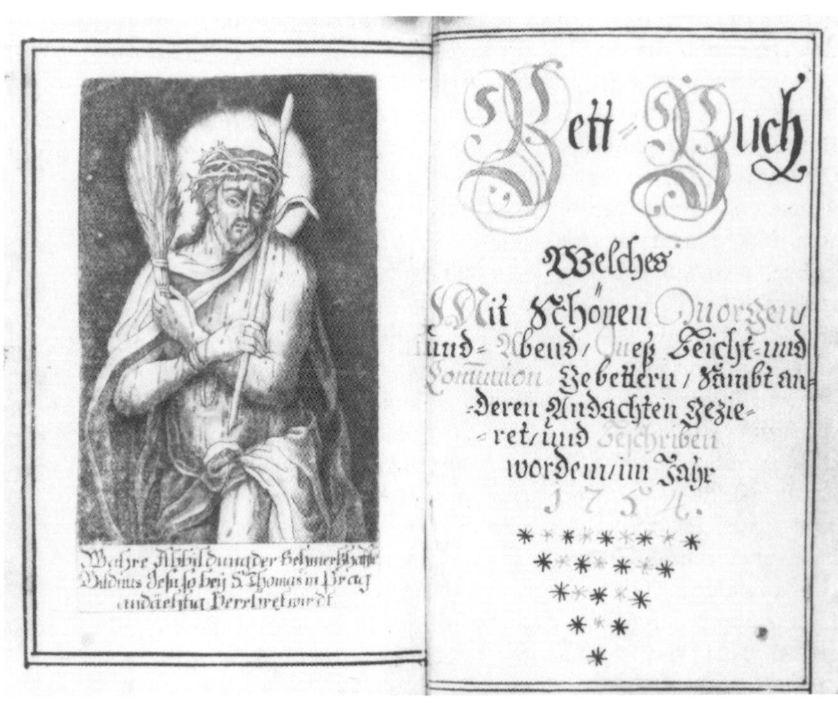

Figure 12.2. Fraktur lettering on title page of a manuscript Catholic prayer book. European, dated 1756. *(Courtesy Roughwood Collection)*

it. The religious notes that are struck range from praise, admonition and exhortation, to the ever-present memento mori. Praise is the note of the Abraham Hübner Vorschrift of 1772—"God, we praise thy goodness in heart and spirit" (*Gott wir loben deine Güte in dem Herzen und Gemüthe*); admonition that of Salome Kriebel, 1801—"Have God and His word before thine eyes and thou shalt prosper here and in eternity" (*Hab Gott vor Augen und sein Wort so geht es dir wohl hier und dort*); and "All men must die" (*Alle Menschen müssen sterben*), from a Lutheran hymn beloved among all Pennsylvania German groups, provides the memento mori. Discipline of children is expressed in the paraphrase of "Remember thy creator in the days of thy youth," on the Eva Kauffman Vorschrift of 1792. Several pieces underscore the Passion—the "bitter cross"—while others point to the Wounds of Christ (*Jesu deine heilge Wunden*—Hiob Hibner, 1763), which as the "Five Wounds" are so widespread a motif in the Catholic folk art of Europe. The Pietist and mystic focus upon Christ—whose beauty transcends the world's beauty—is the thought of the Barbara Schultz Vorschrift of 1806, and of Sarah Reinwald (*Ich weiss ein Blümlein hübsch und fein*), 1787. "Jesus the Christian's Assurance and Refuge" (*Jesus ist dein Zuversicht*) is the central idea of the Peter Ohlinger piece of 1813. And finally the themes of Morning Star, Root of Jesse, Bridegroom, King, and Wondrous Lamb are seen in the bilingual Vorschrift of the Mennonite Huppert Cassel, 1769. The Evangelical Pietist "invitation"—"Come unto me, for my yoke is easy and my burden is light," is engrossed on the David Kriebel Vorschrift of 1805. But through them all shines the call to the devotional life—"But one thing is needful: and Mary hath chosen that good part" (Luke 10:42), calling the Pennsylvania Dutch Hausfrau from her everyday role as busy Martha to the devotion of Mary.

While the vast body of fraktur displays religious themes, there are some secular notes—the four grenadiers with swords and eighteenth-century pigtails on the Johannes Müller Taufschein of 1771; the jaunty unshaven stogie-smoker in beaver hat drawn on a page of Jacob Scherg's *Wahres Christenthum* (1811); the motley dwelling house (or is it a heavenly mansion?) with Pennsylvania tile roof and Pennsylvania two-colored shutters, on the Sarah Jäckel Vorschrift (1788). But birds, stars, hearts, and animals, can all be rationalized as expressions of the divine creation, and for the most part they are combined with religious texts. The human figures, which appear most frequently on the Taufschein, were, according to Walter E. Boyer, sponsors at baptism, the godfather and godmother who were so important a link between the baptized child and the folk community.[10] Even the *"wunder grosser Fisch"*—copied from European broadsides—reputedly caught in the Lake of Geneva in 1740, is invested with crosses, crowns and other religious symbols. The charming Lidia Reinwalt

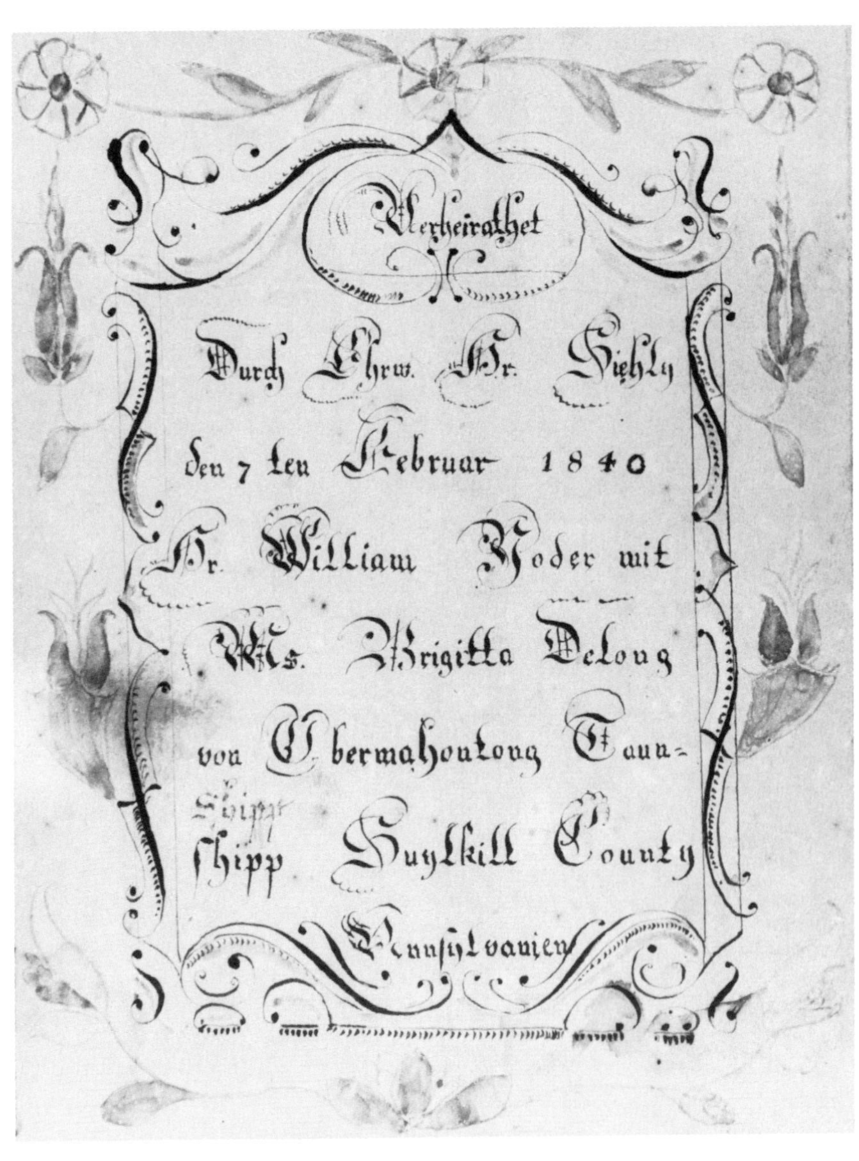

Verheirathet

Durch Ehrw. Hr. Stiehly

den 7 ten Februar 1840

Hr. William Yoder mit

Ms. Brigitta Delong

von Obermahontong Taun-

ſhipp Suylkill County

Pennsylvanien

Figure 12.3. Fraktur marriage certificate of William Yoder and Brigitta Delong, 1840. Work of the Reformed pastor and folk artist Isaac Stiehly (1800–1869) of the Mahantongo Valley.
(Courtesy Roughwood Collection)

Diesen beyden Ehegatten als Georg Joller
und seiner eheligen Hausfrau Elisabeth gebornе Reiner
ist ein Sohn zur Welt geboren im Jahr unsers Erlösers 1812
den December, um 9 Uhr nachmittags, und erhielt den Namen
in der heiligen Taufe Wilhelm von Hrn. Prediger
Hemplin Taufzeugen waren Jacob Reiner
und seine Frau, Großeltern im Staat Pennsylvanien,
Northumberland Launty:

Ich bin getauft ich steh im Bunde,
Durch meine Tauf mit meinem Gott,
So sprech ich steis mit frohem Munde,
In Creuz in Trübsal Angst und Noth,
Ich bin getauft des freu ich mich,
Die Freude bleibet ewiglich.

Ich bin getauft ob ich gleich sterbe,
Was schadet mir das kühle Grab,
Ich weiß mein Vaterland und Erbe,
Das ich bey Gott im Himmel hab,
Nach meinem Tod ist mir bereit,
Die Himmelsfreud, das Freudenkleid.

Figure 12.4. Printed fraktur form with folk-religious symbolism, filled in in manuscript. It records the birth and baptism of Wilhelm Jotter (Yoder), son of Georg and Elisabeth (Reiner) Jotter, in 1812. This piece shows the common orientation of an earth side, out of which the flowers are growing, and a heaven side, complete with three angels.
(Courtesy Roughwood Collection)

valentine (1803), with its eight cut-out hearts, is secular in form but the text is in praise of a maiden—virtuous, devoid of pride, guarded by angels, who listens gladly to God's Word, and fashions her entire life upon it. "Such a maiden I love and her alone," wrote the anonymous scrivener, "and her name is Lidia Reinwalt."

Fraktur as an art, widely practiced and functional in Pennsylvania German culture, was, with minor exceptions, dead by the Civil War period. What had flowered by the time of the Revolution and spread with the migrating Pennsylvania Dutchman in his Conestoga wagon southward to Virginia and North Carolina, westward to Ohio and Indiana, and northward to Ontario, died of natural causes, some of them local and some of them national.

The local reasons for the decline of fraktur can be found in the nineteenth-century disintegration of the folk culture of the Pennsylvania Germans, particularly (1) the disappearance of institutional elements such as the parochial school, which had produced the Vorschrift, (2) the shift to the English language, which brought with it an inevitable loss of German devotional literature as the wellspring of fraktur symbolism, and (3) the decline in the very meaning of baptism, which had produced the Taufschein. In the first half of the nineteenth century baptism declined as a rite in the "churches" as seen in the upgrading of adult conversion, and the downgrading of the custom of choosing godparents for each baptized child. Such religious changes can be partially attributed to the impact of the revivalist movement, which invaded the Pennsylvania German churches and sects from the world of Anglo-America. Fraktur was part of the old-style colonial culture, which, especially in the field of religion, was being challenged and reshaped through acculturation with Anglo-American forms.

National causes were involved too. American nationalism, the industrial revolution, and Victorian sentimentalism also contributed to the decline of fraktur. The symbolic content of fraktur—the mystical and theosophical symbolism of Rose and Tulip and Lily of Jacob Boehme and his medieval sources—faded in the first half of the nineteenth century, and American political symbols—the Spread Eagle, the Flag, the Odd Fellows' or Masonic "Eye" of God, and the iconography of American rural life, in the style of Currier and Ives, took their place. This change in content, this wave of new taste, national in scope and urban in context, destroyed home-made, rustic, do-it-yourself fraktur as it destroyed other traditional arts and crafts in the United States.

As an expression of a past American regional culture, fraktur now ranks with the Puritan tombstones and the New Mexican santos as the principal body of early American religious folk art. It belongs to the formative age of the Pennsylvania German folk culture—the eighteenth and early nineteenth centuries—along with the Conestoga wagon, the Lancaster rifle, and the Pennsylvania barn.

Notes

1. Henry C. Mercer, "The Survival of the Mediaeval Art of Illuminative Writing among Pennsylvania Germans," *Proceedings of the American Philosophical Society* 36 (156) (December 1897): 424–33.
2. Joseph Henry Dubbs, "Rustic Art in Lancaster County," *Papers Read Before the Lancaster County Historical Society* 7 (2–3) (1903): 17–20.
3. Donald A. Shelley, *The Fraktur-Writings or Illuminated Manuscripts of the Pennsylvania Germans,* The Pennsylvania German Folklore Society, vol. 23 (1958–1959), Allentown, Pa., 1961.
4. John Joseph Stoudt, *Pennsylvania German Folk Art: An Interpretation,* The Pennsylvania German Folklore Society, vol. 28, Allentown, Pa., 1966.
5. For valuable hints on how the frakturist combined the various elements in his repertory into the finished piece, see Ellen Shaffer, "Illuminators, Scribes and Printers: A Glimpse of the Free Library's Pennsylvania Dutch Collection," *Pennsylvania Folklife* 9 (4) (Fall 1958): 18–27, especially the photograph of the frakturist's sample kit on p. 20.
6. Conversations with Richard Weiss at his home at Küssnacht, Switzerland, in August 1959. For his valuable analysis of the difference between Catholic and Protestant folk religiosity, see *Volkskunde der Schweiz: Grundriss* (Erlenbach-Zürich: Eugen Rentsch Verlag, 1946), 303–11.
7. See the article by August C. Mahr, "Origin and Significance of Pennsylvania Dutch Barn Symbols," reprinted in Alan Dundes, *The Study of Folklore* (Englewood Cliffs, N.J.: Prentice-Hall, 1965), 373–99.
8. For the most recent research on Daniel Schumacher, see "Daniel Schumacher's Baptismal Register," Frederick S. Weiser, trans. and ed., *Publications of the Pennsylvania German Society,* vol. 1 (Allentown, Pa., 1968), 185–407, with 3 color plates; and John Joseph Stoudt, *Early Pennsylvania Arts and Crafts* (New York: A. S. Barnes and Company, 1964), especially plates 308–12, 332–35.
9. Martin Scharfe, *Evangelische Andachtsbilder: Studien zu Intention und Funktion des Bildes in der Frömmigkeitsgeschichte vornehmlich des schwäbischen Raumes* (Stuttgart: Verlag Müller und Gräff, 1968), 366 pp., 161 plates.
10. Walter E. Boyer, "The Meaning of Human Figures in Pennsylvania Dutch Folk Art," *Pennsylvania Folklife* 11 (2) (Fall 1960): 5–23.

13

Sauerkraut for New Year's

For the Pennsylvania Dutch, New Year's Day is Sauerkraut Day. Every self-respecting Dutchman sits down for dinner that day before a huge *Schissel* of sauerkraut and pork, mounded with big puffy dumplings like cumulus clouds bobbing in the copious juice and served up in style with mashed potatoes, homemade applesauce, and other side dish specialties.

If you ask a Dutchman why he persists in this custom he will tell you that it brings good luck throughout the coming year. Of course he could tell you, too, that he does it because he "chust likes sauerkraut" and welcomes another festive occasion to "enchoy" it, even though it is served on his table many times throughout the winter.

And if you ask him why pork and not the festive American turkey is dished up for New Year's, the answer may be a symbolic one—"The pig roots forward and the turkey scratches backwards." The Dutchman does eat the all-American turkey for Christmas dinner—often also served with sauerkraut—but for New Year's it is pork and sauerkraut, and that's that.

Perhaps it all has something to do with his identity. In Civil War days, when the first Pennsylvania regiments reached Virginia, the natives called them "Sauerkraut Yankees." Pennsylvanians may not have liked it at the time—"Yankee" was a derogatory term in the Dutchman's as well as the Virginian's vocabulary—but they are proud of it today.

In Central Pennsylvania, where there is a large Pennsylvania Dutch population, pork and sauerkraut advertisements appear in the newspapers throughout the dying days of December. One such ad from the *Altoona Mirror* of December 27, 1960, from Pielmeier's Market, urges readers to "Follow the Tradition for New Year's Day" by serving "Sauerkraut and Pork," and adds its bid for confidence: "We make our own kraut." And in the December 29 issue of the same paper the Sanitary Market informs the

This article originally appeared in *The World & I* 4 (1) (January 1989): 612–23.

readers that "Blocher's Fresh Dressed Pork will guarantee the success of your New Year's dinner."

Other evidence that the Pennsylvania Dutch have sanctified sauerkraut is the fact that all over the area, from the Delaware River to the Juniata, and from the north and west branches of the Susquehanna to the Maryland border, most of the Pennsylvania Dutch churches delight in serving gala "sauerkraut suppers" in their parish halls during the fall of the year, usually making the kraut themselves. So in a sense this Pennsylvania Dutch "national dish" is connected intimately with their festival year, their own ethnic identity, and even their religion.

Holidays are important to every group because they break into the routine of everyday life and work, offering a chance to be different for a change and to celebrate. For our European ancestors, feasting on holidays not only heightened the sense of celebration, but was viewed as increasing the possibilities for abundance, wealth, and health. In the magical world in which they lived, what they did on New Year's, that symbolic hinge of the year, was important for its foretokening of their condition during the coming twelve months. Hence holiday foods became major items in all of Europe's traditional regional cultures.

In the German-speaking areas of central Europe, certain foods were traditionally associated with both Christmas and New Year's—for example, fish. Carp was the most important dish in many parts of Germany for the two holidays. Herring was also widespread as a festival dish; even herring roe with its countless eggs was a symbol of the good luck one hoped that the new year would bring.

New Year's cakes—usually large, flat cookies cut in shapes or stamped with designs—were another almost universal holiday food. Even today, many European cultural regions bake their favorite New Year's cakes in the shape of horses, hares, pigs, trees, and the Three Kings. Geometrical shapes such as circles, rings, squares, oblongs, diamonds, and stars were also popular, with their flat surfaces decorated or stamped with religious impressions. In northwest Germany, New Year's cakes featuring symbolic designs were baked in waffle or wafer irons. And everywhere pretzels were given as New Year's gifts, especially to children by their godparents.

Remnants of many of these diverse customs survived in Pennsylvania and can occasionally still be found today. The classic region for large stamped New Year's cakes is New York's Hudson Valley, where the custom came from Holland along with the habit of New Year's visiting. In the eighteenth and nineteenth centuries, such festival cakes were also commonly baked in Pennsylvania cities from carved molds. Country housewives made cakes or puddings in the shape of fish curved into a circle from ceramic molds that are now collectors' items. The Christmas frenzy of baking produced batches for New Year's, Epiphany, and the month of January in general.

These seasonal delicacies were welcomed by all, from grandfather and grandmother to the youngest child, as part of the holiday's function of providing an alternative to everydayness and even allowing a bit of excess for everyone.

"Shooting in" the New Year

If "eating in" the New Year was customary for Pennsylvania Dutchmen, their custom of "shooting in" the New Year was even more spectacular. There are numerous descriptions of this practice, many of them published in upstate Pennsylvania newspapers at the turn of the century, when the custom was dwindling away.

On New Year's Eve, parties of men would be formed in the rural communities to march around to each neighboring farmhouse in succession. They wished each household a happy new year and went through the ritual of "shooting the New Year in" with a volley of rifle shots that echoed for miles.

A typical shooting party usually consisted of about eight men who made the rounds of the neighborhood from midnight till sunup. All carried guns except for the professional "wisher," the man who knew the complicated High German New Year's wish. The visitors gathered under the window of the room where the farmer and his wife slept. The wisher called out the man's name until he appeared, then chanted the wish. It was usually a very long one, at least a hundred lines. (The recitation obviously took a specialist with a good memory.) When the end was reached, the couple was asked if the guests might shoot in the New Year. The shots were made successively, with the unarmed wisher tapping each shooter on the back as a signal to pull the trigger.

When the echoes of the last shot died away, the farmer invited the group into the house, where he served them refreshments. Since this was only one stop of a long night's performance, most of the men went easy on both food and hard liquor. The whole proceeding was done in the soberest manner possible, since this was a traditional ceremony that had to be carried out exactly, not a "frolic."

An account written in 1895 by an old farmer who remembered going in 1828 over the mountain from Schuylkill to Berks County to celebrate the New Year tells us that by 3:00 A.M. his party had visited thirty-seven different farmhouses over a distance of ten miles. There was snow on the ground, and they traveled by sleigh. They took bundles of straw along, setting one on fire when they left a stop and dragging it after the sleigh to illuminate the night. They joined a parade in Rehrersburg at 8:00 A.M. At least thirty sleigh teams lined up, about half of them with six or eight horses each. The drivers were dressed in all sorts of "fantastic" costumes—a word then used for the Pennsylvania versions of European Carnival (*Fastnacht*) costumes. Young women "dressed in the most ludicrous fashion" were part of the picture. The teams were followed by about seventy men on foot, carrying guns. The tinkling of the horse bells as the sleighs glided over the country roads in the early morning sun made the parade a treat for the ears as well as the eyes.

In the eighteenth century, the custom of firing guns on New Year's was so widespread that on December 24, 1774, the Pennsylvania Assembly passed "An Act to Suppress the Disorderly Practice of Firing Guns, &c. on the Times Therein Mentioned." The act began, "Whereas a disorderly practice prevails in many parts of this province of firing guns at or near New Year's Day, which disturbs the public peace." Henceforth anyone caught shooting guns, squibs, fireworks, etc., on December 31, or January 1 or 2, was subject to a fine of ten shillings (then a considerable sum), to be given to the poor. The constabulary had the right to sell the offender's goods and chattels to collect the fine. Secondly, anyone who "permits" such pernicious activities at his house was subject to a fine of twenty shillings. It was a little late to stop the shoots for that year, and the act accomplished very little in its purpose. The war clouds were then gathering over Pennsylvania; after the Revolution the Dutchmen continued to shoot in the New Year whether authorities objected or not.

This description of the rural New Year's parade touches on an additional aspect of the Pennsylvania Dutch New Year's celebration. On New Year's Day the young people often dressed up in fantastic garb and rode into the neighboring towns, whooping it up. The "fantasticals," as they were called, paraded the streets on horseback, in wagons or sleighs, or on foot. The parade of fantasticals took place either at Christmas (usually on Second Christmas Day) or on New Year's morning. On other occasions, too, like the Fourth of July or Battalion Day, when the militia mustered at a local tavern, fantasticals often made up the tail end of the military parade, in a sense parodying it. Both of these rural phenomena joined hands with the urban English mumming tradition to lead to the present-day Mummers' Parade, which is a spectacular feature of Philadelphia's New Year festivities.

"Wishing in" the New Year

"Wishing in" the New Year involved elaborate, formal wishes that were chanted, almost sung, at each farmhouse on the shooters' route. The texts of the New Year's wishes were of two varieties. First there were the solemn

Figure 13.1. Philadelphia mummers, fantasticals, or "belsnickles," from *Scribner's Monthly,* July 1881. *(Courtesy Roughwood Collection)*

blessings given to the farmer, his wife and children, hired man and hired girl, and even to the animals of the farm, wishing them peace, health, and good crops for the coming year. There were also humorous wishes, parodies of the older original solemn blessings.

A New Year's wish as recited in German by William Brown of the Mahantongo Valley in Schuylkill County, Pennsylvania, recorded in 1948 by Walter Boyer, Albert Buffington, and myself, gives the flavor of the solemn blessing. It begins, as translated:

> I wish you and your wife, manservants and maidservants, and all who enter and depart from your house, a Happy New Year! God grant that it may truly be so. I wish you great happiness; and may all your misfortune remain far away. May this 1949th year begin in the name of Jesus Christ, for the New Year is at hand. The former year has passed away; today we begin a new one. Thanks and praise be to God, that this time is one of peace and joy, and that you and all Christendom will experience what God the Father has prepared.

Then, after quoting a favorite German New Year's hymn, the wisher expresses the hope

> that God may guard your house from fire and flood, from sickness and sudden death. This last year, O Lord and God, much fear and need did threaten us, yet thou hast gloriously shielded us from all this, like the good Father thou art.

The wish continues for long life and reception in heaven, "where your dwelling place is prepared." Peace and guidance in life are finally wished "for these people and to all of Christendom, in this blessed New Year." The wish is much longer than these excerpts may suggest; it also rhymes, and is moving and beautiful in its archaic High German language.

This was a deeply religious performance, a blessing and prayer for each individual household as well as for the entire Christian world. Delivery of the wish was a solemn act on the part of the wisher. In the old days, every farmer wanted to have his household and farm blessed in this way. Any farmer who was left out on any New Year's night felt slighted indeed. European folklorists tell us that a folk ritual has to be performed exactly, with any text letter-perfect, otherwise the ritual is considered to fail in its purpose. Hence only the rare individual could "perform" the difficult text of the wish-blessing. The wishing and shooting therefore were solemn acts, actually religious rites in the old days, albeit folk-religious rather than ecclesiastical. But once the company was invited inside, the solemn note was dispelled and pleasantry, even revelry, could begin.

Some shorter, humorous wishes arose to lighten the solemnity of the

Neu-Jahr-Wunsch.

Ich wünsche euch und eurer Hausfrau, Söhnen und Töchtern, Knechten und Mägden und allen denjenigen die zu diesem Hause aus- und eingehen:

Ein glückselig neues Jahr,
Gott gebe daß es werde wahr,
Wir wünschen euch ein großes Glück
Und alles Unglück weit zurück,
Das 183— Jahr tritt ein,
Nun auf im Namen Jesu Christ
Weil das neue Jahr vorhanden ist,
Das alte Jahr ist nun hin,
Dann heute fangen wir ein neues an.
Gott Lob und Dank daß diese Zeit
Erlebet ist in Ruh und Freud,
Und es kommt noch über euch
Und der ganzen Christenheit,
Was Gott und Vater hat bereit;
Und wir gehen dahin und wandern,
Von einem Jahr zum andern,
Wir leben und gedeihen,
Vom Alten bis zum Neuen,
Durch so viel Angst und Plagen,
Durch Zittern und durch Zagen,
Durch Krieg und große Schrecken
Die alle Welt bedecken.
Uund weiter wünschen wir euch
Ein glückseliges neues Jahr,
Das Gott euer ganzes Haus bewahr,
Für Feuer und für Wassersnoth,
Für Krankheit und für schnellem Tod.
Es hat uns zwar O Herr und Gott,
Dies letzte Jahr gedroht,
Viele Angst und Noth,
Doch hat er alles gnädiglich,
Von uns gewendet väterlich.
Und weiter wünschen wir euch
Das hochgelobte neue Jahr
Bis ihr bekommet graue Haar,
Und mit Ehren werdet alt
Und hernach den Himmel erhalt,
Himmels Lust und Gottes Segen
Gottes Geist bleibt euch bewogen,
Bis eure Seel mit der Zeit,
Kommt gen Himmel aufgeflogen,
Und euer Sitz der bleibt bereit
Dort in der ewigen Seligkeit;
Der Herr der breite über euch seine rechte Hand,
Und segne dieses Haus und Land,
Es gebe euch auch Gott der Herr,
Das täglich Brod und was noch mehr gebricht
Voraus Geduld durch Jesum Christ,
So wollen wir hier allzugleich
O höchster Gott ins Himmelreich,
Dich loben an dem neuen Jahr
Und darnach werden es Immerdar,
So wohl auf Erden in dieser Zeit
Als dort in der ewigen Seeligkeit.
Und wieder wünschen wir euch
Ein glückseliges neues Jahr,
Eine Friedenszeit,
Gott helf euch all ins Himmelreich,
Dieses alles wollst du geben,
O meines Lebens, Leben,
Euch und der ganzen Christenschaar,
Zu diesem seeligen neuen Jahr,
Nun will ich mit euch wachen,
Und euch in Ehren fragen,
Ob auch das Schießen und das Krachen,
Heut an eurem Haus darf schallen,
Denn wir sind so fremd hieher gekommen,
Das neue Jahr mit euch anzufangen,
So behüt euch Gott wohl vor dem Schrecken,
Wann wir euch so früh aufwecken,
Ich hoff es wird euch nicht verdrießen,
Wann wir euch das neue Jahr anschießen,
Wann's euch aber thut verdrießen,
So müßt ihr es sagen ehe wir schießen.

Figure 13.2. New Year's Wish, Pennsylvania German, ca. 1830. A blessing of farmers, their wives, children, and hired servants.
(Courtesy Roughwood Collection)

original wishes. One of these was for "a mild winter, a house full of children, a barn full of grain, a stall full of horns!" Another, more common, wishes the listeners "a sausage as big as a stove-pipe, and a New Year's cake [cookie] as big as a barn door!" This latter wish has also been recorded in the Palatinate, the German area from which so many of the ancestors of the Pennsylvania Dutch emigrated. It reads: "A Happy New Year, a pretzel as big as a barn door, a *lebkuchen* as big as a stove-plate, then we'll all eat ourselves full!" (*Lebkuchen* were large cookies of hard gingerbread, stamped with designs from a carved mold. These as well as pretzels were also favorite New Year's gifts in Pennsylvania.)

In addition to the New Year's wish chanted at each farmhouse were manuscript and printed wishes for the new year. In his journals the colonial Lutheran pastor Henry Melchior Muhlenberg (1711–1787) referred to the custom of composing a long German poem to convey formal New Year's wishes. This was usually done by ministers or schoolmasters. One upcountry Lutheran pastor, Daniel Schumacher, was famous in the eighteenth century for his fraktur New Year's verses, which he decorated in watercolors and gave to members of his congregation. Muhlenberg mentioned such verses in his entry for December 31, 1762: "[I] corrected the verse for the New Year; stayed up; was annoyed by much foolish shooting. At twelve midnight I received a serenade from Mr. Hafner, etc., etc., and heard the ringing of the bells"—which tells us his attitude toward the people's celebration of the holiday. And on January 1, 1765, he wrote that "since it is still the custom here to express wishes and make prayers [on New Year's Day]," he evidently read to his congregation twelve wishes, probably in verse, including those for "our gracious king and the royal family"; for the provincial government; for the whole Protestant Church "in all four parts of the world"; for all Protestant congregations—Swedish, German, and English—in America; for Lutherans especially; for teachers, elders, deacons, parishioners, youth, widows, orphans, patrons, and benefactors. That covered everybody.

These formal New Year's verses, read ceremonially in churches or given as gifts, were paralleled by printed New Year's addresses written by, or usually for, city watchmen, newspaper carriers, and newspaper editors. These date from the eighteenth and nineteenth centuries, and are now collectors' items. They customarily feature a serious poem about the future along with the calendar for the coming year. They were dutifully, and hopefully, carried round the city by watchmen and newsboys to their clients' homes, where in return for this gift they were given refreshments and the expected tip. All this was part of the network of New Year's visiting, which was so much a feature of the day's celebration.

Self-examination, Gift Giving, and Watch Night Services

There were other components of the festival that were individual and ecclesiastical responses to New Year's and its significance as a turning point in life. Not every Pennsylvania Dutchman shouldered his rifle and marched out into the frosty midwinter night to traipse around the neighborhood, shooting and wishing the New Year in. We could hardly expect the aforementioned Pastor Muhlenberg, the leading Lutheran minister in colonial Pennsylvania, to have joined his neighbors in such activities. But it is interesting to leaf through his journals, checking his entries for December 31 and January 1 to see just how far he and his family included elements of the Pennsylvania Dutch New Year in their family celebration.

For the pastor, New Year's was always a solemn time, one of self-examination and prayer. He wrote on December 31, 1779:

> In the evening I stayed up alone and meditated on my many transgressions and sins of the past year and the countless blessings of God, His great goodness, mercy, patience, longsuffering, and forbearance for Jesus Christ's sake, and sought pardon and cleansing at the throne of grace.

He usually began New Year's Day by drawing a card from Bogatzky's *Schatzkästlein* (Little Treasure Chest), a favorite devotional work of the times, and meditating on the Bible verse it contained. Unless the roads were impassable due to a heavy snowfall, he and the family attended church services. Whether or not there was church, he led his household in domestic devotions.

Muhlenberg also recorded the giving and receiving of New Year's presents, a common custom among the Pennsylvania Dutch in the eighteenth century. In those days, New Year's, more than Christmas, was the time for giving gifts to one's friends and family. While pastor in Philadelphia in the 1760s, Muhlenberg mentioned gifts of bottles of wine, confections, and New Year's cake. During the Revolution, when he lived upcountry, he recorded rural gifts from parishioners. For example on January 1, 1781: "A number of old friends brought us pudding broth instead of wearisome New Year's wishes." This tells us that the neighbors had butchered on New Year's—a common custom also—and shared with the pastor's family the *Metzelsupp,* or butchering day soup. Shortly after New Year's 1786, the pastor sent his son-in-law and daughter "a goose and some apples as a New Year's present," and he wrote the word *present* in English in his otherwise German journal. At the same time he received from his son, General Peter Muhlenberg, late of Washington's staff, "as a present, a fish and a bushel of oysters."

One of Muhlenberg's most unusual references to gifts came on December 31, 1763, when he wrote that "Ernst Duperger's wife brought an iron pepper mill as a New Year's gift, and selected her funeral text, because she expects to die soon." She also left instructions about what hymn was to be sung at her funeral, whenever that event should take place.

The official religious approach to New Year's Eve centered on church services and self-examination. Both are still important in Pennsylvania Dutch communities—many churches of the pietist and evangelical persuasion still hold what is called a "Watch Night" in the church on New Year's Eve to "watch and pray the New Year in." Such services are a substitute for the secular New Year's "Auld Lang Syne" party, with its drinking and revelry. Groups like the Methodists led in this custom, and many other denominations followed. In his book ***This Is How It Was,*** William J. Laubenstein recalls bringing in not only the New Year in 1899/1900 but also the twentieth century, as a small boy in Minersville:

> In all the churches people gathered for Watch Night services. As the bells rang and the whistles tooted, worshipers prayed for their dead of the dying year and prayed for God's guidance in the brand new century just born.

What Does It All Mean?

Several routes of interpretation help unravel the meaning of New Year and its festivities: the work of the historian, the folklorist, and the ethnologist.

The historian can tell us the external history of New Year's Day itself—that the January 1 date for beginning the year, like our calendar, came to us from ancient Rome. The Romans celebrated the turning of the year with feasting and revelry, derived or continued from the earlier festival of Saturnalia, which also left its mark on Christmas customs. In the Middle Ages, various dates were used by the church for New Year's Day, among them March 1 and even March 25, the Feast of the Annunciation, nine months before the birth of Christ. It was not until 1691 that Pope Innocent XII re-set New Year's at January 1. The historical approach can also help us sift through the massive written materials from the past for references to New Year's, especially the changes that the celebration has undergone.

European folklorists have gathered the lore of New Year's and written much about the special, magical character of New Year's Eve and New Year's Day. Customs and folk beliefs associated with specific days are among the folklorist's stock-in-trade for such events as New Year's. From earliest times, the European New Year was a time of feasting, gift giving, revelry, predicting the future, and masking and dancing. New Year's night, straddling the years as it does, was used for oracular activities—pouring molten lead into water to observe the shapes it formed, paring apples to see how long a paring you get—to predict matters of love, death, weather, and harvest.

Examples of the lore of New Year's from the Pennsylvania Dutch world were gathered by Edwin M. Fogel, a Pennsylvania Dutchman who taught German at the University of Pennsylvania earlier in this century. Fogel unearthed many unusual beliefs dealing with New Year, especially about what was permitted or forbidden on that day. For example, if you sweep your parlor backward on New Year's Eve, you will see your future husband in the mirror. Or eating sausage for breakfast on New Year's will make one robust all year. Bad luck will come to anyone spinning between Christmas and New Year, or taking a bath or changing clothing in the same period. One throwing a bullet under a tree on New Year's Eve will see the Devil. Cleaning or dunging out stables between Christmas and New Year's will bring trouble with witches. Finally, there were some tokens of death. If there are any open graves between Christmas and New Year, there will be many funerals in that congregation during the following year. And if the wind is perfectly still on New Year's, watch out: many old folk will die that year.

Several of these beliefs deal with the critical period between Christmas and New Year's or between Christmas and Epiphany (January 6). In the pagan religions of northern Europe, during this time the "Wild Huntsman" or the "Wild Horde"—fearsome figures connected with the prehistoric cult of Wotan—were supposed to rage through the heavens causing storms. Storms were considered normal weather in northern Europe for that time period; hence if it was windy between Christmas and New Year's, it was believed that there would be plenty of fruit for the next harvest. Lack of winds on New Year's was abnormal and hence a precursor of death.

Fogel also says that the animal shapes of the New Year's cakes are prehistoric. When animals were required for the yule sacrifice, persons without animals offered substitutes in the form of cakes shaped like animals. Fogel relates the taboo on cleaning stables to the fact that the broom, which plays so great a part in witchcraft, was also sacred to Wotan and Thor, the principal Nordic gods, because of its relation to lightning. Not all of Fogel's findings deal with taboo and death; one delightful "superstition" states: If you want your fruit trees to bear well in the coming harvest, go out to the orchard on January 1 and wish each one a happy new year.

In his book on the folk culture of Switzerland, Richard Weiss, professor of European ethnology at the University of Zurich, also wrestled with the question of meanings, but approached them on another level. He, too, makes the point that our customs of the year, even though they are now set in a Christian framework, cannot be understood unless we look at their pagan roots. In doing so, we must search for the underlying function that the rituals had in pre-Christian times. The people of northern Europe, he explains, had two principal seasons around which their main holidays clustered. These were the winter festivals surrounding the winter solstice (December 21), and the spring festivals signaling the end of winter and the beginning of summer. Christmas and New Year's were originally midwinter festivals; Carnival (*Fastnacht*) and Easter were spring festivals.

Both of these festival times, Weiss claims, found their original meanings in two pagan cults: the cult of the dead spirits and the cult of fertility. The former involved the powers of the spirits of the dead to punish and to bless the living. The latter dealt with the eternal riddle of life and the unexplainable power of growth, on which our peasant ancestors were especially dependent. The cult of the dead was predominantly a midwinter cult, when in the long nights the spirits were believed to be abroad, revisiting the living. Spring was the main time for fertility rites.

Yet the two areas seem confusingly mixed in ritual and meaning. Masks were worn in both festival cycles. Were they to protect the wearer by disguising his identity from the spirits, or as in the case of the green-leaf costumes and masks, were they not connected with fertility? Noisemaking—ringing bells, shooting guns, cracking whips—was involved in both sets of holidays. Was this to chase away the spirits of the dead, or to "wake up" the fertility powers to produce a good harvest that year? In the winter and carnival festivals, is the casting forth of seeds, baked offerings, fruits, and nuts a present for the roving spirits, or is it fertility magic? Note that among the Pennsylvania Dutch, the masks and fantastical costumes worn on both Second Christmas and New Year's Day connect very definitely with the European practice.

And we still throw rice at weddings.

"Liberty Cabbage"

We began not with rice, but with sauerkraut—so let us end with sauerkraut. The Dutchmen of Pennsylvania's hills and valleys loved sauerkraut so much that they not only honored New Year's dinner with it, they even wrote poems and songs in its honor. During the First World War, when an edgy government attempted to rename sauerkraut "Liberty Cabbage," a fighting Dutchman named Charles Calvin Ziegler wrote these lines in its defense:

"Liberty Cabbage" now's the name,
But the thing remains the same.
Has it not the old aroma?
Is not "Liberty" a misnomer?

Why discard the name as hellish
When the thing itself you relish?
You may flout it and may scold—
No name fits it like the old.

When applied to Sauer Kraut,
Liberty, beyond a doubt,
Loses something of her halo.
Should this little bit of reason
Be adjudged an act of treason
You may thrust me into jail O,
But in spite of all your pains,
Sauer Kraut it still remains.

Bibliography

Berwin, Solomon. "New Year's Celebration in Berks County in 1828." *The Pennsylvania Dutchman* 3 (15) (January 1, 1952): 1,4.

Boyer, Walter E., Albert F. Buffington, and Don Yoder, eds. *Songs along the Mahantongo: Pennsylvania Dutch Folksongs.* Hatboro, Pa: Folklore Associates, 1964.

Oswald, Erich A., and Richard Beitl. *Wörterbuch der Deutschen Volkskunde.* 2d ed., Richard Beitl, ed. Stuttgart: Alfred Kröner Verlag, 1955.

Fogel, Edwin Miller. *Beliefs and Superstitions of the Pennsylvania Germans.* Philadelphia: Americana Germanica Press, 1915.

Laubenstein, William J. *This Is How It Was.* Cleveland: Dillon/Lieferbach, 1971.

Leh, Leonard L. "Shooting in the New Year." *The Pennsylvania Dutchman* 4 (9) (January 1, 1953): 3.

Oswald, Erich A. "Pennsylvania Legislators in 1774 Oppose Shooting in the New Year." *The Pennsylvania Dutchman* 3 (15) (January 1, 1952): 1, 3–4.

Shoemaker, Alfred L. *Christmas in Pennsylvania: A Folk-Cultural Study.* Don Yoder, intro. Kutztown, Pa.: Pennsylvania Folklife Society, 1959.

Tappert, Theodore G., and John W. Doberstein, eds. *The Journals of Henry Melchior Muhlenberg.* 3 vols., Philadelphia: The Muhlenberg Press, 1942, 1945, 1958.

Weaver, William Woys. *Sauerkraut Yankees: Pennsylvania-German Foods and Foodways.* Don Yoder, Foreword. Philadelphia: University of Pennsylvania Press, 1983.

Weiss, Richard. *Volkskunde der Schweiz.* Erlenbach-Zurich: Eugen Rentsch Verlag, 1946.

Yoder, Don. "Sauerkraut in the Pennsylvania Folk Culture." *Pennsylvania Folklife* 12 (2) (Summer 1961): 56–69.

———. "Gifts of the Pennsylvania Dutch." *The World & I* 3 (11) (November 1988): 642–53.

Selected Bibliography of Don Yoder (1944–1990)

[The following titles were selected from a much larger number which includes reviews, reports, as well as articles in periodicals and symposia. The serial publications involved are the following: *American Folklife Festival Yearbook* (Smithsonian Institution), *The American-German Review, American Philosophical Society Transactions, American Quarterly, Bulletin of Franklin and Marshall College, Bulletin of the Theological Seminary of the Evangelical and Reformed Church in the United States, The Christian Advocate, The Christian Century, Church History, Congressional Record, Ethnologia Scandinavica, F & M Today* (Franklin and Marshall College), *Genealogisches Jahrbuch, Hessische Blätter für Volks- und Kulturforschung, Jahrbuch des Historischen Vereins Alt-Wertheim, Journal of American Folklore, Journal of Religious Thought, Keystone Folklore Quarterly, The Mennonite Quarterly Review, Minnesota History, The Northumberland County Historical Society Proceedings and Addresses, The Pennsylvania Dutchman, Pennsylvania Folklife, The Pennsylvania Genealogical Magazine, The Pennsylvania German Folklore Society* (Yearbook), *The Pennsylvania German Society* (Yearbook), *Pennsylvania History, The Pennsylvania Magazine of History and Biography, Quaker History, Western Folklore, Western Pennsylvania Historical Magazine, Winterthur Portfolio, The World & I,* and *Yearbook of German-American Studies.*]

1944 "Der Fröhliche Botschafter: An Early American Universalist Magazine." *The American-German Review* 10 (5) (June 1944): 13–16.

1944 "He Rode with McKendree: Selections from the Autobiography of Jacob Bishop Crist." *Western Pennsylvania Historical Magazine* 37 (1–2) (March-June 1944): 51–78.

1944 "On Recording Methodist History." *The Christian Advocate* 119 (15) (April 13, 1944): 447.

1945 "Emigrants from Württemberg: The Adolf Gerber Lists." *The Pennsylvania German Folklore Society* 10 (1945): 103–237.

1946 "Lutheran-Reformed Union Proposals, 1800–1850: An American Experiment in Ecumenics." *Bulletin Theological Seminary of the Evangelical and Reformed Church in the United States* 17 (1) (January 1946): 39–77.

1947 "Hegins Valley in Song and Story." *'S Pennsylfawnisch Deitsch Eck,* Allentown *Morning Call,* January 11, 18, 25; February 1, 8, 1947.

1947 "Folklore from the Hegins and Mahantongo Valleys." *'S Pennsylfawnisch Deitsch Eck,* Allentown *Morning Call,* October 4, 11, 18, 25; November 2, 8, 15, 22, 1947.

1947 "Pennsylvania German Pioneers from the County of Wertheim." *The Pennsylvania German Folklore Society* 12 (1947): 147–289.

1947 "Church Union Efforts of the Reformed Church in the United States to 1934." Ph.D. diss., The University of Chicago, September 1947.

1951 Co-author, with Walter E. Boyer and Albert F. Buffington, *Songs along the Mahantongo: Pennsylvania German Folksongs.* Lancaster, Pa.: Pennsylvania Dutch Folklore Center, 1951; 2d ed., Hatboro, Pa.: Folklore Associates, 1964.

1954 "Christian Unity in 19th Century America." In Ruth Rouse and Stephen C. Neill, eds., *A History of the Ecumenical Movement.* London: S.P.C.K. Press, 1954, 219–59; "Christliche Einheit in Amerika des 19. Jahrhunderts," in *Geschichte der Oekumenischen Bewegung, 1517–1948.* Göttingen: Vandenhoeck & Ruprecht, 1957. Vol. 1: 300–358.

1958 "Harvest Home." *Pennsylvania Folklife* 9 (4) (Fall 1958): 2–11.

1958 "Research Needs in Pennsylvania Church History." *Pennsylvania Folklife* 9 (3) (Summer 1958): 48–52.

1959 "The Bench versus the Catechism: Revivalism and Pennsylvania's Lutheran and Reformed Churches." *Pennsylvania Folklife* 10 (2) (Fall 1959): 14–23.

1959 "Through the Traveler's Eye." In Alfred L. Shoemaker, ed., *The Pennsylvania Barn.* Kutztown, Pa.: Pennsylvania Folklife Society, 1959, 12–21.

1960 Introduction to *Christmas in Pennsylvania: A Folk-Cultural Study.* Alfred L Shoemaker, ed. Lancaster, Pa.: Pennsylvania Folklife Society, 1960, 1–18.

1961 *Pennsylvania Spirituals.* Lancaster, Pa.: Pennsylvania Folklife Society, 1961.

1961 "Sauerkraut in the Pennsylvania Folk-Culture." *Pennsylvania Folklife* 12 (2) (Summer 1961): 56–69.

1961 "Schnitz in the Pennsylvania Folk-Culture." *Pennsylvania Folklife* 12 (3) (Fall 1961): 44–53.

1962 "Pennsylvanians Called It Mush." *Pennsylvania Folklife* 13 (3) (Winter 1962–1963): 27–49.

1962 "Witch Tales from Adams County." *Pennsylvania Folklife* 12 (4) (Summer 1962): 29–37.

1963 "The Folklife Studies Movement." *Pennsylvania Folklife* 13 (3) (July 1963): 43–56.

1965 "Folklife Studies Bibliography 1964." *Pennsylvania Folklife* 14 (4) (Summer 1965): 60–64.

1965 "Official Religion versus Folk Religion." *Pennsylvania Folklife* 15 (2) (Winter 1965–1966): 36–52.

1966 "Historiography of Religion in America." *American Quarterly* 18 (2) pt. 1 (Summer 1966): 234–36.

1966 "Twenty Questions on Powwowing." *Pennsylvania Folklife* 15 (4) (Summer 1966): 38–40.

1967 "Folklife Studies and American History." *Pennsylvania Folklife* 16 (4) (Summer 1967).

1968 "Folklore and Folklife." *Festival of American Folklife 1968,* Smithsonian Institution, 1968: 9.

1968 "Folklife." In *American Folklore,* Tristram Coffin, III, ed. Washington, D.C.: Voice of America Forum Lectures, 1968, 53–63.

1968 "Report of the American Folklore Society Delegate to the Deutscher Volkskunde-Kongress, October 1–5, 1967, Würzburg, West Germany." *Journal of American Folklore* Supplement (May 1968): 27–28.

1968 "Trance-Preaching in the United States." *Pennsylvania Folklife* 18 (2) (Winter 1968–1969): 12–18.

1969 Introduction to *Pennsylvania German Fraktur and Color Drawings.* Lancaster, Pa.: Pennsylvania Farm Museum of Landis Valley, Pennsylvania Historical and Museum Commission, 1969.

1969 "The Relevance of Folklife Studies." In *Congressional Record*, 1969.

1969 "Sectarian Costume Research in the United States." In Austin and Alta Fife and Henry H. Glassie, eds., *Forms Upon the Frontier: Folklife and Folk Arts in the United States.* Logan, Utah: Utah State University Press, 1969, 41–75.

1969 "What to Read on the Amish." *Pennsylvania Folklife* 18 (4) (Summer 1969): 14–19.

1970 "Proposals for Academic Participation in the Bicentennial." Memorandum circulated at the University of Pennsylvania, presented to the Bicentennial Corporation, Philadelphia, and read as a paper at the Middle States Conference on Folk Culture, Pittsburgh, Pennsylvania, April 1971.

1971 "The First International Symposium on Ethnological Food Research." *Keystone Folklore Quarterly* 16 (4) (Winter 1971): 185–88.

1971 "Historical Sources for American Foodways Research and Plans for an American Foodways Archive." *Ethnologia Scandinavica* 1 (1971): 41–55.

1971 "Historical Sources for American Traditional Cookery: Examples from the Pennsylvania German Culture." *Pennsylvania Folklife* 20 (3) (Spring 1971): 16–29.

1971 "Pennsylvania German Folklore Research: A Historical Analysis." In Glenn G. Gilbert, ed., *The German Language in America: A Symposium.* Austin: University of Texas Press, 1971, 70–105, 148–63.

1971 "The Saint's Legend in the Pennsylvania German Folk Culture," in Wayland D. Hand, ed., *American Folk Legend: A Symposium.* Berkeley: University of California Press, 1971, 157–83.

1971 "The Pennsylvania Germans: A Preliminary Reading List." *Pennsylvania Folklife* 21 (2) (Winter 1971–1972): 2–17.

1972 Chapters on "Folk Medicine" (191–215), "Folk Costume" (295–323), and "Folk Cookery" (325–50). In Richard M. Dorson, ed., *Folklore and Folklife: An Introduction.* Chicago: University of Chicago Press, 1972.

1973 "Akkulturationsprobleme deutscher Auswanderer in Nord-Amerika." *Kultureller Wandel im 19. Jahrhundert: Verhandlungen des 18. Deutschen Volkskunde-Kongresses in Trier vom 13. bis 18. September 1971,* Günter Wiegelmann, ed. Göttingen: Vandenhoeck & Ruprecht, 1973, 184–203.

1973 "Problems and Resources in Pennsylvania German Genealogical Research." *Genealogisches Jahrbuch* 13 (1973): 5–27.

1974 "Toward a Definition of Folk Religion." Lead article in *Symposium on Folk Religion,* Don Yoder, ed. *Western Folklore* (University of California Press) 33 (1) (January 1974): 1–87.

1975 "Die Volkslieder der Pennsylvanien-Deutschen." In *Handbuch des Volksliedes,* Rolf Wilhelm Brednich, et al., eds. Munich: Wilhelm Fink, 1975, 2:221–70.

1976 *American Folklife.* Don Yoder, ed. Austin: University of Texas Press, 1976, with introductory essay, "Folklife Studies in American Scholarship," 3–18.

1976 "Hohman and Romanus: Origins and Diffusion of the Pennsylvania German Powwow Manual." In *American Folk Medicine: A Symposium,* Wayland D. Hand, ed. Berkeley: University of California Press, 1976, 235–48.

1976 "The Pennsylvania Germans and the American Revolution." *Pennsylvania Folklife* 25 (3) (Spring 1976): 2–17.

1977 Folk-Cultural Questionnaires, Nos. 1–50 (1977). The last one (No. 50), on "Work and Work Attitudes," appeared in *Pennsylvania Folklife* 27 (2) (Winter 1977–1978), inside back cover. The fifty questionnaires, although focused on the cultures of Pennsylvania, form a useful guide to field research in traditional cultures in the United States.

1978 "The Dialect Church Service in the Pennsylvania German Culture." *Pennsylvania Folklife* 27 (4) (Summer 1978): 2–13.

1978 "The Spiritual Lineage of Shakerism." *Pennsylvania Folklife* 27 (3) (Spring 1978): 2–14.

1980 "European Chapbook Literature in the Pennsylvania German Culture." In Leland Phelps, ed., *The Harold Jantz Collection*. Durham, N.C.: Duke University Press, 1980. This is the conference volume for the Symposium on German-American Literary Relations held at Duke University, 1979.

1980 *Palatine Church Visitations, 1609: Deanery of Kusel*. Ricardo W. Staudt, trans., Don Yoder, intro. Baltimore: Genealogical Publishing Company, 1980.

1980 "Palatine, Hessian, Dutchman: Three Images of the German in America." In *Ebbes fer Alle-Ebber, Ebbes fer Dich: Something for Everybody, Something for You*. The Pennsylvania German Society 14 (1980): 107–29.

1980 *Pennsylvania German Immigrants, 1709–1786*. Baltimore: Genealogical Publishing Company, 1980. 2d ed. 1984.

1980 "Pennsylvania Germans." In *Harvard Encyclopedia of American Ethnic Groups*, Stephan Thernstrom, ed. Cambridge, Mass.: The Belknap Press of Harvard University Press, 1980, 770–72.

1981 "The Dialect Church Service in the Pennsylvania German Culture." In *Pfälzer-Palatines: Beiträge zur pfälzischen Ein- und Auswanderung sowie zur Volkskunde und Mundartforschung der Pfalz und der Zielländer pfälzischer Auswanderer im 18. und 19. Jahrhundert*, Karl Scherer, ed. Kaiserslautern: Heimatstelle Pfalz, 1981, 349–60.

1981 "The Sausage Culture of the Pennsylvania Germans." In *Food in Perspective: Proceedings of the Third International Conference on Ethnological Food Research, Cardiff, Wales, 1977*, Alexander Fenton and Trefor M. Owen, eds. Edinburgh: John Donald, 1981, 409–25.

1982 Introduction to *Genealogies of Pennsylvania Families*. Baltimore: Genealogical Publishing Company, 1982. 3 vols. Vol. 1: xi–xix.

1982 *Rhineland Emigrants*. Baltimore: Genealogical Publishing Company, 1982.

1983 Introduction to *The Germanic Heritage: An Exhibition of the Washington County Museum of Fine Arts, October 2–November 23, 1983*, by Jean Woods. Hagerstown, Md.: Washington County Museum of Fine Arts, 1983.

1983 Introduction to *Pennsylvania German Church Records of Births, Baptisms, Marriages, Burials, Etc.: From the Pennsylvania German Society Proceedings and Addresses*. Baltimore: Genealogical Publishing Company, 1983. 3 vols. Vol. 1:v-xii.

1983 Introduction to *Pennsylvania Vital Records from the Pennsylvania Genealogical Magazine and the Pennsylvania Magazine of History and Biography*. Baltimore: Genealogical Publishing Company, 1983. 3 vols. Vol. 1:vii-xii.

1983 "The Reformed Church and Pennsylvania German Identity." In *Yearbook of German-American Studies* 18 (1983): 63–82.

1983 Foreword to *Sauerkraut Yankees: Pennsylvania-German Foods and Foodways*, by William Woys Weaver. Philadelphia: University of Pennsylvania Press, 1983.

1984 "The Baptismal Records of St. Jacob's (Howerter's) Lutheran and Reformed Union Church, Upper Mahanoy Township, Northumberland County, Pennsylvania, 1803–1869." *The Northumberland County Historical Society Proceedings and Addresses* 29 (1984): 127–250.

1984 "The Palatine Connection: The Pennsylvania German Culture and Its European Roots." In Randall M. Miller, ed., *Germans in America: Retrospect and Prospect*. Philadelphia: German Society of Pennsylvania, 1984, 92–109.

1985 "Palatine, Hessian, Dutchman: drei Bezeichnungen für Deutsche in Amerika." *Der grosse Aufbruch: Studien zur Amerikaauswanderung,* in *Hessische Blätter für Volks- und Kulturforschung,* Neue Folge 17 (1985): 191–213.

1985 "The Pennsylvania Germans: Three Centuries of Identity Crisis." In *America and the Germans,* Frank Trommler and Joseph McVeigh, eds. Philadelphia: University of Pennsylvania Press, 1985. Vol. 1:40–65.

1986 "Beauveau Borie IV: An Appreciation." Foreword to *Farming and Folk Society: Threshing among the Pennsylvania Germans,* by Beauveau Borie IV, Gregory Sharrow, ed. Ann Arbor, Mich.: UMI Research Press, 1986, xi-xiii.

1986 "Die Pennsylvania-Deutschen: Eine dreihundertjährige Identitätskrise." In *Amerika und die Deutschen: Bestandsaufnahme einer 300jährigen Geschichte.* Opladen: Westdeutscher Verlag GmbH, 1986, 65–88.

1987 "A Mahantongo Furniture Maker's Account Book." In *Decorated Furniture of the Mahantongo Valley,* by Henry M. Reed. Lewisburg, Pa.: Center Gallery of Bucknell University, 1987, 70–87. Distributed by University of Pennsylvania Press.

1987 "The Schwenkfelder-Quaker Connection: Two Centuries of Interdenominational Friendship." In *Schwenkfelders in America: Papers Presented at the Colloquium on Schwenckfeld and the Schwenkfelders, Pennsburg, Pa., September 17–22, 1984,* Peter C. Erb, ed. Pennsburg, Pa.: Schwenkfelder Library, 1987, 113–62.

1988 "The 'Dutchman' and the 'Deitschlenner': The New World Meets the Old." In *Yearbook of German-American Studies* 23 (1988), 1–17.

1988 "Fraktur: An Introduction." In *Pennsylvania German Fraktur and Printed Broadsides: A Guide to the Collections in the Library of Congress,* Paul Connor and Jill Roberts, comps., for the American Folklife Center. Washington, D.C.: Library of Congress, 1988, 8–19. Publications of the American Folklife Center, No. 16.

1988 "Gifts of the Pennsylvania Dutch." In *The World & I,* 3 (11) (November 1988): 642–653.

1988 "Sects and Religious Movements of German Origin." In *Encyclopedia of the American Religious Experience: Studies of Traditions and Movements,* Charles H. Lippy and Peter W. Williams, eds. New York: Charles Scribner's Sons, 1988. Vol. 1:615–33.

1989 *Hex Signs: Pennsylvania Dutch Barn Symbols and Their Meaning,* by Don Yoder and Thomas E. Graves, with a Foreword by Alistair Cooke. New York: E. P. Dutton, 1989.

1989 *Lamp of My Heart: The Picture-Bible of Ludwig Denig,* Don Yoder, trans. and ed. New York: Hudson Hills Press, 1989, in association with the Museum of American Folk Art and the Pennsylvania German Society.

1989 "Sauerkraut for New Year's." In *The World & I* 4 (1) (January 1989): 612–23.

1990 *Discovering American Folklife: Studies in Ethnic, Religious, and Regional Culture.* Ann Arbor, Mich.: UMI Research Press, 1990.

[1990] *A Gentleman's War: The Revolutionary Journal of Karl Heinrich Philipp von Feilitzsch,* Don Yoder, trans. and ed. (forthcoming).

Ph.D. Dissertations Directed (1962–1990)

1962 Hugh George Anderson, "A Social History of Lutheranism in the Southeastern States." (American Civilization)

1967 James William Hall, "The Tune-Book in American Culture, 1800–1820." (American Civilization)

1968 Philip Wesley Ott, "The Mind of Early American Methodism, 1800–1844." (Religious Thought)

1969 Hilda Adam Kring, "The Harmonists: A Folk-Cultural Approach." (Folklore and Folklife)

1969 Joseph R. Sweeny, "Elhanan Winchester and the Universal Baptists." (Religious Thought)

1970 Eugene Phillip Clemens, "The Social Gospel Background of the Federal Council of Churches." (Religious Thought)

1970 Kathryn Lawson Morgan, "The Ex-Slave Narrative as a Source for Folk History." (Folklore and Folklife)

1970 Scott Trego Swank, "The Unfettered Conscience: A Study of Sectarianism, Spiritualism, and Social Reform in the New Jerusalem Church, 1840–1870." (History)

1971 Jay Allen Anderson, "'A Solid Sufficiency': An Ethnography of Yeoman Foodways in Stuart England." (Folklore and Folklife)

1971 Toni Flores Fratto, "Samplers: The Historical Ethnography of an American Popular Art." (Folklore and Folklife)

1971 Keith Hardman, "Jonathan Dickinson and the Course of American Presbyterianism, 1717–1747." (Religious Thought)

1972 Robert Abraham Barakat, "Tobaccuary: A Study of Tobacco Curing Sheds in Southeastern Pennsylvania." (Folklore and Folklife)

1972 Kay Lorraine Cothran, "Such Stuff as Dreams: A Folkloristic Sociology of Fantasy in the Okefenokee Rim, Georgia." (Folklore and Folklife)

1972 Frank M. Mealing, "Our People's Way: A Study of Doukhobor Hymnody and Folklife." (Folklore and Folklife)

1972 David John Winslow, "The Rural Square Dance in the Northeastern United States: A Continuity of Tradition." (Folklore and Folklife)

1973 Syed Abedin, "In Defense of Freedom: The United States and the Barbary Wars." (American Civilization)

1973 John A. Burrison, "Georgia Jug Makers: A History of Southern Folk Pottery." (Folklore and Folklife)

1973 Phyllis Della Vecchia, "Rhetoric, Religion, Politics: A Study of the Sermons of Lyman Beecher." (American Civilization)

1974 Beauveau Borie, IV, "Threshing Methods in the Pennsylvania German Area." (Folklore and Folklife)

1974 Bonita A. Freeman, "The Development of Spiritualist Mediums: Apprenticeship to a Tradition." (Folklore and Folklife)

1974 David J. Hufford, "Folklore Studies and Health: An Approach to Applied Folklore." (Folklore and Folklife)

1974 Julia Anna Roth, "Popular Attitudes to Mental Illness in Southern Chile." (Folklore and Folklife)

1974 Robert T. Teske, "Votive Offerings Among Greek-Philadelphians: A Ritual Perspective." (Folklore and Folklife)

1975 Angus K. Gillespie, "The Contributions of George Korson to American Intellectual Life." (American Civilization)

1975 Yvonne Lange, "Santos: The Household Wooden Saints of Puerto Rico." (Folklore and Folklife)

1976 Richard M. Candee, "Wooden Buildings in Early Maine and New Hampshire: A Technological and Cultural History, 1600–1720." (American Civilization)

1976 Carter W. Craigie, "A Moveable Feast: The Picnic as a Folklife Custom in Chester County, Pennsylvania, 1870–1925." (Folklore and Folklife)

1976 Harry Ernest Winter, "Catholic, Evangelical and Reformed: The Lord's Supper in the (United) Presbyterian Church USA, 1945–1970." (Religious Thought)

1977 Scott Hambly, "Mandolins in the United States Since 1880: An Industrial and Socio-Cultural History of Form." (Folklore and Folklife)

1977 Beulah Stauffer Hostetler, "Franconia Mennonite Conference and American Protestant Movements, 1840–1940." (Religious Thought)

1978 John Charles Camp, "America Eats: Toward a Social Definition of American Foodways." (Folklore and Folklife)

1978 Bernard L. Herman, "Continuity and Change in Traditional Architecture: Folk Housing on Virginia's Eastern Shore." (Folklore and Folklife)

1979 Gerald L. Pocius, "Calvert: A Study of Artifacts and Spatial Usage in a Newfoundland Community." (Folklore and Folklife)

1979 Angela-Marie Varesano, "Charles Godfrey Leland: The Eclectic Folklorist." (Folklore and Folklife)

1982 Barbara Reimensnyder, "Powwowing in Union County: A Study of Pennsylvania German Folk Medicine in Context." (Folklore and Folklife)

1983 George Albert Boeck, Jr., "The Market Report: A Folklife Ethnography of a Texas Livestock Auction." (Folklore and Folklife)

1983 James Moss, "Land and Legend: The Role of Place in the Folk Narrative of Chester County, Pennsylvania." (Folklore and Folklife)

1984 Thomas E. Graves, "The Pennsylvania German Hex Sign: A Study in Folk Proceess." (Folklore and Folklife)

1985 Michael Ann Williams, "Homeplace: The Social Use and Meaning of the Folk Dwelling in Southwestern North Carolina." (Folklore and Folklife)

1986 Maria Boynton, "Springtown, New Jersey: Explorations in the History and Culture of a Black Rural Community." (Folklore and Folklife)

1987 Una Mary Cadegan, "All Good Books are Catholic Books: Literature, Censorship and the Americanization of Catholics, 1920–1960." (American Civilization)

1987 Leanna Lee-Whitman, "Silks and Simplicity: A Study of Quaker Dress as Depicted in Portraits, 1718–1815." (American Civilization)

1989 The following students are working at present on doctoral dissertations under Don Yoder's direction:

American Civilization: Gloria Goode, Melissa Hough, Steven L. Jones.

Religious Studies: Jill Gill.

Folklore and Folklife: Ruth Cary, Michael Chiarappa, John Eilertsen, Susan Isaacs, Mario Montaño, Karen Pfeiffer, Leonard Primiano, Caroline H. Roston, Diane Sidener.

Index